UNDERSTANDING AND USING

ENGLISH GRAMMAR

Third Edition

Teacher's Guide

Betty Schrampfer Azar
Barbara F. Matthies
Shelley Hartle

Longman

Understanding and Using English Grammar
Teacher's Guide, Third Edition

Copyright © 2001, 1993 by Betty Schrampfer Azar

A Pearson Education Company

Vice President, director of publishing: Allen Ascher
Editorial director: Louisa Hellegers
Editorial manager: Shelley Hartle
Senior development manager: Penny Laporte
Development editor: Janet Johnston
Vice president, director of design and production: Rhea Banker
Associate director of electronic production: Aliza Greenblatt
Executive managing editor: Linda Moser
Production manager: Ray Keating
Production editor: Robert Ruvo
Senior manufacturing buyer: Dave Dickey
Cover design adaptation: Pat Wosczyk
Text composition: Clarinda Co.

ISBN: 0-13-958679-2

3 4 5 6 7 8 9 10—BAH—05 04 03 02

Contents

Preface

This *Teacher's Guide* is intended as a practical aid to teachers. You can turn to it for notes on the content of a unit and how to approach the exercises, for suggestions for classroom activities, and for answers to the exercises in the main text and the practices in the *Workbook*.

General teaching information can be found in the *Introduction*. It includes
- the rationale and general aims of *Understanding and Using English Grammar*
- the classroom techniques for presenting charts and using exercises
- suggestions on the use of the *Workbook* in connection with the main text
- supplementary resource texts
- comments on differences between American and British English
- a key to the pronunciation symbols used in this *Guide*

The rest of the *Guide* contains notes on charts and exercises. The notes about the charts may include
- suggestions for presenting the information to students
- points to emphasize
- common problems to anticipate
- assumptions underlying the contents
- additional background notes on grammar and usage.

The notes that accompany the exercises may include
- the focus of the exercise
- suggested techniques as outlined in the introduction
- possible specialized techniques for particular exercises
- points to emphasize
- problems to anticipate
- assumptions
- answers
- expansion activities
- item notes on cultural content, vocabulary, and idiomatic usage.
  (Some of these item notes are specifically intended to aid any teachers who are non-native speakers of English.)

NOTE: All of the answers to the exercises in the student book are in this *Teacher's Guide*. In addition, a separate *Answer Key* for the student book is printed in a slim gray booklet. Some teachers like to keep copies of it on hand to use in group work in the classroom. The first printing of the separate *Answer Key* booklet contains some errors, unfortunately. Please see page 243 of this *Guide* for the corrections to these errors.

Introduction

General Aims of *Understanding and Using English Grammar*

The principal aims of *Understanding and Using English Grammar* are to present clear, cogent information about English grammar and usage, to provide extensive and varied practice that enourages growth in all areas of language use, and to be interesting, useful, and fun for student and teacher alike. The approach is eclectic, with the text seeking to balance form-focused language-learning activities with abundant opportunities for engaged and purposeful communicative interaction.

Most students find it helpful to have special time set aside in their English curriculum to focus on grammar. Students generally have many questions about English grammar and appreciate the opportunity to work with a text and teacher to make some sense out of the bewildering array of forms and usages in this strange language. These understandings provide the basis for advances in usage ability in a relaxed, accepting classroom that encourages risk-taking as the students experiment, both in speaking and writing, with ways to communicate their ideas in a new language.

Teaching grammar does not mean lecturing on grammatical patterns and terminology. It does not mean bestowing knowledge and being an arbiter of correctness. Teaching grammar is the art of helping students make sense, little by little, of a huge, puzzling construct, and engaging them in various activities that enhance usage abilties in all skill areas and promote easy, confident communication.

The text depends upon a partnership with a teacher; it is the teacher who animates and directs the students' language-learning experiences. In practical terms, the aim of the text is to support you, the teacher, by providing a wealth and variety of material for you to adapt to your individual teaching situation. Using grammar as a base to promote overall English usage ability, teacher and text can engage the students in interesting discourse, challenge their minds and skills, and intrigue them with the power of language as well as the need for accuracy to create understanding among people.

Classroom Techniques

Following are some techniques that have proven useful.

- *Suggestions for Presenting the Grammar Charts* are discussed first.
- Next are some notes on interactivity: *Degrees of Teacher and Student Involvement.*
- Then *Techniques for Exercise Types* are outlined.

Suggestions for Presenting the Grammar Charts

A chart is a concise visual presentation of the structures to be learned in one section of a chapter. Some charts may require particular methods of presentation, but generally any of the following techniques are viable.

Presentation techniques often depend upon the content of the chart, the level of the class, and the students' learning styles. Not all students react to the charts in the same way. Some students need the security of thoroughly understanding a chart before trying to use the structure. Others like to experiment more freely with using new structures; they refer to the charts only incidentally, if at all.

Given these different learning strategies, you should vary your presentation techniques and not expect students to "learn" or memorize the charts. The charts are just a starting place for class activities and a point of reference.

Technique #1: Use the examples in the chart, add your own examples to explain the grammar in your own words, and answer any questions about the chart. Elicit other examples of the target structure from the learners. Then go to the accompanying exercise immediately following the chart.

Technique #2: Elicit oral examples from the students before they look at the chart in the textbook. To elicit examples, ask leading questions whose answers will include the target structure. (For example, for the present progressive, ask: "What are you doing right now?") You may want to write the elicited answers on the board and relate them to the examples in the chart. Then proceed to the exercises.

Technique #3: Assign the chart and accompanying exercise(s) for out-of-class study. In class the next day, ask for and answer any questions about the chart, and then immediately proceed to the exercises. (With advanced students, you might not need to deal with every chart and exercise thoroughly in class. With intermediate students, it is generally advisable to clarify charts and do most of the exercises.)

Technique #4: Lead the students through the first accompanying exercise PRIOR to discussing the chart. Use the material in the exercise to discuss the focus of the chart as you go along. At the end of the exercise, call attention to the examples in the chart and summarize what was discussed during the exercise.

Technique #5: Before presenting the chart in class, give the students a short written quiz on its content. Have the students correct their own papers as you review the answers. The quiz should not be given a score; it is a learning tool, not an examination. Use the items from the quiz as examples for discussing the grammar in the chart.

The here-and-now classroom context: For every chart, try to relate the target structure to an immediate classroom or "real-life" context. Make up or elicit examples that use the students' names, activities, and interests. The here-and-now classroom context is, of course, one of the grammar teacher's best aids.

Demonstration techniques: Demonstration can be very helpful to explain the meaning of structures. You and the students can act out situations that demonstrate the target structure. Of course, not all grammar lends itself to this technique. For example, the present progressive can easily be demonstrated (e.g., "I *am writing* on the board right now"). However, using gerunds as the objects of prepositions (e.g., "instead *of writing*" or "thank you *for writing*") is not especially well suited to demonstration techniques.

Using the chalkboard: In discussing the target structure of a chart, use the chalkboard whenever possible. Not all students have adequate listening skills for "teacher talk," and not all students can visualize and understand the various relationships within, between, and among structures. Draw boxes and circles and arrows to illustrate connections between the elements of a structure. A visual presentation helps many students.

<u>Oral exercises in conjunction with chart presentations</u>: Oral exercises usually follow a chart, but sometimes they precede it so that you can elicit student-generated examples of the target structure as a springboard to the discussion of the grammar. If you prefer to introduce any particular structure to your students orally, you can always use an oral exercise prior to the presentation of a chart and written exercises, no matter what the given order is in the textbook.

<u>The role of terminology</u>: The students need to understand the terminology, but don't require or expect detailed definitions of terms, either in class discussion or on tests. Terminology is just a tool, a useful label for the moment, so that you and the students can talk to each other about English grammar.

Degrees of Teacher and Student Involvement

The goal of all language learning is to understand and communicate. The teacher's main task is to direct and facilitate that process. The learner is an active participant, not merely a passive receiver of rules to be memorized. Therefore, many of the exercises in the text are designed to promote interaction between learners as a bridge to real communication.

The teacher has a crucial leadership role, with "teacher talk" a valuable and necessary part of a grammar classroom. Sometimes you will need to spend time clarifying the information in a chart, leading an exercise, answering questions about exercise items, or explaining an assignment. These periods of "teacher talk" should, however, be balanced by longer periods of productive learning activity when the students are doing most of the talking. It is important for the teacher to know when to step back and let the students lead. Interactive group and pair work plays an important role in the language classroom.

INTERACTIVE GROUP AND PAIR WORK

Many of the exercises in this text are formatted for group or pair work. The third edition of *UUEG* has many more exercises explicitly set up for interactive work than the last edition had. Interactive exercises may take more class time than they would if teacher-led, but it is time well spent, for there are many advantages to student–student practice.

When the students are working in groups or pairs, their opportunities to use what they are learning are greatly increased. In interactive work, the time they spend actually using English is many times greater than in a teacher-centered activity. Obviously, the students in group or pair work are often much more active and involved than in teacher-led exercises.

Group and pair work also expand the students' opportunities to practice many communication skills at the same time that they are practicing target structures. In peer interaction in the classroom, the students have to agree, disagree, continue a conversation, make suggestions, promote cooperation, make requests, be sensitive to each other's needs and personalities—the kinds of exchanges that are characteristic of any group communication, in the classroom or elsewhere.

Students will often help and explain things to each other during pair work, in which case both students benefit greatly. Ideally, students in interactive activities are "partners in exploration." Together they go into new areas and discover things about English usage, supporting each other as they proceed.

Group and pair work help to produce a comfortable learning environment. In teacher-centered activities, students may sometimes feel shy and inhibited or may experience stress. They may feel that they have to respond quickly and accurately and that *what* they say is not as important as *how* they say it—even though you strive to convince them to the contrary. When you set up groups or pairs that are non-competitive and cooperative, the students usually tend to help, encourage, and even joke with each other. This encourages them to experiment with the language and speak more.

Some students may not adjust well at first to interactive activities: they may expect the teacher to fulfill the traditional role of bestower of knowledge and may not understand the value of peer interaction in the language classroom. Openly discuss the use of group and pair work with your class to arrive at an understanding of its benefits. Explore reservations your students might have about devoting their time in class to interactive work and seek to involve them in determining how much class time should be devoted to it. The directions in the text are frequently set up with options for group, pair, or teacher-led work; let the students help decide at times which format should be used.

MONITORING ERRORS IN INTERACTIVE WORK

Students should be encouraged to monitor each other to some extent in interactive work, especially when monitoring activities are specifically assigned. (Perhaps you should remind them to give some *positive* as well as corrective comments to each other.) You shouldn't worry about "losing control" of the students' language production; not every mistake needs to be corrected. Mistakes are a natural part of learning a new language. As students gain experience and familiarity with a structure, their mistakes in using it begin to diminish.

And the students shouldn't worry that they will learn each other's mistakes. Being exposed to imperfect English in this kind of interactive work in the classroom is not going to impede their progress in the slightest. In today 's world, with so many people using English as a second language, students will likely be exposed to all levels of proficiency in people they will interact with in English, from airline reservation clerks to new neighbors from a different land to a co-worker whose native language is not English. Encountering imperfect English is not going to diminish their own English language abilities, either now in the classroom or later in different English-speaking situations.

Make yourself available to answer questions about correct answers during group and pair work. If you wish, you can take some time at the end of an exercise to call attention to mistakes that you heard as you monitored the groups. Another possible way of correcting errors is to have copies of the *Answer Key* available in the classroom so that students can look up their own answers when they need to.

Techniques for Exercise Types

The majority of the exercises in the text require some sort of completion, transformation, combination, discussion of meaning, or a combination of such activities. They range from those that are tightly controlled and manipulative to those that encourage free responses and require creative, independent language use. The techniques vary according to the exercise type.

FILL-IN-THE-BLANKS AND CONTROLLED COMPLETION EXERCISES

The label "fill-in-the-blanks" refers to those exercises in which the students complete the sentences by using words given in parentheses. The label "controlled completion" refers to those exercises in which the students complete sentences using the words in a given list. Both types of exercises call for similar techniques.

Technique A: A student can be asked to read an item aloud. You can say whether the student's answer is correct or not, or you can open up discussion by asking the rest of the class if the answer is correct. For example:

TEACHER:	Juan, would you please read Number 2?
STUDENT:	Diane *washes* her hair every other day or so.
TEACHER (to the class):	Do the rest of you agree with Juan's answer?

The slow-moving pace of this method is beneficial for discussion not only of grammar items but also of vocabulary and content. The students have time to digest information and ask questions. You have the opportunity to judge how well they understand the grammar.

However, this time-consuming technique doesn't always, or even usually, need to be used, especially with more advanced classes.

Technique B: You, the teacher, read the first part of the item, then pause for the students to call out the answer in unison. For example:

> TEXT entry: "Diane (*wash*) _____ her hair every other day or so."
> TEACHER (with the students looking at their texts): Diane . . . .
> STUDENTS (in unison): washes (plus possibly a few incorrect responses scattered about)
> TEACHER: . . . washes her hair every other day or so. *Washes.* Do you have any questions?

This technique saves a lot of time in class, but is also slow-paced enough to allow for questions and discussion of grammar, vocabulary, and content. It is essential that the students have prepared the exercise by writing in their books, so it must be assigned ahead of time as homework.

Technique C: With an advanced class for whom a particular exercise is little more than a quick review, you can simply give the answers so the students can correct their own previously prepared work in their textbooks. You can either read the whole sentence ("Number 2: Diane washes her hair every other day or so") or just give the answer ("Number 2: washes"). You can give the answers to the items one at a time, taking questions as they arise, or give the answers to the whole exercise before opening it up for questions. As an alternative, you can have one of the students read his/her answers and have the other students ask him/her questions if they disagree.

Technique D: Divide the class into groups (or pairs) and have each group prepare one set of answers that they all agree is correct prior to class discussion. The leader of each group can present their answers.

Another option is to have the groups (or pairs) hand in their set of answers for correction and possibly a grade.

It's also possible to turn these exercises into games wherein the group with the best set of answers gets some sort of reward (perhaps applause from the rest of the class).

Of course, you can always mix Techniques A, B, C, and D—with the students reading some aloud, with you prompting unison response for some, with you simply giving the answers for others, with the students collaborating on the answers for others. Much depends on the level of the class, their familiarity and skill with the grammar at hand, their oral–aural skills in general, and the flexibility or limitations of class time.

Technique E: When an exercise item has a dialogue between two speakers, A and B, ask one student to be A and another B and have them read the entry aloud. Then, occasionally, say to A and B: "Without looking at your text, what did you just say to each other?" (If necessary, let them glance briefly at their texts before they repeat what they've just said in the exercise item.) The students may be pleasantly surprised by their own fluency.

OPEN COMPLETION EXERCISES

The term "open completion" refers to those exercises in which the students use their own words to complete the sentences.

Technique A: Exercises where the students must supply their own words to complete a sentence should usually be assigned for out-of-class preparation. Then in class, one, two, or several students can read their sentences aloud; the class can discuss the correctness and appropriateness of the completions. Perhaps you can suggest possible ways of rephrasing to make a sentence more idiomatic. Students who don't read their sentences aloud can revise their own completions based on what is being discussed in class. At the end of the exercise discussion, you can tell the students to hand in their sentences for you to look at, or simply ask if anyone has questions about the exercise and not have the students submit anything to you.

Technique B: If you wish to use an open completion exercise in class without having previously assigned it, you can turn the exercise into a brainstorming session in which students try out several completions to see if they work. As another possibility, you may wish to divide the students into small groups and have each group come up with completions that they all agree are correct and appropriate. Then use only these completions for class discussion or as written work to be handed in.

Technique C: Some open completion exercises are designated WRITTEN, which usually means the students need to use their own paper, as not enough space has been left in the textbook. It is often beneficial to use the following progression: (1) assign the exercise for out-of-class preparation; (2) discuss it in class the next day, having the students make corrections on their own papers based on what they are learning from discussing other students' completions; (3) then ask the students to submit their papers to you, either as a requirement or on a volunteer basis.

TRANSFORMATION AND COMBINATION EXERCISES

In transformation exercises, the students are asked to change form but not substance (e.g., to change the active to the passive, a clause to a phrase, a question to a noun clause, etc.).

In combination exercises, the students are asked to combine two or more sentences or ideas into one sentence that contains a particular structure (e.g., an adjective clause, a parallel structure, a gerund phrase, etc.).

In general, these exercises, which require manipulation of a form, are intended for class discussion of the form and meaning of a structure. The initial stages of such exercises are a good opportunity to use the chalkboard to draw circles and arrows to illustrate the characteristics and relationships of a structure. Students can read their answers aloud to initiate the class discussion, and you can write on the board as problems arise. Another possibility is to have the students write their sentences on the board. Also possible is to have them work in small groups to agree upon their answers prior to class discussion.

The text has many speaking–listening exercises. The following example of a typical oral exercise is taken from page 242 of the student book:

EXERCISE 3.   Noun clauses beginning with a question word.   (Chart 12-2)
  Directions: Work in pairs, in groups, or as a class.
  Speaker A: Your book is open. Ask the question.
  Speaker B: Your book is closed. Begin your response with "I don't know . . . ."

  Example:
  SPEAKER A *(book open):* What time is it?
  SPEAKER B *(book closed):* I don't know what time it is.

  1. Where does (. . .) live?
  2. What country is (. . .) from?
  3. How long has (. . .) been living here?
  4. What is (. . .)'s telephone number?
  5. Where is the post office?
  6. Etc.

You and the class decide how to use the exercise.

  1. If you use an exercise for <u>pair work</u>:

     a. Tell Speaker A that he or she is the teacher for this exercise and must listen carefully for correct responses. Remind Speaker A that it is important to enunciate clearly.

     b. Vary the ways in which the students are paired up, ranging from having them choose their own partners to drawing names or numbers from a hat.

     c. Roam the room and answer questions as needed.

  2. If you use an oral exercise for <u>group work</u>:

     a. Speaker A is the leader of the group. The others in the group have their books closed and can respond either individually or chorally.

     b. The role of Speaker A can be passed around the group, or one student can lead the entire exercise.

     c. Vary the ways in which you divide the students into groups and choose leaders.

  3. If you use an oral exercise as a <u>teacher-led exercise</u>:

     a. You, the teacher, take the role of Speaker A. (You can always choose to lead an oral exercise, even when the directions specifically call for pair work; treat exercise directions calling for pair or group work as suggestions, not iron-clad instructions for teaching techniques that must be employed.)

     b. You don't have to read the items aloud as though reading a script from which there should be no deviation. Modify or add items spontaneously as they occur to you. Change the items in any way you can to make them more relevant to your students. (For example, if you know that some students plan to watch the World Cup soccer match on TV soon, include a sentence about that.) Omit irrelevant items.

     c. Sometimes an item will start a spontaneous discussion of, for example, local restaurants or current movies or certain experiences the students have had. These spur-of-the-moment dialogues are very beneficial to the students. Being able to create and encourage such interactions is one of the chief advantages of a teacher leading an oral exercise.

WRITING EXERCISES

Some writing exercises require sentence completion, but most are designed to produce short, informal compositions. Generally, the topics or tasks concern aspects of the students' lives in order to encourage free and relatively effortless communication as they practice their writing skills. While a course in English rhetoric is beyond the scope of this text, many of the basic elements are included and may be developed and emphasized according to your purposes.

For best results, whenever you give a writing assignment, let your students know what you expect: "This is what I suggest as content. This is how long I expect it to be." If at all possible, give your students composition models, perhaps taken from good compositions written by previous classes, perhaps written by you, perhaps composed as a group activity by the class as a whole (e.g., you write on the board what the students tell you to write, and then you and the students revise it together).

In general, writing exercises should be done outside of class. All of us need time to consider and revise when we write. And if we get a little help here and there, that's not unusual. The topics in the exercises are structured so that plagiarism should not be a problem. Use in-class writing if you want to appraise the students' unaided, spontaneous writing skills. Tell your students that these writing exercises are simply for practice and that—even though they should always try to do their best—mistakes that occur should be viewed simply as tools for learning.

Encourage the students to use their dictionaries whenever they write. Point out that you yourself never write seriously without a dictionary at hand. Discuss the use of margins, indentation of paragraphs, and other aspects of the format of a well-written paper.

ERROR-ANALYSIS EXERCISES

For the most part, the sentences in this type of exercise have been adapted from actual student writing and contain typical errors. Error-analysis exercises focus on the target structures of a chapter but may also contain miscellaneous errors that are common in student writing at this level, e.g., final -s on plural nouns or capitalization of proper nouns. The purpose of including them is to sharpen the students' self-monitoring skills.

Error-analysis exercises are challenging and fun, a good way to summarize the grammar in a unit. If you wish, tell the students they are either newspaper editors or English teachers; their task is to locate all mistakes and write corrections. Point out that even native speakers—including you yourself—have to scrutinize, correct, and revise what they write. This is a natural part of the writing process.

The recommended technique is to assign an error-analysis exercise for in-class discussion the next day. The students benefit most from having the opportunity to find the errors themselves prior to class discussion. These exercises can, of course, be handled in other ways: seatwork, written homework, group work, pair work.

PRETEST EXERCISES

The purpose of these exercises is to let the students discover what they do and do not know about the target structure in order to get them interested in a chart. Essentially, PRETEST exercises illustrate a possible teaching technique: quiz the students first as a springboard for presenting the grammar in a chart.

Any exercise can be used as a pretest. You do not need to follow the ordering of material in the text. Adapt the material to your own needs and techniques.

DISCUSSION-OF-MEANING EXERCISES

Some exercises consist primarily of you and the students discussing the meaning of given sentences. Most of these exercises ask the students to compare the meaning of two or more sentences (e.g., *You should take an English course* vs. *You must take an English course*). One of the main purposes of discussion-of-meaning exercises is to provide an opportunity for summary comparison of the structures in a particular unit.

Basically, the technique in these exercises is for you to pose questions about the given sentences, then let the students explain what a structure means to them (which allows you to get input about what they do and do not understand). Then you summarize the salient points as necessary. Students have their own inventive, creative way of explaining differences in meaning. They shouldn't be expected to sound like grammar teachers. Often, all you need to do is listen very carefully and patiently to a student's explanation, and then clarify and reinforce it by rephrasing it somewhat.

GAMES AND ACTIVITIES

Games and activities are important parts of the grammar classroom. The study of grammar is and should be fun and engaging. Some exercises in the text and in this *Guide* are designated as "expansion" or "activity." They are meant to promote independent, active use of target structures.

If a game is suggested, the atmosphere should be relaxed, not competitive. The goal is clearly related to the chapter's content, and the reward is the students' satisfaction in using English to achieve the goal. (For additional games and activities, see *Fun with Grammar* by Suzanne W. Woodward, © Prentice Hall Regents, 1997; available from Pearson Education, 10 Bank Street, White Plains, NY 10606).

PRONUNCIATION EXERCISES

A few exercises focus on pronunciation of grammatical features, such as endings on nouns or verbs and contracted or reduced forms.

Some phonetic symbols are used in these exercises to point out sounds that should not be pronounced identically; for example, /s/, /əz/, and /z/ represent the three predictable pronunciations of the grammatical suffix spelled -s or -es. It is not necessary for students to learn a complete phonetic alphabet; they should merely associate each symbol in an exercise with a sound that is different from all others. The purpose is to help students become more aware of these final sounds in the English they hear to encourage proficiency of use in their own speaking and writing.

In the exercises on spoken contractions, the primary emphasis should be on the students' hearing and becoming familiar with spoken forms rather than on their production of these forms. The students need to understand that what they see in writing is not exactly what they should expect to hear in normal, rapidly spoken English. The most important part of most of these exercises is for the students to listen to your oral production and become familiar with the reduced forms.

Language learners are naturally conscious that their pronunciation is not like that of native speakers of the language. Therefore, some of them are embarrassed or shy about speaking. In a pronunciation exercise, they may be more comfortable if you ask groups or the whole class to say a sentence in unison. After that, individuals may volunteer to speak the same sentence. The learners' production does not need to be "perfect," just understandable. You can encourage the students to be less inhibited by having them teach you how to pronounce words in their languages (unless, of course, you're a native speaker of the students' language in a monolingual class). It's fun—and instructive—for the students to teach the teacher.

SEATWORK

It is generally preferable to assign exercises for out-of-class preparation, but sometimes it's necessary to cover an exercise in class that you haven't been able to assign previously. In "seatwork," you have the students do an unassigned exercise in class immediately before discussing it. Seatwork allows the students to try an exercise themselves before the answers are discussed so that they can discover what problems they may be having with a particular structure. Seatwork may be done individually, in pairs, or in groups.

HOMEWORK

The textbook assumes that the students will have the opportunity to prepare most of the exercises by writing in their books prior to class discussion. Students should be assigned this homework as a matter of course.

The use of the term "written homework" in this *Guide* suggests that the students write out an exercise on their own paper and hand it in to you. How much written homework you have the students do is up to you. The amount generally depends upon such variables as class size, class level, available class time, your available paper-correcting time, not to mention your preferences in teaching techniques. Most of the exercises in the text can be handled through class discussion without the necessity of the students' handing in written homework. Most of the written homework that is suggested in the text and in the chapter notes in this *Guide* consists of activities that will produce original, independent writing.

Using the *Workbook*

The *Workbook* contains selfstudy exercises for independent study, with a perforated answer key found at the end of the book.

Encourage your students to remove this answer key and put it in a folder. It's much easier for the students to correct their own answers if they make their own answer key booklet.

If you prefer the students not have the answers to the exercises, ask them to hand in the answer key at the beginning of the term. Some teachers may prefer to use the *Workbook* for in-class teaching rather than independent study.

The *Workbook* mirrors the main text. Exercises are called "exercises" in the main text and "practices" in the workbook to minimize confusion when you make assignments. Each practice in the *Workbook* has a content title and refers the students to appropriate charts in the main text and in the *Chartbook*.

The *Workbook* practices can be assigned by you or, depending upon the level of maturity or sense of purpose of the class, simply left for the students to use as they wish. They may be assigned to the entire class, or only to those students who need further practice with a particular structure. They may be used as reinforcement after you have covered a chart and exercises in class, or as introductory material prior to discussing a chart in class.

In addition, the students can use the *Workbook* to acquaint themselves with the grammar of any units not covered in class. Earnest students can use the *Workbook* to teach themselves.

PRACTICE TESTS IN THE *WORKBOOK*

Each chapter in the *Workbook* has Practice Test A and Practice Test B. You may wish to use one as a pretest and the other as a post-test, or simply use both of them as summary review material upon finishing a chapter.

The practice tests are not really intended to be "tests." They are simply another exercise type, to be used as a teaching tool like any other exercise. The students should simply be encouraged to do their best and learn from their mistakes.

You may, however, wish to have the students take a practice test in class under time-pressure conditions for experience in taking that kind of test. (Allow 30 seconds per item.) You could also have the students time themselves if they do the practice test at home.

Supplementary Resource Texts

Two teacher resource texts are available:

One is *Fun with Grammar: Communicative Activities for the Azar Grammar Series,* by Suzanne W. Woodward. The text contains games and other language-learning activities that the author created over a span of years of teaching the Azar texts in her classroom.

The other is *Test Bank for Understanding and Using English Grammar,* written by Mark Wade Lieu (to be published in 2001). The tests are keyed to charts or chapters in the student text. They can be reproduced as is, or items can be excerpted for tests that teachers prepare themselves.

Notes on American vs. British English

Students are often curious about differences between American and British English. They should know that the differences are minor. Any students who have studied British English (BrE) should have no trouble adapting to American English (AmE), and vice versa.

Teachers need to be careful not to inadvertently mark differences between AmE and BrE as errors; rather, they should simply point out to the students that a difference in usage exists.

DIFFERENCES IN GRAMMAR

Many of the differences in grammar are either footnoted in the main text or mentioned in the chart notes in this *Guide*. For example, the footnote to Chart 8-3 contains the information that BrE normally uses a plural verb with *government,* whereas AmE uses a singular verb.

Differences in article and preposition usage in certain common expressions follow. These differences are not noted in the text; they are given here for the teacher's information.

AmE	BrE
*be in **the** hospital*	*be in **Ø** hospital*
*be at **the** university (be in college)*	*be at **Ø** university*
*go to **a** university (go to college)*	*go to **Ø** university*
*go to **Ø** class/be in **Ø** class*	*go to **a** class/be in **a** class*
*in **the** future*	*in **Ø** future (OR in **the** future)*
*did it **the next** day*	*did it **Ø** next day (OR **the** next day)*
*haven't done something **for/in** weeks*	*haven't done something **for** weeks*
*ten minutes **past/after** six o'clock*	*ten minutes **past** six o'clock*
*five minutes **to/of/till** seven o'clock*	*five minutes **to** seven o'clock*

In addition, a few verbs have irregular forms ending in *-t* in the simple past and past participle, with use of the *-t* endings more common in BrE than AmE, especially in the verbs *dreamt, leant, smelt, spelt,* and *spoilt.* Both the *-ed* and *-t* forms are given in Chart 2-7 (Irregular Verbs) since the two forms are used in both BrE and AmE to varying degrees.

DIFFERENCES IN SPELLING

Variant spellings can be noted but should not be marked as incorrect in the students' writing. Spelling differences in some common words follow.

AmE	BrE
jewelry, traveler, woolen	*jewellry, traveller, woollen*
skillful, fulfill, installment	*skilful, fulfil, instalment*
color, honor, labor, odor	*colour, honour, labour, odour*

AmE	BrE
-ize (realize, apologize)	-ise/ize (realise/realize, apologise/apologize)
analyze	analyse
defense, offense, license	defence, offence, licence (n.)
theater, center, liter	theatre, centre, litre
check	cheque (bank note)
curb	kerb
forever	for ever/forever
focused	focused/focussed
fueled	fuelled/fueled
jail	gaol
practice (n. and v.)	practise (v.); practice (n. only)
program	programme
specialty	speciality
story	storey (of a building)
tire	tyre

DIFFERENCES IN VOCABULARY

Differences in vocabulary usage between AmE and BrE usually do not significantly interfere with communication, but some misunderstandings may develop. For example, a BrE speaker is referring to underpants or panties when using the word "pants," whereas an AmE speaker is referring to slacks or trousers. Students should know that when American and British speakers read each other's literature, they encounter only very few differences in vocabulary usage. Similarly, Southerners in the United States and New Englanders have differences in vocabulary, but not so much as to interfere with communication. Some differences between AmE and BrE follow:

AmE	BrE
attorney, lawyer	barrister, solicitor
bathrobe	dressing gown
can (of beans)	tin (of beans)
cookie, cracker	biscuit
corn	maize
diaper	nappy
driver's license	driving licence
drug store	chemist's
elevator	lift
eraser	rubber
flashlight	torch
gas, gasoline	petrol
hood of a car	bonnet of a car
living room	sitting room, drawing room
math	maths (e.g., a maths teacher)
raise in salary	rise in salary
rest room	public toilet, WC (water closet)
schedule	timetable
sidewalk	pavement, footpath
sink	basin
soccer	football
stove	cooker
truck	lorry, van
trunk of a car	boot of a car
be on vacation	be on holiday

Key to Pronunciation Symbols

THE PHONETIC ALPHABET (Symbols for American English)

CONSONANTS

Most consonant symbols are used phonetically as they are in normal English spelling. However, a few additional symbols are needed, and some other letters are more restricted in their use as symbols. These special symbols are presented below. (Note that slanted lines indicate that phonetic symbols, not the spelling alphabet, are being used.)

/ θ / (Greek theta) = voiceless *th* as in **thin, thank**
/ δ / (Greek delta) = voiced *th* as in **then, those**
/ ŋ / = *ng* as in *sing, think* (but not in *danger*)
/ š / = *sh* as in **shirt, mission, nation**
/ ž / = *s* or *z* in a few words like *pleasure, azure*
/ č / = *ch* or *tch* as in *watch,* **church**
/ ǰ / = *j* or *dge* as in *jump, le***dge**

The following consonants are used as in *conventional spelling:*
/b, d, f, g, h, k, l, m, n, o, p, r, s, t, v, w, y, z/

Spelling consonants that are <u>not</u> used phonetically in English: c, q, x

VOWELS

The five vowels in the spelling alphabet are inadequate to represent the 12–15 vowel sounds of American speech. Therefore, new symbols and new sound associations for familiar letters must be adopted.

Front	**Central**	**Back** (lips rounded)
/i/ or /iy/ as in *beat*	/ɚ/ or /ər/ as in *word*	/u/, /u:/, or /uw/ as in *boot*
/ɪ/ as in *bit*		/ʊ/ as in *book*
/e/ or /ey/ as in *bait*		/o/ or /ow/ as in *boat*
		/ɔ/ as in *bought*
/ɛ/ as in *bet*	/ə/ as in *but*	
/æ/ as in *bat*	/a/ as in *bother*	

Glides: /ai/ or /ay/ as in *bite*
/ɔi/ or /ɔy/ as in *boy*
/au/ or /aw/ as in *about*

British English has a somewhat different set of vowel sounds and symbols. You might want to consult a standard pronunciation text or BrE dictionary for that system.

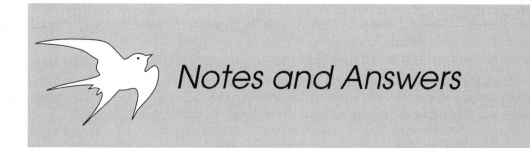

Notes and Answers

Chapter 1: OVERVIEW OF VERB TENSES

ORDER OF CHAPTER	CHARTS	EXERCISES	WORKBOOK
First day of class talking/writing		Ex. 1	
Overview of verb tenses		Ex. 2	
The simple tenses	1-1	Ex. 3	
The progressive tenses	1-2	Ex. 4	
The perfect tenses	1-3	Ex. 5	
The perfect progressive tenses	1-4	Ex. 6	
Summary chart of verb tenses	1-5	Ex. 7 → 9	Pr. 1 → 2
Spelling pretest		Ex. 10	
Spelling of *-ing* and *-ed* forms	1-6	Ex. 11 → 12	Pr. 3

General Notes on Chapter 1

• OBJECTIVE: This chapter begins with an overview of all twelve of the English verb tenses. The intention is for the students to understand that some logical relationships exist among the tenses, i.e., that there is some predictability to the tense system in English.

• APPROACH: Students using this text are probably somewhat familiar with all of the verb tenses (with the possible exceptions of the future perfect and future perfect progressive, two little-used tenses). In presenting the initial charts in this chapter, you can help the learners understand the overall patterns in the English tense system (for example, that all progressive tenses indicate that an activity is/was/will be in progress, or that all perfect tenses indicate that one activity occurs before another activity or time). Then as you proceed through the chapter, you can refer to Chart 1-5 to put each tense within the framework of English verb tenses. For example, you can relate the use of the past progressive *(I was sitting in class at this time yesterday)* to the present progressive *(I am sitting in class right now).*

• TERMINOLOGY: The text calls all twelve verb forms in Chart 1-5 "tenses." Some other analyses of the English verb system may claim that there are only two tenses: past and non-past. They may use the term "aspect" for the perfect and progressive forms.

In this text, the term "tense" is deemed useful because it is easy to use pedagogically to identify twelve verb forms that have particular meanings and uses within a relational system. Whatever these twelve forms are called, the only important consideration for the student is their meaning and use. In sum, it is helpful for purposes of teacher–student communication for the students to learn the names of the tenses. However, one should never lose sight of the fact that the use of grammar labels is simply a means to an end, and that learning them is not an end in itself in the ESL/EFL classroom.

□ EXERCISE 1, p. 1. Introductions and interviews.

ACTIVITY A: First, ask students to suggest questions for topics in the list. Try to elicit idiomatic questions—forms that a native speaker of English would normally use in this situation.

Next, divide the class into pairs, if possible mixing language groups in a multilingual class or mixing proficiency levels in a monolingual class. Discuss two ways to conduct the interview: (1) Student A completes the entire interview of Student B, then Student B conducts an interview of Student A; or (2) Students A and B take turns asking about each topic.

Give the class 10 to 15 minutes for the interviews. Then ask each student to introduce his/her interviewee, giving the person's name and interesting comments about him or her. Either the student or you should write the interviewee's name on the chalkboard. The rest of the class should be encouraged to write down the names of their classmates as a way to start getting to know each other.

As followup to the in-class activity, you could ask the students to write the information from their interviews in a short composition (in class or out of class) and hand it in.

ACTIVITIES B AND C: Discuss what you want the composition to contain before the students begin writing: basic biographical information (name, place of origin, family, education and/or work, etc.); places of residence, travel, and other activities in the past two years; plans for the immediate future (school, work, places of residence, etc.).

ACTIVITY D: You might invite several English speakers to your class so students can interview them in a comfortable setting. Or you could help students identify and contact appropriate interviewees, such as other English teachers, business people, tourists or other visitors. Beforehand, discuss with the class some levels of formality for talking with strangers in an interview.

ACTIVITY E: Assign pairs or small groups of students to go someplace together before or during the next class period and write a report of their experiences. (They could go to an eating place near the school, to a park, to a particular landmark in the city, etc.) Remind them to use only English. You may also wish to use the students' experiences for oral reports. If you assign the students different places to go to, the subsequent oral reports can serve to provide the class as a whole with information about their surroundings.

ASSUMPTIONS: This exercise assumes that students know how to ask and answer basic questions in English. (You may wish to give a short review of question word order if the need arises during class discussion, but primarily this first exercise in class is not intended to focus on any grammar in particular. You may, however, wish to refer the students to Appendix Unit B: Questions if problems such as word order arise, or use that unit as a followup to this exercise.) This exercise also assumes that the students don't know each other. If all of the students are already acquainted, they could pretend to be famous persons being interviewed by television or newspaper reporters and make up entirely different questions.

ACTIVITY A QUESTIONS: **1.** What is your name? **2.** How do you spell your (last) name? / How do you spell that? **3.** Where are you from? / What country are you from? / What is your hometown? / Where were you born? **4.** Where are you living? / Where do you live? **5.** How long have you been living (in this place/here)? How long do you plan to be / are you planning to be / are you going to be (in this place here)? **6.** Why did you (decide to) come here? **7.** [If a student]: What is your major / your field of study? / What are you studying? [If an employee]: What kind of work do you do? / What do you do? **8.** What do you like to do in your spare time? / Do you have any hobbies? **9.** How are you getting along? **10.** How do you like living here? / What do you think of (this place)?

☐ EXERCISE 2, p. 2. Overview of verb tenses. (Chapters 1 → 5)

First have the students go through the items in pairs. Then follow up with a teacher-led review of each item. You can use this exercise to introduce almost all the essential information contained in Charts 1-1 through 1-5 by discussing each item in detail and presenting the diagram of tenses that appears in the following charts. Or you can simply use this exercise as a quick run-through of the tenses prior to your presentation of Charts 1-1 through 1-5.

EXPECTED QUESTIONS: **1.** What do you do every day before you leave home? **2.** What did you do last night? **3.** What were you doing at (this exact time) yesterday? **4.** What are you doing right now? **5.** What have you done since you got up this morning? **6.** What have you been doing for the past five minutes? **7.** What will you do/are you going to do tomorrow? **8.** What will you be doing at (this exact time) tomorrow? **9.** What had you done by the time you got here today? **10.** What will you have done by the time you go to bed tonight? [Note: The past perfect progressive and the future perfect progressive are not included in this exercise. You may wish to add them.]

CHARTS 1-1 THROUGH 1-5: OVERVIEW OF VERB TENSES

• The purpose of these charts is to help the students understand the relationships in form and meaning among verb tenses. Discuss the examples, explain the diagrams, summarize tense forms and meanings, and ask for additional examples from the class.

• Not all the possible uses of each tense are included in these charts. Tense information is expanded in the individual charts for each tense in the chapters that follow.

• In Chart 1-5, point out the tense relationships both vertically and horizontally, especially for the progressive, perfect, and perfect progressive forms and meanings.

• Consider making a wall chart or transparency of Chart 1-5 for reference during class discussions throughout the time spent on Chapters 1 through 5.

• See the *Introduction*, pp. xi-xiii, to this *Guide* for suggestions for presenting the grammar

---

☐ EXERCISE 3, p. 3. The simple tenses. (Chart 1-1)

Ask leading questions to promote the verb tenses you want the students to use. In Exercises 3 through 6, the questions in the text are only suggestions, a springboard. Follow up with questions of your own, using the specific people, place, and time of your classroom as the context.

ERRATUM: Items 3 and 4 were accidentally combined. Item 4 should read: "What are you going to do tomorrow?" These are separated in subsequent printings. Errata are listed on pp. 243-244 following the *Appendix*.

POSSIBLE RESPONSES: **1.** The sun rises in the east. Water and oil don't mix.   **2.** Every day I get out of bed, get dressed, and have breakfast.   **3.** Yesterday I took the bus to school, went to class, and cooked dinner.   **4.** Tomorrow is Saturday, so I am going to do my laundry.

☐ EXERCISE 4, p. 3.   The progressive tenses.   (Chart 1-2)

POSSIBLE RESPONSES: **1.** Right now I am doing Exercise 4. My classmates are looking at their grammar books. It is raining outside the classroom.   **2.** At two o'clock this morning, I was at home. I was sleeping.   **3.** At two o'clock tomorrow morning, I will be at home. I will be sleeping.

☐ EXERCISE 5, p. 4.   The perfect tenses.   (Chart 1-3)

POSSIBLE RESPONSES: **1.** Yes, I have already eaten today. I had lunch at noon.   **2.** Yes, I had eaten supper before I went to bed last night.   **3.** Yes, by the time I go to bed tonight, I will have had dinner.

☐ EXERCISE 6, p. 5.   The perfect progressive tenses.   (Chart 1-4)

POSSIBLE RESPONSES: **1.** Right now I am doing an exercise in my grammar book. I have been doing the exercise for ten minutes.   **2.** Last night at nine o'clock I was doing my English homework. I stopped doing my homework at ten o'clock. I stopped doing my homework because my eyes were tired. I had been doing my English homework for two hours before I stopped.   **3.** At nine o'clock tomorrow night, I am going to be doing my English homework. I am going to stop doing my English homework at ten o'clock. I need to go to sleep at ten o'clock. I will have been doing my English homework for one hour before I stop.

☐ EXERCISE 7, p. 8.   Overview of verb tenses.   (Charts 1-1 → 1-5)

The purpose of this exercise is to consolidate the information the students have received to this point. This exercise is essentially only additional examples of tense usage. It also seeks to promote the learning of the names of the tenses, which is helpful for student–teacher communication during the units on verb tense usage. Students will become more comfortable with the names as they proceed through the chapters on the tenses. After they are done with this course in English, however, they can and probably will forget the names of the tenses and never miss them. Grammar terminology is important only for short-term pedagogy; the learning of grammar terminology is never an end in itself.

If the students work in pairs or groups, you may want to ask them to draw the diagrams that represent the tense used in each item. If you lead the discussion, perhaps draw all the diagrams on the board and ask the students to identify which diagram applies to which example. You could create a game wherein the students match the tense name, diagram, and usage example. For example, write on the board the names of all the tenses and number them. Draw all twelve diagrams and number them. Then ask the students to match the correct numbers of the tense names and diagrams to the numbers of the items in the exercise.

ANSWERS: **2.** The speakers are discussing an activity that began and ended in the past. Tense: the simple past   **3.** The speakers are discussing an activity that is happening (is in progress) at the moment of speaking. Tense: the present progressive   **4.** The speakers are discussing an activity in progress at a particular time in the past. Tense: the past progressive   **5.** The speakers are discussing activities that have occurred (or not occurred) "before now," at unspecific times in the past. Tense: the present perfect   **6.** The speakers are discussing what will happen at a specific time in the future. Tense: the simple future   **7.** This question concerns an activity that will be in progress at a particular time in the future. Tense: the future progressive   **8.** This question concerns the duration of an activity that started in the past and is still in progress. Tense: the present perfect progressive   **9.** The speakers are talking about the duration of an activity that has already started and will end at a specific time in the future. Tense: the future perfect progressive   **10.** This question concerns an activity that started and ended before another time in the past. Tense: the past perfect   **11.** This question concerns an activity that will be finished before a particular time in the future. Tense: the future perfect   **12.** This question concerns the duration of an activity that began before another time in the past. Tense: the past perfect progressive

☐ EXERCISE 8, p. 9.   Overview of verb tenses.   (Charts 1-1 → 1-5)

If teacher-led, this exercise can be a quick summary review of the chapter. If more time is available, ask the students to identify the names of the tenses. Also possible: have one student answer the question while another draws the appropriate diagram on the board.

Also possible is simply to have the students work in pairs, using this review as a quick reinforcement of what they have practiced thus far.

POSSIBLE ANSWERS: **1.** I brush my teeth every day.   **2.** I combed my hair yesterday.   **3.** Tomorrow I will hug my children and kiss my wife/husband.   **4.** Right now I am talking to you. [Note: The answers in the *Teacher's Guide* give the full, uncontracted forms of verbs rather than contracting them with pronoun subjects. Auxiliary verbs such as *will* and *am* are usually contracted in speech. See Appendix Unit C.]   **5.** At this time yesterday, I was watching a game on TV.   **6.** At this time tomorrow, I will be sitting right here.   **7.** Since I got up this morning, I have eaten breakfast and have come to school.   **8.** Before I went to bed last night, I had eaten dinner, done my homework, and read the newspaper.   **9.** By the time I go to bed tonight, I will have watched the news on TV.   **10.** I am talking to you. I have been talking to you for ten minutes.   **11.** Before Ms. Foley walked into the classroom today, I was chatting with the student next to me. I had been doing that for five minutes.   **12.** Tomorrow before Ms. Foley walks into the classroom, I will be talking to the student who sits next to me. I will have been talking to him/her for four or five minutes before Ms. Foley walks into the classroom.

☐ EXERCISE 9, p. 9.   Error analysis: questions and negative verb forms.
(Appendix Charts B-1, B-2, and D-1)

Basic usage ability of question and negative verb forms is assumed in this text. It is assumed that your students know the correct forms of the structures presented in this exercise. If they don't or if you feel a quick review might be appropriate, now might be a good time for you to insert Appendix Charts B-1, B-2, and D-1 into your syllabus.

See the *Introduction*, p. xviii, to this *Teacher's Guide* for suggestions on handling Error Analysis exercises.

ANSWERS:
   1. Does Pedro <u>walk</u> to work every morning?
   2. What <u>are you</u> talking about? I <u>don't</u> understand you.
   3. Did you <u>finish</u> your work?
   4. My friend doesn't <u>like</u> her apartment.
   5. Do you <u>work</u> for this company?   OR   <u>Are you</u> working for this company?
   6. What time <u>did</u> your plane arrive?
   7. How long have you <u>been</u> living in this city?   OR   How long have you <u>lived</u> in this city?
   8. My brother <u>doesn't</u> have <u>a</u> job right now.
   9. Ali <u>won't</u> ~~to~~ be in class tomorrow.
  10. I <u>hadn't seen</u> snow before I moved to Canada last year.   OR   I <u>had</u> never <u>seen</u> snow before I moved to Canada last year.

□ **EXERCISE 10, p. 10.   Spelling pretest.   (Chart 1-6)**

Follow the example: say the word, then the complete sentence, then the word again. Students write only the word on their papers.

   At the end, they can correct their own or each other's papers as you or the students write on the chalkboard. Discuss spelling rules as the papers are being corrected. The order of this exercise follows the order of the spelling rules presented in Chart 1-6.

   ALTERNATIVE: You may wish to tell the students to correct their own papers by referring to Chart 1-6 before you discuss the answers with the class.

ANSWERS: 1. hoped   2. dining   3. stopped   4. planning   5. rained
   6. waiting   7. listening   8. happened   9. beginning   10. occurred
   11. starting   12. warned   13. enjoyed   14. playing   15. studying
   16. worried   17. died   18. lying

CHART 1-6:   SPELLING OF *-ING* AND *-ED* FORMS

• Briefly discuss the spelling rule illustrated by each group of examples so that the students become familiar with the content of the chart and can use it for later reference.

• Discuss this chart in conjunction with giving the correct answers to Exercise 10.

• British and American spelling with these two suffixes sometimes differs. The most notable example is the doubling of "l" in British but not American English. American English follows the rules in this chart; British English does not.

   AmE: *canceling, traveled, fueled, dueling*

   BrE: *cancelling, travelled, fuelled, duelling*

Other variations: AmE = *focused*; BrE = *focussed*

   AmE = *worshiped* or *worshipped*; BrE = *worshipped*

☐ **EXERCISES 11 and 12, p. 11.   Spelling of -ING and -ED forms. (Chart 1-6)**

Complete one exercise at a time. Give students a few minutes to write the answers, then they can check their own work or each other's. Either the students or the teacher can supply answers, preferably written on the chalkboard.

Even if the students don't know the meaning of some of the words in these exercises, they should be able to spell the forms correctly. After the students have written the correct forms, supply vocabulary definitions for the class as necessary.

EX. 11 ANSWERS:
PART I.   **2.** hiding   **3.** running   **4.** ruining   **5.** coming   **6.** writing
7. eating   **8.** sitting   **9.** acting   **10.** patting   **11.** opening   **12.** beginning
13. earning   **14.** frying   **15.** dying   **16.** employing

PART II.   **2.** trying, tried   **3.** staying, stayed   **4.** taping, taped   **5.** tapping, tapped
6. offering, offered   **7.** preferring, preferred   **8.** gaining, gained   **9.** planning, planned   **10.** tying, tied   **11.** helping, helped   **12.** studying, studied
13. admitting, admitted   **14.** visiting, visited   **15.** hugging, hugged
16. raging, raged

EX. 12 ANSWERS:
PART I.   **2.** jarred   **3.** jeered   **4.** dotted   **5.** looted   **6.** pointed   **7.** exited
8. permitted   **9.** intensified   **10.** destroyed   **11.** suffered   **12.** occurred

PART II.   **14.** riding   **15.** bidding   **16.** burying   **17.** decaying   **18.** tying
19. taming   **20.** teeming   **21.** trimming   **22.** harming   **23.** ripening
24. regretting

Chapter 2: PRESENT AND PAST, SIMPLE AND PROGRESSIVE

ORDER OF CHAPTER	CHARTS	EXERCISES	WORKBOOK
Preview: present and past verbs		Ex. 1	
Simple present vs. present progressive	2-1 → 2-2	Ex. 2 → 5	Pr. 1
Stative verbs	2-3	Ex. 6	Pr. 2
Am/is/are being + adjective	2-4	Ex. 7 → 9	
Regular and irregular verbs; pronunciation of *-ed* endings	2-5 → 2-6	Ex. 10 → 12	Pr. 3 → 4
Irregular verbs	2-7	Ex. 13 → 16	Pr. 5 → 9
Raise/rise, set/sit, lay/lie	2-8	Ex. 17 → 18	Pr. 10
Simple past vs. past progressive	2-9 → 2-10	Ex. 19 → 22	
Using progressive verbs with *always* to complain	2-11	Ex. 23	
Using expressions of place with progressive verbs	2-12	Ex. 24	
Cumulative review		Ex. 25	Pr. 11 → 13

General Notes on Chapter 2

• OBJECTIVE: This chapter explores four high-frequency verb tenses, reviewing and reinforcing the students' ability to use them, and introduces some finer points of usage of these tenses.

• APPROACH: The text presents and compares first the simple present and present progressive, including their use with stative verbs, then the simple past and past progressive. The simple past unit includes pronunciation of *-ed* endings and special practice on irregular verbs.

• TERMINOLOGY: "Progressive" is also called "continuous" is some grammars. A clause is a structure containing a subject and a verb. A clause may be either independent (also called a main clause) or dependent (subordinate).

☐ EXERCISE 1, p. 12.   Preview: present and past verbs.
(Chapter 2; Appendix Charts B-1, B-2, and C-1)

This exercise can be used as a pretest. Give the class a few minutes to do the exercise as seat work prior to class discussion. The purpose is for the students to discover which grammar points they need to pay special attention to in this chapter.

The text assumes that the students do not know all the grammar covered in this exercise. If your students can do this exercise without any difficulty or questions, they probably don't need to study this chapter—and indeed may be using a book that is too simple for them.

While this exercise previews the grammar found in this chapter, it also includes grammar not found in this chapter, grammar it is assumed the students are already familiar with, such as word order in questions, parallel structure, and the use of final -s/-es in third person singular simple present verbs. You may wish to take some time in class to review these points. (Question and negative forms can be found in the Appendix, parallel structure in Chapter 16, and final -s/-es in Chapter 6.)

ANSWERS: **2.** I <u>don't know</u> Sam's wife.   **3.** A: What <u>are you</u> talking about?   B: I <u>am</u> talking about the political situation in my country.   **4.** My roommate usually <u>watches</u> TV, <u>listens</u> to music, or <u>goes</u> out in the evening.   **5.** When I turned the ignition key, the car <u>started</u>.   **6.** This class <u>consists</u> of students who <u>want</u> to learn English.   **7.** The children <u>drew</u> some pictures in school this morning.   **8.** While Tom <u>was</u> reading in bed last night, his phone <u>rang</u>. When he <u>answered</u> it, the caller <u>hung</u> up.   **9.** Right now Sally <u>is</u> in the kitchen eating breakfast.   **10.** When the sun <u>rises</u>, it <u>appears</u> from below the horizon.

CHARTS 2-1 and 2-2:   SIMPLE PRESENT AND PRESENT PROGRESSIVE

• Now that the students have covered preliminary material on the English tense system and spelling of -*ing* and -*ed* forms, the text focuses on each tense in more detail.

• Throughout the rest of the chapters on verb tenses, the exercises contain questions, negatives, contractions, and midsentence adverbs. These topics are assumed to be primarily review at this level, but most students still need to work with them. You may wish to refer your students to the Appendix for more information about these topics, or fit the Appendix Units into your class instruction as you see the need and find the time.

☐ Exercise 2, p. 13.   Simple present vs. present progressive.   (Charts 2-1 and 2-2)

SAMPLE ANSWERS: **1.** I get up at 7:00 every morning.   **2.** The sun rises in the east and sets in the west.   **3.** We are working on Exercise 2.   **4.** SIMPLE PRESENT: *(Name of a country)* is at war with *(name of a country)*. PRESENT PROGRESSIVE: These two countries are fighting a war.   **5.** On page 75, the horse is laughing at the rider, who is sitting on the ground.

☐ EXERCISE 3, p. 13. Activity: using the present progressive. (Chart 2-2)

Students write one action on a piece of paper. Collect those papers and redistribute them around the class. (If the class is very large, this can be done in small groups.) A student, without saying anything, performs the action written on his/her piece of paper, and another student describes the activity using the present progressive. This is a lively technique for using English to describe something that is actually happening.

☐ EXERCISE 4, p. 14. Simple present vs. present progressive. (Charts 2-1 and 2-2)

ANSWERS: 2. washes   3. usually sits . . . is sitting   4. am trying   5. Do you always lock   6. am still waiting   7. is shining   8. shines . . . wakes   9. is snowing . . . doesn't snow   10. A: am I doing   B: are rubbing . . . are rubbing

☐ EXERCISE 5, p. 14. Activity: using present verbs. (Charts 2-1 and 2-2)

Tell students not to say the words written for Speakers A and B but to follow the instructions. Set a time limit of five to seven minutes. Be sure that all students have a chance to be both A and B.

Give an example for each item before the pair work begins. For example, for item 1, ask the class to close their eyes. Now, scratch the chalkboard. (Other possibilities for item 1: writing on the chalkboard, tapping one's foot, opening/closing a window or door, closing a book, snapping one's fingers, blowing.) For item 2, lift your eyebrows, look out the window, or lean on the desk. For item 3, describe someone in the room, being purposefully vague but progressively becoming more informative, e.g., "The person I'm thinking of has dark hair. She's sitting in the front half of the room. She's sitting nearer to Abdul-Rahman than to Graciela. She's wearing earrings. She has on a white blouse and jeans." Etc.

CHART 2-3: STATIVE VERBS

• The key point is the difference between "states" and "activities." No verb is inherently stative. The intention of this chart and its terminology is simply to inform the students that certain common verbs are usually not used in the progressive.

• In the list of stative verbs, even the verbs without asterisks can, usually only in rare circumstances, be used in the progressive. The text, however, concentrates only on the usual, most frequent use of these words. [For example: *I am loving being on vacation* is possible. More usual usage of *love: I love* (not *am loving*) *my family very much.*]

• The list of stative (i.e., nonprogressive) verbs is by no means complete. For the most part, it stresses only those verbs used in the exercises. A few other verbs you may or may not wish to mention as being nonprogressive when used to describe states are *amaze, astonish, concern, equal, exist, impress, involve, lack, measure, please, regret, resemble, satisfy, sound, surprise, wish.*

□ Exercise 6, p. 16. Verbs that have both stative and progressive meanings. (Chart 2-3)

See the *Introduction,* p. xix, for suggestions on handling discussion-of-meaning exercises.

ANSWERS:

1. a. *smell* describes a state that exists, i.e., the flowers have a smell, and that smell is good.
   b. *is smelling* describes the action of using one's nose.
2. a. *think* means "believe" in this sentence and describes a state.
   b. *am thinking* is an action; thoughts are going through the speaker's mind.
3. a. *see* describes a perception that exists right now as a result of the speaker using his/her eyes.
   b. *is seeing a doctor* means "is going to a doctor for help," a general activity in progress at present.
   c. *are seeing* means they are dating each other, a general activity in progress at present.
4. a. *looks* means "appears" or "seems to be" and describes an apparent state that exists: Kathy is apparently cold.
   b. *is looking* describes the action of using one's eyes.
5. a. *appears* means "seems" and describes an apparent state that exists.
   b. *is appearing* describes the action of performing on stage in a theater, a general activity in progress at present.
6. a. *is feeling* describes the action of using one's sense of touch. Sue is using her hands to touch the cat's fur. The activity is in progress at the present moment.
   b. *feels* describes a state that exists, the state of the cat's fur; i.e., it is soft.
   c. *am not feeling* describes the speaker's physical feelings of illness, in progress at the present. [Note: The simple present is also possible here with little difference in meaning (*I don't feel well today*) to describe a state that exists.]
   d. *feel* means "think" or "believe" in this sentence and describes a state.
7. a. *has* means "owns" here and describes a state that exists.
   b. *am having* and *is having* mean "experiencing" and describe activities in progress.
8. a. *remember* describes a state that exists.
   b. *is remembering* describes an activity in progress: memories are going through Aunt Sara's mind.
9. a. *weighs* describes a state that exists.
   b. *is weighing* describes an activity in progress: the grocer is putting the bananas on a scale and reading what the scale says.

CHART 2-4: *AM/IS/ARE BEING* + ADJECTIVE

• *Be* is usually a stative verb. When used in the progressive with an adjective, it gives a special meaning. Clarify the notion that this form describes temporary behavior in progress by acting out one or more of the adjectives. For example, make a lot of noise and ask the students to describe your behavior: "Am I being loud? noisy? quiet? Who's being quiet?" Or ask three students to role-play riders on a bus: Two people are sitting on the bus. An old, old person gets on. One of those sitting offers his/her seat to the old person, but the other does not. Ask the class "Who is being polite? thoughtful? kind? Who is being impolite?"

• This chart presents a relatively minor point of English grammar, but one advanced students often find of interest. Sentences with *am/is/are being* + *an adjective* are relatively uncommon. The use of *be* in the progressive is more common in the passive voice: e.g., *A new school is being constructed in our neighborhood.* Students will practice *be* + *being* in Chapter 11.

☐ **EXERCISE 7, p. 17. AM/IS/ARE BEING** + adjective. (Chart 2-4)

> *ANSWERS:* **2.** careful, kind, responsible   **3.** polite, quiet   **4.** cruel, unfair, unpleasant   **5.** good, noisy

☐ **EXERCISE 8, p. 18. Simple present vs. present progressive. (Charts 2-1 → 2-4)**

> *ANSWERS:* **2.** is beginning . . . don't have . . . is wearing   **3.** don't own . . . wear
> **4.** sleep . . . get . . . study   **5.** is taking . . . don't want . . . needs   **6.** am looking
> . . . looks . . . has . . . isn't having   **7.** am looking . . . is writing . . . is biting . . . is
> scratching . . . is staring . . . seems . . . is thinking . . . do you think . . . is doing
> **8.** want . . . know . . . means . . . does "sword" mean   **9.** is doing . . . is being . . .
> doesn't want . . . is always

☐ **EXERCISE 9, p. 19. Activity: using present verbs in writing. (Charts 2-1 → 2-4)**

> To introduce this assignment, have the class brainstorm ideas for a sample composition that might begin with *I am sitting in my English class* as a way of explaining to them what you want them to write at home.

CHART 2-5:   REGULAR AND IRREGULAR VERBS

• Review the terminology.

CHART 2-6:   REGULAR VERBS: PRONUNCIATION OF *-ED* ENDINGS

• These three pronunciations are automatic for speakers of English. If the wrong one is used (e.g., *save* + /əd/ or *look* + /əd/), the result is a "foreign accent" that may be difficult to understand.

• Failure to include appropriate suffixes such as *-ed* and *-s* is common among learners of English as a second or foreign language. Since these sounds are unstressed, learners often don't hear them, and if they don't hear them, they tend not to use them in their own production, whether oral or written. Concentrating on the spoken forms of the *-ed* suffix may help the students correct ingrained usage problems with this form in their own production. Students are not expected to stop and figure out the correct pronunciation while speaking, but the awareness of the three differing forms may help them hear these suffixes more readily and internalize them more easily.

☐ EXERCISE 10, p. 20.   Pronunciation of -ED endings.   (Chart 2-6)

Have students repeat after you. Discuss the difference between voiceless and voiced sounds. (The voiceless sounds in English are the consonant sounds of /p/, /t/, /k/, /h/, /f/, /θ/, /š/, /č/, /ǰ/. Other consonants and all vowels are voiced.) To explain voiced vs. voiceless sounds, have the students put their hands to their throats so they can feel their voice box vibrate when they make the "v" sound but not when they make the "f" sound. Point out that their teeth and lips are in exactly the same position for both sounds. Other voiceless/voiced pairs that you can similarly use are "t" and "d," "s" and "z," "p" and "b."

See p. xxii of the *Introduction* for information about the phonetic alphabet as used in this *Teacher's Guide*.

ANSWERS: **2.** sob/d/   **3.** grade/əd/   **4.** ask/t/   **5.** help/t/   **6.** watch/t/
7. fill/d/   **8.** defend/əd/   **9.** pour/d/   **10.** wait/əd/   **11.** enjoy/d/
12. load/əd/   **13.** roam/d/   **14.** kiss/t/   **15.** halt/əd/   **16.** laugh/t/
17. dry/d/   **18.** believe/d/   **19.** judge/d/   **20.** count/əd/   **21.** add/əd/
22. box/t/   **23.** rest/əd/   **24.** push/t/

☐ EXERCISE 11, p. 21.   Pronunciation of -ED endings.   (Chart 2-6)

Ask a student to read one sentence aloud. You may then ask the student to tell you which pronunciation he/she attempted for each past tense verb, or ask the rest of the class what they heard.

ANSWERS: **2.** hope/t/   **3.** mop/t/ . . . vacuum/d/ . . . dust/əd/   **4.** last/əd/
5. tap/t   **6.** describe/d/   **7.** demand/əd/   **8.** push/t/ . . . pull/d/
9. hand/əd/   **10.** toot/əd/   **11.** ask/t/   **12.** flood/əd/   **13.** depart/əd/ . . .
land/əd/   **14.** jump/t/ . . . shout/əd/

☐ EXERCISE 12, p. 21.   Activity: pronunciation of -ED endings.   (Chart 2-6)

The point of this exercise is for the students to pronounce precisely and listen attentively.

NOTE: In the example, the question of *spilled* vs. *spilt* may arise. American English generally uses *spilled* (spill/d/), while British English uses *spilt* (spil/t/). Both are correct. Alternatives such are these are noted in Chart 2-7.

ERRATUM: The last blue chart heading should read: /əd/ not /əz/. This is corrected in subsequent printings.

CHART 2-7:   IRREGULAR VERBS: AN ALPHABETICAL LIST

• Review the terminology.

• The list on pp. 19–20 is for reference. Ask the students to look through it to see if they have any questions about vocabulary or pronunciation. Define and pronounce as necessary.

• You may occasionally spend three to five minutes quizzing the class on irregular verb forms as an on-going review throughout several weeks of the term. Give the cue and ask a student to say all three forms, pronouncing and spelling them carefully. This can be done orally or on the chalkboard.

☐ EXERCISES 13–16, pp. 24–25. Oral review of irregular verbs. (Chart 2-7)

The exercises should go at a fast pace, almost like a game. The directions call for pair work, but you may wish to lead the exercises yourself, in which case responses can be individual or the whole class together. Students should be encouraged to respond as quickly as possible rather than formulating their answers mentally first. A mistake is nothing more than a learning opportunity. Tell them just to open their mouths and see what happens. (This encouragement is especially pertinent for those cultural groups that tend to write what they want to say in their minds before they speak and judge themselves harshly if they err.) They may be surprised by how much they already know. And while they're practicing irregular verbs, they're also building fluency.

Instead of either pair work or teacher-led work, you may wish to try group work. After you set the pace and demonstrate the format, the students can continue in small groups with leaders asking the questions. Only the leaders have their texts open. The leaders are responsible for monitoring the responses.

You might explain that the usual response to yes/no questions such as these is a short response ("Yes, I did"), but that for the purposes of practicing irregular verbs, the students are asked to give a long response. The short response can be included or not, as the responding student prefers. Students usually have no problem understanding that some grammar exercises focus on particular points for practice purposes and that not all their utterances in their study of English in the classroom need to be personally meaningful creative self-expression. The text has many other types of exercises for that. And indeed, most students enjoy word games such as these exercises.

In Exercise 13, item 24 is supposed to cause a smile, with the answer being "No!!!!! The dog bit me!" It's included just to keep the students from going entirely on automatic pilot and saying something like "Yes, I bit the dog."

Exercises 13–16 can be done over several class periods, not all at one time. They can also be repeated at a later time, after a few days or weeks, for review. They are good for the last five minutes of a class period. They can also be used as oral test items.

EX. 13 PARTIAL ANSWERS: **1.** Yes, I drank . . . .   **2.** brought   **3.** forgot
4. shook   **5.** caught   **6.** drove   **7.** lost   **8.** mislaid   **9.** found
10. understood   **11.** told   **12.** spread [no change in form]   **13.** fell
14. hurt   **15.** flew   **16.** wore   **17.** hung   **18.** ate   **19.** took   **20.** rode
21. swore [This refers to a formal promise, as in a court of law.]   **22.** forgave
23. wrote   **24.** No! I didn't bite the dog. The dog bit me. [a little humor!]

EX. 14 PARTIAL ANSWERS: **1.** No, someone else made . . . .   **2.** broke   **3.** stole
4. took   **5.** drew   **6.** swept   **7.** taught   **8.** dug   **9.** fed   **10.** hid
11. blew   **12.** threw   **13.** tore   **14.** built   **15.** spoke   **16.** wove

EX. 15 PARTIAL ANSWERS: **1.** Yes, I gave . . . .   **2.** stood   **3.** chose [Note the spelling
and differing pronunciations of *choose* and *chose*.]   **4.** ran [If the class does not meet in the
morning, substitute another time word.]   **5.** slept   **6.** heard   **7.** withdrew
8. woke up [also possible: *waked*]   **9.** swam   **10.** went   **11.** bent   **12.** sent
13. sang   **14.** stuck   **15.** ground   **16.** struck   **17.** lit [also possible:
lighted]   **18.** meant   **19.** held   **20.** spoke

EX. 16 PARTIAL ANSWERS: **1.** Yes, it began . . . .   [Add the correct time.] **2.** rose
3. cut [no change in form]   **4.** bled   **5.** grew   **6.** stung   **7.** rang
8. froze   **9.** quit [no change in form; also possible in BrE: *quitted*]   **10.** fought
11. crept   **12.** shot   **13.** fled   **14.** won   **15.** slid   **16.** swung   **17.** blew
18. burst [no change in form]   **19.** broadcast [no change in form]   **20.** knew

---

CHART 2-8:   TROUBLESOME VERBS: *RAISE/RISE, SET/SIT, LAY/LIE*

- If necessary, refer students to Appendix Chart A-1 for further information about transitive and intransitive verbs.

- Mention that native speakers find these verbs troublesome, too, especially *lay* and *lie*.

- There is one other difference between *raise* and *rise* that you may wish to mention to advanced students or to those who have studied principally British English: As nouns meaning "an increase in salary," Americans get "a raise in pay," while Brits get "a rise in pay."

☐ **EXERCISE 17, p. 26.   Troublesome verbs.   (Chart 2-8)**

ANSWERS: **1.** raised **2.** rises **3.** sat **4.** set **5.** lay **6.** lying
7. laid **8.** lie **9.** lies **10.** raises **11.** rose **12.** lays **13.** laid
14. set **15.** sat **16.** lies

☐ **EXERCISE 18, p. 27.   Troublesome verbs.   (Chart 2-8)**

POSSIBLE ANSWERS: **1.** The following things rise: smoke, the sun, the moon, the temperature, airplanes, a helium-filled balloon, mountains, the stock market, someone's voice, prices, emotions.   **2.** I raised my book above my head.   **3.** I set my book on my desk. I laid my book on my desk.   **4.** My book is sitting on the desk. It is lying on the desk.   **5.** Canada lies to the north of the United States. The Pacific Ocean lies to the west and the Atlantic to the east.

CHARTS 2-9 AND 2-10:   SIMPLE PAST AND PAST PROGRESSIVE

- Chart 2-9 is the first appearance of the word "clause." You may wish at this point to explain that a clause is a structure that has a subject and a verb, and make the distinction between a main or independent clause and a dependent clause. (Students will concentrate on complex sentences in later chapters.) Adverb clauses of time are in Chapter 5. You may wish to refer the students to Charts 5-1 and 5-2, but at this point it is usually sufficient to refer simply to *when*-clauses and *while*-clauses. The text assumes that the students are quite familiar with sentences containing basic adverb clauses of time with subordinating conjunctions such as *when, while, before,* and *after.* Keep the focus on verb tenses, with minimal attention to complex sentence structure for the time being.

- Note in (g) and (h): In sentences with *when,* the progressive usually occurs in the main clause. In sentences with *while,* the progressive usually occurs in the *while*-clause. [Sometimes *when* has the same meaning as *while,* and the progressive is used in a *when*-clause: e.g., *When (i.e., while) I was walking home last night, I suddenly remembered that it was my wife's birthday.*]

- Suggestion: If you wish to review some of the information in the Chapter 1 overview, compare the tenses in the pictured examples with other tenses. For example:

    Rita **stood** under a tree when it **began** to rain. vs. Rita **was standing** under a tree when it **began** to rain. vs. Rita **had stood** under a tree when it **began** to rain. vs. Rita **had been standing** under a tree for several minutes when it **began** to rain. vs. Rita **will stand** under a tree when it **begins** to rain. vs. Rita **will be standing** under a tree when it **begins** to rain.

☐ EXERCISE 19, p. 28.   Simple past vs. past progressive. (Charts 2-9 and 2-10)

Some items are dialogues between Speakers A and B. Two students can read a dialogue aloud. Then you can ask them to repeat it with their books closed. This is a good technique to use occasionally for improving fluency.

ANSWERS: **2.** didn't want . . . was raining   **3.** called . . . wasn't . . . was studying **4.** didn't hear . . . was sleeping   **5.** was shining . . . was blowing . . . were singing **6.** were arguing . . . walked   **7.** opened . . . found   **8.** was reading . . . fell . . . closed . . . tiptoed   **9.** was waiting   **10.** A: Did you hear   B: wasn't listening . . . was thinking   **11.** A: did you break   B: slipped . . . was crossing   **12.** was she wearing   **13.** finally found . . . was already . . . were talking busily . . . were speaking . . . were conversing . . . were just sitting . . . chose . . . sat . . . walked . . . stopped **14.** was snowing . . . was shining . . . were shoveling . . . was lying

☐ EXERCISE 20, p. 30.   Activity: using past verbs in speaking. (Charts 2-9 and 2-10)

A pantomime is performed silently. Ideas are communicated by gestures and movements, not by words. Individual students choose incidents to pantomime. They need to think for a while about how they will perform them.

Demonstrate a pantomime yourself or possibly select a volunteer. Then ask a student to describe what happened using past verbs. Other students can then add details that were missed. Your task is to focus attention on the correct use of verb tenses because, in the excitement of describing the details, students may tend to slip into present or uninflected forms. The grammar focus should be on consistent use of past verbs. You may wish to let other errors go by unremarked.

ALTERNATIVE: Students can divide into small groups and follow the above steps. A leader in each group can watch the time limit. Tell the students to monitor each other on using past verbs.

☐ EXERCISE 21, p. 30.   Activity: using past verbs in writing. (Charts 2-9 and 2-10)

A written description can be done either before or after an oral description of a pantomime. The writing can be done either in or out of class. Usually the students are able to produce better writing when it follows class discussion of a pantomime.

ALTERNATIVE: Prior to assigning written homework, write one description as a group activity, with you writing on the chalkboard as students suggest sentences. Then revise the writing with the help of the class and focus the students' attention on chronological organization and using "time words" as connective devices.

☐ EXERCISE 22, p. 30.   Activity: using present and past verbs in writing. (Chapter 2)

When you mark the papers, focus mainly on the use of verb tenses. Other errors should be given less attention. Add an enthusiastic note of praise or encouragement for good work and success.

CHART 2-11:	USING PROGRESSIVE WITH *ALWAYS* TO COMPLAIN

- Call the students' attention to word order: *always* occurs immediately before the main verb.

- The structure in this chart may not be especially significant in a student's overall language usage ability, but it's fun and can be used to point out that a grammatical form can convey a speaker's emotional attitude. This chart and the following exercise are also good places for students to practice conveying emotion in speech through sentence stress and intonation.

☐ **EXERCISE 23, p. 31.   Using progressive verbs with ALWAYS.   (CHART 2-11)**

Encourage the students to be a bit theatrical as they produce their sentences. Model some of the sentences for the students: say the sentences with annoyance or disgust in your voice, emphasizing the word "always." Use a gesture of annoyance such as rolling your eyes upward and lifting your eyebrows while saying "always," or make some forceful gesture with your hands and arms. Students should repeat your sentence with the same voice and gestures. In some sentences, use *constantly* or *forever* instead of *always* for variation.

Item 8 is a dialogue for completion. (See the *Introduction,* pp. xiv–xvi, for ways of handling completion exercises.) Encourage the students to use voice and gestures to show annoyance.

ANSWERS: **2.** [e] He's always leaving his dirty dishes on the table.   **3.** [c] He's forever borrowing my clothes without asking me.   **4.** [a] He's constantly bragging about himself.   **5.** [f] He's always trying to show me he's smarter than me.   **6.** [g] He's constantly cracking his knuckles while I'm trying to study.   **7.** [d] He's always forgetting to give me my phone messages.   **8.** *(free response)*

CHART 2-12:	USING EXPRESSIONS OF PLACE WITH PROGRESSIVE VERBS

- The point is that the prepositional phrases of place can have two positions: (1) the neutral position at the end of the clause or (2) the focus position, which emphasizes the expression of place, between *be* and the main verb.

- The neutral position is used in answer to *what*-questions because the focus is then on the activity. The focus position is used in answer to *where*-questions.

☐ **EXERCISE 24, p. 32.   Using expressions of place with progressive verbs   (Chart 2-12)**

PART I QUESTIONS: **3.** He was in his bedroom watching TV.   **4.** He was watching TV in his bedroom.   **5.** He's taking a nap on the couch in the living room.   **6.** He's on the couch in the living room taking a nap.   **7.** She's in Singapore attending a conference.

PART II POSSIBLE COMPLETIONS: **9.** He's upstairs getting his books.   **10.** She's in her office correcting test papers.   **11.** She's in the kitchen washing dishes.   **12.** He was at home resting from his long trip.   **13.** He was in New York attending a basketball game.

PART III POSSIBLE COMPLETIONS: **15.** I'm back to work now, but a month ago I was <u>on the beach</u> lying in the sun. **16.** We are <u>in Ritter Hall</u> studying English grammar. **17.** No one could see the thief because he was <u>in the garbage can</u> hiding from the police. **18.** When I saw Diana, she was <u>in the Registrar's Office</u> trying to find out what she was supposed to do.

SUGGESTION: Extend the exercise into free response oral work. Make up cues asking questions about familiar persons: "Where is *(name of a school administrator)* now, and what is s/he doing? Where were you last night at nine, and what were you doing?" Etc.

☐ **EXERCISE 25, p. 33. Error analysis: present and past verbs. (Chapter 2)**

ANSWERS:
1. <u>I</u> always <u>eat</u> breakfast.
2. <u>While</u> I was working in my office yesterday, my cousin <u>stopped</u> by to visit me.
3. Portual <u>lies</u> to the west of Spain.
4. Yuki <u>stayed</u> home because she <u>caught</u> / <u>was catching</u> / <u>had caught</u> a bad cold.
5. My brother <u>looks</u> like our father, but I <u>resemble</u> my mother.
6. As a verb, "sink" <u>means</u> "move downward." What <u>does</u> it <u>mean</u> as a noun?
7. Sang-Joon, are you <u>listening</u> to me? I am <u>talking</u> to you!
8. I <u>rewound</u> the rented video before I <u>returned</u> it to the store yesterday.
9. Abdallah <u>wants</u> a snack. <u>He's</u> ~~being~~ <u>hungry</u>.
10. Anna <u>raised</u> her eyebrows in surprise.
11. Yesterday I was working at my computer when Shelley <u>came</u> to the door of my office. I <u>didn't know</u> she was there. I was <u>concentrating</u> hard on my work. When she suddenly <u>spoke, I jumped.</u> She <u>startled</u> me.
12. While I was surfing the net yesterday, I <u>found</u> a really interesting website.
   [also possible: *Web site* or *web site.* As of this printing, all three forms are found in current publications.] ["surfing the net" = exploring the Internet with a computer]

Chapter 3: PERFECT AND PERFECT PROGRESSIVE TENSES

ORDER OF CHAPTER	CHARTS	EXERCISES	WORKBOOK
Review of regular and irregular past participles		Ex. 1 → 2	
Present perfect	3-1	Ex. 3 → 9	Pr. 1 → 3
Present perfect progressive	3-2	Ex. 10 → 13	Pr. 4 → 5
Past perfect	3-3	Ex. 14 → 16	Pr. 6 → 7
Past perfect progressive	3-4	Ex. 17	Pr. 8
Cumulative review		Ex. 18 → 22	

General Notes on Chapter 3

• OBJECTIVE: The focus is on perfect and perfect progressive tenses, which have complex references to time and duration of activities or situations.

• TERMINOLOGY: A "past participle" is the third principal part of a verb (e.g., *go-went-gone-going*). (See Chart 2-5.) The past participle is used with an auxiliary in the perfect tenses (or aspects) and in the passive voice. It can also function as an adjective. (See Chart 11-8.)

☐ **EXERCISE 1, p. 34. Review of regular past participles. (Charts 2-5 and 2-7)**

The teacher can always play the role of Speaker A; in other words, even though the directions suggest pair work, the exercise can be teacher-led. It depends upon availability of time for pair work, the level of your class, your objectives (e.g., quick review of surface grammar or intensive developmental skills work), the composition of your class (monolingual or multilingual), the size of your class, etc.

If necessary, remind students that a question with *your* requires an answer with *my*, as in item 14.

As a follow-up activity, ask students to spell some of the past participles in the exercise, especially those that are sometimes troublesome, such as *hidden* (not *hiden*), *stolen* (not *stollen*), *forgotten* (not *forgoten*). You might write problem words on the chalkboard.

QUESTIONS ONLY: Have you ever . . .?

1. bought   2. broken   3. hidden   4. taught   5. made   6. won
7. flown   8. spoken   9. stolen   10. fallen   11. held   12. fed
13. built   14. forgotten   15. understood   16. eaten

□ **EXERCISE 2, p. 35.   Review: regular and irregular past participles.**
(Charts 2-5 and 2-7)

You may need to explain that *ever* in a present perfect question means "at least once in your lifetime." It is not used in the answer to a question.
   An acceptable alternative to the answer "No, I haven't" is "No, I never have."
   Instead of pair work, this exercise can be teacher-led. The students' books are closed. You say the cue phrase. Then Speaker A asks B a question, and B answers truthfully. If you wish, you may expand some of these short dialogues. After Speaker B replies "Yes, I have," you might ask when or where the event occurred.

QUESTIONS ONLY: Have you ever . . . ?

1. climbed   2. written   3. been   4. told   5. smoked   6. ridden
7. taught   8. seen   9. met   10. given   11. eaten   12. studied
13. played   14. gone   15. walked   16. watched   17. taken   18. driven
19. fallen   20. had   21. driven   22. read   23. drawn   24. ridden
25. caught   26. slept   27. written   28. lost   29. had   30. brought
31. worn   32. drunk   33. left   34. dug   35. shaken   36. sung

---

CHART 3-1:   PRESENT PERFECT

• Compare the example sentences with similar sentences in the simple past; e.g., *They have moved into a new apartment* vs. *They moved into a new apartment last week.*

• The use of the present perfect illustrated by examples (l) though (p) carries the same meaning as the present perfect progressive: it expresses the <u>duration</u> of an activity that began in the past and continues to the present. The present perfect is used to express the duration of a "state," but the present perfect progressive is used to express the duration of an "activity." Note that all the verbs in (l) through (p) are stative. (See Chart 2-3.)

• Special attention may need to be paid to (h) and (n), where *have* is an auxiliary and *had* is the main verb.

□ **EXERCISE 3, p. 36.   Present perfect vs. simple past.   (Charts 2-9 and 3-1)**

ANSWERS: **2.** went   **3.** arrived   **4.** has been   **5.** have already missed . . . missed   **6.** have had   **7.** has drawn . . . drew   **8.** has called . . . called   **9.** has worn . . . wore   **10.** has risen . . . rose   **11.** saw
12. has never seen [*never saw* would mean that either Fatima is now dead or you are telling a story about a fictional character whose story took place in the past.]   **13.** have known [*knew* would mean that Greg Adams is, in all likelihood, dead.]   **14.** has just arrived / just arrived   **15.** haven't been . . . hasn't responded . . . started . . . have faxed . . . have phoned . . . have sent

□ EXERCISE 4, p. 37. Present perfect. (Chart 3-1)

If teacher-led, this exercise can be expanded by eliciting similar sentences using the simple past: e.g., *How many books have you bought since the beginning of the semester?* can be followed by *When did you buy this book?*

As with any teacher-led oral exercise, omit items irrelevant to your particular class and make up additional items directly related to your students' lives and situations.

This kind of question-and-answer oral exercise is a good opportunity to get your students talking about themselves. Ask more than one student the same question. Follow up interesting responses by engaging in short dialogues with your students. Questions that you ask conversationally on the topics suggested in the exercise can provide the students with excellent oral practice of verb tenses. In addition, you can learn more about your students and they about each other. They may discover, for instance, that others in the class are having trouble meeting people and making friends (item 7), or that others miss home cooking and dislike what is offered in the student cafeteria (item 11).

POSSIBLE RESPONSES: **1.** I've bought six books . . . . OR I haven't bought any . . . . **2.** I've gotten two . . . . OR I haven't gotten any . . . . **3.** I've written three . . . . OR I haven't written any . . . . **4.** You've asked three questions . . . . **5.** I've flown many times . . . . **6.** I have made dinner many times . . . . **7.** I've met lots of people . . . . **8.** I haven't missed any classes . . . . **9.** I've had two cups . . . . **10.** I've had four classes . . . . **11.** I've eaten at a restaurant several times . . . . **12.** I've ridden a bike lots of times.

□ EXERCISE 5, p. 38. Present perfect. (Chart 3-1)

Frequent problems occur with the word "since." *Since* may be followed by (1) a specific day or date *(1998, Friday, last January, etc.)* or (2) a clause with a past tense verb *(since I was twelve years old, since he came to this city, etc.)*. Point out that it is incorrect to use durational phrases like *since two years* or *since a long time*. In those cases, *for* is used.

It is advisable to discourage the use of time phrases with *ago* following *since* (e.g., *since three days ago*). Such phrases are sometimes used very informally by native speakers, for instance in a short answer, but are likely to be misused by the learners at this point. Example of possible informal usage:

A: *You can't drive. You don't have a license.*
B: *Yes I do.*
A: *You do? Since when?*
B: *Since two weeks ago!*

NOTE: In usual usage, a person would say: "I've had my driver's license **for two weeks**" NOT "I've had my driver's license since two weeks ago."

SAMPLE RESPONSES: **2.** two weeks . . . two weeks . . . the twenty-second of September **3.** October 2 . . . September 2 OR one month ago . . . September 2 . . . one month **4.** 1999 . . . 1981 . . . eighteen years . . . 1981 **5.** In October . . . three months . . . October

□ EXERCISE 6, p. 39. Present perfect. (Chart 3-1)

FORMAT: After one student replies, the leader asks another student about the first one's response.

If student-led, this exercise gives small groups the opportunity to begin with a structured format and then, it is hoped, proceed to incidental communicative interaction.

If the exercise is teacher-led, some of your exchanges with students might lead to expansion of the dialogue into a brief conversation. If it seems natural and interesting, keep it going for a minute or two.

□ **EXERCISE 7, p. 39.   Present perfect. (Chart 3-1)**

You can either have the students repeat after you, or have the students read the sentences with the contracted forms first and then repeat after you. Make up additional sentences as you and the students wish. (E.g., *How long've you been living here? Why's Juan stopped coming to class? Etc.*)

It is not necessary for students to use these contractions when they speak, but they are natural for native speakers of English. The main point here is to make the class aware that these contractions with nouns and question words exist so that the students might be more likely to notice them when listening to native speakers.

Students sometimes hesitate to use contractions. The result is that their speech sounds stilted and formal in conversations. Comfortable use of contractions comes through experience. You can encourage your students to use contractions but should not require it.

ITEM NOTES: **3.** "weather's" been   **4.** "neighbors've" asked   **5.** "teacher's" never eaten   **6.** *(no contraction; "has" is the main verb)*   **7.** "parents've" lived   **8.** *(no contraction; "have" is the main verb)*   **9.** "Where've" you been?   **10.** "What've" you done

□ **EXERCISE 8, p. 40.   Present perfect vs. simple past. (Charts 2-9 and 3-1)**

Point out spoken contractions.

ANSWERS: **1.** came . . . have you made   **2.** haven't had . . . have had   **3.** had . . . went [*Last night* signals the simple past; both actions occupied the same time period.]   **4.** have gotten/got [*got* is principally British usage.] . . . saw . . . have also gotten/got [*got* is principally British usage.]   **5.** advanced   **6.** have made   **7.** have changed . . . were . . . have become [*today* = in modern times, in contemporary life, these days] . . . has also changed . . . were   **8.** have already taken . . . took   **9.** A: Have you ever met   B: haven't   **10.** have never eaten   **11.** [The most common use of the present perfect is without time signals, as illustrated in the first two blanks.] Have you eaten . . . have already eaten . . . have just finished   OR   Did you eat . . . already ate . . . just finished   **12.** A: have you visited [no time signal]   B: have been [no time signal]   A: have never been . . . were you [asking for a specific time signal]   B: also visited [no time signal—<u>not</u> two years ago, but a different trip] . . . took [six years ago]   A: did you visit [referring to the trip six years ago]*   A: have always wanted . . . haven't had . . . went . . . haven't gone

□ **EXERCISE 9, p. 41.   Activity: using the present perfect. (Chart 3-1)**

You might want to give students some limit on the length of (or amount of detail in) their written answers. A lengthy or detailed answer will require use of the simple past as well as the present perfect and could serve as practice in using both tenses. In evaluating the answers, reward each correct use of the present perfect. You might choose simply to note misspellings and other errors without focusing on them.

In preparation for (or possibly instead of) writing their answers, students could discuss them in small groups. Each member of the group could give an answer as the rest of the group listens for the use of the present perfect. At the end of the speaker's answer, the others could identify (orally or in writing) what the speaker said, copying or correcting the speaker's use of the present perfect.

---

*The separate *Answer Key* booklet mistakenly gives the present perfect as a possible answer for this blank. The author apologizes for the confusion—and sometimes wonders what little grammar gremlins sneak in and cause printed errors! The correct completion for this blank is *did you visit; have you visited* is NOT correct.

Another alternative is to divide the class into five groups. Each group discusses one item. Each student writes a summary of everything that was said in his/her group, or the leader of each group presents an oral summary to the rest of the class. (You might want to expand the scope of item 3 to include "Why?" "Do you ever expect to do these things?" and "What are some interesting and unusual things that you have done and want to do again?")

CHART 3-2:   PRESENT PERFECT PROGRESSIVE

• Compare the examples with the present progressive. (See Chart 2-2.) Explain that both tenses deal with actions in progress, but that the present progressive simply states that an action is in progress at the moment of speaking, while the present perfect progressive gives the duration up to now of an action in progress now.

• Expect students to have difficulty understanding the use of this tense in examples (g), (h), and (i).

• As noted in (j) and (k), sometimes there is little or no difference between the present perfect and the present perfect progressive in sentences with *since* or *for,* often depending on the type of action the verb describes. There is, however, often a subtle preference for one or the other by native speakers in certain situations. The present perfect may be preferred for longstanding activities *(Jack has worked at the ABC Company since he graduated from college 40 years ago)* and the present perfect progressive for temporary or recent activities *(Jack has been working on the X Project since its inception two months ago).* In these cases, however, either tense is usually possible and correct *(Jack has been working at the ABC Company since he graduated from college 40 years ago* AND *Jack has worked on the X Project since its inception two months ago).*
   The present perfect progressive is generally preferred over the present perfect to express the duration of an activity from a point in the past to the present—except, of course, in the case of stative verbs, which are not used in any progressive and use the present perfect to express duration: *I have known Jack since he graduated from college.*

□ **EXERCISE 10, p. 42.   Error analysis: present perfect progressive.   (Chart 3-2)**

This exercise is intended solely as further clarification of the information in the preceding chart. It is intended for discussion. Give the students two or three minutes to find the errors themselves prior to class discussion.
   The items present situations in which only the present perfect progressive is appropriate. Review the meanings of the incorrect tenses and compare them to the present perfect progressive.

ANSWERS: **1.** They <u>have been</u> playing for almost two hours.   **2.** He <u>has been talking</u> on the phone for more than half an hour.   **3.** I <u>have been trying</u> to study for the last hour, but something always seems to interrupt me.   **4.** He <u>has been</u> waiting there for the last twenty minutes.

□ EXERCISE 11, p. 43.   Present perfect vs. present perfect progressive. (Charts 3-1 and 3-2)

Notice in items 1, 3, maybe 6 and 7B, and possibly 12 that the present perfect simple instead of progressive would not necessarily be grammatically incorrect, but native speakers would use the progressive form.

ANSWERS: **1.** has been snowing   **2.** have had   **3.** have been studying   **4.** have written   **5.** has rung   **6.** has been ringing   **7.** Have you been . . . have been trying   **8.** haven't seen . . . have you been doing   **9.** have never had   **10.** Have you been crying?   **11.** A: has he been   B: has been teaching/has taught   **12.** has been playing

□ EXERCISE 12, p. 44.   Present perfect and present perfect progressive with SINCE and FOR. (Charts 3-1 and 3-2)

Students may use either the present perfect or the present perfect progressive. You may choose to ask them for both.

The exercise can be done as a teacher-led oral review, as group or pair work, or as written work.

□ EXERCISE 13, p. 45.   Activity: using the present perfect and present perfect progressive in writing. (Charts 3-1 and 3-2)

This is a summary review activity for both the present perfect and present perfect progressive, as well as the simple past.

Perhaps brainstorm a sample composition with the students by discussing both topics. It could be fun for the class to share some of their experiences and will get them thinking about what they might write. Prior discussion of topics often leads to better compositions. For item 1, if the students seem shy about speaking frankly of their experiences in this class, ask leading questions: "What was your first impression of this building? this room? What do you remember about your classmates the first day? your teacher? Who did you talk to? What did we do the first day of class? How did you feel about taking this class in (grammar, composition, etc.)? Were you excited about studying grammar? Did you think the class was going to be too easy? too hard? What were your concerns? Were you concerned about the level of your English ability?" Etc. Then move into questions with the present perfect: "How long have you been attending this class? What topics of English grammar have we studied? What are some of the fun things we've done in this class since that first day?" (NOTE: The responses to some of these questions might appropriately slip into the simple past; for example, a student might say: "I really enjoyed the pantomimes we did.") "What is one of the things you've enjoyed most in this class? How many compositions have you written? How many tests have we had? How many grammar exercises have we done?" Etc.

Prepare some leading questions for item 2 also.

CHARTS 3-3 AND 3-4: PAST PERFECT AND PAST PERFECT PROGRESSIVE

• Compare the examples with similar sentences containing (1) the present perfect and present perfect progressive; and (2) the simple past. For example, in Chart 3-3: *Sam **has** already **left*** and *Sam **left*** vs. *Sam **had** already **left.*** In Chart 3-4: *The police **have been looking** for the criminal for two years* vs. *The police **had been looking** for the criminal for two years before they caught him.*

• Point out that <u>two</u> past events or times are necessary in order to use the past perfect. The <u>earlier</u> event uses the past perfect tense. The progressive form may be used to express duration or recency.

• You might anticipate that students sometimes have the erroneous idea that the past perfect is used to express an event that happened a long, long time ago. In using the past perfect, <u>when</u> an event occurred in the past is important only in relation to another time in the past.

• The expression "by the time" usually needs some explanation. It conveys the idea that one event was, or will be, completed before another event. It usually signals that either the past perfect (simple or progressive) or the future perfect (simple or progressive) needs to be used in the main clause. In fact, this phrase is used to signal only those tenses in the exercises in the text—even though it is possible to use other tenses when a "state" rather than an "event" is being expressed: e.g., *The doctor came at six. By that time, it **was** too late* (state). *The patient **was** dead* (state) OR ***had died*** (event).

• In (b) and (c), the simple past may be used in informal English. In other words, it is often, but by no means always, possible to use the simple past in place of the past perfect. The past perfect is relatively formal; the past perfect progressive is relatively infrequent. Students can expect to find these tenses more useful in written English than in everyday spoken English, with the possible exceptions of their use in conditional sentences (Chapter 20) and in noun clauses that report speech (Chapter 12).

□ **EXERCISE 14, p. 46. Contracting HAD. (Appendix Chart C)**

Items 1 and 2 review contractions with pronouns. Item 2 points out that the contraction for *had* and *would* is the same: apostrophe (') + *d*. One can determine which auxiliary is being contracted by looking at the verb form that follows *'d*. If it's the past participle, *'d = had.* If it's the simple form of a verb, *'d = would.*

Items 3, 4, and 6 require students to supply the spoken contractions with nouns.

Item 5 distinguishes between *had* as an auxiliary and *had* as a main verb, and how that affects its contractibility. Main verb *had* is not contracted—except rarely and perhaps a bit poetically to show possession; for example, *I'd a lamb for a pet when I was a boy.* By comparison, a native speaker would probably not say, "We'd a test yesterday" OR "They'd dinner last night at Luigi's."

Items 7 and 8 contain contractions with question words (with the contracted forms both spoken and written).

ANSWERS: **3.** children/əd/ **4.** roommates/əd/ **5.** [No contraction is possible because *had* is the main verb.] **6.** flood/əd/ **7.** Where'd [spoken as a single syllable /wɛrd/, but note that /d/ before /y/ in *you* becomes /ǰ/ = Where-/ǰu/] **8.** Who'd [hud]

□ EXERCISE 15, p. 46. Simple past vs. past perfect. (Charts 2-9 and 3-3)

Note the contracted forms for the students.

ANSWERS: **1.** was/had been . . . became   **2.** felt . . . took/had taken   **3.** had already given . . . got   **4.** was . . . had stopped   **5.** roamed [Emphasize that the past perfect is NOT used simply because something happened a long time ago; the use of the past perfect requires two events in the past, one of which occurred before the other.] . . . had become . . . appeared   **6.** had never seen . . . visited   **7.** saw . . . hadn't seen . . . didn't recognize . . . had lost   **8.** emigrated . . . had never traveled . . . settled . . . grew . . . went . . . had always wanted

□ EXERCISE 16, p. 47. Past perfect. (Chart 3-3)

In these sentences, review once again that the earlier or first action is in the past perfect and the later or second action is in the simple past.

It's possible to expand the scope of this exercise by asking the students to write a short paragraph (for each item, one item, or several items) in which the sentence based on the cue in the text is embedded in a context that the student creates. For example, in item 2:

I was supposed to pick my cousin up at the airport last Friday at five in the afternoon. I left my apartment at three and thought I would have plenty of time to get to the airport before his flight arrived. Unfortunately, I got caught in rush hour traffic. **By the time I got to the airport, he'd already left.** *He thought I'd forgotten to meet him, so he took a taxi to my apartment.*

ANSWERS: [These depend on students' creativity.]

□ EXERCISE 17, p. 48. Present perfect progressive and past perfect progressive. (Charts 3-2 and 3-4)

The past perfect progressive is not a common tense. This is the only exercise that focuses on it, although it will be revisited in the chapter on conditional sentences and (briefly) in the noun clause chapter. The intention here is simply to clarify its meaning and use by comparing it to a tense the students are already familiar with, the present perfect progressive.

ANSWERS: **3.** have been studying   **4.** had been studying   **5.** had been daydreaming   **6.** have been sleeping

□ EXERCISE 18, p. 48. Review of verb tenses. (Chapters 1 → 3)

ANSWERS: **2.** Gloria [Riding her bicycle was in progress at the time the rain stopped, meaning she began to ride her bike before the rain stopped. Paul rode his bicycle <u>after</u> the rain stopped; the *when*-clause happens first when both clauses contain the simple past.]   **3.** Ken [Ann went to the store <u>after</u> she had run out of food. Ken went to the store while running out of food was in progress.]   **4.** Mr. Sanchez [*taught for nine years*—the simple past indicates that the activity was completed in the past; *has taught for nine years*—he is still teaching; the activity is not completed.]   **5.** Alice [George walked to the door only <u>after</u> the doorbell rang. Alice knew someone was coming to ring her doorbell because she began to walk toward the door <u>before</u> the bell rang.]   **6.** Joe [Maria finished eating before I arrived. Joe ate <u>after</u> I got there, so he was the one who was still hungry.]   **7.** Carlos. [similar to item 4]   **8.** Jane [Sue's lying in the sun was still in progress when she applied lotion. Jane's lying in the sun had been recently completed when she applied lotion.]   **9.** Mr. Fox. [Mr. Fox's waving was already in progress when I looked across the street.]

□ EXERCISE 19, p. 49.   Error analysis: present and past verbs.   (Chapters 1 → 3)

See the *Introduction*, p. xviii, for suggestions for handling error analysis exercises.

ANSWERS:

1. Since I came to this country, I <u>have learned</u> a lot about the way of life here.
2. Before I <u>came</u> here, I <u>had never bought</u> anything from a vending machine.
3. I <u>arrived</u> here only a short time ago. I <u>have been</u> here only since last Friday.
4. When I arrived here, I <u>didn't know</u> much about the United States. I <u>had seen</u> many movies about America, but that wasn't enough.
5. My understanding of this country <u>has</u> changed a lot since I arrived.
6. When I was in my country, I <u>coached</u> a children's soccer team. When I came here, I <u>wanted</u> to do the same thing. Now I am coaching a soccer team at a local elementary school. I <u>have been</u> coaching this team for the last two months.
7. My grandfather <u>lived</u> in a small village in Italy when he was a child. At nineteen, he <u>moved</u> to Rome, where he <u>met</u> and <u>married</u> my grandmother in 1947. My father <u>was</u> born in Rome in 1950. I <u>was</u> born in Rome in 1979.
8. I <u>have been living</u> / <u>have lived</u> in my cousin's apartment since I <u>arrived</u> here. I <u>haven't been</u> able to find my own apartment yet. I <u>have looked</u> at several places for rent, but I <u>haven't found</u> one that I can afford.
9. How long <u>have</u> you been living here? I <u>have</u> been here for almost two <u>years</u>.
10. Why <u>haven't</u> you been in class the last couple of days?

□ EXERCISE 20, p. 49.   Activity: using verb tenses.   (Chapters 1 → 3)

The stories may get a little silly, but it is hoped the students will have fun.

Be sure students understand that their contributions need to contain the cue words, chosen by them at random.

□ EXERCISE 21, p. 50.   Activity: using verb tenses.   (Chapters 1 → 3)

Each person in the group is to begin a story. In a group of six people, six different stories will be circulating at the same time.

A time limit (two to three minutes per contribution) is advisable, unless you wish to make this an activity that takes up an entire class period. If you use a strict time limit, an unfinished sentence can be completed by the next writer.

After the stories are written and you are discussing them in class, you may or may not wish to bring up the possibility of using present tenses in a narrative. For example: *Let me tell you about Pierre's day yesterday. He gets in trouble as soon as his alarm clock rings. When he hears the alarm and gets out of bed, he steps on a snake! Would you believe that? He's nearly frightened to death, but the snake slithers away without biting him. Etc.* The text doesn't deal with this use of the simple present, but you might want to explore it with an advanced class. This use of the simple present is common when telling jokes.

□ EXERCISE 22, p. 50.   Using verb tenses in writing.   (Chapters 1 → 3)

Suggest a desirable length for the assignment, e.g., six to ten sentences, or 300–400 words, depending on your purposes and the emphasis on writing and composition in your particular class.

The questions are intended only to guide the students' ideas. Tell the students not to simply answer each question in order. The questions in the text are only prompts to start the students thinking about the topic.

If you wish, ask the students to try to use each of the tenses studied so far at least once. List them on the chalkboard or identify them in Chart 1-5.

As preparation for the writing assignment, ask leading questions about the topics to get the students thinking about what they might write about. Discuss the meaning of "the state of the world" by asking the students to describe the state of the world today.

In marking the papers, focus mainly on verb tenses. Praise emphatically correct verb tense usage. One suggestion: mark but do not correct errors in verb tense; correct all other errors yourself. If development of all writing skills is one of the principal goals in your class, however, you will probably want the students to correct most of their errors themselves.

SUGGESTION: Make up your own error analysis exercise by copying incorrect sentences from the students' writing and giving them to the class for discussion. Focus on verb tense errors. Include other miscellaneous errors if you know that the class knows the correct underlying grammar. Edit the student writing somewhat; don't include errors that would get you into a whole new discussion of unfamiliar grammar. For example:

Student writing: *I enjoied to grow myself up in Mexico City. I had had a happy child time there. My parents taked good care of there childrens.*

Used as an error analysis exercise item: *I enjoied growing up in Mexico City. I had had a happy childhood there. My parents taked good care of there childrens.*

One last note: You may notice that some errors in verb tense usage seem to be the result of the students' study of verb tenses. For example, you may notice students trying to use the past perfect more than they had previously, but not always using it correctly. Don't despair. It's natural and does not seem to be of any lasting harm. View the students as experimenting with new tools. Praise them for reaching out toward what is new usage for them, even as you correct their errors. Their study of verb tenses is providing a foundation for growth as they gain experience and familiarity with English. Grammar usage takes time to gel. Don't expect sudden mastery—and make sure your students don't expect that either. Encourage risk-taking and experimentation; students should never be afraid of making mistakes. In language acquisition, a mistake is nothing more than a learning opportunity.

Chapter 4: FUTURE TIME

ORDER OF CHAPTER	CHARTS	EXERCISES	WORKBOOK
Simple future	4-1	Ex. 1	
Will vs. *be going to*	4-2	Ex. 2	Pr. 1
Expressing the future in time clauses	4-3	Ex. 3 → 5	Pr. 2
Using the present progressive and the simple present to express future time	4-4	Ex. 6 → 9	Pr. 3
Future progressive	4-5	Ex. 10	Pr. 4
Future perfect	4-6		
Future perfect progressive	4-7		
Review of perfect and progressive tenses		Ex. 11	Pr. 5
Review of future time		Ex. 12 → 13	

General Notes on Chapter 4

• OBJECTIVE: The chapter emphasizes the common verb forms used to express future time (including present tenses) and briefly touches on the less frequently used future perfect, simple and progressive.

• TERMINOLOGY: Some grammarians maintain that English has only two tenses, past and non-past, which are indicated by having one-word verb forms for them (e.g., *went* for past and *go(es)* for non-past) and does not have a future tense because there is no one-word verb form with a future meaning. However, this text uses traditional terminology by calling ***will*** + *simple form* the simple future tense, and for ease of classroom communication calls ***be going to*** + *simple form* the simple future, too. The text defines the simple future as a verb form that expresses an event or situation that will, to the best of the speaker's knowledge, occur in future time. Using other modals and periphrastic (i.e., phrasal) modals to express future time is covered in Chapters 9 and 10.

CHART 4-1: SIMPLE FUTURE: *WILL* AND *BE GOING TO*

• This chart merely introduces the two basic forms for expressing the future. It does not show their differences in function or meaning. (See Chart 4-2.)

• Model *gonna* for the students. Don't rush them to use it in their speech; remind them that good enunciation is important to second language learners and that normal contracted speaking will occur naturally as they gain experience with the language. Point out that *gonna* is not used in writing.

• Some learners ask about *shall* vs. *will*. *Shall* is rarely used in American English to express future time. It is found more commonly in British English. It also occurs in some questions seeking agreement, e.g., *Shall we go now?* (See Chart 9-10.)

□ **EXERCISE 1, p. 51. Simple future. (Chart 4-1)**

Contraction of *will* is natural in conversation; this exercise gives students practice in hearing these forms and trying to produce them themselves. Most of the personal pronoun contractions are pronounced as a single syllable: *I'll* /ayl/, *you'll* /yul/, *he'll* /hiyl/, *she'll* /siyl/, *we'll* /wiyl/, they'll /ðeyl/. Other words add a syllable for the contraction: it'll /ɪtəl/, that'll, /ðætəl/, etc.

Items 1–4 show the commonly written contracted forms. In other items, the forms are not usually written but should be spoken in this exercise.

ANSWERS: **6.** weather'll   **7.** Mary'll   **8.** Bill'll   **9.** children'll   **10.** Who'll
[This is sometimes a very informal written form also.]   **11.** Where'll   **12.** long'll
13. Nobody'll   **14.** That'll   **15.** What'll

CHART 4-2: *WILL* vs. *BE GOING TO*

• Students often want to know the difference between *will* and *be going to* even though in their own independent production most students rarely make the mistake of using one where the other is required.

• Define "prior plan" as a "preconceived notion" and explain what that means. Ask the students about their future plans to generate sentences that require *be going to* and are inappropriate for *will*. For example:
    A: What are your plans for this evening?
    B: I'm going to go to a movie with my friends this evening.

• For comparison, create a situation that requires *will* by asking for volunteers. For example:
    A: It's warm in here. We need to open a window. Are there any volunteers?
    B: I'll do it.

□ **EXERCISE 2, p. 52. WILL vs. BE GOING TO. (Chart 4-2)**

In the items, which are dialogues between Speaker A and Speaker B, students can work out the answers in pairs, then speak the dialogues in a natural manner (glancing only briefly at their texts). Discuss contracted forms with *will*.

PART I ANSWERS: [Note: There is <u>no</u> difference in meaning between *will* and *be going to* in these sentences.] **2.** will be/is going to be . . . will come/is going to come **3.** will probably see/am probably going to see **4.** A: won't be/isn't going to be . . . Who will be/Who's going to be B: will teach/is going to teach . . . will be/am going to be **5.** will the damage we do to our environment today affect/is the damage we do to our environment today going to affect

PART II ANSWERS: [Note: There <u>is</u> a difference in meaning between *will* and *be going to* in these sentences: *will* expresses willingness and *be going to* expresses a prior plan.] **8.** B: will do C: will do **9.** is going to erase **10.** will meet **11.** am going to meet **12.** will get **13.** am going to enroll . . . am going to take **14.** will get **15.** will go **16.** am going to sell **17.** will look

---

CHART 4-3: EXPRESSING THE FUTURE IN TIME CLAUSES

• The focus is on verb usage in complex sentences containing dependent (subordinate) adverb clauses, called "time clauses" here. The structure of sentences with these clauses is discussed more thoroughly in Chapters 5 and 17.

• Learners naturally feel that it is "logical" to use the future tense in the time clause as well as in the main clause. Point out that this is not "traditional" in English usage. There are certain patterns and systems within a language, but a language should not be expected to be logical.

• The meaning of *until* is sometimes difficult for learners to grasp, as in (e). It means that a situation will exist, then change.

☐ **EXERCISE 3, p. 55. Expressing the future in time clauses. (Chart 4-3)**

ANSWERS: **2.** [After the rain <u>stops</u>,] **3.** [before my wife <u>gets</u> home from work today.] **4.** [until Jessica <u>comes</u>.] **5.** [As soon as the war <u>is</u> over,] **6.** [when the tide <u>comes</u> in,] **7.** [While I'<u>m driving</u> to work tomorrow,]

☐ **EXERCISE 4, p. 55. Expressing the future in time clauses. (Chart 4-3)**

Keep attention focused on the time clause. Problems may occur because students try to use future tense instead of the simple present.

In items 7 and 8, the verbs "plan," "hope," and "intend" are used. These words refer to a present condition, a thought or feeling "at this moment" about a future activity. Therefore, they are in a present, not a future, tense form. Plans, hopes, and intentions occur in the present but concern future activities.

ANSWERS: **2.** eat [*have eaten* is also correct, but try to keep the focus on the two choices in the directions: *will/be going to* or the simple present] . . . will probably take/am probably going to take **3.** get . . . I'll call/am going to call **4.** watch . . . will write/am going to write **5.** will wait/am going to wait . . . comes **6.** stops [also possible: *has stopped*] . . . will walk/am going to walk **7.** graduate [also possible: *am graduated*] . . . intend [present tense because it is my plan <u>now</u>] . . . will go . . . get **8.** am going to listen . . . sleep **9.** A: are you staying/are you going to stay B: plan/am planning . . . hope/am hoping A: will you do/are you going to do . . . leave B: will return/am going to return . . . get A: will be/am going to be . . . return . . . get

□ **EXERCISE 5, p. 57.   Expressing the future in time clauses.   (Chart 4-3)**

Emphasize again the use of the simple present in a future time clause. Tense errors in future time clauses are common among second language learners of English.

VERB FORMS IN ANSWERS: **2.** [simple present . . . future]   **3.** [future . . . simple present]   **4.** [future . . . simple present]   **5.** [simple present . . . future]
6. [future . . . simple present]   **7.** [simple present . . . future]   **8.** [*(someone)* . . . future]

┌───┐

**CHART 4-4:   USING THE PRESENT PROGRESSIVE AND THE
SIMPLE PRESENT TO EXPRESS FUTURE TIME**

• The present progressive, when used to express future time, must relate to a plan or intention.

• The simple present, when used to express future time, is limited to scheduled events.

• These tenses are frequently used to express future time, especially in conversational English. The difficulty for students is to learn the limitations on the use of the tenses to mean future time.

└───┘

□ **EXERCISE 6, p. 57.   Using the present progressive and the simple present to express future time.   (Chart 4-4)**

See the *Introduction*, p. xix, for information about discussion-of-meaning exercises.

ANSWERS: **4.** in the future   **5.** in the future   **6.** now   **7.** in the future
8. habitually   **9.** in the future   **10.** in the future   **11.** habitually   **12.** A: now
B: now   A: in the future [*do you want* asks about a present plan for a future activity.]
13. A: in the future   B: in the future   C: in the future   **14.** in the future   **15.** in the future   **16.** in the future   **17.** in the future   **18.** in the future

□ **EXERCISE 7, p. 59.   Using the present progressive to express future time.
(Chart 4-4)**

Note that *be going to* and sometimes *will* are also possible completions. The purpose of the exercise is to familiarize the learners with common situations in which the present progressive is used to express future time.

EXPECTED COMPLETIONS: **2.** am taking   **3.** are having . . . are coming   **4.** am seeing   **5.** is going   **6.** are driving   **7.** is playing   **8.** am stopping

□ **EXERCISE 8, p. 60.   Using the present progressive to express future time.
(Chart 4-4)**

Students may be comfortable with *be going to* and produce it naturally. Encourage explicit practice with the use of the present progressive here.

□ **EXERCISE 9, p. 60.   Using the present progressive and the simple present to express future time.   (Chart 4-4)**

Explain what an itinerary is: a plan for a trip that shows the places to be visited, the route, the dates of arrival and departure, and sometimes the means of transportation.

As preparation for this writing assignment, perhaps photocopy and bring to class an itinerary from a travel agency for a future trip. Have the class describe the trip on that itinerary using present tenses.

CHART 4-5: FUTURE PROGRESSIVE

• Relate the examples to similar sentences with the present progressive and past progressive.

• In the exercises in the text, the future progressive is associated with an activity that will be in progress at a specific moment of future time. However, as in (d), the future progressive is also used to express predicted activities that will be in progress at a vague or nonspecific future time: e.g., *I'll be seeing you!* OR *I'll be waiting to hear from you* OR *Just wait. Before you know it, the baby will be walking and talking.*

☐ **EXERCISE 10, p. 60.   Using the future progressive.   (Chart 4-5)**

ANSWERS: **1.** will be attending   **2.** arrive . . . will be waiting   **3.** get . . . will be shining . . . will be singing . . . will still be lying   **4.** B: will be lying [Call attention to the spelling of *lying.*]   A: will be thinking   **5.** will be staying   **6.** will be doing . . . will be attending school . . . (will be) studying [Point out the ellipsis (i.e., omission of the subject and auxiliary verb) in parallel structure.]   **7.** is . . . will probably be raining   **8.** will be in Chicago visiting   **9.** will be at the library working   **10.** will be living . . . will be driving

---

CHARTS 4-6 AND 4-7:   FUTURE PERFECT AND FUTURE PERFECT PROGRESSIVE

• These are the two most infrequently used tenses in English. There's no need to belabor them.

• Relate these tenses to perfect simples and perfect progressives in the present and the past. Refer again to Chart 1-5 to show how these two tenses fit into a larger pattern.

☐ **EXERCISE 11, p. 62.   Perfect and perfect progressive tenses.
(Chapter 3; Charts 4-6 and 4-7)**

This exercise includes past, present, and future perfect and progressive tenses. The text seeks to promote an understanding of the future perfect and future perfect progressive by comparing them to other tenses with which the students are more familiar.

ANSWERS: **1.** have been . . . had been . . . will have been   **2.** get . . . will already have arrived / will have already arrived   **3.** got . . . had already arrived   **4.** have been sitting . . . had been sitting . . . will have been sitting   **5.** will have been driving [also possible: *will have driven*]   **6.** had been living / had lived . . . will have been living / will have lived   **7.** get . . . will have taken   **8.** will have been running   **9.** will have had . . . dies   **10.** will have been

☐ EXERCISE 12, p. 63. Review: future time. (Charts 4-1 → 4-7)

Point out the parallels in the use of past and future verb forms. For example, in item 1, the sentences describe an activity in progress, first in the past, then in the future. The situation is progressive in both sentences; only the time is different. Perhaps refer once again to Chart 1-5 to point out the relationships among the tenses.

With an advanced class, you might do this exercise with books closed, with you reading the cue from the text about Bill's activities yesterday and asking the questions about tomorrow.

Suggest that the students use *will* (just for the sake of uniformity in the answers and to avoid having to give two possible answers for each item); forms of *be going to* are also possible and should of course be accepted.

The answers below don't give the contractions for *will*. It is hoped that contractions will occur naturally in at least some of the students' oral production.

ANSWERS: **2.** He will shave and shower, and then make a light breakfast. **3.** After he eats breakfast tomorrow, he will get ready to go to work. **4.** By the time he gets to work tomorrow, he will have drunk three cups of coffee. **5.** Between 8:00 and 9:00, Bill will answer his e-mail and (will) plan his day. **6.** By 10:00 tomorrow, he will have called his new clients. **7.** At 11:00 tomorrow, Bill will be attending a staff meeting. **8.** He will go to lunch at noon and have a sandwich and a bowl of soup. **9.** After he finishes eating, he will take a short walk in the park before he returns to the office. **10.** He will work at his desk until he goes to another meeting in the middle of the afternoon. **11.** By the time he leaves the office, he will have attended three meetings. **12.** When Bill gets home, his children will be playing in the yard. **13.** They will have been playing since 3:00 in the afternoon. **14.** As soon as he finishes dinner, he will take the children for a walk to a nearby playground. **15.** Afterward, the whole family will sit in the living room and discuss their day. **16.** They will watch television for a while, then Bill and his wife will put the kids to bed. **17.** By the time Bill goes to bed tomorrow, he will have had a full day and will be ready for sleep.

☐ EXERCISE 13, p. 64. Review: future time. (Chapter 4)

Have the students brainstorm ideas about the future. If necessary, ask provocative leading questions. You may wish to have one student ask another a question about a given topic. You may wish to divide the students into groups and just let them talk, with no written or oral reports.

ALTERNATIVE: Divide the class into small groups. Assign one topic to each group, or allow them to choose a topic. Give them about 10 minutes to develop a presentation of their ideas. Then ask one person in each group to give the information to the class orally.

ALTERNATIVE: Assign one topic to each student and ask for an oral presentation of ideas. As a followup, students can write their paragraphs and hand them in to you.

In previous exercises, such as descriptions of pantomimes, you have stressed to the students the importance of being consistent in tense usage; e.g., if you begin to tell a story in the past tense, stay in the past tense and don't slip into the present. However, now point out that a paragraph of sentences on a single topic may <u>require</u> a mixing of past, present, and future.

Chapter 5: ADVERB CLAUSES OF TIME AND REVIEW OF VERB TENSES

ORDER OF CHAPTER	CHARTS	EXERCISES	WORKBOOK
Review of verb tenses		Ex. 1 → 5	
Adverb clauses of time	5-1 → 5-2	Ex. 6 → 10	Pr. 1 → 4
Review of verb tenses		Ex. 11 → 18	Pr. 5 → 9
General review		Ex. 19	

General Notes on Chapter 5

• OBJECTIVE: This chapter brings together the verb tense grammar presented in Chapters 1 through 4 and, in addition, consolidates and formalizes the presentation of adverb clauses of time. Adverb clauses of time occur frequently throughout Chapters 1 through 4; the charts in this chapter draw attention to them and provide a basis for a thorough review of the interrelatedness of time and tense, and ways of communicating about time relationships in complex sentences.

See Chapter 17 for a presentation of other kinds of adverb clauses.

• TERMINOLOGY: "Adverb clauses of time" may also be called "dependent or subordinate adverbial clauses." Words that introduce adverb clauses (e.g., *after, when, since*) are called "subordinating conjunctions." In this text, they are simply called "words that introduce adverb clauses."

• APPROACH: Chapter 5 provides practice with all the verb tenses. When students have to choose the appropriate tense(s) according to context and meaning, it is important that they have opportunities to discuss their choices and explore misunderstandings. One of your many roles is to help them become sensitive monitors and effective editors of their own English use.

Now that the foundation for verb tense usage has been laid, the students need both guided and free practice and, most important, lots of out-of-class language experiences as the complex process of adult second language acquisition proceeds. You may wish to tell your students that they shouldn't expect to become instant experts in verb tense usage after studying these five chapters, but that you expect their development to be excellent and their ultimate goal easily reachable. (Sometimes students equate second language learning with other academic pursuits. They may feel that once they study a chapter in mathematics or chemistry, they are now masters of the information it contains—and expect the same results in a second language class. You may wish to discuss with your students the many ways in which the study of a second language is different from other courses of study.)

□ EXERCISE 1, p. 65. Error analysis: review of verb tenses. (Chapters 1 → 4)

The focus in this exercise is almost completely on verb tense usage. One miscellaneous error in singular–plural is also included, in item 7, for the alert student to catch.

ANSWERS: **2.** By the time I return to my country, I <u>will have been</u> away from home for more than three years. **3.** As soon as I ~~will~~ graduate, I <u>am</u> going to return to my hometown. **4.** By the end of the 21st century, scientists will <u>have</u> discovered the cure for the common cold. **5.** I want to get married, but I <u>haven't met</u> the right person yet. **6.** I have <u>seen</u> that movie three times, and now I <u>want</u> to see it again. **7.** Last night, I ~~have~~ <u>had</u> dinner with two <u>friends</u>. I <u>have known</u> both of them for a long time. **8.** I <u>don't</u> like my job at the restaurant. My brother wants me to change it. I <u>think</u> he is right. **9.** So far this week, the teachers <u>have given</u> us a lot of homework every day. **10.** There <u>have been</u> more than forty presidents of the United States since it became a country. George Washington <u>was</u> the first president. He <u>became</u> the president in 1789. **11.** While I <u>am</u> studying tonight, I'm going to listen to Beethoven's Seventh Symphony. **12.** We washed the dishes and <u>cleaned</u> up the kitchen after our dinner guests <u>left/had left</u>. **13.** My neighbors are Mr. and Mrs. Jones. I <u>have known</u> them ever since I <u>was</u> a child. **14.** It <u>will rain</u> tomorrow morning. / It is <u>probably going to rain</u> tomorrow morning. **15.** Many scientists believe there <u>will be</u> / is <u>going to be</u> a major earthquake in California in the next few years. **16.** When I got home to my apartment last night, I <u>used</u> my key to open the door as usual. But the door didn't open. [The question of beginning a sentence with *but* may arise. In informal written English, sentences frequently begin with a coordinating conjunction. (See Chart 16-3.) Beginning a sentence with *but* is a question of style and register, not grammaticality.] I <u>tried</u> my key again and again with no luck. So I <u>knocked</u> on the door for my wife to let me in. Finally the door <u>opened</u>, but I <u>didn't see</u> my wife on the other side. I saw a stranger. I had been <u>trying</u> to get into the wrong apartment! I quickly <u>apologized</u> and <u>went</u> to my own apartment.

□ EXERCISE 2, p. 66. Review of verb tenses. (Chapters 1 → 4)

The important part of this lesson is for the learners to understand and attempt to explain the meaning of each sentence, noting the differences among similar sentences with different verb tenses. They may or may not name the verb tenses. They may or may not use the same sort of explanations used in this text and by the teacher. See the *Introduction,* p. xix, for information about discussion-of-meaning exercises.

If you have a wall chart or transparency of Chart 1-5, this might be a good time to bring it out again.

ANSWERS:
1. (a) frequently, repeatedly, again and again. (b) at this moment, right now.
2. (a) right now. (b) at this time on a past day. (c) at this time on a future day, or at a specific point of future time.
3. (a) completed before now. (b) completed before another event or time in the past. (c) a plan to complete in the future before another event or time.
4. (a), (b), and (c) have the same meaning. (d) means that the teacher's arrival was a signal for the students to leave immediately. (e) means that the students had gotten up to leave shortly before the teacher arrived, but they had not yet left the room.

5. (a) The waiting began two hours ago and is still in progress at present. (b) The waiting began two hours before another event or time in the past. (c) The waiting will have been in progress for two hours by the time another event occurs; the waiting may begin in the future or may have begun in the past.

6. (a) not finished yet. (b) finished at an unspecified time before now. (c) at a specific time in the past (. . . *last night, last weekend, etc.*).

7. (a) in progress recently, but not yet completed. (b) completed, but no date or time is specified.

8. (a) and (b) are the same: You come, <u>then</u> I will begin to study. (c) and (d) are the same: Studying begins before you come and is in progress upon your arrival. (e) Studying will be completed before you come. (f) The studying will have been in progress for two hours by the time another event occurs; the studying may begin in the future or may have begun in the past.

9. (a) completed activity. [He probably works in another place now.] (b) present activity that began two years ago.

10. All four sentences mean the same. Although sentences (c) and (d) are both in the present tense, they describe an event that will happen in the future.

□ EXERCISE 3, p. 67. Review of verb tenses. (Chapters 1 → 4)

If the exercise is teacher-led, approach each item conversationally; add extra words, rephrase the questions, put the questions in relevant contexts. These questions are in the text merely to suggest ideas as you engage the students in an oral review of verb tenses.

In items where there are several related questions, ask a question and wait for the response, then follow that answer with the next question to the same student. Don't stop for corrections or explanations until the item (the conversation) is completed.

Short answers are natural in conversations. However, in this exercise students are practicing verb tenses, so they should answer in complete sentences. Students easily understand that this exercise is a sort of "grammar game," especially an item such as 15.

If the exercise is used for pair or group work, the students can simply monitor each other and check with you as necessary.

POSSIBLE ANSWERS: 1. We've been studying verb tenses. We've studied the present perfect tense. We studied it two weeks ago.   2. We'll have studied adjective clauses, gerunds, and many other grammatical structures.   3. Yes, I had. [BrE: Yes, I had done.] We studied some tenses last year.   4. We'll have been studying it for about three weeks.
5. I was practicing English. After that, I went to the next class.   6. I'm answering your question. I've been doing that for about 30 seconds.   7. I'm probably going to be sitting in this room again.   8. I'll be sleeping. Last night at midnight I was sleeping.
9. I'll be living in my own home. I was living in another city.   10. I've been to the zoo. I went there last month.   11. I eat, study, and listen to the radio.   12. Since I came here, I've done a lot of grammar homework.   13. I've flown across the Pacific two times, climbed mountains, and written songs. I flew across the Pacific once last year, climbed Mt. Fuji in 1999, and wrote a song last month.   14. I've given some roses to my mother-in-law.   15. *(review of all tenses)*

□ EXERCISE 4, p. 68. Review of verb tenses. (Chapters 1 → 4)

This exercise is a straightforward review of verb tenses, using uncomplicated sentences, contexts, and vocabulary. Students should be able to complete it on their own, or in pair or group work, with little difficulty.

ANSWERS: **1.** is studying [Check the spelling "yi."] . . . is also taking . . . begin **2.** had already eaten . . . left . . . always eats . . . goes [Check for -*s* endings.] . . . goes . . . will eat/will have eaten **3.** called . . . was attending **4.** will be attending **5.** got . . . was sleeping . . . had been sleeping **6.** is taking . . . fell . . . has been sleeping **7.** started . . . hasn't finished . . . is reading **8.** has read . . . is reading . . . has been reading . . . intends . . . has read . . . has ever read **9.** eats [no *will* in the time clause] . . . is going to go . . . will have eaten . . . goes [no *will* in the time clause]

□ EXERCISE 5, p. 69.   Review of verb tenses.   (Chapters 1 → 4)

Make sure the students understand the format.

While the main point of this exercise is to practice verb tenses, the intention is that at least some of the exercise items develop into short natural dialogues between classmates.

You may wish to walk around the room and listen to the exchanges—but don't interrupt. Answer individual questions, but make longer explanations to the class only after the exercise is completed.

A and B should exchange roles in Part II.

CHART 5-1:   ADVERB CLAUSES OF TIME: FORM

• Students were introduced to adverb clauses in Charts 2-9 and 2-10 in conjunction with the presentation of the simple past and past progressive. This chart is an expansion on a complex sentence structure that the students have been using throughout Chapters 2, 3, and 4. It defines the term "adverb clause," describes its form, and focuses on some of its features in written English, such as punctuation and sentence completeness. You might note for the students that the comma usually reflects a pause in speaking.

• The use of a comma in a sentence begun by an adverb clause is less common in British English than American English. And even in American English, the comma may be omitted at times. The text focuses on usual usage as a way of providing a pattern that students can use as a guideline in their own production—without getting into too many refinements too soon, refinements that receptive students will later acquire as they gain experience with English.

□ EXERCISE 6, p. 70.   Adverb clauses of time.   (Chart 5-1)

ANSWERS: [The adverb clauses are underlined.]
1. We went inside <u>when it began to rain.</u>   **2.** It began to rain. **We** went inside.
3. <u>When it began to rain,</u> we went inside.   **4.** <u>When the mail comes,</u> my assistant opens it.   **5.** My assistant opens the mail <u>when it comes.</u>   **6.** The mail comes <u>around ten o'clock every morning.</u> **My** assistant opens it.

□ EXERCISE 7, p. 71.   Preview of Chart 5-2.

This exercise provides a review of verb tenses while presenting adverb clauses. Students will probably have questions about both points. This exercise is another summary overview of the English tense system as presented in Chart 1-5. If you have it as a wall chart or a transparency, you might want to pull it out again.

ERRATUM: Item 12 has as its intended completion the habitual past *used to go*. Presentation of the habitual past was deleted from the third edition of this book because it is covered thoroughly in *Fundamentals of English Grammar* (*FEG* = the black book). But this exercise item mistakenly was not changed in the revision. Instead of being deleted in a reprint, the item will remain here with the suggestion that you use this as an opportunity to review the habitual past. If students need more information, refer them to *FEG* by Azar.

EXPECTED COMPLETIONS: **2.** [after I <u>did</u> my homework.] **3.** [after I <u>do/have done</u> my homework.] **4.** [Ever since I was a child,] I <u>have been</u> afraid of dogs. **5.** [while she <u>was playing</u> basketball] (*a contact lens* = a corrective piece of glass or plastic worn on the surface of the eyeball) **6.** [before you <u>hand</u> it in to the teacher tomorrow.] **7.** [By the time I left my apartment this morning,] the mail carrier <u>had already delivered</u> the mail. **8.** [since he <u>was</u> ten years old] **9.** [as I <u>was driving</u> my car to work this morning.] (Note: One superstition holds that a black cat crossing one's path will bring bad luck. What other superstitions do the students know that will bring bad luck? Walking under a ladder? Breaking a mirror?) **10.** [By the time I leave this city,] I <u>will have been</u> here for four months. **11.** [Whenever Mark <u>gets</u> angry,] **12.** I <u>used to go</u> to the beach [whenever the weather was nice,] but now I don't have time to do that [because I have to study.] **13.** [when <u>my parents arrive from Moscow</u>.] **14.** [The next time I <u>go</u> to Hawaii,] **15.** [the last time I <u>ate</u> at that restaurant]

> **CHART 5-2: USING ADVERB CLAUSES TO SHOW TIME RELATIONSHPS**
>
> • Point out the punctuation rule in Chart 5-1, then show how it works in the examples in Chart 5-2.
>
> • Also call attention to the first note in this chart: future verbs are NOT used in an adverb clause of time. (See Chart 4-2.) Discuss the other tenses in the examples; refer the students to Chapters 1 through 4 as necessary.

☐ **EXERCISE 8, p. 73. Using adverb clauses to show time relationships. (Chapters 1 → 4; Charts 5-1 and 5-2)**

Notice that Exercise 8 looks like a regular multiple-choice exercise in which one chooses a single correct answer. It is not that kind of exercise. It is a combination exercise with multiple choices of connecting words. By contrast, Exercise 9 (which follows) is a traditional multiple-choice exercise.

ANSWERS: **3.** Whenever/Every time Susan feels nervous, she chews her nails. (~~before~~) **4.** The frying pan caught on fire while I was making dinner. (~~by the time, as soon as~~) **5.** Someone knocked on the door just as we were sitting down to eat. Just after we sat down to eat, someone knocked on the door. (~~just before~~) **6.** As soon as the singer finished her song, the audience burst into applause. The audience burst into applause immediately after the singer finished her song. (~~as long as~~) **7.** We have to wait here until Nancy comes. (~~as soon as, after~~) **8.** After / As soon as /When Nancy comes, we can leave for the theater. **9.** I knew that something was wrong just as soon as/when my roommate walked into the room yesterday. (~~whenever~~) **10.** Just before I stood up to give my speech, I got butterflies in my stomach. (~~until, while~~) **11.** The first time I saw the great pyramids of Egypt in the moonlight, I was speechless. (~~until, before~~) **12.** Jane has gotten three promotions since she started working at this company six months ago. (~~before, when~~) **13.** The phone rang shortly after / not long after / a short time after I had gone to bed. **14.** When/Once the weather gets warmer, we can start playing tennis again. (~~while~~) **15.** By the time Shakespeare died in 1616, he had written more than 37 plays. (~~while, once~~) **16.** The next time Sam goes to the movies, he'll remember to take his glasses. (~~as long as, by the time~~) **17.** As long as I live, I will not forget Mr. Tanaka. (~~as, so long as~~) **18.** Mohammad had never heard about Halloween before/until he came to the U.S. (~~since~~)

☐ EXERCISE 9, p. 74.   Verb tenses in adverb clauses of time. (Chart 5-2)

This is a traditional multiple-choice exercise. If the students complete it as seat work, give them seven minutes. (Thirty seconds per item is standard for multiple-choice tests.)

ANSWERS: **1.** B   **2.** D   **3.** C   **4.** D   **5.** D   **6.** A   **7.** B   **8.** C
9. B   **10.** B   **11.** B   **12.** A   **13.** D   **14.** B

☐ EXERCISE 10, p. 75.   Using adverb clauses to show time relationships. (Chart 5-2)

Encourage students to use a variety of verb tenses.

See the *Introduction*, p. xvi, for suggestions on ways of handling open completion exercises.

ANSWERS: [Answers depend on students' creativity.]

☐ EXERCISE 11, p. 76.   Review of verb tenses. (Chapters 1 → 5)

Students can perform some of these dialogues dramatically, with appropriate gestures and emotional voices. This can be great fun. You might want to assign the dialogues to be memorized by pairs of students and then presented to the class without their looking at their books. It should take them only a few minutes to memorize their dialogue.

ANSWERS: **1.** am listening   **2.** A: Have you met   B: have never had   **3.** A: are you doing   B: am trying   A: will electrocute / are going to eletrocute   **4.** A: is lying   B: see . . . certainly looks   **5.** A: went   B: Was it   A: enjoyed   B: did you see   A: had never seen   B: have seen . . . saw . . . was . . . wasn't   **6.** A: had never been   B: were you doing   A: were driving   **7.** A: Are you taking   B: am not   A: Have you ever taken   B: have   A: did you take . . . was . . . is/was he   B: is/was   **8.** A: was . . . haven't received . . . don't have/haven't   B: do you need   A: will pay . . . get   **9.** A: isn't   B: will be sitting   **10.** A: do you know . . . have been looking   B: is seeing . . . received   A: sounds . . . has . . . will be working

☐ EXERCISE 12, p. 78.   Review of verb tenses. (Chapters 1 → 5)

Students in pairs can work out the answers. Then one pair can read the whole exercise aloud to the class. Other students should note any errors, but should not interrupt the dialogue. At the end, discussion can always clear up the mistakes.

ANSWERS: **(1)** Are you studying   **(2)** am   **(3)** have been . . . studied / was studying / had been studying   **(4)** are you taking   **(5)** am taking . . . are you taking   **(6)** am studying . . . need . . . take   **(7)** have you been   **(8)** have been . . . arrived . . . have been studying . . . lived / was living   **(9)** speak . . . Did you study / Had you studied . . . came   **(10)** studied / had studied / had been studying . . . spent . . . picked . . . was living/lived   **(11)** were . . . came . . . had never studied . . . started   **(12)** do you plan / are you planning   **(13)** I'm not . . . return . . . will have been   **(14)** hope / am hoping

☐ EXERCISE 13, p. 79.   Review of verb tenses. (Chapters 1 → 5)

Students in pairs or individually can work out the answers. As a variation, you could ask the students to write the letter (without the numbers in parentheses). When they finish, they can exchange letters and look for each other's mistakes. (Copying from a text is usually more beneficial for lower- or mid-level students than for advanced students, who make few mistakes and generally find it busywork.)

This exercise is intended as a model for the student writing assignment that follows in Exercise 14.

ANSWERS: **(1)** received **(2)** have been trying . . . have been **(3)** have had **(4)** has been staying **(5)** and **(6)** have spent / have been spending **(7)** have been **(8)** went . . . watched **(9)** have barely had **(10)** is . . . am sitting **(11)** have been sitting **(12)** leaves . . . decided **(13)** am writing **(14)** am getting **(15)** will take / am going to take . . . get **(16)** are you getting **(17)** are your classes going

☐ **EXERCISE 14, p. 79. Writing. (Chapters 1 → 5)**

You may wish to require the students to use each of the 12 tense forms at least once. That sometimes results in forced sentences, but the students usually find it challenging and fun. Refer the students once again to Chart 1-5 so they can see which verb forms they need to try to include.

☐ **EXERCISE 15, p. 80. Review of verb tenses. (Chapters 1 → 5)**

ANSWERS: **(1)** has experienced **(2)** will experience / is going to experience **(3)** began **(4)** have occurred **(5)** causes **(6)** have developed **(7)** waves **(8)** hold **(9)** moves **(10)** know **(11)** happened **(12)** struck **(13)** were sitting **(14)** suddenly found **(15)** died . . . collapsed **(16)** sent **(17)** will the next earthquake occur / is the next earthquake going to occur **(18)** have often helped **(19)** are studying **(20)** and **(21)** also appear **(22)** seem **(23)** have developed **(24)** will be **(25)** strikes

☐ **EXERCISE 16, p. 81. Activity: review of verb tenses. (Chapters 1 → 5)**

When you make this assignment, announce a time limit (perhaps five minutes) so that the stories are not long. This is not a dictation exercise, so Student A should listen to Student B's complete story, then report it in a written paragraph. Both students should tell their stories to each other first; then they can both write at the same time.

☐ **EXERCISE 17, p. 81. Activity: review of verb tenses. (Chapters 1 → 5)**

Only a few students each day should speak. Thus, the exercise can continue over several days. Students who are not speaking should be instructed to take notes in order to practice listening skills. They can also note (1) questions to ask for additional information and (2) problems with verb tenses or pronunciation. These notes can be used for discussion after the speaker is finished.

Remind students of the time limit. During the reports, you may wish to appoint one student as a timekeeper.

As preparation for this exercise, you may wish to bring a newspaper article to class and have the class work together in making a two- or three-minute summary so that the students will understand exactly what you expect. The article may also be used for a discussion of verb forms; you can discuss the verb forms that the students have already studied and point out the forms that they are going to study later (e.g., modals, sequence of tenses in noun clauses, gerunds and infinitives, passives).

☐ **EXERCISE 18, p. 81. Activity: review of verb tenses. (Chapters 1 → 5)**

The purpose of this exercise is to promote a wide range of tense usage in meaningful communication.

Use item 1 to get the students thinking about things they should consider. For example: What means of transportation were available to prehistoric human beings? How did the invention of the wheel change things? What kinds of animals have been used for transportation? What are modern means of transportation? How has the invention of these modern means of transportation changed human life? Etc.

SUGGESTION: Assign one group of students one topic and ask them to make a list of discussion questions. The list of questions can be handed to one other group, or passed around to all the groups—depending on how much time you decide to devote to this discussion exercise.

ALSO POSSIBLE: Make up a few discussion questions yourself for each item to expedite the process of getting the students thinking about the discussion topics.

The written summary can be quite short. Ask the students simply to list the main points of their discussion. The assignment is not intended to be developed into a formal composition with an introduction, body, and conclusion—but you could, of course, choose to do so if the organization and presentation of ideas in written English is a focus in your class.

□ EXERCISE 19, p. 81. Error analysis: general review. (Chapters 1 → 5)

Not all of the mistakes are verb tenses; some involve capital letters, singular–plural agreement, and pronoun usage. All of the mistakes are typical of many learners at this level of proficiency and are the kinds of errors they should look out for in their own writing. As always, the items are directly adapted from student writing.

ANSWERS:
1. I <u>have been</u> living at 3371 **G**rand **A**venue since last September.
2. I have been in New York **C**ity <u>for two weeks</u> <s>ago.</s>   OR   I <u>was</u> in New York **C**ity two <u>weeks</u> ago.
3. My country <u>has changed</u> its capital city five <u>times</u>.
4. Dormitory life is not quiet. Everyone <u>shouts</u> and <u>makes</u> a lot of noise in the halls.
5. My friends will meet me when I <s>will</s> <u>arrive</u> at the airport.
6. Hasn't anyone ever <u>told</u> you to knock on the door before you enter someone else's room? Didn't your parents <u>teach</u> you that?
7. When I was a child, I viewed <u>things</u> from a much lower height. Many physical objects around me <u>appeared</u> very large. When I <u>wanted</u> to move something such as a chair, I <u>needed</u> help.
8. I <s>will</s> <u>intend</u> to go back home when I <u>finish</u> my education.
9. The phone <u>rang</u> while I was doing the dishes. I <u>dried</u> my hands and <u>answered</u> it. When I <u>heard</u> my <u>husband's</u> voice, I <u>was</u> very happy.
10. I <u>have been</u> in the United States for the last four months. During this time, I <u>have</u> done many <u>things</u> and <u>(have) seen</u> many <u>places</u>.
11. When the old man started to walk back to his cave, the sun <u>had</u> already <u>hidden</u> itself behind the mountain.
12. While I <u>was</u> writing my composition last night, someone <u>knocked</u> on the door.
13. I'm <u>studying</u> English at an English conversation school two <u>times</u> a week.
14. Getting accustomed to a different <u>culture is</u> not easy.
15. I'm really glad you <u>visited / are going to visit / will visit / will be visiting</u> my hometown this year.
16. While I was <u>visiting</u> my cousin in Los Angeles**,** **w**e went to a Thai restaurant and <u>ate</u> Thai food.
17. <u>After</u> we ate dinner**,** **w**e watched TV.   OR   We ate dinner. We watched TV <u>afterwards</u>.
18. When I was in my country, I <u>was</u> afraid to come to the United States. I thought I couldn't walk outside at night because of the terrible crime. But now I <u>have</u> a different opinion. I <u>have lived</u> in this small town for three <u>months</u> and <u>(have) learned</u> that there is very little crime here.
19. Before I came to the United <u>States</u>, I pictured the U.S. as an exciting place with <u>honest</u>, hard-working, well-mannered <u>people</u>. <u>Since</u> I came to the United <u>States</u> four <u>months</u> ago, this picture <u>has</u> changed. The manners of the students while [also possible: *when*] they are in the cafeteria are really bad. I also <u>think</u> that office workers here <u>are</u> lazy. People in my country <u>work</u> a lot harder.

Chapter 6: SUBJECT-VERB AGREEMENT

ORDER OF CHAPTER	CHARTS	EXERCISES	WORKBOOK
Preview: final -s/-es	6-1	Ex. 1 → 7	Pr. 1 → 2
Basic subject–verb agreement	6-2	Ex. 8 → 9	Pr. 3
Using expressions of quantity	6-3	Ex. 10	Pr. 4
Using *there + be*	6-4	Ex. 11 → 12	Pr. 5
Some irregularities	6-5	Ex. 13 → 15	
Review	6-2 → 6-5	Ex. 16 → 17	Pr. 6

General Notes on Chapter 6

• OBJECTIVE: Correct use of final -s/-es is a common problem among learners of English. Even though students may "know" the grammar for using the final -s/-es suffix, they are still not consistent in using it correctly in their own production, both oral and written. To abet self-monitoring and development of correct patterns of production, this chapter focuses attention on final -s/-es and singular–plural distinctions, beginning with a review of some rules for spelling and pronouncing the final -s/-es suffix. The main sections deal with the problem of number: quantities and various aspects of singular–plural agreement between subject and verb.

• TERMINOLOGY: The term "expression of quantity" is used for any quantifier (e.g., *some of, a lot of, several of, two of*), determiner (e.g., *no, each, every, some, any*), or predeterminer (e.g., *all, both*) that expresses amount or size.

☐ EXERCISE 1, p. 83.   Preview: using -S/-ES.   (Charts 2-1, 6-1, 6-2, and 7-4)

This is a kind of pre-test or preview. Give the students a few minutes to add -s/-es, then discuss. Possible points of discussion:

- grammatical explanations for final -s/-es

- pronunciation of -s/-es: /s/, /z/, and /əz/ (See the *Introduction,* p. xxiii, for pronunciation symbols.)

- variations in spelling: -s vs. -es; -ys vs. –ies

- basic grammar terminology: noun, verb, adjective, singular, plural

- the basic structure of the simple sentence: subjects and verbs and complements

- count vs. noncount nouns: items 5 and 6 have the noncount noun *water*, to which no final -s is added (see the following chapter, Chart 7-4)

- expressions of quantity: *every, nine, many, a lot of*

The students are assumed to be familiar with most of the above-mentioned points, so the class can provide much of the information. You may wish to tell them that you know this exercise is "too easy," but that for the average learner, problems with singular–plural persist through many years of English study and use; hence, this review of basics.

Use the chalkboard so that everyone can focus on a word that requires -s/-es. Also discuss why other words do NOT have an -s/-es ending.

EXPANSION ACTIVITY (for use now or later in the unit): Using copies of any paragraph(s) you choose, have the students circle and discuss every word that ends in -s. (Some words, of course, are simply spelled with a final -s, e.g., *bus.*)

ANSWERS: **2.** works /s/ = *singular verb* [Note: *every* is a "singular word" followed by a singular, never plural, noun; therefore, *day* does not take a final -s here.] **3.** consists /s/ = *singular verb* [a present tense verb; subject: *system*] planets /s/ = *plural noun* **4.** rotates /s/ = *singular verb* **5.** animals /z/ = *plural noun* [*water* is a noncount noun, so it has no final -s.] **6.** needs /z/ = *singular verb* **7.** Students /s/, tests /s/ = *plural nouns* **8.** wings /z/ = *plural noun* [Note: The bird pictured in the chapter heading is a swallow—specifically a barn swallow. Other kinds of swallows have shorter tails.] **9.** Swallows /z/, creatures /z/ = *plural nouns* **10.** Butterflies /z/ = *plural noun* [-y is changed to -i. Also: an adjective, *beautiful,* does NOT take a final -s.] **11.** sunsets /s/ = *plural noun* [An adjective, *beautiful,* does not take a final -s.] **12.** contains /z/ = *singular verb,* books = *plural noun* **13.** Encyclopedias /z/, things /z/ = *plural nouns* **14.** watches /əz/ = *singular verb* [-es is added, not just -s, and pronunciation adds a syllable.] **15.** changes /əz/ = *singular verb* [Only -s added, but the pronunciation adds a syllable.]

CHART 6-1: FINAL -*S*/-*ES*: USE, PRONUNCIATION, AND SPELLING

• Most of your students are probably well aware of the elementary grammar in this chart but still sporadically or even frequently omit final -s/-es. The text seeks to reinforce student awareness of -s/-es by a review of rules and an emphasis on oral production.

Encourage the clear and correct pronunciation of -s/-es in your students' speaking throughout the term. Perhaps mention that the use of the wrong pronunciation of final -s/-es contributes to having a "foreign accent." Although there's nothing wrong with having a foreign accent as long as others can understand the speaker, students may wish to work on minimizing their accents.

□ EXERCISE 2, p. 85. Pronunciation of final -S/-ES. (Chart 6-1)

See p. 13 of this *Teacher's Guide* for information about voiced and voiceless sounds.

EXPANSION ACTIVITY: After the three groups of words have been practiced, you may want to try a game in which you spell a word aloud or write it on the chalkboard, and a student must pronounce it correctly, with special attention to the -s/-es pronunciation.

NOTE: Almost all students find *th* + final -s a difficult mouthful. Words you can use if you want to practice *th* + final -s follow:

voiceless /θs/: *months, tenths, strengths*
voiced /ðz/: *clothes* (Few words end in /ðz/. Others: *soothes, loathes, seethes*)
voiceless vs. voiced: *baths (n.)* vs. *bathes (v.), breaths (n.)* vs. *breathes (v.)*

ERRATUM: In the first printing of the student textbook, the second column in Group C contains two items numbered 30. Instead of 30 through 34, the second column should be numbered 30 through 35. This is corrected in subsequent printings.

GROUP A ANSWERS: **2.** feeds /z/ **3.** hates /s/ **4.** lids /z/ **5.** sleep /s/ **6.** robs /z/ **7.** trips /s/ **8.** grabs /z/ **9.** wishes /əz/ **10.** matches /əz/ **11.** guesses /əz/

GROUP B ANSWERS: **12.** books /s/   **13.** homes /z/   **14.** occurs /z/   **15.** fixes /əz/
16. sizes /əz/   **17.** pages /əz/   **18.** unlocks /s/   **19.** fills /z/   **20.** ashes /əz/
21. sniffs /s/   **22.** miles /z/   **23.** rugs /z/

GROUP C ANSWERS: **24.** arranges /əz/   **25.** itches /əz/   **26.** relaxes /əz/   **27.** rises /əz/
28. laugh /s/   **29.** days /z/   **30.** pies /z/   **31.** agrees /z/   **32.** faces /əz/
33. quizzes /əz/   **34.** judges /əz/   **35.** asks /s/

☐ EXERCISE 3, p. 85.   Spelling of final -S/-ES.   (Chart 6-1)

ANSWERS: **3.** talks /s/   **4.** blushes /əz/   **5.** discovers /z/   **6.** develops /s/
7. seasons /z/   **8.** flashes /əz/   **9.** halls /z/   **10.** touches /əz/   **11.** coughs /s/
12. presses /əz/   **13.** methods /z/   **14.** mixes /əz/   **15.** tries /z/   **16.** trays /z/
17. enemies /z/   **18.** guys /z/

☐ EXERCISE 4, p. 86.   Pronunciation and spelling of final S/-ES.   (Chart 6-1)

Have a student say a word that ends with the suffix *-s/-es.* You can supply the words or let
the students make up their own, using plural nouns or singular verbs. Or take three cards
with the symbols on them, show one card privately to a student, and have that student say a
word with that ending. Everyone writes down the word under the symbol for the correct
pronunciation. This exercise is useful for developing both listening and speaking skills.

If you wish, divide the class into two teams. The winning team has the most correct
answers in the correct columns.

☐ EXERCISE 5, p. 86.   Pronunciation of final -S/-ES.   (Chart 6-1)

Students could work in pairs and correct each other's pronunciation. They could note
pronunciation in their books using the symbols /s/, /z/, and /əz/. Another possibility is to
have each student make three cards with symbols /s/, /z/, and /əz/. When a student says a
word with a final *-s/-es,* someone (the speaker, another student, you, the rest of the class, or
everyone) holds up the card that represents the sound being said.

PRONUNCIATION NOTES: **1.** encourages /jəz/ . . . students /nts/   **2.** chickens /nz/, ducks
/ks/ . . . turkeys /iz/ . . . eggs /gz/   **3.** possesses /səz/ . . . qualities /iz/   **4.** wages /jəz/ . . .
taxes /ksəz/   **5.** serves /vz/ . . . sandwiches /čəz/   **6.** coughs /fs/, sneezes /zəz . . .
wheezes /zəz/   **7.** shapes /ps/ . . . sizes /zəz/   **8.** practices /səz/ . . . sentences /səz/
9 shirts /ts/, shoes /uz/, socks /ks/, dresses /səz/, slacks /ks/, blouses /səz/, earrings /ŋz/ . . .
necklaces /ləsəz/ [Note: *slacks* has no singular form; there is no such thing as "one slack."]
10. scratches /čəz/   OR   /čɪz/ . . . itches /čəz/   OR   /čɪz/

☐ EXERCISE 6, p. 87.   Use of final -S/-ES. (Chart 6-1)

This exercise could be led by the teacher giving the cue, or used for group or pair work, with the students monitoring each other's pronunciation.

A note on sentence stress: In these sentences, the loudest (stressed) words are the **second** word and the **last** word.

ANSWERS: **1.** A stamp collector colle<u>cts</u> /kts/ stam<u>ps</u> /ps/.   **2.** An animal trainer trai<u>ns</u> /nz/ anima<u>ls</u> /lz/.   **3.** A bank robber ro<u>bs</u> /bz/ ba<u>nks</u> /ŋks/.   **4.** A dog catcher ca<u>tches</u> /čəz/ do<u>gs</u> /gz/.   **5.** A book publisher publi<u>shes</u> /šəz/ boo<u>ks</u> /ks/   **6.** A tax collector colle<u>cts</u> /kts/ ta<u>xes</u> /ksəz/.   **7.** A ticket taker ta<u>kes</u> /ks/ ticke<u>ts</u> /ts/.   **8.** A fire extinguisher extingui<u>shes</u> /šəz/ fi<u>res</u> /rz/. [Note: A fire extinguisher is a metal bottle that contains a special liquid to spray on a small fire to put it out.]   **9.** A mind reader rea<u>ds</u> /dz/ mi<u>nds</u> /ndz/. [Note: This term is used humorously when someone seems to know what another is thinking without being told.]   **10.** A bullfighter fig<u>hts</u> /ts/ bu<u>lls</u> /lz/. [Note: It is traditional to write *bullfighter* and *storyteller* (item 12) as one word.]   **11.** A wage earner ea<u>rns</u> /rnz/ wa<u>ges</u> /ǰəz/.   **12.** A storyteller te<u>lls</u> /lz/ sto<u>ries</u> /riz/.

☐ EXERCISE 7, p. 87.   Use of final -S/-ES. (Chart 6-1)

The students should have fun trying to make generalizations about the given nouns. Provide additional vocabulary for the completions as needed. Keep calling attention to final *-s/-es*.

As an alternative format, you could give plural cues, e.g., *birds* instead of *bird*. Or you could vary singular and plural cues so that the students have to listen carefully for final *-s/-es* sounds. If you say "bird," the sentence has to begin with "A bird . . . ." If you say "birds," the sentence must begin with "Birds . . . ."

EXPANSION ACTIVITY: Add nouns for vocabulary discussion and further practice with *-s/-es*. For example, students often find it interesting and entertaining to find out what sounds animals make in English: a duck quacks, a cow moos, a snake hiss**es**, a horse whinni**es** or neighs, a chicken clucks, a rooster (American) or a cock (British) crow**s** "cockadoodledoo," a goose honks, a pig oinks, a mule or donkey brays, etc. You could also include nouns about professions (an architect, a welder, a day-care worker, a banker, etc.); machines or devices (a computer, a camera, a toaster, a bulldozer); and things in nature (fire, a planet, a volcano, a tree, etc.).

POSSIBLE ANSWERS: **1.** A baby cri**es** / drinks milk / sleeps a lot.   **2.** A telephone rings. **3.** A star shines / twinkles.   **4.** A dog barks / runs / fetches.   **5.** A duck quacks / swims.   **6.** A ball bounces / rolls.   **7.** A heart beats / pounds / races / pumps. **8.** A river flows / overflows / dries up.   **9.** A cat purrs / chases mice.   **10.** A door closes / shuts / opens / swings.   **11.** A clock ticks / chimes / tells time.   **12.** An airplane fli**es** / lands / takes off.   **13.** A doctor heals / sees patients / prescribes medicine. **14.** A teacher teach**es** / instructs / educates / lectures.   **15.** A psychologist studi**es** human behavior / helps people with problems.

☐ **EXERCISE 8, p. 87.   Preview: subject–verb agreement.   (Charts 6-2 → 6-5)**

Students should complete this exercise before studying the next section of this chapter. It contains the subject–verb agreement rules in Charts 6-2 through 6-5. You can give an overview of these charts when you discuss the answers to this exercise. Advanced classes that have little trouble with this exercise can review the material on pages 88–98 quickly. Students who have difficulty identifying subjects and verbs should be referred to Appendix Chart A-1.

ANSWERS: **2.** gets   **3.** are   **4.** is   **5.** is   **6.** are   **7.** is   **8.** are   **9.** is
10. is   **11.** are   **12.** has   **13.** has   **14.** was/were   **15.** is   **16.** speak
17. are [also possible and common, but informal and substandard: *is*]   **18.** is   **19.** is
20. is   **21.** is   **22.** like   **23.** are   **24.** Japanese (language) is   **25.** Japanese
(people) have   **26.** are   **27.** works   **28.** are   **29.** is   **30.** is

---

CHART 6-2:   BASIC SUBJECT–VERB AGREEMENT

• The grammatical term "third person" refers to this pattern:

SINGULAR: *I* = the person who is speaking, the "first person"
you = the person who is being spoken to, the "second person"
he/she/it OR **a singular or noncount noun** = the person or thing that is being discussed, the "third person"

PLURAL: *we* = the speaker and included persons, the "first person plural" form
you = all persons who are being spoken to or included in the audience, the "second person plural" form
they OR **a plural noun** = people or things that are being discussed, the "third person plural" form

• In (g) and (l): Errors in subject–verb agreement are common for second language learners (and to some degree for native speakers, too) when the subject is separated from the verb by an intervening noun of a different number. For example, in (g) the plural noun "parties," being closer to the verb than the singular subject, may influence the writer to use a plural verb. This is a point learners need to be aware of to improve their self-monitoring skills in their writing.

☐ **EXERCISE 9, p. 89.   Subject-verb agreement. (Chart 6-2)**

Students must be able to identify the grammatical subject, then select the correct form of the verb. The grammatical subject may not be the logical subject. Subjects with *every* and *each* (e.g., *every man, woman, and child*) may seem to be plural because the expression can logically be seen to refer to many people, but the grammatical concept of *every* and *each* is singular. Naturally, this is a difficult point for learners.

ANSWERS: **1.** astounds   **2.** are   **3.** is   **4.** are   **5.** agree   **6.** approves
7. has   **8.** is   **9.** is   **10.** was   **11.** do   **12.** were   **13.** Is   **14.** has

```
┌─────────────────────────────────────────────────────────────────────────┐
│                                                                           │
│  CHART 6-3:  SUBJECT–VERB AGREEMENT: USING EXPRESSIONS                     │
│              OF QUANTITY                                                   │
│                                                                           │
└─────────────────────────────────────────────────────────────────────────┘
```

• Explain how and why examples (a) and (b) are different: (a) deals with only one book, whereas (b) deals with more than one book, and point out how that affects the verb. Emphasize that the expression of quantity preceding the noun does NOT determine the verb in (a) through (f). It is the noun that determines the verb, not the quantifier.

• Refer the students to Chart 7-11, p. 125, for a list of expressions of quantity with *of*.

• In addition to *none of* [examples (j) and (k)], **neither of** and **either of** + *plural count noun* can be followed by either a singular or plural verb, with the singular verb usually preferred in formal English: *Neither of the boys is* (formal) OR **are** (common informally) *here*. [Chart 16-2 covers agreement when the subject includes paired (correlative) conjunctions: *Neither the boy nor the girl is* . . . . *Neither the boy nor the girls are* . . . . *Neither Tom nor I am* (formal) OR **are** (common informally) . . . .]

☐ **EXERCISE 10, p. 90.   Using expressions of quantity. (Chart 6-3)**

        ANSWERS: **1.** is   **2.** are   **3.** are   **4.** is   **5.** are   **6.** is   **7.** is   **8.** has
        9. has   **10.** is   **11.** is/are . . . are   **12.** are   **13.** is   **14.** is   **15.** Do
        16. Does   **17.** were   **18.** was   **19.** is   **20.** is   **21.** Do [Note: Approximately 70% of the earth's surface is covered by water.]

```
┌─────────────────────────────────────────────────────────────────────────┐
│                                                                           │
│  CHART 6-4:   SUBJECT–VERB AGREEMENT: USING THERE + BE                     │
│                                                                           │
└─────────────────────────────────────────────────────────────────────────┘
```

• *There + be* is very different in meaning from *They are* <u>there</u>, in which *there* represents a particular place, substituting for a prepositional phrase of place or other place expression. In fact, it is not unusual to say "There are lots of people there." Be sure students understand that the expletive "there" has no meaning in and of itself. The structure itself (**there + be** + *noun*) conveys the meaning that something exists.

• Stress that the verb agrees with the noun following *be; there* is neither singular nor plural.

• In (f): The use of a singular verb when the noun is plural *(There's some books on the shelf)* jars the ears of many native speakers, but it would seem that sometimes our brains don't always leap ahead to know that the noun following is going to be plural, so a singular verb slips out. Even some well-educated sticklers for correct grammar sometimes find themselves slipping up with a singular verb here. A singular verb is even more commonly used when the subject consists of two singular nouns: *There's a pen and a piece of paper on the desk.* vs. *There are a pen and a piece of paper on the desk.* OR *There's a man and a woman in the car behind us.* vs. *There are a man and a woman in the car behind us.* Formal grammar would insist on a plural verb in these examples, but a singular verb is exceedingly common in actual usage and is the form preferred by many native speakers in daily speech. With an advanced class, ask the students which verb, singular or plural, "sounds best" to them in these examples. If the singular verb "sounds best," that might indicate a near-native familiarity with the structure. Also ask the students which verb they would choose if these sentences were items on a standardized test (in which case they should choose the one considered correct in standard written English, i.e., the plural verb).

☐ **EXERCISE 11, p. 91.   Using THERE and BE. (Chart 6-4)**

ANSWERS: **1.** aren't   **2.** isn't   **3.** are   **4.** is   **5.** are   **6.** are   **7.** isn't
8. was   **9.** is   **10.** are   **11.** has been   **12.** have been

☐ **EXERCISE 12, p. 91.   Using THERE and BE. (Chart 6-4)**

Tell students to begin with "There is/are . . ." and not merely respond with a list of
nouns. This exercise is intended only as a quick check to see if the students are having
any problems with this structure. No problems are anticipated, but sentences with
informal singular rather than plural verbs (e.g., *There's one door and three windows is this
room*) might spur a discussion of actual usage of this structure in everyday spoken
English.

CHART 6-5:   SUBJECT–VERB AGREEMENT: SOME IRREGULARITIES

• The footnote about the word "people" may need further explanation. This word has two
meanings, each requiring a different grammatical interpretation.

(a) the *people* of Great Britain = the British (plural)
(b) They are *one people*. = one nation (singular)

(a) the *people* of Canada = the Canadians (plural)
(b) They are *one people*. = one nation (singular)

(a) *Most people* in Great Britain and Canada *speak* English. (plural)
(b) *The peoples* of Great Britain and Canada *are* loyal to the Queen. (the peoples = two
nations)

☐ **EXERCISE 13, p. 93.   Irregularities in subject-verb agreement. (Chart 6-5)**

The answers below also give the pronouns that would be used to refer to the nouns in
question. Sometimes it helps students decide on number if they try to substitute a pronoun
for the noun. For example, in item 1 most students easily recognize that the correct
pronoun to refer to *the United States* is the singular *it*, not the plural *they*.

ANSWERS: **1.** The United States *(it)* has   **2.** news *(it)* . . . is   **3.** Massachusetts *(it)*
is   **4.** Physics *(it)* seeks   **5.** Statistics *(it)* is   **6.** The statistics *(they)* . . . are
7. Fifty minutes *(It)* is   **8.** Twenty dollars *(It)* is   **9.** Six and seven *(It)* is
10. Many people *(They)* . . . do   **11.** police *(they)* are   **12.** Rabies *(It)* is
13. The English *(They)* are   **14.** English *(It)* is   **15.** Many Japanese *(They)*
commute   **16.** Portuguese *(It)* is . . . isn't   **17.** The poor *(They)* are
18. effect *(it)* . . . depends . . . Most people *(They)* are . . . there have been instances

☐ **EXERCISE 14, p. 93.   Review: subject-verb agreement. (Charts 6-2 → 6-5)**

This can be a fast drill; you say the cue, and students respond with *is* or *are*. Or students
could work in pairs/small groups. In addition to oral practice, you could ask the students to
write out complete sentences.

ANSWERS: **1.** is   **2.** are   **3.** are   **4.** is   **5.** is   **6.** are   **7.** is   **8.** is
9. is   **10.** is [the language]   **11.** are [the people/they]   **12.** is   **13.** is   **14.** are
15. are   **16.** is   **17.** are   **18.** is   **19.** is   **20.** are [clothes are/clothing is]
21. is   **22.** is   **23.** are   **24.** is   **25.** is   **26.** are   **27.** are   **28.** is/are
29. are   **30.** is   **31.** are   **32.** are   **33.** is   **34.** are   **35.** is

☐ EXERCISE 15, p. 94.   Error analysis: subject-verb agreement.   (Charts 6-2 → 6-5)

ANSWERS:

3. All of the employees in that company <u>are</u> required to be proficient in a second language.

4. A lot of the people in my class <u>work</u> during the day and <u>attend</u> class in the evening.

5. Listening to very loud music at rock concerts <u>has</u> caused hearing loss in some teenagers. [The subject is *listening*.]

6. Many of the satellites orbiting the earth <u>are</u> used for communications.

7. *(no errors)*

8. Chinese [the language] <u>has</u> more than fifty thousand written characters.

9. About two-thirds of the Vietnamese <u>work</u> in agriculture.

10. *(no errors)*

11. *(no errors)*

12. *(no errors)*

13. Every girl and boy <u>is</u> required to have certain immunizations before enrolling in public school.

14. Seventy-five percent of the people in New York City <u>live</u> in upstairs apartments, not on the ground floor.

15. Unless there <u>is</u> a profound and extensive reform of government policies in the near future, the economic conditions in that country will continue to deteriorate.

16. While I was in Paris, some of the best food I found <u>was</u> not at the well-known eating places, but in small out-of-the-way cafes.

17. <u>Where are</u> my gloves? Have you seen them anywhere? I can't find them.

18. *(no errors)*

19. *(no errors)* OR [possible but extremely formal: *are*]

20. *(no errors)*

21. Studying a foreign language often <u>leads</u> students to learn about the culture of the <u>country</u> where it is spoken.

22. *(no errors)*

23. Some of the <u>movies</u> about ~~the~~ gangsters <u>are</u> surprisingly funny.

24. *(no errors)*

25. How many people <u>are</u> there in Canada?

26. *(no errors)*

27. Which one of the continents in the world <u>is</u> uninhabited? [*answer:* Antarctica]

28. One of the most common names for dogs in the United States <u>is</u> Rover.

29. Everybody in my family <u>enjoys</u> music and reading.

30. Most of the mountain peaks in the Himalayan Range <u>are</u> covered with snow the year round.

□ EXERCISE 16, p. 96. Review: subject–verb agreement. (Charts 6-2 → 6-5)

ANSWERS: **2.** are **3.** keeps **4.** makes **5.** is **6.** is **7.** Does **8.** Do **9.** is **10.** are **11.** are **12.** Are **13.** is **14.** beats **15.** provides **16.** oversimplifies **17.** is **18.** plan **19.** concerns **20.** is **21.** is **22.** appears **23.** are **24.** is **25.** speaks

□ EXERCISE 17, p. 98. Review: subject–verb agreement. (Charts 6-2 → 6-5)

POSSIBLE ANSWERS: **1.** All of the rooms in . . . are/have, etc. **2.** In my country, there is + *singular noun* / are + *plural noun* **3.** A lot of + *singular noun* + is / *plural noun* + are **4.** people . . . are/have, etc. **5.** The number . . . is **6.** A number . . . are/have, etc. **7.** Each of . . . is/has, etc. **8.** The United States is/has, etc. **9.** The English language is/has, etc. **10.** The English [people] are/have, etc. **11.** English [the language] is/has, etc. **12.** One of my . . . is/has, etc. **13.** Most of the food . . . is/has/tastes, etc. **14.** Most of my classmates are/have, etc. **15.** Linguistics is, etc. **16.** Linguists are/study . . . **17.** The news about . . . was, is, etc. **18.** There are + *plural noun* . . . **19.** Greece, as well as Italy and Spain, is/has/etc. . . . . **20.** Fish is nutritious. Fish live in water. [Note: The use of *fish* is tricky; this item previews some of the information in Chapter 7. In the sentence "Fish is nutritious," *fish* refers to fish as a food and is used as a noncount noun (like *meat*). In the sentence "Fish live in water," *fish* refers to animals and is a count noun with an irregular plural form (i.e., the plural form is the same as the singular).]

Chapter 7: NOUNS

ORDER OF CHAPTER	CHARTS	EXERCISES	WORKBOOK
Regular and irregular plural nouns	7-1	Ex. 1 → 3	Pr. 1 → 3
Possessive nouns	7-2	Ex. 4 → 6	Pr. 4 → 5
Using nouns as modifiers	7-3	Ex. 7 → 8	Pr. 6 → 7
Count and noncount nouns	7-4 → 7-6	Ex. 9 → 11	Pr. 8
Article usage	7-7 → 7-8	Ex. 12 → 17	Pr. 9
Expressions of quantity	7-9	Ex. 18 → 22	Pr. 10
Using *a few* and *few; a little* and *little*	7-10	Ex. 23 → 24	Pr. 11
Using *of* in expressions of quantity	7-11	Ex. 25	Pr. 12
All (of) and *both (of)*	7-12	Ex. 26 → 27	
One, each, every	7-13	Ex. 28 → 29	Pr. 13
Review: expressions of quantity		Ex. 30 → 31	

General Notes on Chapter 7

• OBJECTIVE: Students review and gain control of such important features of English grammar as the singular/plural and count/noncount distinctions, possessive forms, articles, and some expressions of quantity.

• TERMINOLOGY: Some grammar books and dictionaries refer to "noncount" nouns as "mass" or "uncountable" nouns. The term "expression of quantity" is used for any quantifier (e.g. *some of, a lot of, two of*), determiner (e.g., *no, each, every, some, any*), or predeterminer (e.g., *all, both*) that expresses amount or size.

☐ EXERCISE 1, p. 99. Preview: plural nouns.

Students could write their answers on the chalkboard for everyone to check.

ANSWERS: **3.** mice   **4.** monkeys   **5.** industries   **6.** women   **7.** foxes
8. geese   **9.** sheep   **10.** series   **11.** beliefs [The <u>verb</u> "believe" is always spelled with a
"*v*": *believes.*]   **12.** leaves   **13.** selves [usually in words like *ourselves, yourselves, themselves*]
14. echoes [pronounced /ɛkowz/]   **15.** photos   **16.** analyses [pronounced /ənǽləsiz/]
17. hypotheses [pronounced /haipɑθəsiz/]   **18.** curricula [also possible: *curriculums*]
19. phenomena   **20.** stimuli [pronounced either /stɪmyulai/ or /stɪmyuli/]
21. offspring   **22.** bacteria

EXPANSION ACTIVITY: A traditional classroom game is a spelling bee. Students all stand.
The teacher says a word to one student. The student repeats the word, then must spell it
correctly letter by letter from memory. If the spelling is incorrect, the student sits down.
The next student who is standing must then spell the same word. If the spelling is correct,
he or she remains standing and the teacher says a new word to the next student. The game
continues in this way until only one student, the "champion speller," remains standing. (If
your class is large, you may want to ask for only a few volunteers to play the game. The
others can "bet" on who the winner will be.)

In the case of a bee with plural endings, the teacher can say the word and the student
spell it, adding the appropriate ending. Some possible words for a bee: *custom, disease,
skyscraper, appearance, hospital, career, calendar, label, succeed, surround, describe, mask, ladder,
mirror, ghost, ticket, passenger, occasion* (or consult a list of frequently misspelled words*); *wish,
ash, splash, crash, leash, push; pass, boss, kiss, cuss, mess, embarrass, lose, choose, choice; itch, pitch,
patch, fetch, ditch; fix, hoax, six, wax, hex, fox; decay, fairy, balcony, diary, destroy, berry, penalty,
mystery, enemy, holiday, category;* and any of the words in Chart 7-1. (If your class is advanced
and you want to keep them on their toes, throw in the word "homework" or "fun" and see if
they recognize that it's used only as a noncount noun and does not have a final -*s* form.)

---

* Avoid words with variant American/British spelling, e.g., *color/colour, airplane/aeroplane,
program/programme, judgment/judgement.*

CHART 7-1: REGULAR AND IRREGULAR PLURAL NOUNS

• This chart is an introduction and a reference, not something to be memorized precisely. Encourage students to consult their dictionaries when in doubt about the plural form of a noun—just as native speakers have to do. Sometimes native speakers (including, you might tell your students, the author of this text) need to look up, for example, the spelling of the plural form of words that end in *-o.*

• In (c): Words ending in *-ch* add the *-es* suffix—except for *stomach,* whose plural form adds *-s* only: *stomachs.* The difference is that in *stomach,* the *-ch* is pronounced /k/ rather than /č/. You may or may not wish to mention this exception.

• In (f): you can point out that final *-o* is followed by *-s,* not *-es,* when the noun is a shortened form (e.g., *auto–automobile, memo–memorandum*) and when the *-o* is preceded by another vowel. Again, encourage students to consult their dictionaries when in doubt.

• The list in the chart is not inclusive. Others that could be mentioned: in (g): *buffaloes/buffalos, haloes/halos, grottoes/grottos;* in (i): *waifs, oafs, serfs, sheriffs, tariffs;* in (j): *one moose–two moose, one reindeer–two reindeer;* in (m): *vita–vitae.*

• Many of the foreign plurals in examples (k) through (p) are used primarily in academic English; the text seeks only to make the learners aware that some nouns in English have these odd plural forms. Students will learn and remember only those that are useful to them.

• If students ask why some nouns are irregular, you might explain that throughout its history, the English language has had close contact with other European languages. It has been influenced by German, Danish, Latin, Greek, and French, especially; a few forms from those languages occur in some English words today.

☐ **EXERCISE 2, p. 101. Plural nouns. (Chart 7-1)**

    ANSWERS: **3.** teeth **4.** boxes . . . oxen **5.** mice **6.** beaches . . . cliffs **7.** leaves **8.** attorneys **9.** discoveries . . . laboratories **10.** fish **11.** wolves, foxes, deer . . . sheep **12.** echoes **13.** pianos **14.** phenomena **15.** media

☐ **EXERCISE 3, p. 102. Plural nouns. (Chart 7-1)**

If your students find this content too difficult, you could stop after paragraph (3). Not every exercise needs to be done in its entirety by every student. You could make this optional homework.
    Call attention to the information in the footnotes.

    ANSWERS: **(1)** Bacteria . . . things . . . organisms **(2)** Bacteria . . . bodies . . . creatures **(3)** thousands . . . kinds . . . bacteria **(4)** Viruses . . . organisms . . . viruses . . . cells . . . things . . . particles . . . hundreds . . . times **(5)** Viruses . . . diseases . . . beings . . . illnesses **(6)** Viruses **(7)** officials . . . conditions **(8)** officials . . . infections . . . bacteria . . . forms **(9)** infections . . . infections . . . doctors

CHART 7-2: POSSESSIVE NOUNS

• Another way to explain the possessive form is to say that a noun always adds *'s* in writing, e.g., *boy's, men's.* However, in the case of a noun that already ends in *-s*, we take away the second *-s* and leave the apostrophe.

    boy + 's = boy's   (singular, possessive)
    men + 's = men's   (irregular plural, possessive)
    boys + 's = boys's   (plural, possessive) you take away the second *-s*: boys**'**

☐ **EXERCISE 4, p. 103.   Possessive nouns.   (Chart 7-2)**

    ANSWERS: **2.** boy's **3.** boys' **4.** children's **5.** child's **6.** baby's **7.** babies'
    8. wives' **9.** wife's **10.** Sally's **11.** Phyllis'/Phyllis's [pronounced /fɪlɪsəz/]
    12. boss's [pronounced /bɔsəz/] **13.** bosses' [also pronounced /bɔsəz/] **14.** woman's
    15. women's **16.** sister's **17.** sisters' **18.** yesterday's **19.** today's **18.** month's

☐ **EXERCISE 5, p. 104.   Possessive nouns.   (Chart 7-2)**

    ANSWERS: **3.** father's **4.** I have four aunts. All of my aunts' homes . . . mother's
    5. aunt's **6.** Five astronauts were . . . The astronauts' safe return **7.** children's
    8. child's **9.** secretary's **10.** people's **11.** Bill's **12.** Bess's/Bess'
    13. Quite a few diplomats are . . . Almost all of the diplomats' children **14.** diplomat's

☐ **EXERCISE 6, p. 104.   Using apostrophes.   (Chart 7-2; Appendix Chart C)**

This exercise is a general review of apostrophe use, showing that it is used both in possessives and in contractions.

    Pay some special attention to *its* vs. *it's.* Their misuse is common in both native-speaker and second language writing. Reassure the students that they are not the only ones who have trouble remembering when to use an apostrophe with ***it*** + *-s*. Even grammar teachers may have to stop and think through whether to use *its* or *it's* in a particular sentence!

    ANSWERS: **2.** bear's [Note: No apostrophe in *its* (possessive adjective)] **3.** It's . . . world's
    4. individual's **5.** heroes' . . . hero's **6.** Children's . . . they're . . . Adults' toys
    . . . children's toys

CHART 7-3: USING NOUNS AS MODIFIERS

• Some grammar books use the term "noun adjunct" for a noun that modifies another noun.

• Some grammars refer to noun-noun combinations as one type of "compound noun."

• There is an instance in which a noun adjunct <u>is</u> in a plural form. Some nouns are usually or always plural; these nouns often refer to things people wear that have two parts, such as *trousers* or *glasses,* or to instruments that have two parts, such as *scissors* or *binoculars.* When these nouns are used as noun adjuncts, they frequently retain their plural form: *glasses case, jeans pocket, pants pockets, scissors drawer.* They may, however, revert to the singular form, as in *binocular case* and *trouser pocket.* Students rarely encounter or have questions about this minor point of grammar, but the teacher might find it of interest—and then there is always the occasional student who finds the odd exception to what is said in a grammar book and eagerly lays it before the unwary teacher.

□ **EXERCISE 7, p. 105.   Using nouns as modifiers. (Chart 7-3)**

When you read or listen to the students' answers, pay special attention to two common problems: (1) the modifying noun must be singular in form, and (2) the article "a/an" is required for singular count nouns.

Point out the use of hyphens (-) in adjective phrases containing numbers. It is useful to have students write their answers on the chalkboard, as some of them may be unfamiliar with the use of the hyphen.

NOTE: In general, a hyphen is used when two (or more) words used as a modifer to a noun have one meaning when they appear together: *a man-eating tiger* (it's not *a man tiger* or *an eating tiger;* it's *a man-eating tiger* — two words which together give one meaning, as though they were one word), i.e., *salt-and-pepper hair, a part-time job, a matter-of-fact attitude, a heart-breaking story, a two-hour movie.*

ANSWERS: **2.** flowers . . . flower   **3.** beans . . . bean   **4.** babies . . . baby
5. children . . . child   **6.** salads . . . salad   **7.** faxes . . . fax   **8.** cans . . .
can . . . potatoes . . . potato   **9.** airplanes . . . Airplane   **10.** mosquitoes . . .
mosquito   **11.** two-hour . . . two hours   **12.** ten years old . . . ten-year-old
13. ten . . . speeds . . . ten-speed   **14.** six games . . . six-game   **15.** three-letter
. . . three letters

□ **EXERCISE 8, p. 107.   Using nouns as modifiers. (Chart 7-3)**

POSSIBLE RESPONSES: **1.** a cotton shirt, cotton balls, cotton wool [British English]   **2.** a
grammar book, a grammar test   **3.** a birthday card, a birthday present   **4.** chicken
salad, chicken soup   **5.** an airplane trip, an airplane ticket   **6.** a telephone book, a
telephone call   **7.** a mountain peak, a mountain climber   **8.** a government official, a
government program   **9.** a football game, a football uniform [Note: In most parts of the
world, *football* is synonymous with *soccer.* American football and Australian rules football are different
games.]   **10.** a bedroom table, bedroom slippers   **11.** a silk scarf, silk pajamas
12. a morning newspaper, the morning news   **13.** a street sign, a street light   **14.** a
newspaper headline, a newspaper article   **15.** a hotel lobby, a hotel room   **16.** a
kitchen table, a kitchen sink   **17.** baby food, a baby bottle   **18.** vegetable soup, a
vegetable brush   **19.** an office building, office furniture   **20.** a bicycle tire [BrE:
tyre], a bicycle lane

┌───┐
│ **CHART 7-4:   COUNT AND NONCOUNT NOUNS**   │
└───┘

• Some noncount nouns, like *furniture,* are also called "mass nouns" in other grammar books.

• The count/noncount distinction is one of the most difficult points for students to control.

• Some common mistakes that students make are the following:

INCORRECT	CORRECT COUNT FORM	CORRECT NONCOUNT FORM
many homeworks	*many assignments*	*a lot of homework*
some slangs	*some slang expressions*	*some slang*
many vocabularies	*many vocabulary words/items*	*a large vocabulary*

• ERRATUM: In the first printing of the textbook there is a misprint. The first line in Chart 7-4 on the right should read " . . . chairs are items that can **be** counted." This is corrected in subsequent printings.

□ **EXERCISE 9, p. 107.   Count and noncount nouns. (Chart 7-4)**

The purpose of this exercise is to help students understand the two charts that follow (7-5 and 7-6). As you go through the exercise, discuss the ideas presented in Chart 7-5. In item 1, point out that a noncount noun refers to a "whole" that is made up of different parts. *Furniture* is the "whole" and *chairs, tables, desks* are the "different parts." In 4 and 5, compare noncount and count usages of the same word "iron"; the meaning is different. In item 6, point out that the first *baseball* is an "abstract whole" and the second *baseball* (a count noun) is a concrete thing.

You might give each student two cards (or the students can use their own paper). On one is a large letter "C," and on the other is "NC." As you read each sentence aloud, pause after each noun while the students hold up the piece of paper that identifies the noun as "C" or "NC." In this way, you can quickly see if students are incorrectly identifying any nouns, and the students can have a little fun. They can use these cards in the exercises that follow, too.

ANSWERS: **2.** jewelry (NC) . . . rings (C) . . . bracelets (C) . . . necklace (C) **3.** mountains (C) . . . fields (C) . . . lakes (C) . . . scenery (NC)   **4.** Gold (NC) . . . iron (NC)   **5.** iron (C)   **6.** baseball (NC) . . . baseball (C)

┌───┐
CHARTS 7-5 AND 7-6:   NONCOUNT NOUNS
└───┘

• The concept of a noncount noun is covered in Chart 7-5, followed by a list of common examples in Chart 7-6.

• If it helps your students to understand, use the term "mass" to explain the idea of "a whole."

• As pointed out in examples (e) and (f) of Chart 7-5, some nouns can be used as either count or noncount. Some of the nouns in Chart 7-6 also have count uses. A noun is count or noncount depending on how it is used and the speaker's intended meaning. No noun is inherently count or noncount. The words listed in Chart 7-6 are usually or always used as noncount nouns, but you may wish to discuss some of those with dual uses: *glass* (a material) vs. *a glass* (a container for drinking); *tea* (a drink) vs. *teas* (kinds of tea); *pepper* (a spice) vs. *a pepper* (a vegetable); *bridge* (a card game) vs. *a bridge* (a way across a river); *time* (an abstract concept) vs. *times* (occurrences).

□ **EXERCISE 10, p. 109.   Count and noncount nouns. (Charts 7-5 and 7-6)**

In item 1, *change* is a noncount noun that means "coins" or "non-paper money." For particular nouns of your choosing, ask the students to raise their cards with "C" or "NC" on them.

ANSWERS: **3.** music   **4.** traffic   **5.** garbage   **6.** junk   **7.** stuff   **8.** thunder **9.** screwdrivers   **10.** hardware   **11.** homework   **12.** luggage/baggage   **13.** this information   **14.** advice [Note the spelling: *advice* = noun; *advise* = verb]   **15.** progress

□ **EXERCISE 11, p. 110.   Count and noncount nouns; nouns as modifiers. (Charts 7-5 and 7-6)**

A student can read an answer aloud to the class, but he or she should say the complete sentence, not only the nouns. The answers must be spoken loudly and clearly so everyone can hear. You might also review the pronunciation of *-s/-es*. (See Chart 6-1.)

For particular nouns of your choosing, ask the students to raise their cards with "C" or "NC" on them.

ANSWERS: **3.** trees, bush**es**, grass *(no change)*, dirt *(no change)*, and flowers **4.** advice *(no change)* . . . suggestions **5.** words . . . vocabulary *(no change)* **6.** two glass**es** . . . water *(no change)* **7.** Windows . . . glass *(no change)* **8.** glass**es** . . . eyesight *(no change)* **9.** time *(no change)* . . . homework *(no change)*. . . . assignments **10.** three times . . . a lot of time *(no change)* **11.** typewriters, copiers, telephones, and staplers . . . equipment *(no change)* **12.** air *(no change)* . . . smoke, dust, and carbon monoxide *(no changes)* . . . substances . . . air pollution *(no change)* **13.** literature *(no change)* . . . novels, poetry *(no change)*, and essays . . . poets . . . poems **14.** seasons . . . weather *(no change)* **15.** happiness *(no change)* . . . patience *(no change)* . . . rewards **16.** machines . . . a modern factory *(no change)* . . . Modern factor**ies** . . . machinery *(no change)* **17.** travelers . . . luggage *(no change)* . . . suitcases . . . days . . . months . . . traveler *(no change)* . . . stuff *(no change)* . . . day *(no change)* **18.** garbage *(no change)* . . . magazines, envelopes . . . box**es** . . . phone books . . . glass bottles, jars . . . copper *(no change)* . . . brass *(no change)* . . . tin cans **19.** stars . . . grains . . . sand *(no change)*

CHARTS 7-7 AND 7-8: BASIC ARTICLE USAGE

• Articles are very difficult for students to understand and use correctly. Many languages do not have articles. Languages that do have articles use them differently from English. Articles are, in many teachers' experiences, difficult to teach. There are many nuances, complex patterns of use, and idiomatic variations. Students who are frustrated trying to understand and use articles should be reminded that articles are just a small component of English. Proficiency in using articles improves with experience; it cannot be obtained overnight by learning "rules."

• The exercises point out some contrasts in usage that should help the students understand the differences among *a/an, the,* and the absence of any article (symbolized by **Ø**).

• Some students may need a reminder about using *an* instead of *a.* English speakers prefer not to pronounce a vowel sound after the article "a." Therefore, they put "n" between the two vowel sounds. For example:

  a + apple → an apple; a + old man → an old man; a + umbrella → an umbrella
  (But note that *a university* has no "n" because the "u" begins with a sort of "y" or consonant sound.)
  a + other → another (Tradition causes this to be written as one word.)

• These two charts are by no means exhaustive on the topic of article usage. Their goal is simply to give the learners a general understanding of the basics. Students who wish more in-depth information should be referred to texts that deal solely with article usage.

☐ **EXERCISE 12, p. 113. Article usage with generic nouns. (Chart 7-7)**

ANSWERS: **4.** A concert **5.** An opera **6. Ø** **7.** A cup **8. Ø** **9.** An island **10. Ø** **11.** A bridge **12.** A valley **13. Ø** **14.** An adjective **15. Ø** **16. Ø** **17.** A (tennis) player **18.** A tree **19. Ø** **20. Ø** **21. Ø** **22.** A sentence **23. Ø** **24. Ø** **25.** An orange **26. Ø** **27. Ø** **28.** An iron **29.** A basketball **30. Ø**

□ EXERCISE 13, p. 113.   Article usage with indefinite nouns.   (Chart 7-7)

ANSWERS: **5.** an accident   **6.** some homework   **7.** a table   **8.** some furniture
9. some chairs   **10.** some advice   **11.** a suitcase   **12.** some luggage
13. an earthquake   **14.** some letters   **15.** a letter   **16.** some mail   **17.** a machine
18. some new machinery   **19.** Some machines   **20.** some junk   **21.** an old
basket   **22.** some old boots

□ EXERCISE 14, p. 114.   Count and noncount nouns.   (Charts 7-4 → 7-7)

Divide the class into groups of six to ten. Each group can try to do the entire alphabet; set
a time limit (15–20 minutes) and let the groups get as far in the alphabet as they can. To
shorten the game, you could asign only half of the alphabet to a group.

Make sure the students focus on the correct use of *a/an* and *some*. Also tell them that
items can begin with an adjective; for example, *a bald monkey* could be used for the letter "B"
(but not the letter "M"). Explain that strange or funny answers are fine; the only
requirement is that the first word (other than *a/an* or *some*) begin with the appropriate letter
of the alphabet.

One way to play the game is to eliminate each player who can't remember the whole
list beginning with "A." The game continues until there is only one player who can recite
the whole list, or until everyone left can recite the whole list from A to Z. For the
classroom, however, it's better to make the game noncompetitive. The purpose is for the
students to have fun while they are practicing a grammar point. Tell them to try to play
without taking a lot of notes, but it would be all right if they needed to jot down a few
notes to jog their memory when it's their turn to speak. It would also be all right for the
students to help each other remember the list and remind each other about the use of
a/an and *some*.

□ EXERCISE 15, p. 115.   Article usage.   (Charts 7-7 and 7-8)

Exercise 15 is a series of dialogues. Students can work in pairs, or two students can read
one dialogue to the whole class.

Explain to the class that what is in the speaker's mind determines which article to use.
If the speaker believes the listener knows which thing or person the speaker is referring to,
the speaker will use *the*. If not, the speaker will use *a/an, some,* or Ø.

ANSWERS: **3.** a good reason   **4.** the reason   **5.** the washing machine . . . a different
shirt   **6.** a washing machine   **7.** A: The radiator . . . a leak . . . the windshield
wipers   B: the leak   **8.** A: The front wheel   B: a parked car . . . a big pothole [A
pothole /pathol/ is a hole in a street caused by water and traffic.]   A: the car   B: a note . . . the
owner . . . the car   A: the note   B: an apology   **9.** the closet . . . the front hallway

□ EXERCISE 16, p. 116.   Article usage.   (Charts 7-7 and 7-8)

ANSWERS: **4.** Ø   **5.** A hat . . . an article   **6.** Ø . . . Ø   **7.** The brown hat
8. Ø . . . Ø   **9.** a long life   **10.** the life   **11.** an engineer   **12.** an engineer
13. the name . . . the engineer . . . an infection . . . the bridge   **14.** Ø . . . Ø
15. The jewelry

☐ **EXERCISE 17, p. 117.   Article usage. (Charts 7-7 and 7-8)**

ANSWERS: **1.** a new phone   **2.** the phone   **3.** Ø . . . Ø . . . Ø . . . Ø . . . Ø . . .
Ø . . . Ø   **4.** a sandy shore . . . Ø . . . the surface . . . Ø . . . Ø, Ø, Ø, Ø . . . Ø
. . . Ø   **5.** the sand . . . Ø . . . a crab . . . The crab . . . a good time . . . the beach
6. Ø, Ø . . . Ø . . . a person   **7.** Ø . . . Ø . . . the universe   **8.** Ø . . . Ø . . . a
thin layer . . . Ø . . . Ø   **9.** a recent newspaper article . . . an Australian swimmer
. . . a shark [indefinite] . . . a group . . . the shark [now definite] . . . the swimmer . . . the
dolphins . . . the swimmer's life   **10.** Ø . . . Ø . . . Ø . . . an average . . . Ø
11. Ø . . . Ø   **12.** a fly . . . the ceiling . . . the fly . . . the ceiling

☐ **EXERCISE 18, p. 118.   Preview: expressions of quantity. (Chart 7-9)**

Give the class a couple of minutes to do the exercise, then review the correct answers.
Discuss the term "expressions of quantity" and point out differences in their usage between
count and noncount nouns.

ANSWERS:

1. i. ~~too much~~   **2.** a. ~~two~~   h. ~~too many~~
   k. ~~a little~~   b. ~~a couple of~~   j. ~~a few~~
   m. ~~a great deal of~~   c. ~~both~~   l. ~~a number of~~
                             d. ~~several~~

CHART 7-9:   EXPRESSIONS OF QUANTITY

- *A lot of* and *lots of* have the same meaning. Both are somewhat informal, with *lots of* being
the more informal.

- See Appendix Chart D-2 for *not any* vs. *no*.

☐ **EXERCISE 19, p. 119.   Expressions of quantity. (Chart 7-9)**

ANSWERS:

1. b. ~~several~~   g. ~~a few~~   **2.** e. ~~too much~~
   f. ~~too many~~   i. ~~a number of~~   h. ~~a little~~
                                                    j. ~~a great deal of~~

☐ **EXERCISE 20, p. 120.   MUCH vs. MANY. (CHART 7-9)**

Note that *much* is most often used in negative sentences or in questions. (See the footnote
in the text on page 122.)
      You might want to have your students lift their "C" and "NC" cards again.

ANSWERS: **3.** much mail   **4.** many letters   **5.** aren't many hotels   **6.** is too much
furniture   **7.** isn't much traffic   **8.** aren't many cars   **9.** much work   **10.** many
sides [Answer: A pentagon has five sides.]   **11.** much information   **12.** much
homework   **13.** many people   **14.** much postage   **15.** is too much violence
16. much patience   **17.** many patients   **18.** many teeth   [Answer: The average person
has 32 teeth.]   **19.** isn't much international news   **20.** many fish are   **21.** many
continents are [Your students may disagree on the answer to this question. By some calculations
there are seven continents; by other calculations, there are six, with Europe and Asia considered as
one. Technically, Europe is a peninsula of Asia rather than a continent, but traditionally Europe has
been accorded the status of a continent.]   **22.** much progress

□ EXERCISE 21, p. 121. Expressions of quantity. (Chart 7-9)

ANSWERS:

4. Ø
   loaves of bread
   Ø
   jars of honey

5. novels
   Ø
   poems
   Ø

6. orange juice
   light bulb<u>s</u>
   hardware
   computer software

7. sleep
   information
   fact<u>s</u>
   help

8. wom<u>e</u>n
   movie<u>s</u>
   scene<u>s</u>
   Ø

9. shirt<u>s</u>
   Ø
   pen<u>s</u>
   Ø

10. patience
    wealth
    Ø
    Ø

11. luck
    money
    advice
    Ø

12. idea<u>s</u>
    theor<u>ies</u>
    hypothe<u>ses</u>
    Ø

□ EXERCISE 22, p. 122. Expressions of quantity. (Chart 7-9)

This can be a rapid exercise with two-word answers, or a more thorough review with whole-sentence answers (remind the students to use *much* only in questions or negative sentences). Pay special attention to pronunciation of *-s/-es.*

ANSWERS: **1.** much furniture **2.** many desks **3.** many branches **4.** much equipment **5.** much machinery **6.** many machines **7.** many women **8.** many pieces **9.** many mice **10.** much advice **11.** many sheep **12.** much homework **13.** many prizes **14.** many geese **15.** much music **16.** much progress **17.** many races **18.** much knowledge **19.** many marriages **20.** much information **21.** much luck **22.** many hypotheses **23.** much mail **24.** many offices **25.** much slang **26.** many roofs **27.** many shelves **28.** many teeth

CHART 7-10: USING *A FEW* AND *FEW*; *A LITTLE* AND *LITTLE*

• This is difficult grammar for most learners, and it can be difficult to explain. The text compares the meanings by saying *a few* and *a little* indicate that something is "largely present," and *few* and *little* indicate that something is "largely absent." *Largely* (meaning "for the most part") may need your interpretation, as some learners may not be familiar with the term.

• Sometimes students think there must be a difference in quantity between *a few* and *few*. They ask, "How many is 'a few' and how many is 'few'?" They think that "few friends" is less than "a few friends." But the real difference can rest in the speaker's <u>attitude</u>: *a few* reflects a positive opinion of the quantity, and *few* reflects a negative or diminishing opinion, even if the quantity is the same in both cases.
  For example, Sam and Sara are new students in school. In two weeks, Sam has made three friends, and Sara has made three friends. Sam's mother is very pleased. She says, "Sam's getting along fine. He's made *a few* friends and likes his teachers." Sara's mother, however, thinks Sara should have made lots of friends by now and worries that she's not adjusting to her new school. She says, "Sara doesn't like her classes and has *few* friends. I'm worried about her." In each case, the number of friends is the same, but the speaker's attitude is different.

• The following chart may be helpful for students.

COUNT	NONCOUNT
few = not many *a few = some*	*little = not much* *a little = some*

☐ **EXERCISE 23, p. 123.   Using A FEW and FEW; A LITTLE and LITTLE.   (Chart 7-10)**

This exercise approaches the grammar by using parallel meanings. Discuss the meaning of each sentence in terms of what is "largely present" or "largely absent."
  Students could bring out their "C" and "NC" cards again. (See comments on Exercise 9, p. 57 of this *Guide*.)

ANSWERS: **3.** a little sunshine **4.** very little sunshine **5.** a few programs **6.** very few television programs **7.** a few drops **8.** a little oil **9.** very little jewelry

---

☐ **EXERCISE 24, p. 124.   Using A FEW and FEW; A LITTLE and LITTLE.   (Chart 7-10)**

ANSWERS: **3.** a little salt **4.** very little salt **5.** a little music **6.** very little traffic **7.** very few friends **8.** a few days . . . a few days **9.** a few more minutes **10.** a little more time **11.** a few nuts **12.** very few toys **13.** a little rain **14.** a little honey . . . a little milk **15.** very little patience **16.** very few problems

CHART 7-11: USING *OF* IN EXPRESSIONS OF QUANTITY

• When to use *of* with expressions of quantity can be a confusing point for students. The problem is that sometimes *of* is used whether the following noun is specific or nonspecific (as with *a lot of*), and sometimes it is used only when the noun is specific. Students are justifiably confused by this.

• A common point of difficulty is the difference between *most* and *the most*. (See the note at the bottom of page 126 in the textbook.)

• A common mistake is the use of *almost of: almost of the (students)*. Mention the two correct possibilities: *most of the (students)* OR *almost all of the (students)*.

☐ **EXERCISE 25, p. 125. Using OF in expressions of quantity. (Chart 7-11)**

Pairs of sentences in this exercise look similar. Compare the meanings of items to be sure students understand the important differences.

ANSWERS: **3.** Ø . . . Ø   **4.** of   **5.** Ø   **6.** of   **7.** Ø   **8.** of   **9.** Ø
10. of   **11.** Ø   **12.** of   **13.** of   **14.** of   ["junk mail" = advertisements, magazine contests, solicitations for money, etc.]   **15.** Ø   **16.** of   **17.** Ø . . . of   **18.** Ø
19. of   **20.** Ø

CHART 7-12: *ALL (OF)* AND *BOTH (OF)*

• This chart gives more information about using nouns as specific or nonspecific. The concept is not an easy one, but the following exercises help clarify it for most learners.

• The special (and confusing) thing about *all* and *both* is that *of* can be either omitted or included when used with specific nouns (contrary to the other expressions of quantity in GROUP TWO in Chart 7-11, which require *of* to be used with specific nouns).

• With an advanced class, you might mention that *half* has the same pattern as *all* and *both*: *half (of) the children*. And indeed, sometimes *most* is also used without *of*: *Most boys have their own uniforms*. There comes a point in the teaching of grammar, however, when too much information is indeed too much. As a text writer, the author has to decide where to draw the line between what is helpful and what is burdensome information. Teachers have to do the same, especially when it comes to deciding how much class time certain grammar discussions are worth. The grammar in the last parts of this chapter could, for example, be handled quickly and without emphasis, saving class time in order to focus on other grammar topics more useful to the learners.

☐ **EXERCISE 26, p. 126. ALL (OF) and BOTH (OF). (Chart 7-12)**

The concept of an optional *of* here may be confusing. You may need to explain the directions more clearly. Students need to understand that both *all of the children* and *all the children* are correct, but that *all of children* is not correct.

ANSWERS: **3.** (of)   **4.** Ø   **5.** Ø   **6.** Ø . . . Ø . . . (of)   **7.** (of)   **8.** (of)
9. (of)   **10.** Ø . . . Ø

☐ **EXERCISE 27, p. 127.   Using OF in expressions of quantity. (Charts 7-11 and 7-12)**

ANSWERS: **4.** Ø   **5.** of   **6.** of   **7.** Ø . . . Ø . . . Ø   **8.** of   **9.** Ø . . . Ø
10. of . . . of   **11.** Ø   **12.** Ø . . . of

CHART 7-13: SINGULAR EXPRESSIONS OF QUANTITY:
**   *ONE, EACH, EVERY***

- You might recall Chart 6-2 (Basic subject–verb agreement), which identified *each* and *every* as singular in number.

- *Each, every,* and *one of* are common sources of errors. For that reason, they receive special emphasis here.

- Note the concept of "specificity" as introduced in Chart 7-11: a noun is made specific by fronting it with *the,* a possessive, or a demonstrative adjective. One can say *one of **the** students, one of **my** students,* or *one of **those** students,* but one cannot say *one of students.*

☐ **EXERCISE 28, p. 128.   Using ONE, EACH, and EVERY. (Chart 7-13)**

This should be an oral exercise with discussion of similarities and differences between the sentences.

ANSWERS: **2.** girls   **3.** children   **4.** child   **5.** member   **6.** members

☐ **EXERCISE 29, p. 129.   Using ONE, EACH, and EVERY. (Chart 7-13)**

ANSWERS: **3.** countries   **4.** each student / each of the students   **5.** *(no change)*
6. All (of) the furniture / Each piece of furniture   **7.** Some of the equipment / One piece of equipment / One of the pieces of equipment   **8.** each woman / each of the women / all of the women   **9.** places   **10.** *(no change)*   **11.** language   **12.** each of the errors / each error

☐ **EXERCISE 30, p. 129.   Activity: expressions of quantity. (Charts 7-9 → 7-13)**

This can be done during a class period, with the students polling each other. Each student should make up his or her own list of questions. Give the students ample time—perhaps even overnight—to think of good, interesting questions.

Another possibility would be for your class to poll other classes in a language program and then report their findings. Taking a poll in, for example, a lower-intermediate level English class could be fun not only for your students but also for those in the other class, giving all the students a good opportunity for interaction.

☐ **EXERCISE 31, p. 130.   Review: expressions of quantity. (Charts 7-9 → 7-13)**

The sentences in this exercise are NOT TRUE. That's the point of this exercise: expressions of quantity are important. Unqualified statements are inaccurate. Discuss the importance of qualifying a generalization in order to make it accurate. The sentences in the text are examples of overgeneralizations that need expressions of quantity to make them reasonable, true, supportable statements.

ANSWERS: [These depend on students' opinions.]

Chapter 8: PRONOUNS

ORDER OF CHAPTER	CHARTS	EXERCISES	WORKBOOK
Personal pronouns	8-1	Ex. 1 → 3	Pr. 1
Agreement with nouns	8-2 → 8-3	Ex. 4 → 8	Pr. 2
Reflexive pronouns	8-4	Ex. 9 → 10	Pr. 3
Impersonal pronouns	8-5	Ex. 11 → 12	Pr. 4
Forms of *other*	8-6 → 8-7	Ex. 13 → 16	Pr. 5
Summary review, chapters 6–8		Ex. 17 → 21	Pr. 6 → 8

General Notes on Chapter 8

• OBJECTIVE: This chapter reviews most aspects of personal pronoun use, with emphasis on the problem areas of agreement and the use of *other* as both a pronoun and an adjective.

• TERMINOLOGY: A "possessive adjective" (e.g., *my, your, her*) is a pronoun (i.e., a noun substitute) that functions as a determiner. Some grammars call it a "possessive determiner" or a "determinative possessive pronoun." The terminology may be confusing for students because a possessive adjective is indeed a pronoun, but the term "possessive pronoun" (e.g., *mine, yours, hers*) is used in this text and most others to refer to an independent possessive pronoun that is used alone as a noun substitute.

In an effort to minimize grammatical terminology, the text does not use the term "determiner," finding other ways to present these function words (such as *a/an/the, one, no, this/that/these/those, many, other, my/you/her, some/any*). If you are comfortable with the term "determiner" and find it useful, by all means introduce it to your class and explain that what this text calls a "possessive adjective" may be called a "possessive determiner."

☐ EXERCISE 1, p. 131. Preview: personal pronouns. (Chart 8-1)

ANSWERS: **1.** Some North American food is very good, but I don't like most of <u>it</u>.   **2.** When we were schoolgirls, my sister and <u>I</u> used to play badminton after school every day.   **3.** If you want to pass <u>your</u> exams, you had better study very hard for <u>them</u>.   **4.** The work had to be finished by my boss and <u>me</u> after the store had closed for the night. [You might point out to the students that they may hear native speakers misuse the pronoun "I" in noun phrases with *and* that are used as objects (e.g., *by my boss and **I**,* in which the noun phrase is the object of the preposition *by*). Even well-educated speakers of English misuse the pronoun "I" in this way in their regular speech. It's quite an interesting and curious linguistic phenomenon. Evidently, to many native speakers the use of a subject pronoun after *and* simply sounds right, for they use it even though they know that correct, standard grammar requires an object pronoun. It's baffling.] **5.** A hippopotamus spends most of <u>its</u> time in the water of rivers and lakes. **6.** After work, Mr. Gray asked to speak to Tim and <u>me</u> about the company's new policies. He explained <u>them</u> to us and asked for <u>our</u> opinions. **7.** <u>Children</u> should learn to respect other people. They need to learn how to treat other people politely, including their playmates. **8.** My friends asked to borrow my car because <u>theirs</u> was in the garage for repairs.

CHART 8-1: PERSONAL PRONOUNS

• Most of this information should be familiar to the students, so they can use this chart as a reference.

• Note the definition of *antecedent* in (a).

• Pay attention to possessive pronouns vs. possessive adjectives, pointing out that possessive adjectives occur <u>with</u> a noun, but possessive pronouns occur <u>without</u> a noun.

• Give additional examples of *its* vs. *it's;* this is a frequent source of errors (by native speakers, too).

☐ **EXERCISE 2, p. 132. Personal pronouns: antecedents. (Chart 8-1)**

> *ANSWERS:*
> **2.** they . . . they = *pronouns;* monkeys = *antecedent*
> **3.** She = *pronoun;* teacher = *antecedent*
>   them = *pronoun;* papers = *antecedent*
> **4.** her . . . She = *pronouns;* Nancy = *antecedent*
>   it = *pronoun;* apple = *antecedent*
> **5.** it = *pronoun;* dog = *antecedent*
> **6.** She . . . She = *pronouns;* cat = *antecedent*
>   His . . . him = pronouns; Tom = antecedent
>   They = *pronoun;* dogs = *antecedent*
>   him = *pronoun;* Tom = *antecedent*

☐ **EXERCISE 3, p. 133. Possessive pronouns and adjectives. (Chart 8-1)**

> If necessary, again point out the difference between possessive pronouns and possessive adjectives in Chart 8-1. And remind students that *it's* = *it is,* not a possessive adjective.
>
> *ANSWERS:* **2.** mine . . . yours **3.** their books . . . hers . . . his **4.** its **5.** It's true . . . its way . . . its trip **6.** Its name . . . It's a turtle . . . It's been [*It's been* = It has been] **7.** Our house . . . Our neighbor's house . . . ours . . . theirs **8.** It . . . its prey . . . its long, pointed bill . . . it . . . it . . . it . . . It's interesting . . . them

CHART 8-2:

CHART 8-2: PERSONAL PRONOUNS: AGREEMENT WITH GENERIC NOUNS AND INDEFINITE PRONOUNS

• The English language traditionally used only male pronouns when speaking of people in general, e.g. *A doctor treats **his** patients kindly,* as though no women were doctors (which, in fact, was true during certain periods of Western history). Language reflects social change; today women have more equal representation in language usage because they do in society in general. Now English speakers try to use *he or she, she or he, s/he, his or her, etc.* The easiest way to avoid the problem is to use a plural rather than a singular generic noun so that *they/them/ their* (which are neither masculine nor feminine) may be used, e.g., *Doctors treat **their** patients kindly.*

• Not so long ago, it would have been unthinkable for an educated speaker to use *their* (a plural pronoun) to refer to *someone* (singular). Today it seems to have become the norm rather than the exception in everyday spoken English, and it avoids a feminine/masculine pronoun problem. However, singular personal pronouns are still expected in formal writing. Discuss with your class guidelines for feminine/masculine and singular/plural pronoun usage.

□ **EXERCISE 4, p. 132.   Personal pronouns use with generic nouns. (Chart 8-2)**

ANSWERS: **3.** <u>Students</u> in Biology 101 <u>have</u> to spend three hours per week in the laboratory, where <u>they do</u> various experiments by following the directions in <u>their</u> lab <u>manuals</u>.   **4.** <u>Pharmacists fill</u> prescriptions, but <u>they are</u> not allowed to prescribe medicine.   **5.** *(no change)*   **6.** <u>Citizens have</u> two primary responsibilties. <u>They</u> should vote in every election, and <u>they</u> should serve willingly on a jury.   **7.** *(no change)*   **8.** <u>Lecturers need</u> to prepare <u>their</u> notes carefully so that <u>they do</u> not lose <u>their</u> place while <u>they are</u> delivering <u>their</u> speech(<u>es</u>). [Note that the nouns "place" and "speech" can remain singular even though the subject noun and pronouns are plural. It is also possible to use plural nouns here. The choice is a matter of style and clarity rather than grammar. Indeed, in this sentence one would probably choose to keep *place* in the singular and change *speech* to the plural. Both of the following examples are correct grammatically: *Dogs wag their **tail** to show they are happy. Dogs wag their **tails** to show they are happy.* Some stylists might argue that the singular, *tail*, is preferable because a dog has only one tail and maintain that the plural, *tails*, might misleadingly indicate that a dog has more than one tail. Other stylists would argue that everyone knows a dog has only one tail, so the meaning is clear with the plural noun; and the plural *tails* is appropriate because the sentence concerns more than one dog.]

□ **EXERCISE 5, p. 135.   Personal pronoun use with indefinite pronouns. (Chart 8-2)**

Students could discuss the various possibilities in small groups, but the principal purpose of the exercise is to provide material for discussion of the usage problems in Chart 8-2. Students will want your advice.

ANSWERS: **2.** s/he wants; he or she wants; they want   · **3.** his/her; their   **4.** his/her; their   **5.** anyone; his/her; their   **6.** him/her; them   **7.** s/he . . . his/her; they . . . their   **8.** s/he pleases; they please

┌───┐
│ **CHART 8-3:   PERSONAL PRONOUNS: AGREEMENT WITH**   │
│   **COLLECTIVE NOUNS**   │
└───┘

• The speaker's view of the collective unit determines the grammatical usage of the words in this chart. The English language is somewhat flexible on this point. If the speaker wants to emphasize unity or wholeness, the collective noun will be singular, and this number will influence both the pronoun and the verb. On the other hand, if the speaker wants to emphasize the individuals within the group, the collective noun will be considered plural (but it will not add *-s/-es*).

• Other collective nouns: *army, community, company, crew, enemy, gang, herd, media, press.*

□ **EXERCISE 6, p. 136.   Personal pronoun use with collective nouns. (Chart 8-3)**

The purpose of this exercise is to help students develop an understanding of the difference between singular and plural uses of collective nouns. In general, the singular usage is impersonal or statistical, while the plural usage emphasizes the people involved.

ANSWERS: **2.** it consists [a statistical unit, not a group of real people]   **3.** It   **4.** They   **5.** they [the people on the team]   **6.** It doesn't   **7.** they   **8.** It was   **9.** They are . . . their . . . them [*class* = the individuals in the group]   **10.** It is [*class* = an organized unit of people taught together]

□ **EXERCISE 7, p. 137.   Preview of reflexive pronouns. (Chart 8-4)**

In a natural, conversational style, lead the class to answer these questions about their drawings. The questions in the book are simply suggestions for the teacher. Cover as many of the reflexive pronouns as you can by asking leading questions.
   If you wish, supply drawing paper and colored pencils or crayons. Reassure those students who believe they can't draw by first drawing a self-portrait of yourself—a drawing that is simple and funny, requiring no special artistic skill. The self-portraits should be a fun task.

□ **EXERCISE 8, p. 137.   Preview of reflexive pronouns. (Chart 8-4)**

ANSWERS: **2.** himself   **3.** herself   **4.** themselves   **5.** ourselves   **6.** yourself   **7.** yourselves   **8.** oneself

CHART 8-4: REFLEXIVE PRONOUNS

- In informal English, reflexive pronouns are sometimes substituted for object pronouns, especially in prepositional phrases. To some degree, the reflexive pronoun adds emphasis. This use of reflexive pronouns is variously deemed to be incorrect, nonstandard, questionable, or perfectly acceptable.

INFORMAL USAGE: She gave the gift *to* Bob and ***myself***.

PREFERRED USAGE: (a) She gave the gift *to* Bob and *me*.
(b) *I gave a gift to myself.*

Other examples: *What happened between my girlfriend and **myself** is no one's business.*
*No one on the bus spoke English except a few Italians and **ourselves**.*

In the vast majority of instances, reflexive pronouns cannot be substituted for personal pronouns used as objects: *I sit in the front row in class; Mustafa sits behind **me*** (not *myself*). *When Tom arrived, Alice spoke to **him*** (not *himself*).

As with any other grammar structure, idiomatic use of reflexive pronouns develops as learners gain experience with the language. Grammar basics can be taught and provide a good foundation for growth, but idiomatic usage ability grows only with time and exposure. Engaging in lots of reading, listening, and communicative interaction is essential for second language learners. The study of grammar is but a foundation and springboard; it is neither desirable nor possible to explain every possible structure in the English language. Students who believe they need to know a "rule" for every possible variation of an English structure should be disabused of that notion—and encouraged to go to a movie in English or make an English-speaking friend.

- Some other exceptions are given in the footnote. The text focuses on the basic patterns of any given structure, but also tries to anticipate questions students may have about exceptions that they note. The old saying about there being an exception to every rule is a good one for students of language to keep in mind.

☐ **EXERCISE 9, p. 138. Reflexive pronouns. (Chart 8-4)**

ANSWERS: **2.** herself **3.** themselves **4.** herself **5.** yourself . . . himself . . . myself . . . ourselves . . . themselves **6.** myself **7.** himself **8.** yourself
9. themselves **10.** herself

☐ **EXERCISE 10, p. 139. Reflexive pronouns. (Chart 8-4)**

ANSWERS: **2.** enjoy himself **3.** proud of yourselves **4.** pat yourself ["pat someone on the back" = congratulate, praise] **5.** killed himself **6.** entertained themselves
7. introduced myself **8.** feeling sorry for yourself **9.** talking to yourself
10. laugh at ourselves **11.** promised herself **12.** angry at himself

- Point out that when a speaker is using impersonal *you,* the *you* does not refer specifically to the listener. For example:

    A: *What are some of the customs in your country about touching another person?*
    B: *Well,* **you** *shouldn't touch someone else's head.*

Speaker B means "people in general should not do this." She is not giving personal instructions to the listener; the "you" does not refer specifically and only to Speaker A.

□ **EXERCISE 11, p. 141. Impersonal YOU and THEY. (Chart 8-5)**

> *ANSWERS:* **3.** The pronouns refer to people in general.   **4.** The pronouns refer to Alex.   **5.** people in general   **6.** Sonya   **7.** people in general   **8.** people in general   **9.** people in the orchestra   **10.** people in general

□ **EXERCISE 12, p. 141. Review of nouns and pronouns, singular and plural. (Chapters 7 and 8)**

> This exercise marks the end of the unit on pronouns and the beginning of a general review of nouns and pronouns. Help students recall what they have learned about singular and plural in Chapters 7 and 8. Assign the exercise as homework or seatwork prior to discussion or group work. Settle questions that arise during this exercise.

> *ANSWERS:* **2.** <u>Millions</u> of <u>years</u> ago, they had <u>wings</u>. <u>These</u> wings changed as the birds adapted to <u>their</u> environment.   **3.** <u>Penguins'</u> principal food <u>was fish</u>. Penguins needed to be able to swim to find their food, so eventually their <u>wings</u> evolved into <u>flippers</u> that enabled <u>them</u> to swim through water with speed and ease.   **4.** Penguins <u>spend</u> most of their lives in <u>water</u>. However, they lay their <u>eggs</u> on <u>land</u>.   **5.** Emperor penguins have interesting egg-laying <u>habits</u>.   **6.** The female <u>lays</u> one <u>egg</u> on the <u>ice</u> in Arctic regions, and then immediately <u>returns</u> to the ocean.   **7.** After the female lays the egg, the male <u>takes</u> over. <u>He covers</u> the egg with <u>his</u> body until <u>it hatches</u>.   **8.** <u>This</u> process <u>takes</u> seven to eight <u>weeks</u>. During <u>this</u> time, the male <u>doesn't</u> eat.   **9.** After the egg <u>hatches</u>, the female returns to take care of the chick, and the male <u>goes</u> to the ocean to find food for <u>himself</u>, his mate, and their offspring.   **10.** Although the <u>penguins'</u> natural habitat is in polar regions, we can see them in most major zoos in the world. <u>They seem</u> to adapt well to life in confinement, so we can enjoy watching <u>their</u> antics without feeling sorry about <u>their</u> loss of freedom.

CHART 8-6: FORMS OF *OTHER*

• The use of forms of *other* is a common source of errors. Emphasize that *other* has a final *-s* only when it is used as a pronoun, NOT as an adjective.

• Point out that *another* is a combination of the article "an" with "other," so *the* never precedes *another.* *The* and *a/an* are never used together. (A common mistake is, for example, *I bought* ***the another*** *book.*)

□ **EXERCISES 13 and 14, p. 143.   Using OTHER.   (Chart 8-6)**

In items 2 and 3, the students use their fingers and then their hands to illustrate *another* vs. *the other.* It is important for students to understand the difference between these two items. In item 2, emphasize that you are dealing with a known, finite quantity: five. For comparison with the use of *another* (but not *the other*) for a series of items in an unknown, indefinite quantity, walk around the classroom and say, pointing at various books, "This is a book. This is another. This is another. This is another. This is another." Etc. Then stack five books on a desk. "This is one book. This is another. This is another. This is another. And this one, the last of the five, is **the** other."

Have the students do Exercise 13 as seatwork followed by discussion. Then have them do Exercise 14 more independently, perhaps in pairs or small groups, or as a quick teacher-led review in which the students' books are closed and the teacher provides the cues.

EX. 13 ANSWERS: 2. Another . . . Another . . . Another . . . the other   3. The other   4. The others   5. The other   6. others   7. other   8. another   9. Others   10. the other   11. other   12. others   13. another   14. another   15. Another . . . Others   16. others   17. Another . . . Others . . . other   18. the other   19. the others   20. another   21. Another . . . The other

EX. 14 ANSWERS: [These depend on students' creativity.]

CHART 8-7: COMMON EXPRESSIONS WITH *OTHER*

• When the phrase *every other* means "alternate," the vocal emphasis is on *every*: e.g., *I receive that magazine **every** other month.*
    When *every* is used as an expression of quantity that happens to be followed by *other*, the stress is on *other*: e.g., *George is the only student who missed the test; every **other** student took it last Friday.* In this instance *every* has the meaning of *each* or *all: All of the other students took it last Friday.*

• Forms of *other*, especially the reciprocal pronouns in (a), can be used to show possession, in which case an apostrophe is used:, e.g., *They enjoy each other's company.*

☐ EXERCISE 15, p. 145. Using OTHER. (Charts 8-6 and 8-7)

ANSWERS: 2. Another . . . other   3. one another/each other   4. the other
5. other . . . other   6. other   7. others . . . others . . . other   8. each other/one
another . . . each other/one another . . . each other/one another . . . other   9. other
10. other   11. another

☐ EXERCISE 16, p. 147. Using OTHER. (Charts 8-6 and 8-7)

Punctuation depends on the structure of students' sentences. (See Charts 5-1 and 16-3.)

ANSWERS: [These depend on students' creativity.]

☐ EXERCISE 17, p. 147. Summary review. (Chapters 6 → 8)

You might divide the class into competing groups. Set a time limit (about five minutes for
advanced classes, eight or ten for intermediate students). The group that identifies and
corrects the most errors is declared the winner. Deduct one point for each error they
overlook, for each correct word that they mistakenly identify as an error, and for each error
that they correct in an unacceptable way. You may decide how to reward the winners.

ANSWERS:
1. That book <u>contains</u> many different <u>kinds</u> of <u>stories</u> and <u>articles</u>.
2. ~~The~~ English is one of the most important <u>languages</u> in the world.
3. She is always willing to help her friends in every possible <u>way</u>.
4. In the past, horses <u>were</u> the principal <u>means</u> of transportation.
5. He succeeded in creating one of the best <u>armies</u> in the world.
6. There <u>is a lot of equipment</u> in the research laboratory, but undergraduates are not
   allowed to use <u>it</u>.
7. All of the <u>guests</u> enjoyed <u>themselves</u> at the reception.
8. I have a <u>five-year-old</u> daughter and a <u>three-year-old</u> son.
9. Each <u>state</u> in the country <u>has</u> a different language.
10. Most of <u>the</u> people/ Most ~~of~~ people in my apartment building <u>are</u> friendly.
11. A political leader should have the ability to adapt <u>himself/herself</u> to a changing world.
12. In my opinion, ~~an~~ international <u>students</u> should live in a dormitory because they will
    meet many people and can practice their English every day. Also, if <u>they</u> live in a
    dormitory, <u>their</u> food is provided for <u>them</u>. [Note: It is not good style to mix different
    impersonal pronouns (*they, you, one*) in the same paragraph.]
13. When I lost my passport, I had to apply for ~~the~~ another one.
14. When I got to class, all of the <u>other</u> students were already in their seats.
15. Everyone <u>seeks</u> ~~the~~ happiness in <u>their</u> <u>lives</u>. OR Everyone <u>seeks</u> ~~the~~ happiness in <u>his/her</u> life.
16. In my country, there <u>are</u> a <u>lot</u> of schools / ~~a~~ lots of schools.
17. Writing compositions <u>is</u> very hard for me.
18. It's difficult for me to understand English when people <u>use</u> a lot of <u>slang</u>.
19. ~~A~~ <u>Students</u> at the university should attend class regularly and hand in their assignments
    on time.   OR   A student at the university should attend classes regularly and hand in
    <u>his/her</u> assignments on time.
20. In my opinion, ~~the~~ English is <u>an</u> easy language to learn.

☐ EXERCISE 18, p. 148. Summary review. (Chapters 6 → 8)

If you used Exercise 17 as a game, you might use this one in a test format. Give the
students ten minutes to complete it as seatwork prior to discussion. Or give them a longer
time and ask them to rewrite the sentences correctly and hand them in.

ANSWERS:

1. There <u>are</u> many different <u>kinds</u> of <u>animals</u> in the world.
2. My cousin and her husband want to move to <u>another</u> city because they don't like ~~a~~ cold weather.
3. I like to travel because I like to learn about other <u>countries</u> and <u>customs</u>.
4. Collecting stamps is one of my <u>hobbies</u>.
5. I came here three and a half <u>months</u> ago. I think I have made ~~a~~ good progress in English.
6. I was looking for my keys, but I couldn't find <u>them</u>.
7. When my mother was <u>a</u> child, she lived in a small town. Now this town is <u>a</u> big city with tall <u>buildings</u> and many <u>highways</u>.
8. English has borrowed quite a few ~~of~~ <u>words</u> from <u>other</u> languages.
9. There <u>are</u> many <u>students</u> from <u>different</u> countries in this class.
10. <u>Thousands</u> of <u>athletes</u> take part in the Olympics.
11. Education is one of the most important <u>aspects</u> of life. <u>Knowledge</u> about many different things <u>allows</u> us to live fuller lives.
12. All of the <u>students'</u> names were on the list.
13. I live in a <u>two-room</u> apartment.
14. Many ~~of~~ people prefer to live in small towns. Their attachment to their communities <u>prevents</u> them from moving from place to place in search of <u>work</u>.
15. <u>Today's</u> news is just as bad as <u>yesterday's</u> news.
16. Almost <u>all</u> of the students / Almost <u>all</u> ~~of~~ the students / <u>Most</u> (of the) students in our class <u>speak</u> English well.
17. The teacher gave us <u>some</u> homework to hand in next Tuesday.
18. Today <u>women</u> work as <u>doctors</u>, <u>pilots</u>, <u>archeologists</u>, and many other <u>things</u>. Both my mother and father are <u>teachers</u>.
19. Every <u>employee</u> in our company <u>respects</u> Mr. Ward.
20. <u>Children need</u> to learn how to get along with <u>other</u> people, how to spend <u>their</u> time wisely, and how to depend on <u>themselves</u>. [Also possible, but more stylistically awkward in its use of pronouns: *A child needs to learn how to get along with <u>other</u> people, how to spend his or her time wisely, and how to depend on <u>himself or herself</u>*.]

□ EXERCISE 19, p. 149.   Writing: nouns and pronouns.   (Chapters 7 and 8)

This exercise is principally for fun, with a focus on pronoun awareness. The paragraphs should use the simple present tense. Probably there is no reason for you to mark them, because the real test of their effectiveness is whether the class can identify the object described. You could spread this activity over several days.

   Answer to the example: *a bell*.

□ EXERCISE 20, p. 150.   Writing: agreement.   (Chapters 6 → 8)

The purpose of this exercise is to reinforce self-monitoring awareness of final *-s/-es*, first by requiring that mistakes be purposefully made and then by requiring corrections of those mistakes.

□ EXERCISE 21, p. 150. Writing: nouns. (Chapters 6 → 8)

One purpose of this kind of writing assignment is to reduce the students' hesitation to write freely by challenging them to write quickly on a broad topic. This sort of practice is especially good for those students who, unsure of themselves before now, have written only laboriously, wrestling with each word, afraid of making mistakes. Assure them that mistakes are not the end of the world and that even English teachers make changes in their own paragraphs. No one can write perfectly on the first attempt. All writers need to do their own proofreading ("error analysis"), rewording, and reorganizing.

In terms of grammar, the main purpose of this exercise is to let the students see if any old habits of singular–plural misuse remain in their writing. If so, they need to be especially aware of these problems when they monitor their writing and speech. When the students correct each others' papers, ask them to look especially for errors in singular and plural. Many students tend to proofread another student's writing more assiduously than they do their own; point out that they need to apply the same care and effort to their own writing. It's simply part of the writing process for everyone.

This type of exercise, designed to develop speed and fluency as well as to improve proofreading skills, can be repeated periodically throughout the term with topics of your or the students' choosing. You can set the time limit from one to ten minutes. In marking, you may choose to focus only on the points you have recently taught in the class.

Chapter 9: MODALS, PART 1

ORDER OF CHAPTER	CHARTS	EXERCISES	WORKBOOK
Introduction	9-1	Ex. 1	Pr. 1
Polite requests	9-2 → 9-4	Ex. 2 → 7	Pr. 2 → 3
Expressing necessity: *must, have to, have got to*	9-5	Ex. 8	Pr. 4
Lack of necessity and prohibition: *have to* and *must* in the negative	9-6	Ex. 9 → 10	
Review			Pr. 5
Advisability: *should, ought to, had better*	9-7	Ex. 11 → 14	Pr. 6
The past form of *should*	9-8	Ex. 15 → 17	
Expectations: *be supposed to*	9-9	Ex. 18 → 22	Pr. 7 → 8
Making suggestions: *let's, why don't, shall I/we*	9-10	Ex. 23	Pr. 9
Making suggestions: *could* vs. *should*	9-11	Ex. 24 → 27	Pr. 10

General Notes on Chapter 9

• OBJECTIVE: Modal auxiliaries are used in English to express attitudes, give advice, and indicate politeness. Mistakes with modal auxiliaries can, therefore, sometimes cause bad feelings or misunderstandings between speaker and listener. Students should become aware that a small change in a modal auxiliary can signal a large difference in attitudes and meanings.

• APPROACH: Students using this textbook are probably familiar with the most common meanings of the modal auxiliaries. The focus at the beginning of this chapter is on the basic forms, and Exercise 1 calls attention to errors in form that should be avoided. The rest of the chapter takes a semantic approach, grouping together modals and other expressions that have similar meanings. Matters of pronunciation, spoken/written usages, and formal/informal registers are noted in the charts.

• TERMINOLOGY: The terms "modal auxiliary" and "modal" are both used. Most modal auxiliaries are single words (e.g., *must, should*); the exceptions are *ought to* and *had better*. Many have two- or three-word phrases with similar meanings (e.g., *have to, be supposed to*) called "phrasal modals." Phrasal modals are also called "periphrastic modals" in some grammars.

CHART 9-1:   INTRODUCTION

• Use an example to show how modal choice expresses attitude:

> *Would you open the door?*   *You could open the door.*
> *You should open the door.*   *You'd better open the door.*
> *You may open the door.*   *Etc.*

A detailed discussion of the meaning of each modal is not necessary at this point. The students already know enough about modals to understand that examples such as the above express differing "modes" of communicating about the same action. Some general points you could make: There are differences in degrees of politeness (e.g., *Can you open the door for me?* vs. *Could you open the door for me?*). Use of modals sometimes depends on the relationship between the speaker and listener (e.g., the use of *had better* may indicate the speaker has a superior position to the listener, such as a parent speaking to a child). There may be differences in levels of formality/informality (e.g., *may* vs. *can* for permission).

• The chart mentions that each modal auxiliary has more than one meaning or use. These are presented throughout Chapters 9 and 10 and are summarized in Chart 10-10, pp. 199–200. This may be a good time to point out this reference chart to the students. The text itself does not present this chart at the beginning of modal study for fear it will seem too intimidating; however, if the students know they have two chapters to learn what's in the summary chart of modals, the task should seem less daunting.

• If students want to get an idea of how varied the meanings of modals are, refer them to any standard dictionary and ask them to look up the meanings of *can, could, may,* or any of the others. Perhaps point out that this kind of information found in a dictionary is what their grammar text presents more fully and summarizes in Chart 10-10.

• Point out that all the sentences in example (a) express PRESENT and/or FUTURE time. Students should understand that *could* and *would* express present/future time as used in this chart, but that, in some other situations (e.g., in the sequence of tenses in noun clauses), it is also possible to use *could* as the past form of *can* and *would* as the past form of *will*.

• Students are sometimes not aware that *shall* and *should* have meanings as separate modals and are not simply the present and past forms of one modal. **Should** + *simple form* has a present/future meaning. Only in rare instances in the sequence of tenses in noun clauses does *should* represent the past form of *shall* (which makes it curious that in some dictionaries, the first definition of *should* is as the past form of *shall*).

□ **EXERCISE 1, p. 152.   Forms of modals.   (Chart 9-1)**

Ask students to find the error in each sentence and then to say the correct form of the sentence. Explain that modal auxiliaries follow rules that affect the form of other verbs in the sentence. If they ask <u>why</u> modal auxiliaries are so different from other verbs, just tell them that long centuries of use and change have resulted in these forms; they are traditional in English.

ANSWERS: **1.** She can see it. [no *to*]   **2.** [no -*s* on modal auxiliary *can*]
3. [no -*s* on main verb *see*]   **4.** She can see it. [Modals are immediately followed only by the simple form.]   **5.** [no *to*]   **6.** Can you see it? [no *do;* begin questions with the modal]   **7.** They can't go there. [no *do;* add negation after the modal]

76 *CHAPTER 9, Modals, Part 1*

CHARTS 9-2 AND 9-3: POLITE REQUESTS

- Discuss how polite requests allow the speaker to show respect to the listener. A person who says "Give me your pencil" or "Pass the salt" seems to be too abrupt, aggressive, or unfriendly.

- Point out the levels of politeness and formality in these charts; e.g., a change from *may* to *can* usually signals a difference in the relationship between the people who are conversing.

- The word "please" is frequently used in conversation. This is another way to show respect and friendliness.

- Another typical response to a request, especially in informal American English, is "Okay."

- The grammar in these two charts may be quite familar to your students and can probably be covered quite quickly.

- You may wish to point out that imperative sentences can function as polite requests when accompanied by *please* (e.g., *Please close the door*).

□ **EXERCISE 2, p. 153. Polite requests. (Charts 9-2 and 9-3)**

When you set up each situation for two students to role-play, add specific details. Set the scene for them.

SAMPLE QUESTIONS AND ANSWERS: **1.** B: May I please use your phone? A: Sure. **2.** B: Mr. Jones, may I have permission to leave early today? A: Only if it's absolutely necessary, Sara. **3.** B: Hello. May I speak to Helen? A: She's not at home. This is Joe. Can I take a message? **4.** B: May I talk to you for a minute? A: Certainly. Come in and sit down. **5.** B: Hello. I'd like to make an appointment to see Dr. North. A: He can see you next Wednesday at 3:00 P.M. Are you free then? B: Yes, thank you. **6.** B: I have a meeting tonight. Would you please tape *Star Trek* for me this evening? A: Of course. That's at eight o'clock, isn't it? B: No. It starts at 9:00. **7.** B: I really need to get a drink to wash down an aspirin. Would you mind holding my place in line and watching my suitcase while I find a water fountain? A: No problem. Glad to.

CHART 9-4: POLITE REQUESTS WITH *WOULD YOU MIND*

- An alternative way of asking permission is "<u>Do</u> you mind if I <u>close</u> the window?" Using *would* is a bit more formal or polite than using *do*.

- In casual conversation, the auxiliary and subject pronoun are often omitted and a present—not past—verb is used: "Mind if I sit here?"

- Another informal response is "No. Go ahead," or sometimes (somewhat illogically) even a positive response: "Sure. Go ahead." Both mean "You have my permission to proceed."

- Note that "No" as a response to "Would you mind . . ." is a positive response, not a refusal. It means "No, I don't mind. / It's no problem."

- In (c): A gerund is used following *Would you mind*. Gerunds are not presented until Chapter 14. You may need to explain briefly that a gerund is the *-ing* form of a verb used as a noun.

- Occasionally one hears the form "Would you mind <u>my asking</u> a question?" This has the same meaning as "if I asked." A possessive may be used to modify a gerund; see Chart 15-6.

□ EXERCISE 3, p. 154. Polite requests with WOULD YOU MIND. (Chart 9-4)

This is essentially an exercise on verb forms. It also gives examples of typical situations in which *would you mind* is used.

ANSWERS: **3.** mailing   **4.** if I stayed   **5.** opening/if I opened   **6.** if I asked
7. if I smoked [NOTE: "I'd really rather you didn't" is a polite and indirect way of saying "I don't want you to smoke."]   **8.** speaking   **9.** if I changed/changing   **10.** if I borrowed

□ EXERCISE 4, p. 155. Polite requests with WOULD YOU MIND. (Chart 9-4)

POSSIBLE RESPONSES: **1.** Would you mind drying the dishes for me?   **2.** Would you mind if I turned up the volume?   **3.** Would you mind getting/buying (something) for me?   **4.** Would you mind if I asked you a personal question?   **5.** Would you mind showing me (how to use) that CD-ROM?

□ EXERCISE 5, p. 155. Polite requests. (Charts 9-2 → 9-4)

These controlled-completion dialogues are a preparation for Exercise 6, where the students make up their own dialogues.

POSSIBLE COMPLETIONS: **2.** Could we have a few more minutes? / Could you give us a little more time?   **3.** Could I get a ride with you?   **4.** Would you mind meeting Wednesday instead?   **5.** Could you take a look at them?   **6.** May I help you? . . . Could I see what you have in silk scarves?   **7.** Would you mind changing seats / if we changed seats?   **8.** May I call you this evening?

□ EXERCISE 6, p. 156. Polite requests. (Charts 9-2 → 9-4)

Assign pair work. You may not want every pair of students to work on every item. Give each pair one or two items to prepare in a time limit of five to eight minutes. Allow each group to "perform" its best dialogue for the other students. Then in discussion the class can identify which modals were used and can comment on how appropriately and idiomatically they were used.

This exercise could also be assigned as written homework.

□ EXERCISE 7, p. 157. Polite requests. (Charts 9-2 → 9-4)

To get the students started on this assignment, the class can brainstorm two or three items, trying to think of as many requests as possible. Then pairs can make up dialogues.

You might want to assign roles to students and have them make up a dialogue extemporaneously. For example, for item 1 tell Jose he's the teacher in this classroom and Nadia that she's a student. You could ask them what polite questions the teacher of this class has asked the students, what polite questions students have asked the teacher, and what their typical responses have been.

ADDITIONAL ITEMS: in a bookstore, in a bank, at a post office, in a library, in the headmaster's/director's office, at a doctor's/dentists's office.

EXPANSION ACTIVITY: Assign your students to write down any requests they hear—polite or not—during the coming week. Also suggest that they write down requests that they themselves make. At the end of the week, use the students' papers for discussion.

SAMPLE REQUESTS: **1.** Would you please shut the door? Please repeat your answer. May I borrow a pencil?   **2.** Would you mind checking my oil? How can I help you? Could you check my tire pressure?   **3.** May we have a table in the non-smoking section? Would you direct me to the ladies' room? Could I have my coffee right away?   **4.** Can you tell me where the Children's Department is? May I see some socks in dark blue? Could you please direct me to the gift-wrapping counter?   **5.** Quick! What's the fastest way to get to Terminal C? Can you tell me how often the shuttle bus runs? Please direct me to the nearest telephone.   **6.** Could I speak with Mr. Rodriquez? Could I take a message? Could I leave a message?

CHART 9-5:   EXPRESSING NECESSITY: *MUST, HAVE TO, HAVE GOT TO*

• This chart contains information about pronunciation, formal/informal usage, spoken/written forms, and one past form. Students should note and discuss these points.

• Note especially that *must* is used primarily with a forceful meaning. *Have to* and *have got to* are much more frequently used in everyday English.

• Encourage students to practice (but not to force) conversational pronunciations. These are the most natural and frequent forms in spoken English. The phonetic representations of these pronunciations follow:

> *have to* = /hæftə/   OR   /hæftu/
> *has to* = /hæstə/   OR   /hæstu/
> *got to* = /gadə/   OR   /gɔtə/

• *Have got to* (necessity) is not the same as *have got* (possession). For example:
"I've got to get some money." (I need money.)
"I've got some money." (I have money.)

☐ **EXERCISE 8, p. 158.   MUST, HAVE TO, HAVE GOT TO. (Chart 9-5)**

The directions ask the students to practice usual spoken forms. Reinforce that it is by no means necessary for students to use contracted spoken English; clear enunciation of full forms is always good. Contracted speech can be practiced, but it needn't be forced.

If you prefer not to put the emphasis on spoken forms (which you model), this exercise could be used for pair work.

POSSIBLE ANSWERS: **1.** Tomorrow I have to buy vegetables at the market on my way home. Then I have to mix up a salad to take to the potluck supper at my next door neighbor's house.   **2.** Today (. . .) has to pick up her shoes at the repair shop.   **3.** After class, I have got to ask my teacher about the homework I missed when I was sick.   **4.** After class, Rashid has got to go to the airport to meet his sister.   **5.** I must go to the bank this afternoon before it closes. I need to get some traveler's checks. [BrE: *cheques*]   **6.** Yesterday I had to pick up my new eyeglasses. Now I can see the chalkboard without sitting in the front row.   **7.** What time do you have to be on campus each morning for your first class?

CHART 9-6:   LACK OF NECESSITY AND PROHIBITION: *HAVE TO* AND *MUST* IN THE NEGATIVE

• *Need not* (principally British) and *don't need to* are similar in meaning to *don't have to*.

☐ **EXERCISE 9, p. 158.   HAVE TO and MUST in the negative. (Chart 9-6)**

Allow time for students to think about the meaning of each item. The context determines which answer is appropriate. Help students understand the situational context of each item, perhaps by means of role-playing and discussion.

ANSWERS: **3.** don't have to   **4.** must not   **5.** doesn't have to   **6.** must not   **7.** don't have to   **8.** don't have to   **9.** must not   **10.** don't have to   **11.** must not   **12.** doesn't have to

□ EXERCISE 10, p. 159. HAVE TO and MUST in the negative. (Chart 9-6)

Keep the pace lively, but allow a student to think of a reasonable answer. Then, additional possible answers can be offered by some other students. This could be done in small groups or as written work, but a teacher-led exercise may be preferable.

POSSIBLE ANSWERS: **1.** argue with their parents   **2.** pay taxes   **3.** exceed the speed limit   **4.** renew their licenses every year   **5.** come to school on holidays   **6.** forget our homework   **7. and 8.** [Answers depend on using a familiar name.]   **9.** spill food on a customer   **10.** cook the food, just serve it   **11. and 12.** [Answers depend on personal opinions.]

CHART 9-7:   ADVISABILITY: *SHOULD, OUGHT TO, HAD BETTER*

• Advice or a suggestion is usually friendly. It is often given by one's supervisor, parent, or friend. It is not as forceful as necessity. (Advice can also, of course, be not-so-friendly, depending upon the speaker's tone of voice and attitude.)

• Note the special meaning of *had better*. It is used in giving advice to a peer or a subordinate, but not to a superior.

□ EXERCISE 11, p. 160. SHOULD, OUGHT TO, HAD BETTER. (Chart 9-7)

Discuss who might be talking to whom when *had better* is used.

If this exercise is done as a class rather than as pair work, the teacher's book is open and the students' books are closed. The teacher is Speaker A, in which case students probably would not want to use *had better* in some of the situations. An alternative to teacher-led would be for one student to be the "teacher" and lead the exercise, or for several students to each present four or five items.

If you have the time, contextualize each item for the class by inventing who is talking to whom and what the situation is. Then ask for two students to role-play each situation, with one of them saying the words in the text. The intention of this exercise is to give short examples of situations in which modals of advice are frequently used, but expanding the examples can certainly be helpful. In later exercises, students are given fuller contexts as well as real-life contexts in which to practice giving advice.

One advantage of using this as a teacher-led exercise is to enable you to take advantage of the opportunities for leading a spontaneous discussion of the topics in some of the items.

POSSIBLE ANSWERS: **1.** You'd better look it up   **2.** You ought to get some rest.
3. You should have your eyes tested.   **4.** You'd better put on a sweater.   **5.** You should stomp it on the floor.   **6.** You should wake him/her up.   **7.** You'd better call the airline for the schedule.   **8.** You should start cleaning it up right now.   **9.** You'd better go to the grocery store right now.   **10.** You ought to get more sleep.   **11.** You should see a dentist.   **12.** You should get a tutor.   **13.** You should try blowing into a paper bag. [It's fun to discuss other traditional remedies: drinking a glass of water, drinking a glass of water upside down, holding one's breath, being suddenly startled by someone else, etc.]
14. He should do what his parents expect/do what he wants to do as a career. [This item might provoke a short discussion as students disagree on what William should do.]   **15.** She should talk with him or with some of his good friends. [Perhaps spend some time talking about what one can do to help someone addicted to drugs.]   **16.** *(free response)*

☐ **EXERCISE 12, p. 161.   SHOULD, OUGHT TO, HAD BETTER.   (Chart 9-7)**

This exercise could be used for written pair work.

SAMPLE COMPLETIONS: **2.** hurt my feet . . . return them.   **3.** finish your homework
. . . forbid you to watch TV tonight.   **4.** put antifreeze in the car   **5.** be ready for the
test . . . I don't feel confident.   **6.** help us with dinner . . . We'd be happy to help. Shall
I set the table?   **7.** give up caffeine, but I love coffee . . . listen to your doctor.
8. call your brother if you want him to pick you up at the airport next week . . . do that
now.   **9.** finished your report yet? . . . do it soon.   **10.** swim . . . a lifeguard? . . .
ask him to teach Mary how to swim.   **11.** study or go to a movie? . . . study . . . you
won't be prepared for class tomorrow.   **12.** tired all the time . . . see a doctor . . .
seeing an acupuncturist?

☐ **EXERCISE 13, p. 162.   Necessity, advisability, and prohibition.   (Charts 9-5 → 9-7)**

Lead a brief discussion of each pair of sentences so that students understand the contexts
and meanings. Small groups of advanced learners could do this with some imagination.

ANSWERS: [These are the stronger sentences in each pair.]
1. b.   **2.** b.   **3.** a   **4.** a.   **5.** b.   **6.** a.

☐ **EXERCISE 14, p. 162.   SHOULD vs. MUST/HAVE TO.   (Charts 9-5 → 9-7)**

Students can write their answers as seat work, then discuss them in small groups or as a
class. You should help resolve disagreements. Some of the items have fine distinctions in
meaning which may be confusing for some students. Sometimes there's only a fine line
between *should* and *must/have to,* but students should understand that that line does exist.
In none of the items is the same meaning conveyed when both *should* and *must/have to* are
possible completions.

ANSWERS: **3.** must/have to [This is a statement of fact, not a piece of advice, so *should* is not
appropriate. *Have to* would be more typical of spoken English; *must* would most likely occur in
somewhat formal writing. *Should* would be used to give advice in a situation such as the following:
So you want to be a doctor, do you? Then you should go to medical school and see how it goes.]
4. have to/must [Note: Both *have to* and *must* are correct here, but *have to* is preferable because
the situation is neither formal nor urgent. *Should* is not appropriate here because the speaker is
not dealing with a situation in which walking home is "a good idea." Rather, walking home is a
necessity due to lack of funds for a bus.]   **5.** should [Here the speaker is giving advice, so *should*
is used. Point out that *have to* or *must* would be too strong, as though the speaker were ordering the
listener to walk to work. A listener might take umbrage if the speaker used *have to* or *must* here.
You might also note that *ought to* is synonymous with *should* and could also be used to complete the
sentence. In most circumstances, *had better* would be inappropriate here, again because it is too
strong.]   **6.** *should* [also possible: *have to/must*] [In typical circumstances, one would say
should here—going to Colorado for our vacation is a good idea; the speaker is suggesting Colorado
as a vacation spot. The use of *have to/must* would require very particular circumstances in which the
speaker is saying "We have no choice." It's hard to think what reasons might compel someone to go
to a particular place for vacation.]   **7.** should [it's a good idea; the advisor is simply making a
suggestion]   OR   must/ have to [if it's a requirement of the school]   **8.** must/has to [Rice
will not grow without water.]   **9.** should   **10.** must [spoken with enthusiasm and
emphasis]

CHART 9-8: THE PAST FORM OF *SHOULD*

• Sometimes students confuse the past form of modals with the present perfect tense because the <u>form</u> of the main verb is the same (***have** + past participle*). If students ask about "tense," tell them that ***have** + past participle* here doesn't carry the same meaning as the present perfect tense; it simply indicates past time.

• The information in Chart 9-11, example (f), p. 171, says that the past form of *should* is also used to give "hindsight advice." Here, you may want to introduce the concept of viewing something in hindsight: We use *should have done something* when we look at the past (i.e., we look at something in hindsight), decide that what was done in the past was a mistake, and agree that it would have been better if the opposite had been done.

• The short answer to a question is "Yes, I should've" (British: "Yes, I should've done"). Note the pronunciation of *should've*, which is exactly like *should + of*. In fact, some people (native speakers and second language learners alike) mistakenly spell the contraction as if it were the words "should of."

• Also, students should remember to pronounce *should* like *good*, with no sound for the letter "l."

☐ EXERCISE 15, p. 163. The past form of SHOULD. (Chart 9-8)

Students can work quickly in pairs; the items are straightforward and uncomplicated. Alternatively, a student with clear pronunciation can read the situation aloud (to the whole class or as the leader of a small group), then another student can give an opinion about it, using the past form of *should*. Or, asking for volunteer responses, you can simply run through the items quickly as an extension of your presentation of the information in Chart 9-8.

ANSWERS: **1.** He/She shouldn't have left the door open. **2.** I should have gone to the meeting. **3.** (. . .) should have gone to see a doctor. **4.** (. . .) shouldn't have sold his/her car. **5.** (. . .) should have read the contract more carefully.

☐ EXERCISE 16, p. 164. The past form of SHOULD. (Chart 9-8)

If less advanced students have difficulty, Speakers B can open their books.
And again, even though the directions call for pair work, you can always employ any methodology that suits your particular class.

EXPECTED RESPONSES: **1.** I should have worn a coat. **2.** I should have looked the word up in the dictionary. **3.** I should have written my friend a letter. **4.** I shouldn't have spent my money foolishly. **5.** I shouldn't have opened the window. **6.** I should have gone to the grocery store. **7.** I should have set my alarm clock. **8.** I should have gone to (New Orleans) with my friends. **9.** I should have had a cup of coffee. **10.** John should have married Mary. **11.** John shouldn't have married Mary. **12.** I should have stayed home yesterday. **13.** I should have gone outside and enjoyed the nice weather. **14.** I should have bought my girlfriend/boyfriend a different present. **15.** The little girl shouldn't have told a lie / should have told the truth. **16.** I should not have lent (. . .) my car. [*lent* = loaned]

☐ EXERCISE 17, p. 164. The past form of SHOULD. (Chart 9-8)

In pairs or small groups, students can discuss their opinions about each situation. If you want to include writing in the task, one person in each group can record their answers. Then another person can read the answers to the whole class, or you can ask that they be handed in. You should probably set a time limit for the group work (about three to five minutes per item) and another for each person's report (one minute).

To handle the exercise quickly, lead it yourself and have the students call out their responses. With an advanced class, do the exercise with books closed.

POSSIBLE RESPONSES:

1. John should have discussed his job offer with Julie before he accepted it. John should not have taken the offer on the spot. John should have told the new company that he had to have time to discuss the offer with his wife. John should have realized that in a marriage, both employed partners have equal loyalties to their jobs and to their companies.

2. Ann should not have forgotten about her meeting with Carl. Ann should have first gone to the library to tell Carl that she was no longer available to work with him. If Ann couldn't go to the library, she should have phoned Carl or sent him a message. Ann shouldn't have kept Carl waiting for three hours. Ann should have been more considerate.

3. First, Donna should not have lent nearly all her savings to her brother. She could have lent him some of her savings, but not the bulk of it. Donna also should have set up some repayment schedule, in writing, so she and Larry would know when the loan would be repaid. Larry should not have spent the loan on frivolous things while he was unemployed. Because Donna had grown up with Larry, she should have known that he was irresponsible because he had not saved any of the money he earned from his previous good job. Donna should have realized that Larry was self-indulgent, short-sighted, and self-centered.

4. Although Sarah had no way of knowing that her claim of being fluent in French would get back to her boss, she should not have said she was fluent when she wasn't. And when Sarah was asked to interpret, she should have said that she was not fluent enough to interpret for a negotiation. When she was in the meeting, she should have told the truth instead of claiming to be ill. Sarah should not have put herself in the position of holding up a contract negotiation.

CHART 9-9: EXPECTATIONS: *BE SUPPOSED TO*

• The important difference between expectations and necessity (Chart 9-5: *must, have to, have got to*) is that the notion of necessity can sometimes originate within oneself. Expectations come from outside, from other people; therefore, *be supposed to* is similar to passive verb phrases with no agent. *He is supposed to come* means "He is expected (by someone) to come."

• Similarly, the notion of advisability (Chart 9-7: *should, etc.*) can originate within oneself, as if one's conscience were speaking. But expectations come from other people.

• The negative form of this phrasal modal inserts *not* after *be:* "I'm not supposed . . . ," "He isn't/He's not supposed to . . . ," etc.

• Another meaning of *be supposed to* is "it is generally believed." For example, *Sugar is supposed to be bad for your teeth.*

• An expression similar to *be supposed to* is *be to. Be to* was included in the second edition of the text but omitted here in the third edition due to its relative infrequency of occurrence. (*Be supposed to,* by comparison, is a phrase every learner will need to know and use.) You may wish to introduce the students to *be to* at this juncture. If alert students ever run across it, perhaps on standardized tests, they will find this structure curious. *Be to* is close in meaning to *must* but includes the idea of expectation, the idea that someone else strongly expects, demands, or orders this behavior. For example, if *be to* were used in example (c)—*I am to be at the meeting*—it would convey the idea that *My boss ordered me to be there. He will accept no excuses.*

□ EXERCISE 18, p. 166. Error analysis: BE SUPPOSED TO. (Chart 9-9)

The most common errors: (a) omitting *be* before *supposed to,* and (b) omitting *-d* at the end of *supposed* because it is not clearly pronounced when *to* is the next word. Other errors involve subject–verb agreement and use of the auxiliary "do."

ANSWERS:

1. The building custodian <u>is</u> supposed to unlock the classrooms every morning.
2. We're not <u>supposed</u> to open that door.
3. Where are we <u>supposed</u> to meet?
4. I have a meeting at seven tonight. I <u>am supposed</u> to be there a little early to discuss the agenda.
5. When we go to the store, Annie, you <u>are</u> not <u>supposed</u> to handle the glassware. It might break, and then you'd have to pay for it out of your allowance.
6. I'm <u>supposed</u> to be at the meeting. I suppose I'd better go. [The purpose in this item is to compare *be supposed to* with *suppose.* Make up a few additional items to make the difference clear.]
7. Where have you been? You <u>were supposed</u> to be here an hour ago!
8. A: I can't remember what the boss said. <u>Am</u> I supposed to work in the mail order room tomorrow morning and then the shipping department tomorrow afternoon? Or the other way around?   B: How am I <u>supposed</u> to remember what you <u>are supposed</u> to do? I have enough trouble remembering what I <u>am</u> supposed <u>to do</u> / <u>am</u> supposed <u>to be doing</u>.

□ EXERCISE 19, p. 167. BE SUPPOSED TO. (Chart 9-9)

POSSIBLE RESPONSES:

1. You are supposed to exchange names, addresses, and insurance information with the other driver. You are also supposed to notify the police department within 24 hours of the accident. If the accident is a bad one, you are supposed to wait at the scene until the police arrive. If your car is damaged, you are supposed to report the accident to your insurance company, and they are supposed to send an investigator to examine the damage before you have it repaired.
2. Before take-off in an airplane, you are supposed to fasten your seatbelt, turn off any electronic equipment, such as a laptop computer, and put all loose, carry-on baggage under the seat or in the overhead compartment.
3. Athletes in training are supposed to get lots of sleep, eat lots of protein, and practice hard every day. Athletes are not supposed to keep late hours, eat unwisely, or skip practice.
4. Later today I am supposed to stop at the bank and make a deposit.
5. You are supposed to pull off the road so the ambulance can pass safely and quickly.
6. Yesterday I was supposed to return a phone call, but I forgot.
7. Right now I am supposed to be asking and answering questions with *be supposed to.* [You may wish to note the progressive infinitive: *to be + -ing.* Here the infinitive form carries the progressive meaning of "in progress right now, at the moment of speaking." The text does not specifically present progressive infinitives, but it does, as here, include them passively in a typical context.]
8. When I worked in Yellowstone Park one summer, I was a waitress at Old Faithful Lodge. Every day I was supposed to take orders from the tourists who came to eat in the dining room and serve them their meals.
9. At ten o'clock tomorrow morning, I am supposed to be here in my English class.
10. Last week I was supposed to return a call to my insurance agent, but I put it off.
11. If someone tells you a secret, you are not supposed to tell anyone else.
12. *(free response)*

☐ EXERCISE 20, p. 167. Necessity, advisability, and expectations. (Charts 9-5 → 9-9)

This exercise compares the modal auxiliaries from Charts 9-5, 9-7, and 9-9. Students may create a context for each item and decide who the speakers are. For example, items one to four involve people who are riding in an airplane or automobile; they might be father and son, flight attendant and passenger, two business partners, etc. Students decide which sentence is stronger, and they might also discuss its appropriateness for the context they have created. Some statements are too strong between people of equal status and could cause the listener to become angry.

ANSWERS: [These are the stronger sentences in each pair.]
1. a. **2.** a. **3.** a. **4.** a. **5.** b. **6.** b. **7.** a.

☐ EXERCISE 21, p. 168. Necessity, advisability, and expectations. (Charts 9-5 → 9-9)

This could be a written exercise, including stated reasons. Alternatively, it could be used for group work, with students discussing their intended meanings.

☐ EXERCISE 22, p. 168. Necessity, advisability, and expectations. (Charts 9-5 → 9-9)

The students need to use their imaginations in this exercise; most of them probably haven't had any experience in the roles described in the given situations. You could suggest other, more familiar roles of authority (e.g., the teacher of this class), or the students could invent their own authority roles.

Take a few minutes to discuss item 1 with the whole class. Have them add other answers, using all the rest of the modals and similar expressions in the list. Then assign them one, two, or all of the other topics to discuss, roleplay, or write about.

If you assign this as written work, perhaps the students could write the answers for one of the given situations and also write answers for a situation of their own devising.

CHART 9-10: MAKING SUGGESTIONS: *LET'S, WHY DON'T, SHALL I/WE*

• These three expressions are followed by the simple (i.e., base) form of the main verb. For example: *Let's **be** careful; Why don't you **come** at six?;* and *Shall I **be** your partner in this game?*

• *Shall* is used only with *I* or *we*. It is not appropriate to ask "Shall he," "Shall you," etc.

• These suggestions are similar to polite requests, but also may include both speaker and listener in the suggested activity.

• In informal British usage, *Don't let's* is a possible alternative form of *Let's not.* *Don't let's* is also heard in American English, but is considered nonstandard.

☐ EXERCISE 23, p. 170. LET'S, WHY DON'T, SHALL I/WE. (Chart 9-10)

SAMPLE RESPONSES: **2.** B: we go to a movie   A: I pick you up?   **3.** A: we go eat now or finish the report first?   B: finish the report   A: we make a reservation at the restaurant?   B: to get a table without having to wait.   **4.** A: go to the country B: we go camping?   A: stay in a motel.   **5.** B: we each spend an hour studying alone. A: take a break for ten minutes.   B: test each other.

CHART 9-11: MAKING SUGGESTIONS: *COULD* vs. *SHOULD*

• Make sure the students understand that *could* refers to present or future time here. Sometimes learners mistakenly think of *could* only as the past tense of *can,* but *could* has many uses and meanings. (See Chart 10-10, p. 199, in the textbook for other uses.)

• *Could* is used to make suggestions when there are several good alternatives. It often occurs with *or,* as in *You could do this, or you could try that.*

□ EXERCISE 24, p. 171. Making suggestions. (Chart 9-11)

Students read the dialogues aloud, then paraphrase the *should/could* sentences. The purpose of this type of exercise is to give additional examples of the structure for students to discuss and explore.

EXPLANATIONS: **1.** Speaker B suggests that it is a good idea for Ted to get professional medical advice. **2.** B's suggestions are all possibilities, not recommendations. **3.** B advises taking a bus to save money. **4.** All B's suggestions are possible ways of traveling to the airport. **5.** B's suggestion is hindsight advice: if A had taken the airport bus, s/he would have saved all the money s/he spent on the taxi. **6.** Two hindsight possibilities of ways to avoid the high cost of the taxi.

□ EXERCISE 25, p. 172. Activity: making suggestions. (Charts 9-7 → 9-11)

This could be done as group work, but it's effective to have the students give <u>you</u> advice. They usually enjoy feeling like experts for a change!
  Elicit from the students two or three suggestions with *could.* Then elicit one response with *should.*
  This exercise benefits greatly from the use of names and places that are familiar to the students. Don't feel that you must read every item exactly as it appears in the textbook. You can create a fuller context, change the order of items, and use more natural phrases to make the exercise more meaningful to your students.

□ EXERCISE 26, p. 172. Activity: making suggestions. (Charts 9-7 → 9-11)

This activity calls for the creation of an extended dialogue. Encourage the students to create somewhat dramatic dialogues. They can perform them for the whole class.
  Make it clear that the expressions listed in the nine items are only suggestions; they are prompts for the tongue-tied student who can't think what to say after Speaker A says, "What's the matter?" These listed expressions do not need to be included at all.
  If you wish, of course, you could assign the listed expressions to various pairs, and have other pairs make up their own response to the initial question "What's the matter?"

□ EXERCISE 27, p. 173. Activity: writing. (Chapter 9)

Encourage students to include imagination and good humor in their letters. In marking them, focus on the correct use of modals and praise good efforts. Students should have fun with this exercise. They may enjoy reading their letters aloud.
  You might wish to note the subjunctive in the example letter to Abby: ". . . insists that I *not invite.* . . ." (not "insists that I don't invite"). The use of the subjunctive in a noun clause is covered in Chart 12-8. When the subjunctive is called for, only the simple form is used: it has no singular form, and the negative is formed simply by adding *not* rather than using the auxiliary "do."

Chapter 10: MODALS, PART 2

ORDER OF CHAPTER	CHARTS	EXERCISES	WORKBOOK
Degrees of certainty	10-1 → 10-4	Ex. 1 → 14	Pr. 1 → 2
Progressive and past modals	10-5	Ex. 15 → 17	Pr. 3
Cumulative review		Ex. 18 → 20	
Ability: *can* and *could*	10-6	Ex. 21 → 23	Pr. 4
Would for repeated actions	10-7	Ex. 24	Pr. 5
Would rather	10-8	Ex. 25 → 26	Pr. 6
Combining modals with phrasal modals	10-9	Ex. 27	
Summary chart of modals and similar expressions	10-10	Ex. 28 → 32	Pr. 7 → 8
Review of verb forms		Ex. 33 → 34	

General Notes on Chapter 10

• OBJECTIVE: Continuing from Chapter 9, students will learn additional uses and forms of modal auxiliaries.

• APPROACH: The first half of this chapter concentrates on using modals to express suppositions and logical conclusions, and relates the modals to matters of time and duration. Then attention is paid to a few additional modal usages. The chapter leads to a summary chart of the information presented in Chapters 9 and 10 and review exercises on modal usage.

• TERMINOLOGY: The term "degrees of certainty" is used with those modals that express the strength of a speaker's belief in the sureness of what s/he is saying. In other grammars, terms such as "logical possibility" or "degree of probability" are used in discussions of these modal usages.

□ **EXERCISE 1, p. 174. Preview. (Chapter 10)**

This exercise previews modals used to express degrees of certainty (items 1–11) and progressive and past modals (items 12–14). Item 5 makes the point that if one is sure, no modal is needed; the modals are used when one is not 100 percent sure.

Students should discuss their choices and their reasoning process. In item 1, the speaker is expressing a logical conclusion based upon the evidence available (i.e., that Jeff was offered a scholarship); the speaker is saying that s/he believes Jeff is a good student—but does not know that with 100 percent sureness.

ANSWERS: **2.** B [not sure; is mentioning one possibility]   **3.** A [logical conclusion, but not 100% sure]   **4.** B [not sure; is mentioning one possibility]   **5.** C [100% sure; no modal needed. Note: Speaker could be wrong. The chicken may turn out NOT to be in the freezer, but that doesn't affect the speaker's verb choice. The speaker uses the modal that expresses his belief in his sureness.]   **6.** B [possibility]   **7.** A [logical conclusion, but not 100% sure] **8.** B [possibility]   **9.** C [100% sure]   **10.** A [logical conclusion, but not 100% sure] **11.** B [possibility]   **12.** B [right now]   **13.** B [earlier]   **14.** C [in progress at a past time when another past event (hearing the doorbell) occurred]

CHART 10-1:   DEGREES OF CERTAINTY: PRESENT TIME

- The percentages are, of course, not exact. They show the relative strength of one's certainty.

- Call students' attention to the note about *maybe* and *may be;* confusing the two is a common written error (for native speakers too).

☐ **EXERCISE 2, p. 176.   Degrees of certainty: present time.   (Chart 10-1)**

This exercise can be teacher-led as a quick followup to the discussion of Chart 10-1. It presents simple, everyday situations in which to practice using *must* to express logical conclusions.
   If you wish, have a student pantomime the action in an item. For example, in item 1:
SPEAKER A (you):   Oscar, please yawn.
SPEAKER B (Oscar):   *(yawns)*
SPEAKER A (you):   Oscar is yawning. Why do you suppose that is, Abdul?
SPEAKER C (Abdul):   He must be sleepy.

EXPECTED RESPONSES: **1.** (. . .) must be tired / must be sleepy / must need sleep. **2.** (. . .) must have a cold / must be sick / must not feel well.   **3.** (. . .) must be married.   **4.** (. . .) must be cold.   **5.** (. . .) must be hungry / (. . .)'s stomach must be empty.   **6.** (. . .) must have an itch / must have an insect bite.   **7.** (. . .) must be thirsty.   **8.** (. . .) must be happy / must have heard some good news / must be feeling good.   **9.** (. . .) must be sad.   **10.** The food there must be very good. **11.** The battery must be dead.   **12.** The movie must be very popular / must be really good.   **13.** It must be (around 10:35).

☐ **EXERCISE 3, p. 177.   Degrees of certainty: present time.   (Chart 10-1)**

Point out that the answers in this exercise express less certainty than the answers in Exercise 2.
   You could be Speaker A, asking questions of the class.

POSSIBLE RESPONSES: **1.** I don't know. S/he may/might be at home.   **2.** I don't know. S/he may/might/could live in an apartment near school.   **3.** I don't know. You may/might/could have a ballpoint pen.   **4.** I don't know. It may/might/could be a Seiko watch.   **5.** I don't know. It may/might/could have fallen under your chair.   **6.** I don't know how old Queen Elizabeth is. She may/might/could be 70 or 75.

☐ EXERCISE 4, p. 177.   Degrees of certainty: present time. (Chart 10-1)

Give students time to complete most of this exercise as seatwork. Then lead a discussion of their answers. Emphasize that students can use their own words if they wish.

EXPECTED COMPLETIONS: **2.** must be rich.   **3.** must be crazy.   **4.** may/might/could be at a meeting   **5.** must have the wrong number.   **6.** must be very proud.   **7.** must feel terrible.   **8.** may/might/could fit Jimmy.   **9.** must miss them very much.   **10.** must be about ten.

CHART 10-2:   DEGREES OF CERTAINTY: PRESENT TIME NEGATIVE

- The percentages are not exact; they show only relative certainty.

- Note that while *could* indicates less than 50 percent certainty (Chart 10-1), *couldn't* indicates 99 percent certainty. Tell your students they are right if they complain that language is not always a logical structure!

☐ EXERCISES 5–7, p. 179.   Degrees of certainty: present time. (Charts 10-1 and 10-2)

In Exercise 5, compare *must not* with simple present verbs *(she must not study* vs. *she doesn't study).*

In Exercise 6, compare *can't/couldn't* with simple present verbs *(it couldn't be Mary* vs. *it isn't Mary).*

In Exercise 7, elicit from the students probable/possible reasons for the speakers' verb choices.

EX. 5 POSSIBLE RESPONSES: **2.** be at home [Compare: *He isn't at home.* = The speaker knows this for sure; the speaker, for example, knows that Tarek is in another city visiting his sister.]   **3.** be thirsty [Compare: *She isn't thirsty.* = The speaker knows this for sure because Rosa told the speaker so.]   **4.** like nuts [Compare: *He doesn't like nuts.* = The speaker knows this for sure because Mr. Chang has told the speaker he doesn't like nuts.]   **5.** have many friends [Compare: *She doesn't have any friends.* = The speaker knows Rosa well and knows for a fact that she doesn't have friends.]

EX. 6 POSSIBLE RESPONSES: **2.** Alex wasn't here today. / Alex never wears a hat. [Compare: *It doesn't belong to him.* = The speaker knows who it belongs to.]   **3.** I just saw her yesterday. / She was in class with me last night. [Compare: *She isn't in Norway.* = The speaker knows where she is right now or just saw her recently.]   **4.** There aren't any wolves here. [Compare: *It isn't a wolf.* = The speaker knows it's a dog and is making a statement of fact rather than discussing the impossibility of the notion that the big animal is a wolf.]   **5.** She loves her job. / She needs her job. [Compare: *That's not true.* = The speaker knows for a certainty that Marie still has her job.]

☐ EXERCISE 8, p. 180.   Degrees of certainty: present time.   (Charts 10-1 and 10-2)

This exercise can be done in pairs, then performed and compared.

- Note the parallels between the <u>affirmative</u> expressions in this chart and in Chart 10-1.

- Then note the parallels between the <u>negative</u> expressions here and in Chart 10-2.

- Point out to students that modal auxiliaries are very useful in communicating how one perceives situations for which 100 percent sure facts are not available. Other languages may use very different kinds of expressions for these ideas, so English modals can be difficult to learn.

☐ **EXERCISE 9, p. 181. Degrees of certainty: past time. (Chart 10-3)**

If you lead this exercise, take an active role, helping each dialogue develop in a fairly natural way:
   a. Say the first line to the class, using the name of a student.
   b. Wait for several students to give some good guesses.
   c. Then pose the *What if*-question and wait for new responses.

☐ **EXERCISE 10, p. 182. Degrees of certainty: present time. (Chart 10-3)**

This exercise refers to a game called "Clue" that is often played in the United States. The players are given clues to a murder mystery, then they try to solve the mystery and identify the criminal.

Clarify for the students that they are to assign themselves roles as A, B, C, D, and E, and then complete the conversation on p. 183, using both the information on p. 182 and information they invent.

ERRATUM: On p. 183, the first five speakers in the CONVERSATION should be A, B, A, B, then **C** (not A). This is corrected in subsequent printings.

The outline given for the conversation doesn't need to be followed exactly; it can be viewed as suggestions for talking points. The main purpose of this exercise is communicative practice; so as long as the students are explaining things to each other and figuring things out, all is well. This is not a tightly constructed exercise with "correct" answers; there are no built-in clues as to the certain identity of the murderer. Students need to use both the given information and their own imaginations to create a scenario. Their five-person conversation can take any direction they wish.

POSSIBLE CONJECTURES:

B: It might have been Colonel Mustard because he has a gun, had an argument with Mrs. Peacock, was angry, was unaccompanied by his wife. [His having asthma and a gray mustache are "red herrings" (irrelevant leads).]

C: It could have been Mrs. White because she has a motive (jealousy) and was awake at ten o'clock.

D: [This speaker knows the facts about Colonel Mustard and Mrs. White.] It couldn't have been Colonel Mustard because he went to bed early. It can't have been Mrs. White because she was in the living room playing cards at 10 o'clock last night.

A: It must have been Miss Scarlet because she was deeply in debt and needed Mrs. Peacock's money, which she would have inherited upon Mrs. Peacock's death as her only living relative.

E: It wasn't Miss Scarlet, Colonel Mustard, or Mrs. White because I know who did it.

Then Speaker E makes up the solution to the murder mystery from his/her own imagination.

Note for students that the pronunciation of *Colonel* is the same as *kernel*.

☐ **EXERCISE 11, p. 183.   Degrees of certainty.   (Charts 10-1 → 10-3)**

Assign speaker roles and ask students to present the dialogues without looking at their texts.

ANSWERS: **2.** must not like   **3.** must have been   **4.** must be   **5.** must have forgotten   **6.** must not speak   **7.** must have left   **8.** must be   **9.** must have hurt   **10.** must mean   **11.** must have been   **12.** must have misunderstood

---

CHART 10-4:   DEGREES OF CERTAINTY: FUTURE TIME

• Of course, no one can be 100 percent sure about future events. But we can make promises with *will* and confident predictions (as in Chart 4-2 using *will*).

• This chart is titled "future time," but for convenience in section (b), the past forms *should have* and *ought to have* are included.

• Compare *should have* meaning "unfulfilled expectation" with *should have* in Chart 9-11 meaning "hindsight advice." The forms are identical, but the contexts modify the meanings.

☐ **EXERCISE 12, p. 185.   Degrees of certainty.   (Charts 4-2, 10-1, and 10-4)**

Discuss the fine line between *will* and *should/ought to* to express future certainty, as in item 2. (Learners may sometimes sound more assertive than they intend if they use *will* instead of other "softer" modals.)

ANSWERS: **3.** must   **4.** should / ought to [also possible: *will*]   **5.** should   **6.** will   **7.** should / ought to   **8.** will   **9.** must   **10.** should / ought to / will   **11.** should / ought to   **12.** should / ought to   **13.** should / ought to   **14.** must   **15.** should have / ought to have   **16.** must have

☐ **EXERCISE 13, p. 186.   Degrees of certainty. (Charts 10-1 → 10-4)**

ANSWERS:

2. a. Jane   **3.** a. a rat   **4.** a. Mark   **5.** a. Janet
  b. Ron   b. a cat   b. my neighbor   b. Sally
  c. Sue   c. a mouse   c. Carol   c. Bob
  d. Ann   d. Andy

☐ **EXERCISE 14, p. 187.   Degrees of certainty. (Charts 10-1 → 10-4)**

Assign only one dialogue to each pair. Some students may want to choose their own situations for dialogue construction. Have the pairs (all or only some) perform their dialogues with or without their "scripts."

CHART 10-5: PROGRESSIVE FORMS OF MODALS

- You could elicit more examples. Tell the students: "(. . .) is at home / in the next classroom / in the school office / at the park right now." Then ask them to describe (. . .)'s possible activities at the present moment.

  Use the same situations but in a past context to elicit past progressive modals: what (. . .) could/may/might have been doing.

- Every progressive form must contain both a form of **be** and a *verb* + *-ing*.

- Point out similarities and differences with other progressive verb forms:
  Chart 2-2: Present progressive *(is sleeping vs. might be sleeping)*
  Chart 2-10: Past progressive *(was sleeping vs. might have been sleeping)*

□ **EXERCISE 15, p. 189. Progressive forms of modals. (Chart 10-5)**

Call students' attention to the situations, reminding them that the progressive is necessary for actions that are in progress "right now" or were in progress at a specific point in the past.

ANSWERS: **3.** must be burning **4.** may/might/could be talking . . . may/might/could be talking **5.** must be playing **6.** may/might/could be staying . . . may/might/could be staying **7.** should be studying **8.** must be kidding **9.** may/might/could have been kidding [*kidding* = joking] **10.** must have been kidding

□ **EXERCISE 16, p. 190. Progressive forms of modals. (Chart 10-5)**

POSSIBLE RESPONSES:
The students should be inside the bus, sitting in their seats.
This (pointing at the picture) student shouldn't be throwing a book out the window.
. . . shouldn't be hanging outside the window.
. . . shouldn't be riding on top of the bus.
. . . shouldn't be running in the aisle.
. . . shouldn't be flying a kite out the window.
. . . shouldn't be riding on his skateboard behind the bus.
. . . shouldn't be cutting the skateboarder's rope.
. . . shouldn't be throwing a rock at the skateboarder.

□ **EXERCISE 17, p. 190. Progressive and past forms of modals. (Charts 9-8 and 10-1 → 10-5)**

ANSWERS: **2.** must be waiting **3.** shouldn't have left **4.** might have borrowed **5.** must have been watching . . . must have forgotten **6.** may have been attending [also possible: *may have attended*] **7.** might have been washing **8.** must have left **9.** might be traveling **10.** must not have been expecting **11.** must have been daydreaming . . . should have been paying . . . shouldn't have been staring **12.** A: should have taken B: must be walking A: might have decided . . . could be working . . . may have called

□ **EXERCISE 18, p. 192.   Degrees of certainty.   (Charts 10-1 → 10-5)**

Encourage the class to actually go to a public place (though they can, of course, visit that place in their imaginations to complete the assignment). Perhaps the whole class could go together to a zoo or public square.

As an alternative, show a videotape to the class. You could turn off the sound and have the class guess what the people on the tape are talking about and doing. Or you could show several minutes from the middle of a movie or TV show and have the students guess about the characters and the story.

As another alternative, you could supply pictures such as news photos or posters depicting people and activities for the students to write about. It can be fun for you to supply snapshots of your family and friends for the students to make guesses about.

□ **EXERCISE 19, p. 192.   Degrees of certainty.   (Charts 10-1 → 10-5)**

You may be surprised at how many different conjectures your class can have about this picture. Let them study it for a moment, then ask leading questions, e.g., "What's your guess about the man at the front of the line? What is he doing? What's inside the envelope? Why is it so large? Do you think he's employed? Why is he at the post office at 3:00? What would you guess about his occupation from the clothes he's wearing?" Etc.

□ **EXERCISE 20, p. 193.   Degrees of certainty.   (Charts 10-1 → 10-5)**

Perhaps two students could perform this dialogue in front of the class, using some dramatic expression. Then the discussion will probably be more lively.

CHART 10-6: ABILITY: *CAN* AND *COULD*

- In (b): a common use of *can* is with stative verbs of sense perceptions (see Chart 2-3, p. 15) that are not used in progressive tenses to express the idea of "in progress right now." Compare:

  CORRECT: *I can't hear (right now) the lecture.*

  INCORRECT: *I am not hearing. I don't hear.*

- Pronunciation notes:

  Can't has two acceptable pronunciations. Most Americans say /kænt/. But along the northern Atlantic coast, the pronunciation is similar to the British /kant/.

  Can also has two pronunciations. Before a verb, it is usually /kən/. In a short answer ("Yes, I can") it is /kæn/.

  In typical intonation, *can't* is stressed and *can* is unstressed.

- The modal "could" can be confusing. It has many uses, most of which are close in meaning. Compare the following:

  I could run fast if I wanted to. (present/future contrary-to-fact conditional)

  I could run fast when I was young. (past ability, meaning "used to be able to")

  I could run or I could walk. (50–50 possibility, present/future)

  You could run to improve your physical condition. (present/future suggestion)

- To further complicate things, *could* meaning "past ability/possibility" occurs mostly in the negative:

  I couldn't go to the meeting yesterday afternoon. I had a doctor's appointment.

  However, one does not normally use *could* in the affirmative to indicate past ability:

  INCORRECT: *I could go to the meeting yesterday afternoon. I'm glad I didn't miss it.*

  Rather, one would use *be able to, managed to,* or the simple past:

  I was able to go to the meeting yesterday afternoon.

In sum, if the speaker is talking about an ablity to perform an act at one particular time in the past, *could* is NOT usually used in affirmative sentences. Compare:

  INCORRECT: *Did you read about the mountain climbers? They could reach the top of Mt. Everest yesterday.*

  CORRECT: *They were able to reach the top yesterday.*

  They managed to reach the top yesterday.

  They reached the top yesterday.

In negative sentences, however, there is no difference between using *could* and *was/were able to*:

  They couldn't reach/weren't able to reach the top yesterday.

For an idea of how complicated *could* is, look it up in a dictionary such as the *Collins COBUILD English Language Dictionary.* *Could* in all its aspects can be difficult to explain to learners, and doing so (for most learners) is not necessary.

☐ **EXERCISE 21, p. 194. CAN and COULD. (Chart 10-6)**

Read the sentences aloud, choosing *can* or *can't* at random. (Try not to move your head!) Then ask the students to tell you what you said.

☐ **EXERCISE 22, p. 194. CAN and COULD. (Chart 10-6)**

This exercise is a general review of uses of *can* and *could,* comparing them with other modals.

□ **EXERCISE 23, p. 195.   Degrees of certainty; ability.   (Charts 10-1 → 10-6)**

Prior to having students read this passage, ask them for a show of hands: "How many of you can dance? sing? draw?" Compare the results with those in the passage.

Note how the definition of *can* changes with the age groups in the passage. The college students can, in the literal sense, dance, sing, and draw (just as small children can), but not many define *can* as having a special skill rather than simply an innate ability. The point is that *can* has a wide range of meanings.

There is no "correct" answer to the discussion question. Responses will probably mention that children are less self-conscious than adults and more able to express themselves naturally through their bodies.

You might also discuss how our innate artistic abilities to express ourselves may become suppressed as we get older. This might be because we become sensitive to the judgments of others. It may be because we set new standards for ourselves based on comparisons with others or adopted societal standards. Etc.

This exercise is intended as a short communicative opportunity. It's not necessary to put a great deal of emphasis on modal usage. If good modal usage occurs naturally and appropriately, that's great, but it shouldn't be required or forced.

**CHART 10-7:   USING *WOULD* TO EXPRESS A REPEATED ACTION
IN THE PAST**

• Compared to *used to,* "habitual *would*" is somewhat more formal. *Would* is often preferred in writing, whereas *used to* may be preferred in speech.

• Note the important limitation on *would*: it cannot express a situation, only an action.

• This use of *would* is unusual in British English.

□ **EXERCISE 24, p. 195.   Using WOULD and USED TO.   (Chart 10-7)**

ANSWERS: **2.** would give   **3.** used to be   **4.** used to be . . . would start   **5.** used to be . . . would get . . . would spend . . . would find . . . would gather   **6.** used to ask . . . would never let   **7.** would make . . . would put   **8.** would wake . . . would hike . . . would see   **9.** used to take   **10.** would be sitting . . . would always smile . . . would stand . . . (would) clear

---

CHART 10-8:   EXPRESSING PREFERENCE: *WOULD RATHER*

• In a question, either the word "or" or the word "than" can follow *would rather:*
Would you rather eat fruit or candy?
Would you rather eat fruit than candy?

• In a negative question, only the word "than" is possible for a preference:
Wouldn't you rather eat fruit than candy?

□ **EXERCISE 25, p. 197.   Expressing preference: WOULD RATHER. (Chart 10-8)**

Encourage students to use contractions in their spoken answers. The contraction *'d* is often difficult to hear and may be difficult to pronounce for some learners. Sometimes students omit it because they don't hear it.

SAMPLE RESPONSES: **1.** would rather stay home and watch the ball game on TV.
2. would rather have been catching up on my sleep.   **3.** would rather be riding my bike.   **4.** would rather not.   **5.** A: I would rather read . . . do anything else I can think of.   B: would rather eat . . . do anything else I can think of.

□ **EXERCISE 26, p. 197.   Expressing preference: WOULD RATHER. (Chart 10-8)**

You might try a round-robin sequence like this:
   TEACHER to A: *What would you rather do than go to class?*
   SPEAKER A: *I'd rather go bowling than go to class.*
   TEACHER to B: *What would you rather do than go bowling?*
   SPEAKER B: *I'd rather play chess than go bowling.*
   TEACHER to C: *What would you rather do than play chess?*

SAMPLE RESPONSES: **1.** I would rather be in Italy than in the United States.   **2.** I would rather go to a movie than go to class.   **3.** Last night I stayed home. I would rather have gone to the concert downtown.   **4.** Right now I am doing a grammar exercise. I would rather be watching TV.   **5.** No, I'd rather stay home and watch TV than go to a movie. No, I'd rather rent a movie than go to a concert. No, I'd rather play tennis tomorrow than go to the zoo.   **6.** No, I would rather get on the Internet than play tennis this afternoon. No, I'd rather go bike riding than go bowling. No, I'd rather take a short hike in the woods than shoot pool.   **7.** No, I would rather eat at McDonald's than (at) the cafeteria. No, I'd rather eat at a Thai restaurant than (at) a Chinese restaurant.   **8.** No, I would rather live in Seoul than Singapore.

CHART 10-9:   COMBINING MODALS WITH PHRASAL MODALS

• Some other possible sequences in (c), with a phrasal modal combined with another phrasal modal: *be supposed to be able to, have (got) to be able to, used to have to, used to be able to, didn't use to be able to, be going to have to, be supposed to have to.*

□ **EXERCISE 27, p. 198.   Combining modals with BE ABLE TO and HAVE TO. (Chart 10-9)**

This exercise shows common combinations of both modals and phrasal modals with the two phrasal modals *be able to* and *have to.*

SAMPLE COMPLETIONS: **1.** Roy might not be able to finish writing his report before lunch. **2.** He is going to have to finish the rest of it later this afternoon.   **3.** You have to be able to pass a written driver's test before you can get your driver's license.   **4.** I shouldn't have to go to the dentist again for another year.   **5.** Sam lost his apartment; he must not have been able to pay his rent.   **6.** I would rather not have to take another English course, but it may be required.   **7.** I'm sorry, but I'm not going to be able to accept your invitation.   **8.** Tarek didn't get home at the usual time tonight; he may have had to work late.

```
┌─────────────────────────────────────────────────────────────────┐
│  CHART 10-10:   SUMMARY CHART OF MODALS AND SIMILAR             │
│                 EXPRESSIONS                                      │
├─────────────────────────────────────────────────────────────────┤
│                                                                 │
│  • By the time the students reach this chart, they should be    │
│    familiar with its contents. It summarizes for them what      │
│    they have been learning since the beginning of Chapter 9.    │
│                                                                 │
│  • The term "similiar expressions" in the chart title refers    │
│    to phrasal modals.                                           │
│                                                                 │
└─────────────────────────────────────────────────────────────────┘
```

☐ EXERCISE 28, p. 201.   Review: modals and similar expressions. (Chapters 9 and 10)

Ask leading questions to elicit student interpretations of meaning. In addition to a review of grammar, this kind of exercise provides the students with the opportunity to develop their speaking skills by explaining something they already know and understand. It challenges them to express their understandings in spoken English. Encourage them to invent possible contexts as a way of explaining differences in meaning.

In some items there is no difference in meaning; in other items there are distinct differences in meaning. In still other items, there might be a subtle difference in politeness or in forcefulness.

All of the sentences in this exercise are grammatically correct.

DISCUSSION:
1. a. is a formal, very polite request; b. and c. are informal and much more familiar.
2. a. through c. express increasing degrees of necessity: a. and b. are advice; c. states a fact; d. states an absolute requirement.
3. Again, degrees of necessity: a. is advice; b. is even stronger (the cut seems to definitely need treatment); c. is the strongest possible (the cut looks like it might be infected).
4. a. states prohibition; b. means you can use the door, but there's another possibility as well.
5. a. is a promise; b. is a guess at the time I expect to arrive.
6. a. through c. are all suggestions or possibilities; d. is definite.
7. All are degrees of negative possibility: a. is a suggestion; b. is a stronger negative; c. is 100 percent negative.
8. a. is a possibility; b. is a conclusion; c. is a definite statement.
9. a. is advice; b. is a requirement.
10. a. is a suggestion; b. is advice.
11. a. and b. are the same degree of necessity; c. through e. state the advisability of my going; f. states a preference: it could mean "I'd rather go than stay" or "It's better that I go than you go."
12. a. is hindsight advice; b. is merely another possibility in hindsight.
13. a. and b. mean the same thing: habitual activity.

☐ **EXERCISE 29, p. 202.   Review: modals and similar expressions.   (Chapters 9 and 10)**

The students have to think of only one possible answer, not all of the possibilities. In the following section, the most likely answers are given first and others are in parentheses.

ANSWERS:
1. had better shut (should / ought to / have to / must shut)
2. could / would you hand (can / will you hand)
3. don't / won't have to go
4. can already say (is already able to say)
5. must / have to attend
6. had to wait
7. could / might go
8. would rather go
9. must not have seen
10. had better clean (should / ought to / must / have to clean)
11. can't / couldn't be (must not be) . . . may / might / could belong (must belong)
12. cannot go (must not / may not go)
13. should not have laughed
14. May / Can / Could I speak . . . can't come . . . May / Can I take
15. should / ought to take (could take) . . . can get
16. had to study . . . should have come
17. had better answer (should / ought to / have to answer) . . . might / could / may be
18. should have been / was supposed to be
19. could / might / may be
20. must have been daydreaming

☐ **EXERCISE 30, p. 204.   Error analysis: modals.   (Chapters 9 and 10)**

ANSWERS:
1. If you have a car, you can <u>travel</u> around the United <u>States</u>.
2. During class, the students must ~~to~~ sit <u>quietly</u>. When the <u>students</u> have questions, they must ~~to~~ raise their hands.
3. When you send for the brochure, you should <u>include</u> a self-addressed, stamped envelope.
4. A film director must <u>have</u> control over every aspect of a movie.
5. When I was a child, I ~~can~~ <u>could</u> / <u>would</u> <u>go</u> to the roof of my house and <u>see</u> all the other houses and streets.
6. <u>When</u> I ~~was~~ <u>worked</u> in the fields, my son would <u>bring</u> me oranges or candy.
7. I <u>broke</u> my leg in a soccer game three <u>months</u> ago.
8. <u>Will</u> / <u>Would</u> / <u>Could</u> you please help me with this?
9. Many <u>students</u> would rather ~~to~~ study on their own than <u>go</u> to <u>class</u>.
10. We <u>are</u> supposed to bring our books to class every day.
11. You can <u>have</u> a very good time as a tourist in my country. My country <u>has</u> many <u>different weather areas</u>, [also possible: *different climates,*] so you <u>had</u> better plan ahead before you <u>come</u>.
12. When you visit big <u>cities</u> in my country, you must ~~to be~~ <u>pay</u> attention to your wallet when you are in a <u>crowded</u> place because there <u>are</u> a lot of <u>thieves</u>.

☐ **EXERCISE 31, p. 204.   Activity: modals.   (Chapters 9 and 10)**

Students might work in pairs to complete the dialogues, with one student completing A's sentences and the other completing B's. The completed dialogues can be performed, discussed by the whole class, and/or written out and handed in. (See the *Introduction*, p. xiv for suggestions for using completion exercises.)

☐ EXERCISE 32, p. 205.　Activity: modals.　(Chapters 9 and 10)

You may need to set a time limit for these discussions.　Sometimes students get rather excited about the topics and don't want to stop.　The given ideas are, for the most part, overstated generalizations of opinion that need to be qualified, explained, and supported. So, to conclude the exercise, you might ask the students to rewrite or expand on a sentence given in the textbook so that all members of the group agree with the idea.

If these topics are unfamiliar or uncomfortable for your students, you might add some others that are closer to their immediate interests.　Topics about their school, sports, clothing fashions, etc., may be productive.

These topics can also be used for writing.

☐ EXERCISE 33, p. 206.　Review of verb forms.　(Chapters 1 → 5, 9, and 10)

This entire exercise is a dialogue between two people, so you could choose two good speakers to read it (after everyone has independently completed it by writing in their books).　The other students should listen carefully and offer corrections or alternative answers, if appropriate.

ANSWERS:　**1.** had　　**2.** happened　　**3.** was driving　　**4.** broke　　**5.** did you do　**6.** pulled　　**7.** got　　**8.** started　　**9.** should not have done　　**10.** should have stayed　　**11.** are probably　　**12.** started　　**13.** have been walking / had walked　　**14.** went　　**15.** discovered　　**16.** didn't have　　**17.** can think **18.** could / might have gone　　**19.** could / might have tried　　**20.** could / might have asked　　**21.** asked　　**22.** told　　**23.** was　　**24.** allowed　　**25.** drove　　**26.** must have felt　　**27.** took　　**28.** took　　**29.** might get / might have gotten　　**30.** will know　　**31.** must / have to / should leave　　**32.** have to / must be　　**33.** May / Could/ Can I use　　**34.** need　　**35.** don't have　　**36.** will / can take

☐ EXERCISE 34, p. 207.　Writing: modals.　(Chapters 9 and 10)

A "short paragraph" is usually about five to eight sentences long.　You might want to set a limit for your students.

In marking their papers, focus on modals and verb tenses.　Reward them for correct use of these forms.

Chapter 11: THE PASSIVE

ORDER OF CHAPTER	CHARTS	EXERCISES	WORKBOOK
The passive: form and use	11-1 → 11-3	Ex. 1 → 10	Pr. 1 → 11
The passive form of modals and phrasal modals	11-4	Ex. 11 → 14	Pr. 12 → 14
Review		Ex. 15 → 17	
Stative passive	11-5 → 11-6	Ex. 18 → 22	Pr. 15 → 18
The passive with *get*	11-7	Ex. 23 → 25	Pr. 19 → 20
Participial adjectives	11-8	Ex. 26 → 28	Pr. 21 → 22
Cumulative review		Ex. 29	Pr. 23 → 25

General Notes on Chapter 11

• OBJECTIVE: In speaking and writing, about one sentence in eight uses the passive structure. In scientific, academic, and informative reporting, usage increases to about one passive in every three sentences. The passive allows one to focus on actions and the receivers of actions, but it does not require identification of the act<u>or</u> because often it is not important or necessary to know who did something. Although the passive is a useful structure, learners should be encouraged to continue using active sentences for direct, forceful, or persuasive purposes when the agent/actor is known.

• APPROACH: Students are given plenty of practice in forming and using passive sentences thoughout the chapter. Special attention is given to passive modals, the verb "get" as a passivizer, and the often confusing participial adjectives (e.g., *interesting* vs. *interested*). With the charts and exercises, students learn to use various tenses with the passive and to decide whether to use the passive or active form.

• TERMINOLOGY: It is assumed that students understand the grammatical terms "subject," "object," and "(in)transitive verb." The term "*by*-phrase" is used for the prepositional phrase that includes the agent of the verb's action.

```
┌─────────────────────────────────────────────────┐
│  CHART 11-1:  FORMING THE PASSIVE                 │
└─────────────────────────────────────────────────┘
```

• Students must understand the difference between transitive and intransitive verbs; refer them to Appendix Chart A-1. Some other languages use transitivity in very different ways, leading some students to make mistakes in English.

INCORRECT: *The accident was happened.* OR *My shoe was fallen off.*

• In reviewing the tense forms listed at the bottom of the chart, you might have students change some of the statements into questions or negatives. This focuses their attention on the required use of the auxiliary "be" in every passive sentence.

☐ **EXERCISE 1, p. 209. Forming the passive. (Chart 11-1)**

EXPANSION ACTIVITY: Before or after Exercise 1, you might want to demonstrate the passive in all the tenses. Ask students to assist you, then include their actions in your sentences. For example: *("Omar") touches your book, then takes his hand from it.*

TEACHER: Omar touched the book.
SPEAKERS: The book was touched by Omar.
(You touch the book with your hand and do not take your hand from it.)
TEACHER: I am touching the book.
SPEAKERS: The book is being touched by you.
(Continue with sentences like the following:)
(simple present) Mr. Lee touches the book during class each day.
(simple past) When we started this lesson, Omar touched the book.
(present perfect) Ruth hasn't touched the book yet.
(past progressive) A few minutes ago, Omar was touching the book.
(past perfect) Before I touched the book, Omar had touched it.
(future) Baiwong will probably touch the book next.
(future) Pierre is going to touch the book when I ask him to.
(future perfect) Soon Maria will have touched the book.

ANSWERS: **2.** is being opened   **3.** has been opened   **4.** was opened   **5.** was being opened   **6.** had been opened   **7.** will be opened   **8.** is going to be opened   **9.** will have been opened   **10.** Is . . . being opened   **11.** Was . . . opened   **12.** Has . . . been opened

☐ **EXERCISE 2, p. 209. Forming the passive. (Chart 11-1)**

This exercise may be done individually or in small groups. In an advanced class where this is review only, a "student-teacher" could lead the exercise.

Every sentence in this exercise should include a *by*-phrase in the passive form. Focus attention on the <u>forms</u> at this point in the chapter. Check the students' pronunciation of *-ed* endings.

PART I ANSWERS: **2.** Customers <u>are served</u> by waitresses and waiters.   **3.** The lesson <u>is going to be explained</u> by the teacher.   **4.** A new idea <u>has been suggested</u> by Shirley. **5.** Ann <u>will be invited</u> to the party by Bill.   **6.** That report <u>is being prepared</u> by Alex.   **7.** The farmer's wagon <u>was being pulled</u> by two horses.   **8.** The book <u>had been returned</u> (by Kathy) to the library (by Kathy). [Either position is acceptable.]   **9.** By this time tomorrow, the announcement <u>will have been made</u> by the president.   **10.** That note <u>wasn't written</u> by me. It <u>was written</u> by Jim.   **11.** That pie <u>wasn't made</u> by Alice. <u>Was</u> it <u>made</u> by Mrs. French?   **12.** <u>Is</u> that course <u>taught</u> by Prof. Jackson? I know that it <u>isn't taught</u> by Prof. Adams.   **13.** Those papers <u>haven't been signed</u> (yet) by Mrs. Andrews (yet). [Either position is acceptable.] <u>Have</u> they <u>been signed</u> by Mr. Andrews?
14. <u>Is</u> your house <u>being painted</u> by Mr. Brown?   **15.** I <u>won't be fooled</u> by his tricks.

PART II ANSWERS: **16.** Omar <u>wrote</u> that sentence.   **17.** The teacher <u>is going to collect</u> our papers.   **18.** <u>Did</u> Thomas Edison <u>invent</u> the electric light bulb?   **19.** Most drivers <u>don't obey</u> the speed limit on Highway 5.   **20.** <u>Has</u> the building superintendent <u>informed</u> you of a proposed increase in our rent?

☐ EXERCISE 3, p. 210. Forming the passive. (Chart 11-1)

The items include intransitive verbs that are often used incorrectly in a passive form by learners. (INCORRECT: *My cat was died; I am agree with you.*)

ANSWERS: **3.** *(no change)* [Compare *died* (intransitive verb) and *is dead* (*be* + adjective)] **4.** *(no change)*   **5.** That theory was developed by Dr. Ikeda.   **6.** The cup was dropped by Timmy.   **7.** *(no change)*   **8.** I was interviewed by the assistant manager.   **9.** *(no change)*   **10.** The small fishing village was destroyed by a hurricane.   **11.** *(no change)*   **12.** *(no change)*   **13.** *(no change)*   **14.** After class, the chalkboard is always erased by one of the students.   **15.** *(no change)* **16.** *(no change)*   **17.** *(no change)*   **18.** The fire wasn't caused by lightning. **19.** The dispute is going to be settled by a special committee.   **20.** Was the enemy surrounded by the army?   **21.** *(no change)*   **22.** Windmills were invented by the Persians around 1500 years ago.

CHART 11-2:   USING THE PASSIVE

• Point out that a combination of factors determines when the *by*-phrase is omitted. It is not used:
—when it can easily be assumed who, in general, performs such an action. *(Rice is grown "by farmers." Arithmetic is taught in elementary school "by teachers." etc.)* In such cases, the *by*-phrase is implied.
—when the speaker doesn't know who performed the action. *(The house was built in 1890 "by some unknown people who engaged in house building." My shoes were made in Italy "by some unknown shoemakers." etc.)*
—when the focus is on the action, and it is not important to know who performed the action. *(This olive oil was imported from Spain "by people in a company that imports olive oil." It's not important to know who those people are. The focus is solely on the origin of the olive oil.)*

COMPARE: The active is usually used when the act<u>or</u> is specifically known. *(Mr. Lee grows rice on his farm. Ms. Hill teaches arithmetic in elementary school. My grandfather built our house. The Acme Trading Company imports olive oil from Spain.)*

• The *by*-phrase is included (in other words, the passive is used even when there is an acceptable active equivalent with a known agent) when the speaker wants to focus attention on the <u>receiver</u> of the action, rather than the actor.

☐ EXERCISE 4, p. 211. Using the passive. (Charts 11-1 and 11-2)

You could ask the students some leading questions about the sentences, such as: "Why is the passive used here instead of the active? Who is the actor or agent? Change the sentence to its active form; what's the difference in meaning or forcefulness?"
ADDITIONAL SUGGESTION: For homework, ask the students to find examples of passive sentences, copy them, and bring them to class the next day. Tell them to look in a newspaper, an encyclopedia, a textbook, etc. (This shows them that the passive occurs frequently in many contexts.) At the beginning of the next class, some of the students could write on the chalkboard the sentences they found. Or they could hand in their sentences, which you could then duplicate for further class discussion.

POSSIBLE ANSWERS:

1. We don't know who made the sweater, and it is not important to know. The equivalent active sentence is "Someone (in England) made my sweater (in England)." The passive is preferred here because the actor is unknown and unimportant.

2. The implied *by*-phrase is "by people who build highways." The passive expresses all the necessary information without the *by*-phrase.

3. "by language teachers," no important additional information

4. It's obvious that the symphony was performed "by the symphony orchestra," not by a high school band or by a guitar player. If the symphony had been performed by any agent other than the obvious one, either the active would be used or the *by*-phrase would be included.

5. "by television stations" is understood.

6. The *by*-phrases give necessary details. The active forms of these sentences are equally useful. The difference is that the passive focuses attention on two compositions rather than on their authors. Information about the authors is given to identify or distinguish between the two compositions.

7. The *by*-phrase is used because it contains the important information of "hundreds." The active sentence is equally viable, but the passive focuses attention on the monument.

8. "by banana growers" and "by someone who brought them," no important additional information

9. Except for the third sentence, the agents are unknown and unimportant. The third sentence is active and names the actors in the subject.

10. Sentence one is active. [There is no passive form of main verb "be." *Be* is used in the passive only as an auxiliary.]
    Sentence two: *by people* is uninformative.
    Sentences three and four: Note that there are five passives here. No *by*-phrases are necessary. Point out how useful the passive can be when the speaker's/writer's purpose is to give information about the receivers of actions (in this case, the things that received actions) without knowing who performed those actions.
    Sentence five: The *by*-phrase is necessary because the agent is known. The active equivalent could be used, but the passive focuses attention on *paper* rather than on *the Chinese*. Even though the active could easily be used in the last sentence, point out that the use of the passive allows a parallel contrast between *parchment* and *paper*.

☐ **EXERCISE 5, p. 212.   Using the passive. (Charts 11-1 and 11-2)**

This exercise allows students to apply the rules they have learned so far about the passive: using the correct tense with *be*, omitting or including a *by*-phrase, not using an intransitive verb in the passive, observing singular/plural agreement between subject and verb.

ANSWERS: **3.** This antique table was made in 1734.   **4.** *(no change)*   **5.** My purse was stolen.   **6.** The coffee was being made when I walked into the kitchen. [The active sentence is more direct and preferable.]   **7.** That book has been translated into many languages.   **8.** That picture was drawn by Jim's daughter. This picture was drawn by my son.   **9.** The applicants will be judged on the basis of their originality.   **10.** *(no change)*   **11.** Is that course being taught by Professor Rivers this semester?   **12.** When was the radio invented?   **13.** The mail had already been delivered by the time I left for school this morning.   **14.** When are the results of the contest going to be announced? [Note the plural verb.]   **15.** After the concert was over, the rock music star was mobbed by hundreds of fans outside the theater.   **16.** Ever since I arrived here, I have been living in the dormitory because I was told that it was cheaper to live there than in an apartment.   **17.** The new hospital is going to be built next year. The new elementary school has already been built. [The active sentences with impersonal *they* are acceptable in casual conversation.]   **18.** If a film is exposed to light while it is being developed, the negative will be ruined. [The passive makes the sentence more formal and the speaker/writer more distant from the listener/reader.]

CHART 11-3: INDIRECT OBJECTS AS PASSIVE SUBJECTS
• Students may or may not already be familiar with direct vs. indirect objects.

☐ EXERCISE 6, p. 213. Indirect objects as passive subjects. (Chart 11-3)

You should focus the students' attention on indirect objects. The principal purpose in using the passive in these sentences is to focus attention on the person (I.O.), not on the "thing" (D.O.).

ERRATUM: Item 4 should read: "Someone has given Maria a promotion at her job as a computer programmer at Microsoft." This is corrected in subsequent printings.

ANSWERS:
2. Peggy = indirect object—Peggy has been awarded a scholarship by Indiana University.
3. Fred = indirect object—Fred was paid three hundred dollars in consulting fees.
   [no *by*-phrase]
4. Maria = indirect object—Maria has been given a promotion at her job as a computer programmer at Microsoft. [no *by*-phrase]
5. you = indirect object—You will be sent a bill. [no *by*-phrase]
6. people = indirect object—The starving people will be given a week's supply of rice.
   [no *by*-phrase]

☐ EXERCISE 7, p. 213. Using the passive. (Charts 11-1 → 11-3)

This should be a fast-paced exercise. If you lead the exercise, you may want to add specifics that make the items relevant to your students' lives, e.g., "Someone invited you to a reception for international students at Berg Hall" or "Someone is televising the final match of the French Open on Channel 5 this coming Saturday."

As the students speak, pay special attention to their pronunciation of *-ed* endings. Often they tend to omit them or add unnecessary vowel sounds.

ANSWERS: **1.** You were invited to a party. **2.** Rice is grown in many countries. **3.** The game is being televised. **4.** Reading is taught in the first grade. **5.** You were told to be here at ten. **6.** That hat was made in Mexico. **7.** Dinner is going to be served at six. **8.** The news will be announced tomorrow. **9.** A mistake has been made. **10.** A test is being given (by the teacher) in the next room right now.

☐ EXERCISE 8, p. 214. Using the passive. (Charts 11-1 → 11-3)

Have three students pattern the exercise format before the groups start working together, just to make sure everyone understands the directions.

☐ EXERCISE 9, p. 215. Using the passive. (Charts 11-1 → 11-3)

This exercise can be done as written seatwork and then discussed, or it can be done orally. It works equally well with small groups or as a class exercise. It can also be omitted or assigned as self-study.

ANSWERS: **2.** is surrounded **3.** is spelled [also possible, esp. in British English: *spelt*] **4.** will be built / is going to be built **5.** was divided / has been divided **6.** is worn **7.** was caused **8.** was ordered **9.** who was accidentally killed **10.** was reported **11.** was surprised **12.** was offered **13.** were frightened **14.** was confused **15.** is expected

☐ **EXERCISE 10, p. 216.   Using the passive. (Charts 11-1 → 11-3)**

This exercise is a review of tenses in both active and passive voices.

In passive sentences, discuss why the passive is used and is preferable to the active.

For the longer items (items 10, 11, and 12), ask students to summarize them without looking at their books. Point out and praise good use of the passive in the summaries.

ANSWERS:

1. is produced
2. is being treated
3. will probably be won / is probably going to be won
4. saw . . . was interviewed
5. are controlled / are determined
6. was caught [*purse-snatcher* = a thief who steals a woman's purse] . . . was being chased . . . jumped . . . kept [*kept from* = prevented]
7. appeared [Note that *fish* is plural here.] . . . have been named . . . described [*Have been* is usually not repeated after *and*.] . . . are being discovered / are discovered
8. was informed . . . was told [*age discrimination* = a legal term similar to racial or sex discrimination. It refers to a situation in which someone is treated unfairly because of his/her age.]
9. is exposed . . . affects [*Frostbite* = the formation of small ice crystals under the skin. In serious cases, it can result in severe damage to the skin.] [Point out that *affect* is a verb and *effect* is a noun.]
10. was discovered . . . called . . . was translated . . . had been built . . . do not exist
11. was recognized . . . was asked . . . took . . . knew . . . multiplied . . . came ["came up with" = found, discovered]
12. brought . . . sent . . . were asked [*impromptu* = something devised at the immediate moment, not planned ahead of time] . . . was discovered . . . is still called

---

CHART 11-4:   THE PASSIVE FORM OF MODALS AND PHRASAL MODALS

• ASSUMPTION: Students are familiar with the meanings of modal auxiliaries (Chapter 9).

• Remind students that a modal is always immediately followed by the simple form of a verb, in this case *be* and *have*.

• You might add examples relevant to your students' lives. Have them change passive sentences to active. Examples:
  This room has to be cleaned. → *Someone has to clean this room.*
  Olga should be told about tomorrow's test. → *Someone should tell Olga about* . . . .

☐ **EXERCISE 11, p. 219.   Passive modals. (Chart 11-4)**

Compare similar items so that students can see the differences in pairs of sentences where one is passive and the other is active.

This is principally an exercise on the form of passive modals, but also include discussion of their meaning.

ANSWERS: **4.** must be kept [*spoil* = become bad to eat]   **5.** must keep   **6.** couldn't be opened   **7.** couldn't open   **8.** may be offered   **9.** may offer   **10.** may already have been offered / may have already been offered   **11.** may already have offered / may have already offered [*firm* = a company, a business]   **12.** ought to be divided   **13.** ought to have been divided   **14.** have to be returned   **15.** has to return . . . will have to pay   **16.** had better be finished   **17.** had better finish   **18.** is supposed to be sent   **19.** should have been sent [*belated* /bɪˈleɪtəd/ = after-the-fact]   **20.** must have been surprised

☐ EXERCISE 12, p. 220. Passive modals. (Chart 11-4)

Encourage more than one completion in some of the items where there are choices. Students enjoy experimenting with various combinations. In the following, the most likely completion is given first, i.e., the completion a typical native speaker might use in a typical context in which the sentence might occur.

EXPECTED COMPLETIONS: **2.** must be married [By custom, a wedding ring is worn on the next-to-last finger of the left hand.] **3.** must be written / have to be written [also possible: *are to be written*] **4.** must have been left **5.** should / ought to / has to be postponed [also possible: *had better/must be postponed*) **6.** should not be given [also possible: *must not be/can't be given*] **7.** should / ought to be encouraged [also possible: *must be encouraged*] **8.** may / could / might / will be misunderstood **9.** cannot be explained [A "UFO" is an Unidentified Flying Object, which some people believe comes from advanced civilizations on distant planets.] **10.** must have been embarrassed **11.** must / has to be pushed [*pushed* = encouraged, urged] **12.** should / ought to have been built **13.** must / should be saved [also possible: *have to be/ought to be saved*] **14.** must / has to / should be done [also possible: *ought to be done*] **15.** ought to / should be elected [advisability]; must/has to [necessity]; will be elected [prediction]; may/might/could be elected [possibility]. [Point out how the meaning significantly changes according to choice of modal.]

☐ EXERCISE 13, p. 221. Passive modals. (Chart 11-4)

Students work in pairs. You could assign one or two of the items to each pair for their dialogue. In other words, no one will use all of the items. When the dialogues are performed, all students should listen to identify which items are included, checking them off in their books as they hear them.

☐ EXERCISE 14, p. 222. Using the passive. (Charts 11-1 → 11-4)

This exercise is a general review. Some of the items anticipate Chart 11-7, The Passive with *Get.* You may wish to mention the possible use of *get* in the passive here, or comment upon it only if students supply it or have questions about it.

ANSWERS: **1.** is usually delivered [also possible: *usually gets delivered*] **2.** were working . . . occurred . . . was hurt [also possible: *got hurt*] **3.** was not admitted . . . had already begun **4.** had already been offered **5.** is being organized **6.** will never be forgotten / is never going to be forgotten ["will go down in history" = will be included in historical records] **7.** was . . . happened . . . flunked . . . dropped . . . was walking . . . fell . . . was stolen [also possible: *got stolen*] **8.** had (already) been rented (already) **9.** was being ignored **10.** did you buy . . . didn't buy . . . was given . . . Do you like **11.** is circled . . . are held . . . are circled **12.** worshipped [BrE = *worshiped*] **13.** have been destroyed **14.** were allowed . . . were not invited . . . were forbidden . . . were being held / were held **15.** was built . . . has often been described . . . was designed . . . took [*took* = required] **16.** is being judged . . . will be announced / are going to be announced ["to cross one's fingers" = to wish for good luck]

☐ EXERCISE 15, p. 224. Activity: the passive. (Charts 11-1 → 11-4)

This is the students' chance to make up a grammar exercise. The format of the exercise is one they are well familiar with: fill in the blank with a form of the verb in parentheses. The exercise should be fun as well as a good test of the test-makers' (rather than test-takers') usage ability and understanding. You can expect widely varying levels of skill at creating items. Students shouldn't be surprised if an item they thought was clear turns out to be confusing for the test-taker; such confusions are a good source of discussion.

ERRATUM: The example should read: *(name of a person)* \ offer. This is corrected in subsequent printings.

ANSWERS: [These depend on students' creativity.]

☐ **EXERCISE 16, p. 224. Using the passive. (Charts 11-1 → 11-4)**

Note during discussion that the passage illustrates a typical way in which the passive is advantageously and appropriately used, i.e., in a technical description in which information about the actors is unimportant and/or unknown.

SUGGESTION: Discuss the organization of the passage.
— It has an introduction (that announces the subject) leading to a thesis sentence: "Today people make paper from wood pulp by using either a mechanical or a chemical process."
— The second paragraph discusses one topic: the mechanical process.
— The third paragraph is about the chemical process.
— The fourth paragraph concludes the process of making paper from wood pulp. The description of the process itself is in chronological order.
— The last paragraph contains a conclusion, stating the general belief that this process is important to the modern world.

For further discussion: Will paper ever become outmoded? At some point in the future, will all written communication, including books, be composed, transmitted, received, and read electronically?

ANSWERS:
(1) <u>paper has been made</u> from various plants . . . In the past, <u>paper was made</u> by hand . . . <u>most of the work is done</u> by machines . . . Today <u>paper is made</u> from wood pulp
(2) In the mechanical process, <u>wood is ground</u> . . . During the grinding, <u>it is sprayed</u> . . . Then <u>the chips are soaked</u>
(3) First <u>the wood is washed</u>, and then <u>it is cut</u> into small pieces . . . Then <u>the chips are cooked</u> . . . After <u>the wood is cooked, it is washed</u>
(4) <u>The pulp is drained</u> to form . . . <u>(is) bleached</u> . . . and then <u>(is)</u> thoroughly <u>washed</u> again. Next <u>the pulp is put</u> . . . drier and a press, <u>they are wound</u>
(5) . . . how <u>it is made</u>.

☐ **EXERCISE 17, p. 225. Writing: the passive. (Charts 11-1 → 11-4)**

You might want to set a limit on the length of these compositions—say, 10 to 15 sentences. Expect that your students will have some difficulty in trying to translate explanations from another language into English; tell them to use only English reference books. If your students don't have access to reference books, perhaps they could interview a local expert, parent, or acquaintance about how some common object is made.

Another possibility is for you to invite an expert such as a ceramicist, weaver, or carpenter to speak to the class. The students can take notes as the basis for their compositions.

Another alternative is for you to photocopy a description of a process. First, discuss the process and analyze with the class the use of the passive in the passage. Then tell the students to put the passage aside and describe the process in their own words in writing.

You may choose to ask the students to underline every example of a passive in their papers after they have finished writing and revising them. This helps you in marking their successes and errors. It also helps the students check their own use of the passive. Another possibility is for the students to read each other's compositions and underline each instance of the passive.

You might assign the first of these topics for homework and use the second one later as an in-class writing test.

CHART 11-5: STATIVE PASSIVE

• The stative passive is frequently used in both spoken and written English.

• You may want to demonstrate the relationship between regular passive and stative passive by using things in your classroom. Examples:

(Close a book.) *I just closed the book.*
> *The book was closed by me.* (describes an action)
> *Now the book is closed.* (describes an existing state)

[Have a student (Ali) break a piece of chalk.]
> *Ali broke the chalk.*
> *The chalk was broken by Ali.*
> *Now the chalk is broken.*

• In the following exercise, items 8 and 10 are intended to point out that the stative passive is used to describe an existing state in the <u>past</u> as well as the present. As the chart has only present-time examples, you may wish to mention usage in past time in your discussion of the chart. Example:

Tom tried to open the door (last night), but it **was locked**. = *Someone had locked it prior to Tom trying to open the door.*

It is not a difficult point, which is why it is demonstrated in the exercise rather than in the chart, but you may wish to add it to your presentation of the stative passive prior to Exercise 18.

☐ **EXERCISE 18, p. 226.   Stative passive.   (Chart 11-5)**

ANSWERS: **2.** is shut   **3.** are turned   **4.** is not crowded   **5.** are bent . . . are folded ["Folded" hands have the fingers of one hand between the fingers of the other hand.]   **6.** is finished   **7.** is closed   **8.** was closed   **9.** is stuck ["to stick" = to be unable to move, as if glued]   **10.** was stuck   **11.** is/has been made . . . (is) swept . . . (are) washed   **12.** is set . . . (are) done . . . (are) lighted / (are) lit ["to set a table" = to put the plates, glasses, and utensils in place for each person]   **13.** is gone   **14.** is torn   **15.** is hidden

---

☐ **EXERCISE 19, p. 226.   Stative passive.   (Chart 11-5)**

ANSWERS: **2.** is . . . crowded   **3.** is scheduled   **4.** am exhausted   **5.** am confused   **6.** is stuck   **7.** are turned off   **8.** is insured   **9.** are divorced   **10.** is gone   **11.** are . . . qualified   **12.** am married   **13.** is spoiled/spoilt   **14.** is blocked   **15.** is located   **16.** was born   **17.** Is . . . turned off   **18.** are . . . done [*done* = ready. Perhaps note that the singular word "another" is used with the plural noun phrase "ten minutes." See Chart 8-6, p. 142. In this instance, a block of time, such as *ten minutes, two days,* or *six weeks,* is treated as a singular structure.]

CHART 11-6: COMMON STATIVE PASSIVE VERBS + PREPOSITIONS

• Choice of prepositions is always difficult for students; therefore, these phrases should be learned as whole units. The following exercises help in this process, but perfection at this stage of learning cannot be expected. The list in this chart is intended for reference, not memorization, but learning styles differ. Some students will set about memorizing the list on their own, while others will simply give it a minimal glance and put their learning emphasis into the exercises.

   Discuss with the students the difficulty ALL learners have in learning preposition combinations. Explain that correct usage comes with time and experience. Learning prepositions is definitely worth the students' time and attention, but not worth fretting over. The exercises are intended to help the students "educate their ears" so that eventually the correct prepositions will "sound right."

• You may wish to try to explain the difference between *tired of* and *tired from*. *Tired of* is used to express that one has had enough of something and doesn't feel like doing it anymore. *Tired from* expresses that one is physically tired from doing a certain activity, e.g., *I am pleasantly* **tired** *tonight* **from** *a good day's work in the garden.* Compare:

   I'm **tired of** *working in the garden* = I've been working in the garden and don't want to do it anymore. I've had enough.

   I'm **tired from** *working in the garden* = The reason I'm physically tired is that I worked (or am still working) in the garden.

□ **EXERCISE 20, p. 228. Stative passive + prepositions. (Chart 11-6)**

Ways of reinforcing the prepositions:

1. Ask students to say the entire sentence, not only the preposition. This gives them a chance to say and hear the whole phrase in context.

2. At the end of an entry, ask another student to repeat the information in the item without looking at the book by asking him or her a leading question, e.g., "What can you tell me about (. . .)'s* high school soccer team?" "What did (. . .) say about that man?" "What can you tell me about Mark Twain?" "Who needs professional help?" Etc.

3. At the conclusion of the exercise, review it orally, with students' books closed, by reading an item up to the blank and allowing the class to supply the preposition.

   TEACHER: Our high school soccer team was very excited . . . .
   CLASS: about
   TEACHER: **excited about** going to the national finals.

   TEACHER: I'm not acquainted . . .
   CLASS: by / with / for / of
   TEACHER: Let's take a vote. How many vote for "by"? Etc.
              . . . Okay, "with" wins!
              Again: I'm not acquainted . . .
   CLASS: with!
   TEACHER: Great! **acquainted with** that man.

4. Use the items in the exercise or the chart and ask students questions about their lives: "Maria, is there anything in your future that you are excited about?"

---

*Here (. . .) refers to the name of the student who read the item aloud.

5. Give one student a past participle to use in a question posed to another student:
   TEACHER: accustomed
   SPEAKER A: Kim, are you accustomed to the food here?
   SPEAKER B: No, I'm not accustomed to this kind of cooking.

ANSWERS: **1.** [Perhaps note that the preposition is followed by a gerund *(going)*. See Chart 14-2.] **2.** with **3.** for **4.** to **5.** to **6.** with **7.** in [*a dock* = a quay, a place where a ferry or other boat can land] **8.** with [*a sun roof* = a sliding panel in the car's roof] **9.** to [*the measles* = red spots on the skin] **10.** to **11.** with **12.** of **13.** to **14.** to . . . of [*ban* = prohibition; *disarmament* = destroying/getting rid of weapons] **15.** with **16.** from **17.** with **18.** in **19.** to **20.** with [*seedlings* = new plants beginning to grow from seeds] **21.** to **22.** with **23.** for **24.** in/with . . . to . . . with [*plot* = story] **25.** with . . . in . . . to

☐ EXERCISE 21, p. 230. Stative passive + prepositions. (Chart 11-6)

This exercise is an example of what you could do with the whole list in Chart 11-6 if you wanted to. You begin a sentence, going up to the place where the preposition is needed, and a student finishes it.

   You could use this books-closed, oral format for quick reviews at the beginning or end of class over the next couple of weeks to help your students get used to the correct prepositions for the common expressions in Chart 11-6.

SAMPLE RESPONSES: **1.** Are you related to Abdul-Rahman? **2.** Oscar is worried about his grade in this class. **3.** I'm not accustomed to drinking weak coffee. **4.** Jin Won is dressed in a casual shirt and tan pants. **5.** My foot is connected to my leg. **6.** The walls of this room are covered with ugly green paint. **7.** This class is composed of eleven men and thirteen women. **8.** Giovanni is married to Isabel. **9.** I'm opposed to killing animals to make fur coats. **10.** Are you acquainted with Mr. Wong's wife?

☐ EXERCISE 22, p. 230. Stative passive + prepositions. (Chart 11-6)

You may wish to ask students to spell some of the verbs aloud to review the spelling rules in Chart 1-6. You may also wish to review the pronunciation of *-ed* endings, as presented in Chart 2-6.

ANSWERS: **2.** is composed /d/ of **3.** am accustomed /d/ to [Emphasize that *accustomed* is spelled with two "c's" and one "m."] **4.** is terrified /d/ of **5.** is finished /t/ with **6.** is addicted /əd/ to **7.** is covered /d/ with **8.** am satisfied /d/ with **9.** is married /d/ to [INCORRECT: *with*] **10.** is divorced /t/ from **11.** am . . . acquainted /əd/ with **12.** am tired /d/ of **13.** Are . . . related /əd/ to **14.** is dedicated /əd/ to **15.** is disappointed /əd/ in/with [Emphasize that *disappointed* has one "s" and two "p's."] **16.** is scared /d/ of ["scared of his own shadow" = someone who is very timid or shy.] **17.** is committed /əd/ to [NOTE: two "m's" and two "t's." Perhaps refer to the salient spelling rule in Chart 1-6, p. 10: When adding suffixes, remember to double the consonant in two-syllable words when the stress is on the second syllable.] **18.** are devoted /əd/ to **19.** is dressed /t/ in **20.** are done with

CHART 11-7: THE PASSIVE WITH *GET*

• *Get* has a meaning similar to *become;* in other words, it signals a changing situation or an altered state. To discuss this meaning of *get,* you might ask students to make up their own sentences with ***get*** + *adjective,* using a few of the adjectives in the list in the chart's footnote. Students at this level are generally quite familiar with this use of *get,* although they may not have recognized that it has a passive form, meaning, and use.

• The passive with *get* is common, especially in spoken English. It is a somewhat informal structure although it can at times be found even in formal writing.

□ **EXERCISE 23, p. 232.   The passive with GET.   (Chart 11-7)**

This is an exercise on verb tenses as well as the passive with *get.*
   Students can have fun if they read their answers rather dramatically, accompanied by gestures, as if performing in a theater.

ANSWERS: **2.** am getting sleepy   **3.** is getting late   **4.** got wet   **5.** is getting hot
6. get nervous   **7.** is getting dark   **8.** got light   **9.** am getting full   **10.** is
getting better   **11.** Get busy ["Shake a leg" = "get moving" = "step on it." All are idioms
meaning to move or work faster, to hurry up.]   **12.** Get well [Point out that *well* is an adjective
in this sentence and that a "get-well card" is sent only to someone who is ill.]

□ **EXERCISE 24, p. 233.   The passive with GET.   (Chart 11-7)**

This is also a verb tense review exercise.

ANSWERS: **2.** got hurt   **3.** got lost   **4.** get dressed   **5.** did . . . get married / are
. . . getting / going to get married   **6.** get accustomed   **7.** am getting worried
8. get upset   **9.** got confused   **10.** get done   **11.** got depressed   **12.** Did . . .
get invited   **13.** got bored   **14.** get packed [*pack* = put things into a suitcase]
15. get paid   **16.** got hired   **17.** got fired   **18.** didn't get finished   **19.** got
disgusted   **20.** got engaged . . . got married . . . got divorced . . . got remarried

□ **EXERCISE 25, p. 234.   The passive with GET.   (Chart 11-7)**

This can be teacher-led, with the students' books closed. Students could also work in pairs.
The purpose of the exercise is to elicit from the students familiar contexts in which they
already use many of these expressions with *get.* Ones that may be unfamiliar to them are
items 16, 21, 23, and 24.

ANSWERS: [These depend on students' creativity.]

CHART 11-8:   PARTICIPIAL ADJECTIVES

• The active meaning of the present participle (the *-ing* form of a verb) is also observed in the progressive. (See Chapter 2.)

• A frequent error learners make is the substitution of an active participle (e.g., *interesting*) where a passive one is required. (INCORRECT: *I am interesting in literature.*)

• This grammar point is dealt with in this chapter because it is a structure in which a passive meaning is compared with an active meaning.

□ **EXERCISE 26, p. 235. Participial adjectives. (Chart 11-8)**

Encourage students to raise questions and discuss meanings during this exercise. You may want to explain that the present participle has an active ("giving" or "causing") meaning, but the past participle has a passive ("taking" or "receiving") meaning.

This is a simple, straightforward exercise so that you can make sure the students understand the basics of the information in the chart. One might say this exercise is "too easy," but something is easy only if one already knows how to do it. For some students this is a difficult grammar point, and for many teachers (and this text writer) not always an easy one to explain. This exercise allows you and the students to see how much they understand before proceeding.

ANSWERS: **3.** exciting **4.** excited **5.** surprising **6.** surprised **7.** frightened **8.** frightening **9.** exhausting **10.** exhausted

□ **EXERCISE 27, p. 235. Participial adjectives. (Chart 11-8)**

You could be Speaker A for items one to five. Then let pairs of students take over the rest of the items. Be sure the students understand that they are to ask the question "How would you describe . . . ?" as the second part in each item.

This exercise is designed to reinforce the students' understanding of the concepts underlying the use of participial adjectives.

To review the grammar in real contexts, ask the students "real" questions using the verbs in this exercise, e.g., "Roberto, can you tell us about something you have found confusing? Somchart, have you ever been confused? Who has had an amazing experience? Tell us about a time you were really amazed." Etc.

ANSWERS: **1.** amazing (story) . . . amazed (person) **2.** depressing (story) . . . depressed (person) **3.** tired (person) . . . tiring (work) **4.** boring (movie) . . . bored (person) **5.** interested (person) . . . interesting (painting) **6.** embarrassing (situation) . . . embarrassed (person) [Emphasize the spelling.] **7.** disappointing (book) . . . disappointed (reader) **8.** A person who fascinates me is a fascinating person. I am fascinated by this person. **9.** frustrating (situation) . . . frustrated (person) **10.** annoying (noise) . . . annoyed (person) **11.** shocking (event) . . . shocked (person) **12.** thrilling (experience) . . . (thrilled) person

□ **EXERCISE 28, p. 236. Participial adjectives. (Chart 11-8)**

Now that the students have a thorough understanding of the basics, this exercise begins with review verbs and then branches out into a broader vocabulary.

Check on the spelling of the participles, especially "y" vs. "i" and doubling of consonants.

If you do the exercise orally, students should read complete sentences aloud, not only the participles.

ANSWERS: **2.** satisfying **3.** terrifying **4.** terrified **5.** embarrassing **6.** broken **7.** crowded [*Elbowed* = pushed people aside with one's elbow or arm.] **8.** locked **9.** injured **10.** annoying **11.** challenging **12.** expected **13.** growing . . . balanced **14.** spoiled/ spoilt [A child who is accustomed to receiving immediately everything he/she wants is said to be "spoiled," in other words unpleasant, like rotten food.] **15.** sleeping [This saying means "Don't change anything and cause problems."] **16.** thrilling [*Hair-raising* = so frightening that it causes one's hair to stand up on one's neck or head. For animals such as dogs and cats whose neck hair stands up when riled, one says the animal's "hackles are up."] **17.** abandoned [A *tow truck* = a service vehicle that pulls broken-down cars.] **18.** required **19.** Polluted **20.** furnished **21.** dividing **22.** elected **23.** printing **24.** Experienced **25.** amazing

☐ EXERCISE 29, p. 237.   Error analysis: the passive. (Chapter 11)

ANSWERS:

2. Two people got <u>hurt</u> in the accident and were <u>taken</u> to the hospital by an ambulance.
3. The movie was so <u>boring</u> that we fell asleep after an hour.
4. The students <u>were</u> helped by the clear explanation that the teacher gave.
5. That alloy is <u>composed of</u> iron and tin.
6. The winner of the race hasn't been <u>announced</u> yet.
7. If you are <u>interested</u> in modern art, you should see the new exhibit at the museum. It is <u>fascinating.</u>
8. Progress is <u>being</u> made every day.
9. When and where <u>was</u> the automobile invented?
10. My brother and I have always been <u>interested</u> in learning more about our family tree. [A *family tree* shows relationships between ancestors and descendents.]
11. I <u>don't</u> agree with you, and I don't think you'll ever ~~to~~ convince me. [The incorrect use of *to* after a modal is not related to the passive; it slipped into the exercise because the sentence was taken verbatim from student writing. If the students query why this error is in an exercise on the passive, tell them that miscellaneous errors keep them on their toes.]
12. Each assembly kit is <u>accompanied</u> by detailed instructions.
13. Arthur was <u>given</u> an award by the city for all of his efforts in crime prevention.
14. It was late, and I was getting very <u>worried</u> about my mother.
15. The problem was very <u>puzzling</u>. I couldn't figure it out.
16. Many strange things ~~were~~ happened last night.
17. How many <u>people</u> have you ~~been~~ invited to the party?   OR   How many <u>people</u> have ~~you~~ been invited to the party?
18. When I returned home, everything <u>was quiet</u>. I <u>walked</u> to my room, <u>got undressed</u>, and <u>went</u> to bed.
19. I didn't go to dinner with them because I had already ~~been~~ eaten.
20. In class yesterday, I was <u>confused</u>. I didn't understand the lesson.
21. I couldn't move. I was very <u>frightened</u>.
22. When we were children, we <u>were</u> very afraid of caterpillars. Whenever we saw one of these monsters, we <u>ran</u> / <u>would</u> run to our house before the caterpillars could attack us. I am still <u>scared</u> when I <u>see</u> a caterpillar close to me.
23. One day, while the old man was cutting down a big tree near the stream, his axe <u>fell</u> into the river. He sat down and <u>began</u> to cry because he <u>did</u> not have enough money to buy another axe.

Chapter 12: NOUN CLAUSES

ORDER OF CHAPTER	CHARTS	EXERCISES	WORKBOOK
Introduction	12-1	Ex. 1	
Noun clauses beginning with a question word	12-2	Ex. 2 → 6	Pr. 1 → 5
Noun clauses beginning with *whether* or *if*	12-3	Ex. 7 → 8	Pr. 6
Review		Ex. 9	
Question words followed by infinitives	12-4	Ex. 10	Pr. 7
Noun clauses beginning with *that*	12-5	Ex. 11 → 16	Pr. 8 → 9
Quoted speech	12-6	Ex. 17 → 20	Pr. 10
Reported speech: verb forms in noun clauses	12-7	Ex. 21 → 25	Pr. 11 → 13
Cumulative review		Ex. 26 → 34	
Using the subjunctive in noun clauses	12-8	Ex. 35 → 36	Pr. 14
Using *-ever* words	12-9	Ex. 37	Pr. 15
Cumulative review			Pr. 16 → 17

General Notes on Chapter 12

• OBJECTIVE: One of the most common uses of conversation and writing is to report what was said by someone else. Another very common use is to express an opinion about, or reaction to, some situation. Therefore, speakers begin many sentences with "he/she/they said" and "I think" (or their equivalents) followed by a noun clause. Learners should pay special attention in this chapter to the order of words in a noun clause.

• APPROACH: The chapter focuses attention on the words that introduce noun clauses. It begins by focusing on the use of question words and the confusing similarity between noun clauses and questions. The students transform questions into noun clauses. Then many of the variations in the use of *that*-clauses are presented. Next, the students learn to punctuate quoted speech, and then to make adjustments in verb forms and pronouns as they change quotes into reported speech. Added to the end of the chapter are two short sections, one on the subjunctive in noun clauses and one on words such as *whatever, whoever, whenever, etc.*

• TERMINOLOGY: Noun clauses are referred to variously as "embedded sentences, embedded questions, indirect speech, nominal clauses," or certain kinds of complements. Words used to introduce noun clauses are labeled "conjunctions" in most dictionaries. Quoted and reported speech is also called "direct and indirect address/speech/discourse." Question words are also called "*Wh*-words" or "interrogatives (interrogative pronouns, interrogative adjectives, interrogative adverbs)." Information questions are also called "*Wh*-questions."

CHARTS 12-1 and 12-2:   NOUN CLAUSES BEGINNING WITH A QUESTION WORD

• It is often useful to substitute the pronoun "something" in the place of noun clauses. Then students replace this pronoun with a clause. For example:

Something was interesting.
What he said was interesting.

I heard something.
I heard what he said.

• The main problem for most learners is word order. Also, they may try to use *do* or *did*, as in a question.

☐ **EXERCISE 1, p. 240.   Noun clauses. (Chart 12-1)**

Give students a few silent moments to add the necessary marks. Then lead a discussion of their answers, giving special attention to groups of related items (items 3–5, 6–7, and 8–12).

ANSWERS: [The noun clauses are underlined.]   **3.** Where did Tom go? **N**o one knows. **4.** No one knows <u>where Tom went</u>.   **5.** <u>Where Tom went</u> is a secret.   **6.** What does Anna want? **W**e need to know.   **7.** We need to know <u>what Anna wants</u>.   **8.** What does Alex need? **D**o you know?   **9.** Do you know <u>what Alex needs</u>?   **10.** <u>What Alex needs</u> is a new job.   **11.** We talked about <u>what Alex needs</u>.   **12.** What do you need? **D**id you talk to your parents about <u>what you need</u>?

☐ **EXERCISE 2, p. 241.   Noun clauses beginning with a question word.   (Chart 12-2)**

Ask students to write the complete sentences on the chalkboard, then use these to identify the noun clauses, discuss their grammatical function in the sentence, and label the subjects and verbs in both the independent and dependent clauses.

Be sure students read and say the complete sentence, not only the noun clause, so they see/hear the whole context.

If your students have difficulty with this exercise, you might suggest that they use a two-step approach in developing an answer:

Step 1: *I don't know **something**.*
Step 2: *I don't know **how old he is**.*

Step 1: ***Something** was interesting.*
Step 2: ***What he was talking about** was interesting.*

ANSWERS: **3.** where you live   **4.** What she said   **5.** when they are coming
6. how much it costs   **7.** which one he wants   **8.** who is coming to the party
9. who those people are   **10.** whose pen this is   **11.** Why they left the country
12. What we are doing in class   **13.** Where she went   **14.** how many letters there are
in the English alphabet   **15.** who the mayor of New York City is   **16.** how old a person
has to be to get a driver's license   **17.** what happened   **18.** who opened the door

□ EXERCISE 3, p. 242.   Noun clauses beginning with a question word. (Chart 12-2)

This exercise has an uncomplicated pattern and can easily be used for pair work. Tell the
students to substitute the name of a classmate for the ellipsis that appears in parentheses
(. . .).

If you lead the exercise, you might want to change some of the items so that they are
more directly related to experiences in your students' lives. This exercise can start slowly
and get faster as the students become accustomed to the pattern. There's no need to rush,
however. Allow spontaneous interchanges to develop if students have interesting things
they want to say. You may wish to select students at random instead of in a predictable
order, or sometimes have the whole class respond in chorus to one or two items for a
change of pace.

Alternative format: Have the students tell you to ask someone else the question.

TEACHER: *Where does Ali live?*
SPEAKER: *I don't know. Ask Ali/him where he lives.*

Or start a chain involving three students.

TEACHER: *Maria, what is Ali's favorite color?*
SPEAKER A (Maria): *I don't know. Roberto, ask Ali what his favorite color is.*
SPEAKER B (Roberto): *Ali, what's your favorite color?*
SPEAKER C (Ali): *Blue.*

Write the pattern on the board: A: I don't know. _____, ask _____.
                                 B: _____, _____?
                                 C: (answer)

ANSWERS: I don't know . . . .
1. where (. . .) lives.   **2.** what country (. . .) is from.   **3.** how long (. . .) has been
living here.   **4.** what (. . .)'s telephone number is.   **5.** where the post office is.
6. how far it is to (Kansas City).   **7.** why (. . .) is absent.   **8.** where my book is.
9. what kind of watch (. . .) has.   **10.** why (. . .) was absent yesterday.   **11.** where
(. . .) went yesterday.   **12.** what kind of government (Italy) has.   **13.** what (. . .)'s
favorite color is.   **14.** how long (. . .) has been married.   **15.** why we are doing this
exercise.   **16.** who turned off the lights.   **17.** where (. . .) is going to eat lunch/dinner.
18. when (the semester) ends.   **19.** where (. . .) went after class yesterday.   **20.** why
(. . .) is smiling.   **21.** how often (. . .) goes to the library.   **22.** whose book that is.
23. how much that book cost.   **24.** who took my book.

☐ **EXERCISE 4, p. 242.   Noun clauses beginning with a question word. (Chart 12-2 and Appendix Unit B)**

This exercise allows students to review question formation and then compare that with noun clause formation.

ANSWERS: **2.** Why is he coming? Please tell me why he is coming.   **3.** Which flight will he be on? Please tell me which flight he will be on.   **4.** Who is going to meet him at the airport? Please tell me who is going to meet him at the airport.   **5.** Who is Jim Hunter? Please tell me who Jim Hunter is.   **6.** What is Tom's address? Please tell me what Tom 's address is.   **7.** Where does he live? Please tell me where he lives.   **8.** Where was he last week? Please tell me where he was last week.   **9.** How long has he been working for IBM? Do you know how long he has been working for IBM? [also possible: *at IBM*]   **10.** What kind of computer does he have at home? Do you know what kind of computer he has at home?

☐ **EXERCISE 5, p. 243.   Noun clauses beginning with a question word. (Chart 12-2 and Appendix Unit B)**

This exercise again compares information questions and noun clauses that begin with a question word. The dialogues in this exercise give the students typical contexts in which noun clauses might be used.

ANSWERS: **2.** is my eraser . . . it is   **3.** didn't Fred lock . . . he didn't lock   **4.** has he been . . . he has lived/has been living   **5.** you are taking . . . are you taking   **6.** are we supposed . . . we are supposed

☐ **EXERCISE 6, p. 245.   Information questions and noun clauses. (Charts 12-1 and 12-2; Appendix Unit B)**

Take some time to explain this exercise. The idea is to practice a realistic conversational exchange between two speakers in which the second speaker is verifying that s/he heard the first speaker correctly.

Make sure the students understand to switch roles every five items.

You may want to encourage the students to complete the conversation naturally, as in this example:

SPEAKER A: Who is your roommate?
SPEAKER B: You want to know who my roommate is. (Intonation may rise at the end, like a question.)
SPEAKER A: That's right. / Yes. / Right.
SPEAKER B: His/Her name is (. . .).

ANSWERS: [These depend on students' creativity.]

CHART 12-3:   NOUN CLAUSES BEGINNING WITH *WHETHER* OR *IF*

• The word "whether" always implies a choice—in this case, between *yes* and *no*.

• To avoid problems with the formal sequence of tenses in noun clauses, the main verbs in any material you might add or use for examples should not be in a past form until the students reach Chart 12-7.

□ **EXERCISE 7, p. 246.   Noun clauses beginning with WHETHER or IF.   (Chart 12-3)**

This exercise combines noun clauses that begin with question words and those that begin with *whether* or *if.*

   The exercise can be done rather quickly if you are the first speaker and a student merely gives the response. If, however, you set it up in the format below, the interactions will be more realistic and students' responses will be a little less mechanical. For example:

>   TEACHER: *Where is Yoko?*
>   A to B: *I wonder where Yoko is.*
>   B to C: *A wants to know where Yoko is. Do you know? / What do you think?*
>   C to B: *She's at home. / I don't know where she is.*

If the students work in pairs, have them switch roles once or twice during the exercise.

ANSWERS: I wonder . . . .
1. where my friend is. [also possible: *whether/if my friend is at the library.*]   **2.** whether/if we should wait for him.   **3.** whether/if I should call him.   **4.** where my dictionary is.
5. who took my dictionary. [also possible: *whether/if (. . .) took my dictionary.*]
6. whether/if (. . .) borrowed my dictionary.   **7.** who that woman is. [also possible: *if that woman is Joe's wife.*]   **8.** whether/if she needs any help.   **9.** why the sky is blue.
10. how long a butterfly lives.   **11.** what causes earthquakes.   **12.** when the first book was written.   **13.** who that man is.   **14.** what he is doing.   **15.** whether/if he is having trouble.   **16.** whether/if I should offer to help him.   **17.** how far it is to (Florida).   **18.** whether/if we have enough time to go to (Florida) over vacation.
[*over vacation* = during our vacation/holiday]   **19.** whose book this is.   **20.** whether/if it belongs to (. . .) / who(m) it belongs to.   **21.** why dinosaurs became extinct.
22. whether/if there is life on other planets.   **23.** how life began.   **24.** whether/if people will live on the moon someday.

□ **EXERCISE 8, p. 246.   Noun clauses.   (Charts 12-2 and 12-3)**

Be sure that students respond with a complete sentence, not just the noun clause.

ANSWERS: Could you please tell me . . . .
1. if this bus goes downtown?   **2.** how much this book costs?   **3.** when Flight 62 is expected to arrive?   **4.** where the nearest phone is?   **5.** whether/if this word is spelled correctly?   **6.** what time it is?   **7.** if this information is correct?   **8.** how much it costs to fly from (Chicago) to (New York)?   **9.** where the bus station is?   **10.** whose pen this is?

□ **EXERCISE 9, p. 247.   Error analysis: noun clauses.   (Charts 12-1 → 12-3)**

   ANSWERS:
   2. No one seems to know when <u>Maria will arrive</u>.
   3. I wonder why <u>Bob was late</u> for class.
   4. I don't know what ~~does~~ that word <u>means</u>.
   5. I wonder ~~does~~ <u>whether/if</u> the teacher <u>knows</u> the answer.
   6. What <u>they should</u> do about the hole in their roof is their most pressing problem.
   7. I'll ask her <u>whether/if she would like</u> some coffee or not.
   8. Be sure to tell the doctor where ~~does~~ it <u>hurts</u>.
   9. Why <u>I am</u> unhappy is something I can't explain.
   10. I wonder ~~does~~ <u>whether/if</u> Tom <u>knows</u> about the meeting or not.
   11. I need to know who <u>your teacher is</u>.
   12. I don't understand why <u>the car is not running</u> properly.
   13. My young son wants to know where ~~do~~ the stars go in the daytime.

CHART 12-4: QUESTION WORDS FOLLOWED BY INFINITIVES

• This is an example of language flexibility—two ways to say exactly the same thing. The emphasis here is on the meaning of the infinitives in this structure.

☐ **EXERCISE 10, p. 247. Question words followed by infinitives. (Chart 12-4)**

The first six items require only a change from noun clause to infinitive, but items 7–13 require students to supply an appropriate infinitive phrase. Those items also contain some challenging vocabulary, so they might require some discussion.

ANSWERS: [The infinitives are underlined.]
2. The plumber told me how <u>to fix</u> the leak in the sink. [*plumber* = a person who installs and repairs water pipes, etc.; *fix* = repair, mend; *leak* = water dripping slowly through a hole; *sink* = a wash basin in a kitchen or bathroom]   **3.** Please tell me where <u>to meet</u> you.   **4.** . . . Sandy didn't know whether <u>to believe</u> him or not. [*elaborate* /ɪlǽbərət/= involved, complex]   **5.** . . . deciding which one <u>to buy</u>.   **6.** . . . I don't know what else <u>to do</u>. [*straightened out* = in order, normal; *else* = additional]

POSSIBLE COMPLETIONS: **7.** to say [*tongue-tied* = unable to speak due to fear or surprise]
8. what to wear   **9.** to live in a dormitory or an apartment   **10.** to ski   **11.** to give (. . .)   **12.** to accept the job offer or (to) stay in graduate school   **13.** to go . . . to get there

CHART 12-5: NOUN CLAUSES BEGINNING WITH *THAT*

• Again, as with Chart 12-1, it may be helpful to substitute the pronoun "something" in these examples:
  (c) *We know* **something.**
      We know **(that)** *the world is round.*
  (d) **Something** *is obvious.*
      That she doesn't understand spoken English *is obvious.*

• Sentences beginning with a *that*-clause, such as (d) and (f), are much more common in written than in spoken English.

• Compare uses of *that:*
  (1) *This coat is mine.* **That** *coat/***that** *one/***that** *is yours. (That* is a demonstrative adjective/pronoun; pronounced /ðæt/ with stress.)

  (2) *I don't have a coat.* **That** *is a problem in cold weather.* (The demonstrative pronoun "that" refers to a whole sentence. It is pronounced /ðæt/ with stress.)

  (3) *I bought a coat* **that** *has a hood. I showed my friend the coat* **(that)** *I bought. (That* is an adjective clause pronoun referring to the noun "coat." It is pronounced /ðət/ without stress.)

  (4) *I think* **(that)** *Bob bought a new hat. (That* marks a noun clause and links it to the independent clause. It refers to nothing. It has no semantic meaning. It is not a pronoun. It is pronounced /ðət/without stress.)

☐ EXERCISE 11, p. 249. Noun clauses beginning with THAT. (Chart 12-5)

This exercise may proceed slowly with false starts and discussion. You might point out that A's responses are typical in both spoken and written English, while B's are usually written. Perhaps also include in the exercise the more informal structure shown in the example: *The world is round.* ***That*** *is a fact. (= It is a fact that the world is round. = That the world is round is a fact.)*

Encourage students to vary their responses by using words from the list. They should use the unstressed pronunciation /ðət/ in all these items.

POSSIBLE SENTENCES: **1.** It is a pity that Tim hasn't been able to make any friends. That Tim hasn't been able to make any friends is a pity. **2.** It is a well-known fact that drug abuse can ruin one's health. That drug abuse can ruin one's health is a well-known fact. **3.** It is unfair that some women do not earn equal pay for equal work. That some women do not earn equal pay for equal work is unfair. **4.** It is true that the earth revolves around the sun. That the earth revolves around the sun is true. **5.** It is surprising that Irene, who is an excellent student, failed her entrance examination. That Irene, who is an excellent student, failed her entrance examination is surprising. **6.** It is apparent that smoking can cause cancer. That smoking can cause cancer is apparent. **7.** It is a fact that English is the principal language of the business community throughout much of the world. That English is the principal language of the business community throughout much of the world is a fact.

☐ EXERCISE 12, p. 249. Noun clauses beginning with THAT. (Chart 12-5)

Give the class about three quiet minutes to think of some good ideas for their responses using *it.* Then begin the exercise.

SAMPLE RESPONSES: **1.** It is a fact that the world is round. That the world is round is a fact. **2.** It is surprising that vegetation can survive in a desert. That vegetation can survive in a desert is surprising. **3.** It is obvious that you need to wear warm clothing when it's cold. That you need to wear warm clothing when it's cold is obvious. **4.** It is too bad that prejudice influences so many people. That prejudice influences so many people is too bad. **5.** It is a well-known fact that women on the average live longer than men. That women on the average live longer than men is a well-known fact. **6.** It is unfortunate that Ali had to miss class due to illness. That Ali had to miss class due to illness is unfortunate. **7.** It is true that alcohol can cause birth defects. That alcohol can cause birth defects is true. **8.** It is strange that we are destroying our own natural resources. That we are destroying our own natural resources is strange. **9.** It is unlikely that you will live to be one hundred. That you will live to be one hundred is unlikely. **10.** It is undeniable that the sun rises in the east. That the sun rises in the east is undeniable.

☐ EXERCISE 13, p. 249. Noun clauses beginning with THAT. (Chart 12-5)

Students might produce some interesting personal responses to this exercise. If you think they are shy about expressing their opinions in class, you could have them write their responses to be seen only by you. Then you might also respond with your agreement or a differing point of view, in addition to marking their grammatical structures.

SAMPLE COMPLETIONS: **2.** It seems to me that adequate health care is the right of every citizen. **3.** It is my impression that time seems to go faster as I grow older. **4.** It is my theory that excessively thin models encourage eating disorders in young women. **5.** It is widely believed that herbs can heal. **6.** It is thought that you can't teach an old dog new tricks. **7.** It has been said that teenagers are more influenced by their peers than by their parents. **8.** Given the number of cars on the road these days, it is a miracle that more people aren't killed in automobile accidents.

□ **EXERCISE 14, p. 250. Noun clauses beginning with THAT. (Chart 12-5)**

It's assumed the students are familiar with this common pattern:
subject (a person) + **be** + *adjective/past participle* + **that***-clause*

Other words used in this pattern: *delighted, relieved, sad, upset, proud, ashamed, astonished, shocked, stunned, alarmed, angry, furious, irritated, worried, satisfied, fascinated, interested, impressed, intrigued, aware, sure, certain, lucky, fortunate.*
Students aren't expected to have difficulty with this pattern.

SAMPLE COMPLETIONS: **2.** . . . we had this time together.   **3.** . . . I wasn't able to get a ticket to the soccer finals.   **4.** . . . you have been my teacher this year.   **5.** . . . Yoko quit school.   **6.** . . . you will like this restaurant as much as we do.   **7.** . . . the prices are so reasonable.   **8.** . . . it isn't raining today.   **9.** . . . my bus was late.
10. . . . I can't make it to your wedding.

□ **EXERCISE 15, p. 250. Noun clauses beginning with THAT. (Chart 12-5)**

This exercise contains basics of English rhetoric: topic sentence followed by supporting sentences. Items 3, 4, and 5 could be turned into full compositions if your students are interested in the organization of writing.
When discussing item 4 in class, take some time to let the students share the problems they are having. Ask for completions from several or many students.

SAMPLE COMPLETIONS: **3.** One reason is that I want to study at an American university. Another reason is that I need to pass a written driver's test. A third reason is that I need to find a good part-time job.   **4.** One problem is that I'm homesick. Another problem is that I can't understand people when they speak fast. A third problem I have had is that I am having trouble finding an apartment for my family.   **5.** One advantage of owning your own car is that you don't need to rely on public transportation. Another advantage is that you can travel into the country on weekends. One disadvantage, however, of owning your own car is that it is expensive.

□ **EXERCISE 16, p. 250. Noun clauses beginning with THAT. (Chart 12-5)**

ANSWERS: **2.** The fact that Rosa didn't come made me angry.   **3.** I feel fine except for the fact that I'm a little tired.   **4.** Natasha was not admitted to the university due to the fact that she didn't pass the entrance examination.   **5.** The fact that many people in the world live in intolerable poverty must concern all of us.   **6.** The fact that Surasuk is frequently absent from class indicates his lack of interest in school.   **7.** I was not aware of the fact that I was supposed to bring my passport to the examination for identification.
8. Due to the fact that the people of the town were given no warning of the approaching tornado, there were many casualties.

CHART 12-6: QUOTED SPEECH

• As an example of the importance of using quotation marks correctly, you might put the following sentence on the chalkboard and ask students to add punctuation marks:

My dog said Mary needs a new home.

If the punctuation is incorrect, the dog might appear to be speaking!

INCORRECT: *My dog said, "Mary needs a new home."*
CORRECT: *"My dog," said Mary, "needs a new home."*

• In the chart, *said* and *asked* are used as the reporting verbs. Additional reporting verbs are *cry, exclaim, mutter, reflect, snarl.*

☐ **EXERCISES 17 and 18, p. 252.   Quoted speech.   (Chart 12-6)**

Point out the exact placement of each punctuation mark. Make sure the students are writing the quotation marks above, not on, the line. A good approach to this exercise is to have the students write the items on the chalkboard to provide a focus for class discussion.

Comic strips in a newspaper can also be used to practice writing quotations; the students can describe a comic strip in writing, using quoted speech as appropriate.

EX. 17 ANSWERS:
1. Henry said, "There is a phone call for you."
2. "There is a phone call for you," he said.
3. "There is," said Henry, "a phone call for you."
4. "There is a phone call for you. It's your sister," said Henry.
5. "There is a phone call for you," he said. "It's your sister."
6. I asked him, "Where is the phone?"
7. "Where is the phone?" she asked.
8. "Stop the clock!" shouted the referee. "We have an injured player."
9. "Who won the game?" asked the spectator.
10. "I'm going to rest for the next three hours," she said. "I don't want to be disturbed."
    "That's fine," I replied. "You get some rest. I'll make sure no one disturbs you."

EX. 18 ANSWERS:
When the police officer came over to my car, he said, "Let me see your driver's license, please."

"What's wrong, Officer?" I asked. "Was I speeding?"

"No, you weren't speeding," he replied. "You went through a red light at the corner of Fifth Avenue and Main Street. You almost caused an accident."

"Did I really do that?" I said. "I didn't see a red light."

☐ **EXERCISE 19, p. 253.   Activity: quoted speech.   (Chart 12-6)**

The conversation should be brief (a maximum of six sentences). The two speakers will probably have to repeat their dialogue, for some of the listeners will miss the exact words at first. The speakers must repeat it exactly, so it's a good idea for them to work from a script that they have written.

Have the students compare their written conversations. Emphasize the importance of accuracy in direct quotations.

If your class is very large or the room is noisy, it might be difficult for everyone to hear the conversation. In that case, you might divide the class into groups or simply ask students to imagine a conversation and write it down in order to practice quoted speech.

☐ EXERCISE 20, p. 253. Activity: quoted speech. (Chart 12-6)

In item 1, the fable shows a lazy grasshopper relaxing while ants are busily collecting food. Later, in the cold of winter, the grasshopper must beg for food from the happy ants. Ask the students what the moral of the tale is, something along the lines of "It's important to work hard and prepare for the future" or "Those who don't take care of themselves must rely on the generosity of others."

CHART 12-7: REPORTED SPEECH: VERB FORMS IN NOUN CLAUSES

• Changes in noun-clause verbs to a past form are sometimes called "the formal sequence of tenses in noun clauses."

• Tense usage in noun clauses is by no means as regular and consistent as this chart may indicate. Rules for sequence of tenses are helpful, but there are many exceptions. Encourage your students to practice the sequence of tenses as presented in this chart, but accept any viable responses in the exercises.

• You might have Student A read a quoted speech sentence in the chart, then ask Student B (book closed) to paraphrase that in reported speech. Invite comments from the class about the grammatical differences.

• Point out the changes in modals (h–k) from quoted to reported speech, and note the exceptions in (l).

☐ EXERCISE 21, p. 254. Reported speech. (Chart 12-7)

This exercise requires students: (1) to form noun clauses and (2) to adjust verb forms. The same student should read aloud both sentences in each item.

ANSWERS: **4.** if I was hungry.   **5.** (that) she wanted a sandwich.   **6.** (that) he was going to move to Ohio.   **7.** whether/if I had enjoyed my trip.   **8.** what I was talking about.   **9.** whether/if I had seen her grammar book.   **10.** (that) she didn't want to go.   **11.** where Nadia was.   **12.** whether/if I could help him with his report. **13.** (that) he might be late.   **14.** (that) I should work harder. [also possible: *to work harder*]   **15.** (that) she had to go downtown.   **16.** why the sky is blue.   **17.** why I was tired.   **18.** (that) he would come to the meeting.   **19.** whether/if Ms. Chang would be in class tomorrow / would be in class the next day.   **20.** that the sun rises in the east.   **21.** (that) someday we would be in contact with beings from outer space. [*beings* = living things]   **22.** (that) he thought (that) he would go to the library to study. [Note: In items 22, 23, and 24, the sentences contain two noun clauses, i.e., one of the noun clauses contains another noun clause.]   **23.** whether/if Omar knew what he was doing. **24.** whether/if what I had heard was true.   **25.** (that) sentences with noun clauses are a little complicated.

☐ EXERCISE 22, p. 256. Activity: reported speech. (Chart 12-7)

You might suggest that the students use formal sequence of tenses. However, in this kind of conversation, the present tense may be equally or even more appropriate because the situation is immediate.

ANSWERS: **1.** what time it was.   **2.** whether/if I could speak Arabic.   **3.** whether/if I had seen (. . .).   **4.** whether/if I would be here tomorrow.   **5.** what kind of camera I had.   **6.** what courses I was taking.   **7.** whether/if I had finished my assignment. **8.** (*free response*)   **9.** whether/if I had read . . . .   **10.** how I liked living here. **11.** if he/she could borrow . . . .   **12.** where I would be . . . .   **13.** what I was going to do . . . .   **14.** whether/if I had gone/ went . . . .   **15.** whether/if she/he could use my pen.   **16.** (*free response*)   **17.** how many people I have/had met . . . . **18.** where he/she should meet me . . . .   **19.** whether/if I understood . . . . **20.** whether/if I had gone . . . .   **21.** whether/if what I had said was/were really true. [*Were* is the subjunctive, which emphasizes the speculative nature of the question.   (See Chapter 20.)]   **22.** whether/if what I wanted to talk to her/him about was/were really important.   **23.** how I knew that what I said was really true.

☐ EXERCISE 23, p. 257.   Activity: reported speech. (Chart 12-7)

The directions require a past verb form in the noun clause. This includes the past perfect.

ANSWERS: (. . .) asked me . . . .
[See Exercise 22.]

☐ EXERCISE 24, p. 257.   Reported speech: verb forms in noun clauses. (Chart 12-7)

ANSWERS: **2.** [*leave for* = go to]   **3.** was going . . . didn't know . . . worked **4.** where the chess match would take . . . hadn't been decided   **5.** was . . . didn't think . . . would . . . speak . . . was getting . . . would be speaking   **6.** were . . . might be . . . could develop

☐ EXERCISE 25, p. 258.   Reported speech. (Chart 12-7)

The students are using parallel noun clauses in this exercise. (Parallel structure is presented in Chart 16-1.) They must notice whether the two statements are similar (use *and*) or are in a contrasting relationship (use *but*). The possible use of ellipsis (i.e., the deletion of unnecessary, repetitive words when the meaning is evident) is noted below by parentheses.

ANSWERS: **2.** she was excited about her new job and (that she) had found a nice apartment.   **3.** my Uncle Harry was in the hospital and that Aunt Sally was very worried about him.   **4.** that s/he expected us to be in class every day and that unexcused absences might affect our grades.   **5.** that Highway 66 would be closed for two months and that commuters should seek alternative routes.   **6.** that he was getting good grades but (that he) had difficulty understanding lectures.   **7.** that every obstacle was a steppingstone to success and that I should view problems in my life as opportunities to prove myself. [*steppingstone* = a flat stone to walk on; figuratively, the next step toward a goal] **8.** that she would come to the meeting but (that she) couldn't stay for more than an hour.

☐ EXERCISE 26, p. 259.   Activity: reported speech. (Charts 12-1 → 12-7)

Students can have fun with this exercise if they use their creativity. The "reporter" has to have a good memory!

ANSWERS: [These depend on students' creativity.]

☐ EXERCISE 27, p. 259.   Review: noun clauses. (Charts 12-1 → 12-7)

If students take time to use their knowledge and creativity, they can produce very interesting sentences. Encourage them to do this, then reward their successes.

ANSWERS: [These depend on students' creativity.]

☐ **EXERCISE 28, p. 259.   Activity: noun clauses. (Charts 12-1 → 12-7)**

Students' answers will vary. They can read each other's to discover the variations and to help check for mistakes.

POSSIBLE ANSWERS:
1. Alex asked me what I was doing. I replied that I was drawing a picture.
2. Ann asked Sue if she wanted to go to a movie Sunday night. Sue said that she would like to but that she had to study.
3. The little boy asked Mrs. Robinson how old she was. She told him that it was not polite to ask people their age.
4. My sister asked me if there was anything I especially wanted to watch on TV. I replied that there was a show at 8:00 that I had been waiting to see for a long time. She asked me what it was. When I told her that it was a documentary about green sea turtles, she wondered why I wanted to see that. I explained that I was doing a research paper on sea turtles and thought I might be able to get some good information from the documentary. I suggested that she watch [subjunctive (See Chart 12-8.)] it with me. She declined and said she wasn't especially interested in green sea turtles.

☐ **EXERCISE 29, p. 260.   Activity: noun clauses. (Charts 12-1 → 12-7)**

This exercise asks the students to invent a story based on a picture. It's intended as a fun writing exercise. Tell them to include all five people in the picture in their story.

The point of this exercise is for the students to use reported speech in their writing. They could, of course, also use quoted speech if they wish. Be sure they report the story in the past.

The class might enjoy orally sharing their stories to see how closely their stories resemble each other.

☐ **EXERCISE 30, p. 261.   Error analysis: noun clauses. (Charts 12-1 → 12-7)**

You might want to let the students know that all of the items in this exercise come from the written work of students just like them, and that these errors are common. In language learning, an error in usage is a learning opportunity. Encourage the students to feel good about their ability to spot and correct these typical noun clause errors, and emphasize that self-monitoring is an important part of their own writing process.

ANSWERS:
1. Tell the taxi driver where ~~do~~ you want to go.
2. My roommate came into the room and asked me why <u>I wasn't</u> in class. I <u>told him / said (that) I was</u> waiting for a telephone call from my family.   OR   My roommate came into the room and asked ~~me,~~ "Why aren't you in class?" I said, "I am waiting for a telephone call from my family."
3. It was my first day at the university, and I <u>was</u> on my way to my first class. I wondered who else <u>would</u> be in the class and what <u>the teacher would be like</u>.
4. He asked me what ~~did~~ I <u>intended</u> to do after I <u>graduated</u>.
5. Many of the people in the United States do not know much about geography. For example, people will ask you where <u>Japan is located</u>.
6. What ~~does~~ a patient <u>tells</u> a doctor ~~it~~ is confidential.
7. What my friend and I did ~~it~~ was our secret. We didn't even tell our parents <u>what we did</u>.
8. The doctor asked <u>whether/if</u> I felt okay. I told him that I <u>didn't</u> feel well.
9. <u>It is</u> clear that the ability to use a computer ~~it~~ is an important skill in the modern world.

10. I asked him, "What kind of movies <u>do you like?</u>" He said ~~me~~, "I like romantic movies." OR I asked him what kind of movies <u>he liked</u>. He <u>told</u> me / said <u>(that)</u> he <u>liked</u> romantic movies.

11. "<u>Is it</u> true you almost drowned?" my friend asked me. "Yes," I said. "I'm really glad to be alive. It was really frightening."

12. <u>The fact that</u> I almost drowned makes me very careful about water safety whenever I go swimming.

13. I didn't know where I <u>was</u> supposed to get off the bus, so I asked the driver where <u>the science museum was</u>. She <u>told</u> me the name of the street. She said she <u>would</u> tell me when <u>I should</u> get off the bus.

14. My mother did not live with us. When other children asked me where ~~was~~ <u>my mother was</u>, I told them she <u>was</u> going to come to visit me very soon.

15. When I asked the taxi driver to drive faster, he said, "I will drive faster if you pay me more." OR he said he would drive faster if I paid him more. At that time I didn't care how much <u>it would</u> cost, so I told him to go as fast as he <u>could</u>.

16. We looked back to see where <u>we were</u> and how far <u>we were</u> from camp. We <u>didn't</u> know, so we decided to turn back. We <u>were</u> afraid that we <u>had wandered</u> too far.
    [*wander* = walk with no definite goal]

17. After the accident, I opened my eyes slowly and <u>realized</u> that I <u>was</u> still alive.

18. My country is prospering due to ~~it is a~~ <u>the fact</u> that it has become a leading producer of oil.

19. <u>It is</u> true that one must know <u>**E**</u>nglish in order to study at an <u>**A**</u>merican university.

20. My mother told me ~~what it was~~ the purpose of our visit. OR what ~~it~~ <u>the purpose of our visit was</u>.

□ **EXERCISE 31, p. 262.   Activity: noun clauses. (Charts 12-1 → 12-7)**

You might want to set a limit on length for item 1 (e.g., a minimum of five sentences and a maximum of eight). Students should underline the sentences that include the assigned pattern so that you can find them easily.

When you mark the students' papers, focus mainly on sentences that include reported speech. Reward their grammatical successes.

For item 2, the letter can be written out of class, then the summary in class. You should probably set a length limit for the letter (e.g., one page). Writing a letter to a classmate can be a fun activity. Make sure that each student is the recipient of a letter. Perhaps recipients' names can be drawn from a hat.

□ **EXERCISE 32, p. 262.   Activity: noun clauses. (Charts 12-1 → 12-7)**

This exercise uses meaningful, creative communication as the basis for written work that reinforces the grammar the students have been concentrating on. The written reports can be quite short and succinct.

The topics are designed to engender differing points of view and encourage open discussion. For example, not everyone will agree on what is most important in life, or what jobs women can and cannot do. Also, you or the class can provide other topics for discussion relevant to contemporary world events or issues in your city or school.

Another possibility is to use the items as debate topics, assigning certain students to argue in favor of the statement and others against. Some students, however, find it difficult to argue in favor of something they don't believe.

□ **EXERCISE 33, p. 262.   Activity: noun clauses. (Charts 12-1 → 12-7)**

As an ongoing activity through many classes, have one or two students per day give their one-minute speeches until everyone in the class has had an opportunity to speak. Allow writing time in class.

SUGGESTION: Give the written reports to the student who spoke and ask her/him to correct them. It is enlightening for a speaker to read what others think s/he said.

One problem here is to encourage reticent students to speak in front of the whole class, and to speak clearly so that their classmates can take notes and report what was said. On the other hand, it may be difficult to keep some eager speakers within the one-minute limit.

If some students object to listening to each other's imperfect English, you might remind them that in future years they will probably use English to communicate with people who, like them, are not native speakers of English.

□ **EXERCISE 34, p. 263.   Activity: noun clauses.   (Charts 12-1 → 12-7)**

The interviewee can be a member of your family, a faculty member, a community leader, your next-door neighbor—students enjoy interviewing a native speaker of English. Whoever the interviewee is, prepare the students. Give them information about the person and ask them to prepare questions before they come to class on the day of the interview. Record the interview (on audio or video tape) so that the accuracy of quotations can be checked (and students can proudly hear their own public English).

All students will interview the same person, so their written reports will be similar. Therefore, you might choose the best one for "publication." As an alternative, you could arrange for several people to be available for interviews and divide the class into groups. Then students' reports will differ, and you could publish more than one.

CHART 12-8:   USING THE SUBJUNCTIVE IN NOUN CLAUSES
• The subjunctive is referred to as a "mood" in traditional grammar books. This is unimportant for your students to know. The important point is for them to understand and use the subjunctive appropriately. It is a useful structure because the words used to introduce noun clauses containing a subjunctive verb are common expressions.

□ **EXERCISES 35 and 36, p. 264.   Using the subjunctive in noun clauses.   (Chart 12-8)**

Give students a moment to read and think before they answer.

EX. 35 POSSIBLE ANSWERS: **2.** call   **3.** tell   **4.** speak   **5.** write/send   **6.** see
7. contact   **8.** be

EX. 36 ANSWERS: **1.** take   **2.** be named   **3.** stay   **4.** be postponed   **5.** be admitted   **6.** be controlled . . . (be) eliminated   **7.** have   **8.** be   **9.** know
10. be   **11.** be permitted   **12.** not be [Note the word order with a negative.]
13. return   **14.** be built   **15.** not tell . . . be told

┌───┐
│ **CHART 12-9: USING -*EVER* WORDS**   │
└───┘

• These words are of fairly low frequency, but deserve a moment's notice. Concentrate on meaning here. The text treats these words principally as vocabulary items because the underlying grammatical structures are complicated.

• Mention that *so* might be added with no change in meaning: *whosoever, whatsoever, wheresoever, howsoever.* This is more common in legal or religious contexts than in everyday speech or writing.

☐ **EXERCISE 37, p. 265.   Using -EVER words. (Chart 12-9)**

Lead the class through this exercise fairly quickly, but discuss any questions that arise.

ANSWERS: **2.** whenever   **3.** whatever   **4.** whichever   **5.** whatever
6. Whoever   **7.** whatever   **8.** however   **9.** whoever   **10.** wherever
11. whomever/whoever . . . whomever/whoever   **12.** whatever ["the end justifies the means" = achieving your goal (the end) is more important than the method (means) of achieving it]
13. whichever   **14.** wherever   **15.** whatever . . . wherever . . . whenever . . . whomever/whoever . . . however

Chapter 13: ADJECTIVE CLAUSES

ORDER OF CHAPTER	CHARTS	EXERCISES	WORKBOOK
Introduction	13-1		
Using *who, who(m), which, that, whose*	13-2 → 13-6	Ex. 1 → 13	Pr. 1 → 5
Using *where* and *when*	13-7 → 13-8	Ex. 14 → 16	Pr. 6
Review		Ex. 17 → 18	Pr. 7 → 8
Using adjective clauses to modify pronouns	13-9	Ex. 19 → 20	
Punctuating adjective clauses	13-10	Ex. 21 → 23	Pr. 9 → 12
Special adjective clauses	13-11 → 13-13	Ex. 24 → 32	Pr. 13
Reducing adjective clauses to adjective phrases	13-14 → 13-15	Ex. 33 → 36	Pr. 14
Cumulative review		Ex. 37 → 42	Pr. 15 → 20

General Notes on Chapter 13

• OBJECTIVE: Learners understand their need to express more complex relationships between ideas than is possible in simple sentences alone. Even with a limited vocabulary, those who can employ dependent clauses can greatly increase their communicative competence in the new language.

• APPROACH: The chapter begins with exercises on linking words and their position in the adjective clause. All possible patterns of restrictive adjective clauses using subject pronouns, object pronouns, or *whose* are presented first. Then *where* and *when* are added, followed by a series of summary oral exercises that practice all of these patterns. The use of commas in punctuating restrictive and nonrestrictive clauses is explained next, and then some less frequent uses of adjective clauses. Finally, the reduction of adjective clauses to phrases is practiced.

• TERMINOLOGY: A "clause" is defined as "a structure containing a subject and verb." Clauses can be either independent/main (like a simple, self-standing sentence) or dependent/subordinate (not meaningful by themselves). A "phrase" is defined as "a multiword structure that does not contain a subject-verb combination." There are many kinds of phrases.

The term "relative pronoun" is not used in the text. Relative pronouns (e.g., *who, whom, which*) are called "subject pronouns" and "object pronouns" to emphasize their connection with personal pronouns (e.g., *she, them, it*) in both meaning and grammatical function.

The terms "restrictive" and "nonrestrictive" are footnoted but otherwise not used. Restrictive/essential/identifying clauses are called "clauses that don't need commas," and nonrestrictive/nonessential/nonidentifying clauses are called "clauses that need commas."

CHART 13-1:   INTRODUCTION

• In literature and in academic publications, writers often construct complicated sentences with multiple clauses. This has the effect of highlighting some information while putting other details in the background. Students need not try to produce such exceedingly complex sentences, but they should understand the concept of subordination: that a dependent clause is subordinate in structure as well as in meaning to the independent clause. For intermediate students, the immediate task is to learn to control an independent clause with only one dependent clause correctly attached to it. This can be quite challenging. For advanced students, the task is to review the basic forms of adjective clauses so that they can correct possible problems in their own usage. All learners need to gain experience and fluency in this fundamental and useful structure.

CHART 13-2:   ADJECTIVE CLAUSE PRONOUNS USED AS THE SUBJECT

• The verb "modify" means "change" or "limit the meaning." Thus, the traditional grammarian says that an adjective modifies a noun. Refer students to Appendix Chart A-3, p. A4, for an understanding of the terms "modify" and "adjective." Point out that an adjective changes or limits the meaning of a noun slightly *(a friendly woman, an old woman, a tall woman)* and that an adjective clause likewise changes or limits the meaning of a noun slightly *(the woman who helped me, a woman I saw in the park, the woman the teacher was talking to)*. Point out the useful function of adjective clauses: adding details about a noun in the independent clause, i.e., expanding the amount of information in a sentence.

• Stylistically and idiomatically, *who* is usually preferred to *that*, and *that* is preferred to *which* when they are used as subject relative pronouns. (See Chart 13-5.) At this point, the students are being asked to learn all possible correct patterns.

• Point out that the adjective clause follows immediately after the noun that it modifies. This may interrupt the main clause. (Advise students that an adjective clause should be put as close as possible to the noun it modifies, but at times there may be an interrupting element, usually a modifying prepositional phrase: *I didn't recognize the man **in the blue suit** who waved at me. The student **from Rome** who lives down the hall has invited me to a party.*)

☐ **EXERCISE 1, p. 268.   Adjective clause pronouns used as subjects.   (Chart 13-2)**

ANSWERS: **2.** The girl <u>who/that won the race</u> is happy.   **3.** The student <u>who/that sits next to me</u> is from China.   [Point out subject–verb agreement: In item 3, *who/that* refers to a singular noun *(student)*, so the adjective clause verb *(sits)* is singular. In item 4, *who/that* refers to a plural noun *(students)*, so the adjective clause verb *(sit)* is plural.]   **4.** The students <u>who/that sit in the front row</u> are from China.   **5.** We are studying sentences <u>which/that contain adjective clauses</u>.   **6.** I am using a sentence <u>which/that contains an adjective clause</u>.   **7.** Algebra problems contain letters <u>which/that stand for unknown numbers</u>.   **8.** The taxi driver <u>who/that took me to the airport</u> was friendly.

CHART 13-3:   **ADJECTIVE CLAUSE PRONOUNS USED AS THE OBJECT OF A VERB**

• Review the difference between "subject" and "object" if necessary. Also, recall that the symbol "Ø" means "nothing" (no word is needed here).

• Discuss informal vs. formal usage (e.g., informal = everyday conversation, a letter to a friend; formal = a business or school report, academic journal, encyclopedia). Ask your students when or if they need to use formal English. The object form "whom" is used primarily in formal writing. Even in nonrestrictive clauses (Chart 13-10), *who* seems to be preferred to *whom* by most native speakers (e.g., *My best friend,* **who** *nobody else seems to like, needs to learn how to get along with people*).

• In everyday English, an object relative pronoun is usually omitted from a restrictive clause. Students should have control of all possibilities, however, so that they understand what they are omitting. Also, they will learn in Chart 13-10 that in nonrestrictive clauses they cannot omit the object pronoun.

• Some languages connect clauses similar to these with a conjunction, not a pronoun. Those languages, therefore, keep the object pronoun in its normal position in the dependent clause. For some students, transferring this pattern may lead to an ungrammatical sentence in English. For example:
INCORRECT: *The book that I read* **it** *yesterday was enjoyable.*
INCORRECT: *I didn't know the man who(m) I spoke to* **him.**

☐ **EXERCISE 2, p. 269.   Adjective clause pronouns used the object of a verb.
          (Chart 13-3)**

ERRATUM: Item 5 should read: "The man is standing over there. Ann brought him to the party." This is corrected in subsequent printings.

ANSWERS: **1.** The book <u>which/that/Ø I read</u> was good.   **2.** I liked the woman <u>who(m)/ that/Ø I met at the party last night</u>.   **3.** I liked the composition <u>which/that/Ø you wrote</u>.   **4.** The people <u>who(m)/that/Ø we visited yesterday</u> were very nice.   **5.** The man <u>who(m)/that/Ø I was telling you about</u> is standing over there.   OR   . . . <u>about whom I was telling you</u> is standing over there.

CHART 13-4: ADJECTIVE CLAUSE PRONOUNS USED AS THE OBJECT OF A PREPOSITION

- Common problems:
  - (1) repeating the preposition: . . . *the woman about whom I told you about.*
  - (2) omitting the preposition: . . . *the music that we listened last night.*

- Some older grammar books and style manuals stated that a preposition must never be the last word in a sentence. Today it is quite acceptable to end with a preposition, as in examples (b), (c), and (d), except possibly in the most formal writing. The writer as stylist would have to make that determination, but grammatically there is no error in ending a sentence with a preposition.

☐ **EXERCISE 3, p. 269.** **Adjective clause pronouns used as the object of a preposition. (Chart 13-4)**

ANSWERS: **1.** The meeting <u>which/that/Ø I went to</u> was interesting.   OR   The meeting <u>to which I went</u> was interesting.   **2.** The man <u>to whom I talked yesterday</u> was very kind.   OR   The man <u>who(m)/that/Ø I talked to yesterday</u> was very kind.   **3.** I must thank the people <u>from whom I got a present</u>.   OR   I must thank the people <u>who(m)/that/Ø I got a present from</u>.   **4.** The picture <u>which/that/Ø she was looking at</u> was beautiful.   OR   The picture <u>at which she was looking</u> was beautiful.   **5.** The man <u>about whom I was telling you</u> is over there.   OR   The man <u>who(m)/that/Ø I was telling you about</u> is over there. **6.** I ran into a woman <u>with whom I had gone to elementary school</u>.   OR   I ran into a woman <u>who(m)/that/Ø I had gone to elementary school with</u>.   **7.** The topic <u>about which Omar talked</u> was interesting.   OR   The topic <u>which/that/Ø Omar talked about</u> was interesting.   **8.** The people <u>to whom I spoke</u> were friendly.   OR   The people <u>who(m)/that/Ø I spoke to</u> were friendly. [*spoke **with** is also possible with no difference in meaning*] **9.** Olga wrote on a topic <u>about which she knew nothing</u>.   OR   Olga wrote on a topic <u>which/that/Ø she knew nothing about</u>.   **10.** The candidate <u>for whom I voted</u> didn't win the election.   OR   The candidate <u>who(m)/that/Ø I voted for</u> didn't win the election.

☐ **EXERCISE 4, p. 270.** **Adjective clauses. (Charts 13-2 → 13-4)**

ANSWERS: **1.** <u>I met last night</u>—Did I tell you about the woman <u>who(m)/that I met last night</u>?   **2.** <u>I was dancing with</u>—The woman <u>who(m)/that/Ø I was dancing with</u> stepped on my toe.   OR   The woman <u>with whom I was dancing</u> stepped on my toe.   **3.** <u>Joe is writing</u>—The report <u>which/that/Ø Joe is writing</u> must be finished by Friday.   **4.** <u>who examined the sick child</u>—The doctor <u>who/that examined the sick child</u> was gentle. **5.** <u>I was waiting for</u>—The people <u>who(m)/that/Ø I was waiting for</u> were late.   OR   The people <u>for whom I was waiting</u> were late.   **6.** <u>that occurred in California</u>—Did you hear about the earthquake <u>which occurred in California</u>?

CHART 13-5: USUAL PATTERNS OF ADJECTIVE CLAUSES

• In sum, native speakers generally prefer *who* for people and *that* for things when the relative pronoun is the subject of the clause, and object relative pronouns are usually omitted in restrictive clauses.

• Although usual in everyday usage, omitting the object pronoun is not necessary, and indeed at times speakers/writers consciously choose to include it for clarity. On the other hand, inclusion of the object pronoun regularly can make one's English sound stilted and unnatural.

• You might caution the students that sometimes it is not possible to omit the object pronoun, as they will discover in Chart 13-10, where nonrestrictive adjective clauses are discussed. There are, however, no nonrestrictive adjective clauses in the exercises at this point, so you may prefer simply to keep the students' focus on the typical patterns of restrictive clauses, just as the text does.

□ **EXERCISE 5, p. 270. Adjective clauses. (Charts 13-2 → 13-5)**

Students can discuss these answers in small groups or prepare them individually as written seatwork. You should walk around the classroom as they work and answer any questions they have.

ANSWERS: **1.** She lectured on a topic <u>which/that/Ø I know very little about</u>. OR She lectured on a topic <u>about which I know very little</u>. [usual: *topic I know very little about*] **2.** The students <u>who/that were absent from class</u> missed the assignment. [usual: *students who were absent from class*] **3.** Yesterday I ran into an old friend <u>who(m)/that/Ø I hadn't seen for years</u>. [usual: *friend I hadn't seen for years*] **4.** The young women <u>who(m)/that/Ø we met at the meeting last night</u> are all from Japan. [usual: *women we met at the meeting last night*] **5.** I am reading a book <u>which/that was written by Jane Austen</u>. [usual: *book that was written by Jane Austen*] **6.** The man <u>who(m)/that/Ø I spoke to</u> gave me good advice. OR The man <u>to whom I spoke</u> gave me good advice. [usual: *man I spoke to*] **7.** I returned the money <u>which/that/Ø I had borrowed from my roommate</u>. [usual: *money I had borrowed from my roommate*] **8.** The dogcatcher caught the dog <u>which/that had bitten my neighbor's daughter</u>. [usual: *dog that had bitten my neighbor's daughter*] **9.** I read about a man <u>who/that keeps chickens in his apartment</u>. [usual: *man who keeps chickens in his apartment*]

□ **EXERCISE 6, p. 271. Adjective clauses. (Charts 13-2 → 13-5)**

This is a review exercise.

ANSWERS: **1.** In our village, there were many people <u>who</u> didn't have much money. OR In our village, many people didn't have much money. **2.** I enjoyed the book (that) you told me to read ~~it~~. **3.** I still remember the man who ~~he~~ taught me to play the violin when I was a boy. **4.** I showed my father a picture of the car I am going to buy ~~it~~ as soon as I save enough money. **5.** The woman about <u>whom</u> I was talking ~~about~~ suddenly walked into the room. OR The woman ~~about~~ <u>who(m)/that/Ø</u> I was talking about suddenly walked into the room. I hope she didn't hear me. **6.** Almost all of the people <u>who/that</u> appear on television wear makeup. **7.** I don't like to spend time with people <u>who/that lose</u> their temper easily. **8.** The boy drew pictures of people at an airport <u>who/that were</u> waiting for their planes. OR The boy drew pictures of people <u>who/that were</u> waiting for their planes at an airport. **9.** People who <u>work</u> in the hunger program ~~they~~ estimate that 3500 people in the world die from starvation every day of the year. **10.** In one corner of the marketplace, an old man ~~who~~ was playing a violin. OR In one corner of the marketplace, <u>there was</u> an old man who was playing a violin.

☐ **EXERCISE 7, p. 272.   Adjective clauses.   (Charts 13-2 → 13-5)**

This exercise is good practice for listening comprehension skill and for fluency of oral production.

Note the direction to omit the object pronoun. The intention is to encourage typical usage.

POSSIBLE ANSWERS: **1.** about the letter she/he got (yesterday) from her/his brother (yesterday).   **2.** about the letter he/she wrote to (. . .)   **3.** about the party he/she went to yesterday.   **4.** about some people he/she met at that party.   **5.** about the country he/she took a trip to. . . .   **6.** some experiences he/she had in (. . .)   **7.** the small town she/he used to live in. [Check on the past tense forms.]   **8.** the program he/she watched.   **9.** the job she/he interviewed for.   **10.** the report he/she had to write . . . .   **11.** the person she/he talked to. . . .   **12.** the meeting (for new employees) he/she went to (for new employees).

☐ **EXERCISE 8, p. 273.   Adjective clauses.   (Charts 13-2 → 13-5)**

Note that the first example is in the past tense, so *read* = /rɛd/.

Like the preceding exercise, this kind of practice is intended to promote fluency and ease of usage.

POSSIBLE ANSWERS: **1.** Yes, the chair I am sitting in is comfortable.   **2.** Yes, the man I saw was wearing a brown suit.   **3.** Yes, the woman I talked to answered my questions.   **4.** Yes, the woman who stepped on my toe apologized.   **5.** Yes, most of the students who took the test passed.   **6.** Yes, the meat I had for dinner last night was good.   **7.** Yes, the woman who shouted at me was angry.   **8.** Yes, I know the person who is sitting next to me. [Also possible: *the person sitting next to me.* (See Chart 13-14.)]   **9.** Yes, I recognize the woman who came into the room.   **10.** Yes, the coat I bought keeps me warm.   **11.** Yes, the TV program I watched last night was good.   **12.** Yes, I finished the book I was reading.   **13.** Yes, the hotel I stayed at was in the middle of the city.   OR Yes, the hotel where I stayed was in the middle of the city. [See Chart 13-7 for the use of *where.*]   **14.** Yes, the exercise we are doing is easy.   **15.** Yes, the waiter who served me at the restaurant was polite.   **16.** Yes, the student who stopped me in the hall asked me for the correct time.   **17.** Yes, all the students who are sitting in this room can speak English.   **18.** Yes, I found the book I was looking for.   **19.** Yes, the boots/tennis shoes/loafers I am wearing are comfortable.   **20.** Yes, I had a conversation with the taxi driver who took me to the bus station.   **21.** Yes, I thanked the man who opened the door for me.   **22.** Yes, the clerk who cashed my check asked for identification.   **23.** Yes, the package I got in the mail was from my parents.   **24.** Yes, the man who stopped me on the street asked me for directions.

☐ **EXERCISE 9, p. 274.   Adjective clauses.   (Charts 13-4 and 13-5)**

Encourage omission of relative pronouns, but accept any correct pattern the student produces.

If you lead the exercise, adapt the items to your particular students as much as possible, changing the vocabulary, omitting some items, making up other items of your own.

ERRATUM: In the footnote to item 3, the last word should be "those" not "x." How things like this slip into a book is a mystery to its author and editors, but it is corrected in subsequent printings.

ANSWERS: [These depend on students' creativity.]
   1. [*studying at* = enrolled in; *studying in* = inside the building]

```
┌─────────────────────────────────────────────────────────┐
│  CHART 13-6:   USING WHOSE                                │
└─────────────────────────────────────────────────────────┘
```

• *Whose* can be troublesome for students. It has a relatively low frequency, so they aren't as familiar with these adjective clauses as with the ones in the preceding charts. Emphasize that *whose* functions as a possessive <u>adjective</u> and needs to be paired with a noun.

☐ **EXERCISE 10, p. 275.   Using WHOSE in adjective clauses. (Chart 13-6)**

Word order in this structure is difficult for learners. Take time with this exercise and use the chalkboard so that they can see the patterns.

ANSWERS: [The adjective clauses are <u>underlined</u>.]
2. I apologized to the woman <u>whose coffee I spilled</u>.   **3.** The man <u>whose wallet was stolen</u> called the police.   **4.** I met the woman <u>whose husband is the president of the corporation</u>.   **5.** The professor <u>whose course I am taking</u> is excellent.   **6.** Mr. North teaches a class for students <u>whose native language is not English</u>.   **7.** The people <u>whose house we visited</u> were nice.   **8.** I live in a dormitory <u>whose residents come from many countries</u>.   **9.** I have to call the man <u>whose umbrella I accidentally picked up after the meeting</u>.   **10.** The man <u>whose beard caught on fire</u> when he lit a cigarette poured a glass of water on his face. [Note: *when he lit a cigarette* is an adverb clause connected to an adjective clause.]

☐ **EXERCISE 11, p. 275.   Using WHOSE in adjective clauses. (Chart 13-6)**

For a review of *a/an* vs. *the,* see Chart 7-8 (a) and (b). An adjective clause identifies the noun it modifies, i.e., makes it specific for the listener/reader. Therefore, many nouns modified by an adjective clause will use *the.*

ANSWERS: **1.** Maria is **a** student. I found her book. Maria is **the** student <u>whose book I found</u>.   **2.** Omar is **a** student. I borrowed his dictionary. Omar is **the** student <u>whose dictionary I borrowed</u>.   **3.** I used **a** woman's phone. I thanked her. I thanked **the** woman <u>whose phone I used</u>.   **4.** I broke **a** child's toy. He started to cry. **The** child <u>whose toy I broke</u> started to cry.   **5.** I stayed at **a** family's house. They were very kind. **The** family <u>at whose house I stayed</u> were very kind.   OR   **The** family <u>whose house I stayed at</u> were very kind.   **6.** **A** woman's purse was stolen. She called the police. **The** woman <u>whose purse was stolen</u> called the police.   **7.** (Placido Domingo) is **a** singer. I like his music best. (Placido Domingo) is **the** singer <u>whose music I like best</u>.   **8.** Everyone tried to help **a** family. Their house had burned down. Everyone tried to help **the** family <u>whose house had burned down</u>.

☐ **EXERCISE 12, p. 276.   Using WHOSE in adjective clauses. (Chart 13-6)**

There in these sentences is spoken with emphasis, as if one were pointing at someone. This is very different from the expletive *There + be* (Chart 6-4), which is rarely followed by *the.*

ANSWERS: **3.** There is the boy <u>whose father is a doctor</u>.   **4.** There is the girl <u>whose mother is a dentist</u>.   **5.** There is the person <u>whose picture was in the newspaper</u>.
6. There is the woman <u>whose car was stolen</u>.   **7.** There is the man <u>whose daughter won a gold medal at the Olympic Games</u>.   **8.** There is the woman <u>whose keys I found</u>.
9. There is the teacher <u>whose class I'm in</u>.   **10.** There is the man <u>whose wife we met</u>.   **11.** There is the author <u>whose book I read</u>.   **12.** There is the student <u>whose lecture notes I borrowed</u>.

□ **EXERCISE 13, p. 276. Using WHOSE in adjective clauses. (Chart 13-6)**

ANSWERS: **3.** The students <u>whose names were called</u> raised their hands. **4.** Jack knows a man <u>whose name is William Blueheart Duckbill, Jr.</u> **5.** The police came to question the woman <u>whose purse was stolen outside the supermarket.</u> **6.** The day care center was established to take care of children <u>whose parents work during the day.</u> [*day care center =* a place where very young children are cared for while their parents are at work] **7.** We couldn't find the person <u>whose car was blocking the driveway.</u> **8.** The professor told the three students <u>whose reports were turned in late</u> that he would accept the papers this time but never again.

CHARTS 13-7 and 13-8: USING *WHERE* AND *WHEN*

- *Where* and *when* substitute for prepositional phrases and serve as the link between an adjective clause and the noun that it modifies.

- Note the special rules for the prepositions in all the examples.

□ **EXERCISE 14, p. 277. Using WHERE in adjective clauses. (Chart 13-7)**

ANSWERS: **1.** The city <u>where we spent our vacation</u> was beautiful. OR The city <u>which/that/Ø we took our vacation in</u> was beautiful. OR The city <u>in which we took our vacation</u> was beautiful. **2.** That is the restaurant <u>where I will meet you.</u> OR That is the restaurant <u>which/that/Ø I will meet you at.</u> OR That is the restaurant <u>at which I will meet you.</u> [Either *at* or *in* may be used with nearly the same meaning in these sentences.] **3.** The town <u>where I grew up</u> is small. OR The town <u>which/that/Ø I grew up in</u> is small. OR The town <u>in which I grew up</u> is small. **4.** That is the drawer <u>where I keep my jewelry.</u> OR That is the drawer <u>which/that/Ø I keep my jewelry in.</u> OR That is the drawer <u>in which I keep my jewelry.</u>

□ **EXERCISE 15, p. 277. Using WHEN in adjective clauses. (Chart 13-8)**

You may wish to review the use of prepositions *(in, on, at)* with time phrases: *at* + clock time, *on* + a day, *in* + longer periods.

ANSWERS: **1.** Monday is the day <u>when we will come.</u> OR The day <u>that/Ø we will come</u> is Monday. OR The day <u>on which we will come</u> is Monday. **2.** 7:05 is the time <u>when my plane arrives.</u> OR 7:05 is the time <u>that/Ø my plane arrives.</u> OR 7:05 is the time <u>at which my plane arrives.</u> **3.** July is the month <u>when the weather is usually the hottest.</u> OR July is the month <u>that/Ø the weather is usually the hottest.</u> OR July is the month <u>in which the weather is usually the hottest.</u> **4.** 1960 is the year <u>when the revolution took place.</u> OR 1960 is the year <u>that/Ø the revolution took place.</u> OR 1960 is the year <u>in which the revolution took place.</u>

☐ EXERCISE 16, p. 278. Using WHERE and WHEN in adjective clauses. (Charts 13-7 and 13-8)

ANSWERS: **3.** A cafe is a small restaurant <u>where people can get a light meal.</u> [Note: This is the form of many definitions: *a . . .is a . . . place where/time when/thing that/person who*]
4. Every neighborhood in Brussels has small cafes <u>where customers drink coffee and eat pastries.</u> **5.** There was a time <u>when dinosaurs dominated the earth.</u> **6.** The house <u>where I was born and grew up</u> was destroyed in an earthquake ten years ago.
7. Summer is the time of year <u>when the weather is the hottest.</u> **8.** The miser hid his money in a place <u>where it was safe from robbers.</u> **9.** There came a time <u>when the miser had to spend his money.</u> **10.** His new shirt didn't fit, so Dan took it back to the store <u>where he'd bought it.</u>

☐ EXERCISE 17, p. 278. Adjective clauses. (Charts 13-2 → 13-8)

Students should use *the* in their responses, not because it is required grammatically (except for items 4 and 6 because of the ordinal determiner), but because its use is likely in this context of the speaker remembering someone in particular or something particular s/he has done.

ANSWERS: [These depend on students' life experiences.]

☐ EXERCISE 18, p. 279. Activity: adjective clauses. (Charts 13-2 → 13-8)

The idea of this exercise is to engender as natural a conversation as possible while guiding the grammar structures used. It gives the students the opportunity to practice what they've learned by combining free response with controlled structure use.

Given that this is a somewhat complicated exercise format, it might work best if teacher-led (in terms of time alotted especially), but if the time is available, students enjoy taking responsibility for the quality of their language practice in the interaction of small groups. And this is a good point in the chapter for student-student interactive work.

If you lead the exercise, it is not necessary to use the exact words in the book. Use ideas and things that occur naturally in your classroom with your students. Encourage them to exchange real information or, if they prefer, to invent an interesting response.

TEACHER (looking around the room): *Who got a letter yesterday?*
  (Nod at or name a student with an upraised hand.)
SPEAKER A: *I did.* OR *I got a letter yesterday.* OR *Me.*
  (The use of an object pronoun here, i.e., *me,* is common in everyday informal English although not grammatically correct.)
TEACHER: *Who was it from?*
SPEAKER A: *My brother.*
TEACHER (to another student): *Can you summarize this information?* (Point to the word "The" that you have written on the chalkboard as a way of reminding the student how to begin.)
SPEAKER B: *The letter (. . .) got yesterday was from his brother.*

ANSWERS: [These depend on students' creativity.]

```
┌─────────────────────────────────────────────────────────────────────────┐
│   CHART 13-9:   USING ADJECTIVE CLAUSES TO MODIFY PRONOUNS                │
├─────────────────────────────────────────────────────────────────────────┤
```

• Discourage students from using adjective clauses to modify personal pronouns. Sometimes students get enthusiastic about gaining control of adjective clauses and want to use them everywhere, including following personal pronouns, for example, #*I, who am a student from Malaysia, am studying English.* Explain that such structures, even though grammatically logical, rarely occur idiomatically.

• This chart is included in the text because
  (1) adjective clauses modifying indefinite pronouns are common and useful;
  (2) the patterns in (d) and (e), though less common, are also useful; and
  (3) the text seeks to point out that extending the use of adjective clauses to modify personal pronouns, while logical, is not common and should be avoided.

□ **EXERCISE 19, p. 280.   Using adjective clauses to modify pronouns. (Chart 13-9)**

Since using adjective clauses to modify indefinite pronouns is a very common pattern, it is assumed that the students are familiar with it and will have little difficulty with idiomatic responses for items 2–9. The pronouns to be modified in items 10–14 are included principally for advanced students and may seem unfamiliar to intermediate students.

POSSIBLE COMPLETIONS: **2.** I need to ask you.   **3.** he can trust.   **4.** I can do. **5.** who can help you.   **6.** she meets.   **7.** she said.   **8.** the teacher says. **9.** he says is true.   **10.** who is standing.   **11.** we took last week.   **12.** I took last term.   **13.** who came late   **14.** whose names began with letters in the first half of the alphabet . . . whose names started with letters in the last half of the alphabet . . .

□ **EXERCISE 20, p. 281.   Review: adjective clauses. (Charts 13-1 → 13-9)**

This exercise can be more challenging than it looks. Had you, prior to their studying this unit, given the class an item such as "everyone she" or "woman I" and asked them to create a meaningful sentence, they might have been a bit perplexed. That they can now immediately recognize the structures represented by these word combinations is greatly to your students' credit. Congratulate them for a job well done!

The exercise can be discussed orally, with various students giving responses, assigned as written homework, or worked on in groups or pairs.

ANSWERS: [These depend on students' creativity.]
[Note: Sometimes item 18 confuses some students. A possible completion: When Roberto went to the hospital, the doctor (who/whom/that) he saw recommended surgery.]

CHART 13-10: PUNCTUATING ADJECTIVE CLAUSES

- The use of commas with adjective clauses is rather difficult to learn. In fact, native speakers of English are often uncertain about this point.

- You might point out that commas with adjective clauses are similar to parentheses ( ). They are placed before and after additional, but not essential, information.

- This chart contains several important points, so you should plan to spend time discussing them and providing additional examples. The following exercises should help students understand the usage more easily.

□ **EXERCISE 21, p. 282.   Punctuating adjective clauses. (Chart 13-10)**

You should read the first two items aloud as examples for students to follow. Demonstrate to them how to pause and lower the voice between commas. Read the complete sentence, then comment on the punctuation, as illustrated in items 1 and 2.

ERRATUM: There should be no commas in item 8. This is corrected in subsequent printings.

ANSWERS:
3. *No commas—"who" can be changed to "that."*
4. Matthew, <u>who speaks Russian</u>, applied for the job.—*"who" cannot be changed to "that."*
5. *No commas—"which" can be changed to "that."*
6. Rice, <u>which is grown in many countries</u>, is a staple food throughout much of the world.—*"which" cannot be changed to "that."*
7. *No commas—"who" can be changed to "that."*
8. Paul O'Grady, <u>who died two years ago</u>, was a kind and loving man.—*"who" cannot be changed to "that."*
9. I have fond memories of my hometown, <u>which is situated in a valley</u>.—*"which" cannot be changed to "that."*
10. *No commas—"which" can be changed to "that."*
11. The Mississippi River, <u>which flows south from Minnesota to the Gulf of Mexico</u>, is the major commercial river in the United States.—*"which" cannot be changed to "that."*
12. *No commas—"which" can be changed to "that."*
13. Mr. Brown, <u>whose son won the spelling contest</u>, is very proud of his son's achievement.—*"whose" cannot be changed to "that."* [Second sentence = no commas.]
14. Goats, <u>which were first tamed more than 9,000 years ago in Asia</u>, have provided people with milk, meat, and wool since prehistoric times.—*"which" cannot be changed to "that."*
15. *No commas—"which" can be changed to "that."*

□ **EXERCISE 22, p. 283.   Punctuating adjective clauses. (Chart 13-10)**

ANSWERS: 3. a.   4. b.   5. a.   6. b.   7. Only some apples were rotten.
8. All the apples were rotten.   9. Only some students were excused.   10. All the students were excused.   11. Cindy got one present.   12. Cindy got several presents.
13. There were other maps in the room, hanging on other walls.   14. They were the only maps in the room.

□ **EXERCISE 23, p. 283.   Punctuating adjective clauses. (Chart 13-10)**

This is a summary exercise. Students should do it at home, where they have plenty of time to think. Then in class you can lead a discussion of each item as classmates check their work. Also possible is group work, where students can discuss the punctuation among themselves.

ANSWERS: **1.** *(no change)*   **2.** We enjoyed Mexico City**,** where we spent our vacation.   **3.** An elephant**,** which is the earth's largest land mammal**,** has few natural enemies other than human beings.   **4.** *(no change)*   **5.** At the botanical gardens, you can see a Venus's-flytrap**,** which is an insectivorous plant.   **6.** *(no change)*   **7.** One of the most useful materials in the world is glass**,** which is made chiefly from sand, soda, and lime.   **8.** Glaciers**,** which are masses of ice that flow slowly over land**,** form in the cold polar regions and in high mountains.   **9.** *(no change)*   **10.** Petroleum**,** which some people refer to as black gold, is one of the most valuable resources in the world today.   **11.** You don't have to take heavy clothes when you go to Bangkok**,** which has one of the highest average temperatures of any city in the world.   **12.** *(no change)*   **13.** Child labor was a social problem in late eighteenth-century England**,** where employment in factories became virtual slavery for children.   **14.** *(no change)*   **15.** The man**,** who was wearing a plaid shirt and blue jeans**,** was caught shortly after he had left the bank.   **16.** The research scientist**,** who was well protected before she stepped into the special chamber holding the bees**,** was not stung.

CHART 13-11:   USING EXPRESSIONS OF QUANTITY IN ADJECTIVE CLAUSES

• In (a): this is a pattern where *whom* is always used (not *who*), even in speech.

• This pattern is of low frequency, occurring typically in situations such as complicated journalistic sentences in which the most information possible is packed into a single sentence. This chart needs minimal time and attention in class. Advanced students who find it of interest will get what they need from the text and a quick run-through of the exercises. It is a relatively formal written structure. Even in writing, students at this level can communicate their meanings clearly and accurately without ever using this structure.

□ **EXERCISE 24, p. 285.   Using expressions of quantity in adjective clauses. (Chart 13-11)**

ANSWERS: **2.** Last night the orchestra played three symphonies, <u>one of which was Beethoven's Seventh</u>.   **3.** I tried on six pairs of shoes, <u>none of which I liked</u>.   **4.** The village has around 200 people, <u>the majority of whom are farmers</u>.   **5.** That company currently has five employees, <u>all of whom are computer experts</u>.   **6.** After the riot, over one hundred people were taken to the hospital, <u>many of whom had been innocent bystanders</u>.

□ **EXERCISE 25, p. 285.   Using expressions of quantity in adjective clauses. (Chart 13-11)**

POSSIBLE COMPLETIONS: **2.** which is a Porsche.   **3.** whom are in school at present.   **4.** which is Conversational English.   **5.** whom speaks my native language.   **6.** which were expensive hardbacks.   **7.** whom were newly graduated PhDs.   **8.** which have three or more bedrooms.

> **CHART 13-12: USING NOUN + _OF WHICH_**

- This pattern does not occur often. This chart can be skipped or dealt with quickly, depending on your students' level and needs.

- Sometimes the choice between using _whose_ and _of which_ is not clear when the clause modifies a nonhuman noun. We can use both:
    the table, the top **of which** . . . .   OR   _the table, **whose** top . . . ._

- _jade inlay_ = pieces of jade stone set into the table's surface in an artistic pattern.

□ **EXERCISE 26, p. 286.   Using noun + OF WHICH. (Chart 13-12)**

ANSWERS: **2.** They own an original Picasso painting, <u>the value of which is more than a million dollars.</u>   **3.** I bought a magazine, <u>the title of which is _Contemporary Architectural Styles_.</u>   **4.** My country is dependent upon its income from coffee, <u>the price of which varies according to fluctuations in the world market.</u> [_fluctuations_ = waves of highs and lows]   **5.** The genetic engineers are engaged in significant experiments, <u>the results of which will be published in the _Journal of Science_.</u>   **6.** The professor has assigned the students a research paper, <u>the purpose of which is to acquaint them with methods of scholarly inquiry.</u>

> **CHART 13-13:   USING _WHICH_ TO MODIFY A WHOLE SENTENCE**

- Make sure that students understand that _that_ and _this_ are used here as demonstrative pronouns that refer to a whole sentence.

- This pattern is fairly common in spoken English and is useful. _Which_ is used as a connector of ideas. Often speakers pause before they add this kind of _which_-clause to what they have just said.

- Some grammars and some grammar teachers find this structure unacceptable, if indeed not abhorrent. The text writer views it as normal informal English, and presents it to learners as such with the caveat in the last paragraph of this chart. Indeed the text writer hears herself say sentences with this structure with some regularity and notes to herself its usefulness.

□ **EXERCISE 27, p. 286.   Using WHICH to modify a whole sentence. (Chart 13-13)**

ANSWERS: **2.** My roommate never picks up after herself, <u>which irritates me.</u> [_picks up after herself_ = makes order in her room]   **3.** Mrs. Anderson responded to my letter right away, <u>which I appreciated very much.</u>   **4.** There's been an accident on Highway 5, <u>which means I'll be late to work this morning.</u>   **5.** I shut the door on my necktie, <u>which was really stupid of me.</u>   **6.** Sally lost her job, <u>which wasn't surprising.</u>   **7.** She usually came to work late, <u>which upset her boss.</u>   **8.** So her boss fired her, <u>which made her angry.</u>   **9.** She hadn't saved any money, <u>which was unfortunate.</u>   **10.** So she had to borrow some money from me, <u>which I didn't like.</u>   **11.** She has found a new job, <u>which is lucky.</u>   **12.** So she has repaid the money she borrowed from me, <u>which I appreciate.</u>   **13.** She has promised herself to be on time to work every day, <u>which is a good idea.</u>

□ **EXERCISE 28, p. 287.   Using WHICH to modify a whole sentence. (Chart 13-13)**

SAMPLE SENTENCES: **2.** I didn't do well on the last test, which disappointed me.
3. The taxi driver was speeding, which made me nervous.   **4.** Sandra lied to her surpervisor, which shocked all of us.   **5.** David called from the police station, which means he's probably in trouble.   **6.** My best friend took me to dinner for my birthday, which was a pleasant surprise.   **7.** David didn't keep his date with Maria, which made her very unhappy.   **8.** A friend visited my ailing mother in her nursing home, which I appreciated very much.   **9.** The workmen outside my window were making a lot of noise, which made it difficult for me to concentrate.   **10.** My best friend said something unkind to me, which bothered me so much that I couldn't get to sleep.

□ **EXERCISE 29, p. 288.   Special adjective clauses. (Charts 13-11 → 13-13)**

Students need time to think of appropriate answers. This exercise is best done as seatwork or homework to be discussed or marked later. Some of the students' sentences are likely to be fairly awkward, which is more the fault of the exercise format than the students' lack of familiarity with adjective clause structures. It is an imperfect exercise, but allows students to experiment with the structures introduced in the charts.

SAMPLE COMPLETIONS: [Words already provided in the text are in *italics*.]   **1.** My best friend has four *brothers, all of whom* are older than she is.   **2.** She mailed the package *early, which was fortunate* because she had written down the wrong due date.   **3.** I carpool to school with four *students, three of whom* live in my apartment building. [carpool (noun or verb) = drive or ride together to save fuel]   **4.** The art director asked his staff for *ideas, none of which* he liked.   **5.** The women at the gala were wearing a lot of *jewelry, the value of which* was astronomical.   **6.** This school has many fine *teachers, some of whom* have taught here for more than 20 years.   **7.** I thought of home and my *mother, which made me* homesick.   **8.** The teenager delivered newspapers to earn *a little money, all of which* he spent on a new bicycle.   **9.** I have three *sisters, each of whom* is a college graduate.   **10.** We've just bought a *new car, the inside of which* smells like leather.
11. Anna bought a lot of new *clothes, some of which* she'll probably never wear.   **12.** My long-lost aunt arrived on our doorstep *two days ago, which surprised* everyone in the family.

□ **EXERCISE 30, p. 288.   Adjective clauses. (Charts 13-1 → 13-13)**

This exercise illustrates adjective clause usage in formal written English.

ANSWERS:

2. The blue whale, <u>which can grow to 100 feet and 150 tons</u>, is considered the largest animal that has ever lived. [100 feet = 30 meters]
3. The plane was met by a crowd of three hundred people, <u>some of whom had been waiting for more than four hours</u>.
4. In this paper, I will describe the basic process <u>by which raw cotton becomes cotton thread</u>.
5. The researchers are doing case studies of people <u>whose families have a history of high blood pressure and heart disease</u> to determine the importance of heredity in health and longevity. [*longevity* /lɔnǰɛvɪti/ = living to an old age]
6. At the end of this month, scientists at the institute will conclude their AIDS research, <u>the results of which will be published within six months</u>.
7. According to many education officials, "math phobia" (that is, fear of mathematics) is a widespread problem <u>to which a solution must and can be found</u>.
8. The art museum hopes to hire a new administrator <u>under whose direction it will be able to purchase significant pieces of art</u>.
9. The giant anteater, <u>whose tongue is longer than 30 centimeters (12 inches)</u>, licks up ants for its dinner.
10. The anteater's tongue, <u>which can go in and out of its mouth 160 times a minute</u>, is sticky.

□ EXERCISE 31, p. 289.   Activity: Adjective clauses.   (Charts 13-1 → 13-13)

An ideal is not necessarily real, so explain that students should imagine a type of person, not name someone they know.

□ EXERCISE 32, p. 289.   Activity: Adjective clauses.   (Charts 13-1 → 13-13)

You may want to assure students that any controversial ideals will not affect the way you mark their papers. After all, ideals are not necessarily real.

CHARTS 13-14 and 13-15:   REDUCING AN ADJECTIVE CLAUSE TO AN ADJECTIVE PHRASE

- The structures in these two charts are of relatively high frequency. Although these patterns may not seem immediately familiar to the students, encourage them to include the patterns in their usage repertoire. Understanding of these structures is also important for reading comprehension, especially those sentences that cause the reader to pause to figure out the structure in order to grasp the meaning. It's important to know what parts of a sentence modify other parts of a sentence, and it helps to be able to see the form and meaning underlying reduced structures.

- Some other terms used for adjective phrases (Chart 13-15) are:
  modifying participial phrase: *The man **talking to John** . . . .*
  *The ideas **presented in that book** . . . .*

  appositive: *George Washington, **the first president**, was . . . .*

In these exercises, all of these types are simply called "adjective phrases."

□ EXERCISE 33, p. 291.   Adjective phrases.   (Charts 13-14 and 13-15)

This exercise is intended as immediate followup to the explanation of Chart 13-15. Give students a few minutes to make the necessary changes, then open the discussion, reviewing each sentence carefully.

ANSWERS: [The adjective clauses are <u>underlined</u>.]
2. The people ~~who are~~ <u>waiting for the bus in the rain</u> are getting wet.   **3.** I come from a city ~~that is~~ <u>located in the southern part of the country</u>.   **4.** The children ~~who~~ <u>attend**ing** that school</u> receive a good education.   **5.** The scientists ~~who are~~ <u>researching the causes of cancer</u> are making progress.   **6.** The fence ~~which~~ <u>surround**ing** our house</u> is made of wood.   **7.** They live in a house ~~that was~~ <u>built in 1890</u>.   **8.** We have an apartment ~~which~~ <u>overlook**ing** the park</u>.

□ EXERCISE 34, p. 291.   Adjective phrases.   (Charts 13-14 and 13-15)

After it is clear that the students understand the grammar in Exercise 33, they can do this exercise more independently. They may work in pairs to decide on their answers, or you may assign it for homework.

ANSWERS:
2. Be sure to follow the instructions ~~that are~~ given at the top of the page.
3. The rules ~~that~~ <u>allowing</u> public access to wilderness areas need to be reconsidered.
4. The photographs ~~which were~~ published in the newspaper were extraordinary.
5. There is almost no end to the problems ~~that~~ <u>facing</u> a head of state.
6. The psychologists ~~who~~ <u>studying</u> the nature of sleep have made important discoveries.
7. The experiment ~~which was~~ conducted at the University of Chicago was successful.
8. Kuala Lumpur, ~~which is~~ the capital city of Malaysia, is a major trade center in Southeast Asia.
9. Antarctica is covered by a huge ice cap ~~that~~ <u>containing</u> 70 percent of the earth's fresh water.
10. When I went to Alex's house to drop off some paperwork, I met Jerry, ~~who is~~ his longtime partner.
11. Our solar system is in a galaxy ~~that is~~ called the Milky Way.
12. Two out of three people ~~who are~~ struck by lightning survive.
13. Simon Bolivar, ~~who was~~ a great South American general, led the fight for independence early in the 19th century.
14. Many of the students ~~who~~ <u>hoping</u> to enter the university will be disappointed because only one-tenth of those ~~who~~ <u>applying</u> for admission will be accepted.
15. There must exist in a modern community a sufficient number of persons ~~who~~ <u>possessing</u> the technical skill ~~that is~~ required to maintain the numerous devices upon which our physical comforts depend. [This sentence came from the writing of Bertrand Russell, a British philosopher.]
16. Many famous people did not enjoy immediate success in their early lives. Abraham Lincoln, ~~who was~~ one of the truly great presidents of the United States, ran for public office 26 times and lost 23 of the elections. Walt Disney, ~~who was~~ the creator of Mickey Mouse and the founder of his own movie production company, once was fired by a newspaper editor because he had no good ideas. Thomas Edison, ~~who was~~ the inventor of the light bulb and the phonograph, was believed by his teachers to be too stupid to learn. Albert Einstein, ~~who was~~ one of the greatest scientists of all time, performed badly in almost all of his high school courses and failed his first college entrance exam. [All of the information in this item is true. It should encourage all of us who are less than perfect!]

☐ EXERCISE 35, p. 292. Adjective phrases. (Charts 13-14 and 13-15)

In this exercise, the reverse of the last two exercises, students must expand phrases into clauses. When they read books and articles, it can be important for them to be able to determine what key structure words have been omitted from a complicated sentence.

ANSWERS: [The adjective clauses are <u>underlined</u>.]
2. Corn was one of the agricultural products <u>which/that were introduced to the European settlers by the Indians</u>. Some of the other products <u>which/that were introduced by the Indians</u> were potatoes, peanuts, and tobacco. 3. He read *The Old Man and the Sea,* <u>which is a novel</u> <u>which/that was written by Ernest Hemingway</u>. 4. Mercury, <u>which is the nearest planet to the sun,</u> is also the smallest of the nine planets <u>which/that orbit the sun</u>. 5. The pyramids, <u>which are the monumental tombs of ancient Egyptian pharaohs,</u> were constructed more than 4,000 years ago. 6. The sloth, <u>which is a slow-moving animal</u> <u>which/that is found in the tropical forests of Central and South America</u>, feeds entirely on leaves and fruit. 7. Two-thirds of those <u>who are arrested for car theft</u> are under twenty years of age. 8. St. Louis, Missouri, <u>which is known as "The Gateway to the West,"</u> traces its history to 1763, when Pierre Laclède, <u>who was a French fur trader,</u> selected this site on the Mississippi River as a fur-trading post. 9. Any student <u>who does not want to go on the trip</u> should inform the office. 10. I just purchased a volume of poems <u>that/which were written by David Keller,</u> <u>who is a contemporary poet</u> <u>who is known for his sensitive interpretations of human relationships</u>.

☐ **EXERCISE 36, p. 292.   Adjective phrases.   (Charts 13-14 and 13-15)**

This exercise consists of appositives. The appositive is a useful and common structure in written English. An appositive usually consists of a noun phrase* that follows and is equivalent to another noun phrase; it gives more information about a noun or noun phrase by describing or defining it. Appositives are nonrestrictive, requiring commas; they give additional information about the head noun but are not essential to give meaning to the noun. In item 1, Mt. Everest is Mt. Everest with or without the appositive; the appositive is nonrestrictive or nonessential, giving only additional clarifying information.

ANSWERS: **2.** Baghdad, the capital of Iraq.   **3.** seismographs, sensitive instruments that measure the shaking of the ground.   **4.** The Dead Sea, the lowest place on the earth's surface, ...   **5.** Buenos Aires, the capital of Argentina.   **6.** lasers, devices that produce a powerful beam of light.   **7.** Mexico, the northernmost country in Latin America, ...   **8.** Nigeria, the most populous country in Africa, ...   **9.** Both Mexico City, the largest city in the Western Hemisphere, and New York City, the largest city in the United States . . . .   **10.** The mole, a small animal that spends its entire life underground, . . . The aardvark, an African animal that eats ants and termites, ...

☐ **EXERCISE 37, p. 293.   Review: adjective clauses and phrases.   (Chapter 13)**

"Choppy" sentences are short and not smoothly connected.

This exercise gives students practice in constructing quite complex sentences, an important technique for communicating a lot of related information successfully and succinctly.

ANSWERS:
 2. Disney World, an amusement park located in Orlando, Florida, covers a large area of land that includes / land including lakes, golf courses, campsites, hotels, and a wildlife preserve.
 3. Jamaica, the third largest island in the Caribbean Sea, is one of the world's leading producers of bauxite, an ore from which aluminum is made.
 4. Robert Ballard, an oceanographer, [also possible: *Oceanographer Robert Ballard*] made headlines in 1985 when he discovered the remains of the *Titanic,* the "unsinkable" passenger ship that has rested on the floor of the Atlantic Ocean since 1912, when it struck an iceberg. [*oceanographer* rhymes with *photographer;* the syllable "og" is stressed.]
 5. William Shakespeare's father, John Shakespeare, was a glove maker and town official who owned a shop in Stratford-upon-Avon, a town about 75 miles (120 kilometers) northwest of London.
 6. The Republic of Yemen, located at the southwest tip of the Arabian Peninsula, is an ancient land that has been host to many prosperous civilizations, including the Kingdom of Sheba and various Islamic empires. [Also possible, without using the underlined sentence as the independent clause: *The Republic of Yemen, an ancient land located at the southwest tip of the Arabian Peninsula, has been host to many prosperous civilizations, including the Kingdom of Sheba and various Islamic empires.*]

☐ **EXERCISE 38, p. 294.   Error analysis: adjective clauses and phrases.   (Chapter 13)**

ANSWERS:
 1. One of the people who(m) I admire most/most admire is my uncle.
 2. Baseball is the only sport in (which) I am interested in it.   OR   sport in which I am interested.
 3. My favorite teacher, Mr. Chu, he was always willing to help me after class.
 4. It is important to be polite to people who live in the same building.

---

* Appositives, while consisting of noun phrases, function gramatically as adjective phrases reduced from adjective clauses.

5. She lives in a hotel <u>which/that</u> is restricted to senior citizens.   OR   hotel ~~is~~ restricted to . . .

6. My sister has two <u>children, whose</u> ~~their~~ names are Ali and Talal.   OR   My sister has two children. Their names are Ali and Talal.

7. He comes from Venezuela, (<u>which</u> is) a Spanish-speaking country.

8. There are some people in the government (<u>who are</u>) trying to improve the lives of poor people.

9. I have some good advice for anyone who ~~he~~ wants/anyone want<u>ing</u> to learn a second language.

10. My classroom is located on the second floor of Carver Hall**,** (<u>which</u> is) a large brick building in the center of the campus.

11. A myth is a story <u>which/that</u> expresses traditional beliefs.   OR   A myth is a story <u>expressing</u> traditional beliefs.

12. There is an old legend (<u>which is</u>) <u>told</u> among people in my country about a man <u>living</u> (OR man who lived) in the seventeenth century <u>who</u> saved a village from destruction. [It is better style to use only one *who*-clause in a sentence.]

13. An old man ~~was~~ fishing next to me on the pier was muttering to himself.   OR   An old man <u>who</u> was fishing next to me . . . .

14. When I was a child, I was always afraid of the beggars <u>who</u> ~~they~~ went from house to house in my neighborhood. [*who* is the subject of *went*; thus, *whom* is incorrect.]

15. At the national park, there is a path <u>which/that</u> leads to a spectacular waterfall.   OR   At the national park there is a path <u>leading</u> to a spectacular waterfall.

16. The road (that) we took ~~it~~ through the forest ~~it~~ was narrow and steep.

17. There are ten universities in Thailand, seven of ~~them~~ <u>which are located</u> in Bangkok**,** (<u>which</u> is) the capital city.

18. I would like to write about several <u>problems</u> (which) I have faced ~~them~~ since I <u>came/</u> since <u>coming</u>) to the United <u>States</u>.

19. There is a small wooden screen <u>which/that</u> separates the bed from the rest of the room.   OR   There is a small wooden screen <u>separating</u> the bed . . . .

20. At the airport, I was waiting for some relatives <u>who(m)/that/Ø</u> I had never met ~~them~~ before.   OR   At the airport, I was waiting for some relatives. ~~which~~ I had never met them before.

21. It is almost impossible to find two persons <u>whose</u> ~~their~~ opinions are the same.

22. On the wall, there is a colorful poster which ~~it~~ consists of a group of young people (<u>who are</u>) dancing.   OR   On the wall, there is a colorful poster ~~which it~~ <u>consisting</u> of . . . .

23. The sixth member of our household is Alex**,** ~~that~~ (<u>who</u> is) my sister's son.   OR   The sixth member of our household is Alex**,** ~~that is~~ my sister's son.

24. Before I came here, I didn't have the opportunity to speak with people <u>whose native tongue is English</u>.   OR   people <u>for whom</u> English is their native tongue.

□ EXERCISE 39, p. 295. Activity: adjective clauses. (Chapter 13)

The purpose of this practice is to encourage students to express their own knowledge and opinions while using many of the English structures they have learned. If the students discuss the questions in groups, the groups could later compare their lists of inventions and report their conclusions to the rest of the class.

The questions are just suggestions to stimulate the discussion or writing. It is not necessary to answer the questions in sequence or to answer every one of them.

In class, students could make a list of twentieth-century inventions, then rate them by answering item 1. After discussing their lists and ratings, they could complete the exercise in writing as seatwork or homework. In their writing, they should use several adjective clauses and phrases in their definitions, descriptions, and explanations.

ANSWERS: [These depend on students' creativity.]
[Note: Students may have a little difficulty with conditional verbs in item 5.]

□ EXERCISE 40, p. 295. Activity: adjective clauses. (Chapter 13)

Once they get control of adjective clauses, some students tend to overuse them for a while. This exercise is a way of pointing out that it is possible to use too many adjective clauses. At the same time, students should have fun playing with the structures they now control.

You might look up the children's story "The House That Jack Built," which constructs just such a sentence: "This is the cat that ate the rat that stole the cheese that . . . ."

□ EXERCISE 41, p. 296. Writing: adjective clauses and phrases. (Chapter 13)

Students should now feel relatively comfortable using adjective clauses and phrases in their own writing. However, you should assure them that it is neither necessary nor appropriate to have such structures in <u>every</u> sentence. Reward their successful sentences, especially those with good adjective clauses or phrases. You might want to set a limit on how long or short the essay(s) should be.

□ EXERCISE 42, p. 296. Activity: speaking and writing.

Producing a play, even a short one, can be challenging and time-consuming, so make sure that enough students are willing to cooperate and see it through to the end. Then it can be well worth the effort.

Chapter 14: GERUNDS AND INFINITIVES, PART 1

ORDER OF CHAPTER	CHARTS	EXERCISES	WORKBOOK
Introduction	14-1		
Using gerunds as the objects of prepositions	14-2 → 14-3	Ex. 1 → 4	Pr. 1 → 2
Common verbs followed by gerunds	14-4	Ex. 5 → 6	Pr. 3
Other expressions followed by *-ing*	14-5 → 14-6	Ex. 7 → 10	Pr. 4
Review			Pr. 5
Common verbs followed by infinitives	14-7	Ex. 11 → 14	Pr. 6 → 7
Common verbs followed by either infinitives or gerunds	14-8	Ex. 15 → 18	Pr. 8
Review		Ex. 19	
Reference lists of verbs followed by gerunds or infinitives	14-9 → 14-10	Ex. 20 → 23	Pr. 9
Cumulative review			Pr. 10 → 13
It + infinitive; gerunds and infinitives as subjects	14-11	Ex. 24 → 27	Pr. 14
Cumulative review		Ex. 28	

General Notes on Chapter 14

• OBJECTIVE: Gerunds and infinitives are common features of both spoken and written English (as the following underlines demonstrate). A person who tries <u>to speak</u> English without <u>using</u> gerunds and infinitives will produce very unnatural-sounding sentences. <u>Learning to understand</u> and <u>use</u> these structures fluently is important for students.

• APPROACH: The chapter begins with gerunds and their functions, then introduces infinitives, then special groups of verbs followed by either a gerund or an infinitive. Throughout, the emphasis is on becoming comfortable with these structures through practice, not memorization. Reference lists are also included.

• TERMINOLOGY: Like most traditional terms in grammar, "gerund" and "infinitive" were borrowed from analyses of the Latin language; they do not fit the description of the English language equally as well. In this text, the combination **to** + *simple form of a verb* is called an "infinitive" (e.g., *to be, to fly*). The "simple form of a verb" is the base form with no indication of tense or number (e.g., *be, fly*). A "gerund" is *verb* + **-ing** which functions like a noun (e.g., *being, flying*).

CHART 14-1: GERUNDS: INTRODUCTION

• Students should learn that "gerund" is the name of a <u>form</u> based on a verb. A gerund may have the <u>function</u> of subject or object in a sentence.

• In Chapter 1, students learned that some verbs (e.g., *know, need, want*) usually have no progressive use and may hesitate to use the *-ing* form of these verbs. Point out that these verbs can be used as gerunds:

    INCORRECT: *I <u>am knowing</u> John.* (progressive form is not possible)
    CORRECT: *<u>Knowing</u> John is a pleasure.* (gerund as subject)
    CORRECT: *I insist on <u>knowing</u> the truth.* (gerund as object of a preposition)

• Because a gerund is based on a verb form, it can have an object and can be modified by adverbial phrases.

    I <u>play games</u>. = v. + obj. → *<u>Playing games</u> is fun.* = gerund + obj.
    We <u>play in the park</u>. = v. + prep. phr. → *<u>Playing in the park</u> is fun.* = gerund + prep. phr.
    → *<u>Playing games in the park</u> is fun.* = gerund + obj. + prep. phr.

• A gerund with its associated object or modifier is called a "gerund phrase." In the above examples, *Playing games, Playing in the park,* and *Playing games in the park* are gerund phrases. (These are called "nominals" in some grammars.)

CHART 14-2: USING GERUNDS AS THE OBJECTS OF PREPOSITIONS

• A gerund can immediately follow a preposition, but an infinitive cannot.

• The exception that proves the rule: There is one idiom in which a preposition is followed by an infinitive, not by a gerund: *be about* meaning "ready for immediate action." For example: *I am <u>about to open</u> my book.*

☐ **EXERCISE 1, p. 298. Preview. (Chart 14-3)**

This is a preview of the preposition combinations in the following chart, a way for students to see which ones they already know and which they don't. The exercise also, by unvarying repetition of form, emphasizes that a gerund follows a preposition.

After students do the exercise as seatwork, you might divide the class in half and do this exercise orally rather quickly: you read aloud from the book, pause for one group to say the preposition, signal the other group to say the gerund, then you finish the sentence. For example:

TEACHER: Alice isn't interested (pause)
GROUP A: in
GROUP B: looking
TEACHER: in looking for a new job.

Group B's answer will always be a gerund, thus underscoring the main point of Chart 14-2.

ANSWERS: **2.** about leaving **3.** of doing **4.** for being **5.** to having **6.** from completing **7.** about/of having **8.** of studying **9.** for helping **10.** on knowing **11.** in being **12.** of living [*take advantage of* = do something beneficial that is possible only in this situation] **13.** for not going **14.** in searching **15.** for making **16.** for not wanting **17.** for washing . . . drying **18.** to going **19.** from running [also possible: *by running* (i.e., *I was running*)] **20.** to going **21.** of clarifying **22.** of stealing **23.** of taking . . . (of) keeping **24.** to wearing **25.** to eating . . . (to) sleeping

---

CHART 14-3: COMMON PREPOSITION COMBINATIONS FOLLOWED BY GERUNDS

• Students should check off the phases they already know from having done Exercise 1. Then they can concentrate on learning the rest. The following exercises will help.

☐ **EXERCISE 2, p. 300.** **Using gerunds as the objects of prepositions.**
(Charts 14-2 and 14-3)

Students can simply call out completions. Alternatively, this can be done as individual homework or small group seatwork. Then some sentences can be written on the chalkboard and discussed.

SAMPLE COMPLETIONS: **2.** for lending me his fishing rod. **3.** about going to the opera tonight. **4.** to living in an apartment. **5.** about having a headache. **6.** for not wanting to go to the dentist. **7.** for being late to class. **8.** about missing the bus. **9.** in finding out about the landscape of Mars. **10.** about/of going to Singapore next year. **11.** for being late. **12.** to driving on the left side of the road. **13.** from going to the hockey game! **14.** for taking care of ordering the paper for the copier? **15.** to going to visit my grandparents. **16.** of stealing a car. **17.** to working in the school office, she types manuscripts for graduate students. **18.** for not writing sooner. **19.** of telling a lie. **20.** from traveling [BrE: *travelling*] long distances.

☐ **EXERCISE 3, p. 300.** **Using gerunds as the objects of prepositions.**
(Charts 14-2 and 14-3)

You may wish to point out that short answers ("Yes, she did") are more natural in response to conversational questions. However, in this exercise the students should respond with complete sentences in order to practice using gerunds.

SAMPLE COMPLETIONS: [The prepositions and their gerund objects are underlined.]
1. Yes, I had a good excuse OR No, I didn't have a good excuse <u>for being</u> late for class yesterday. **2.** Yes, I am looking forward OR No, I'm not looking forward <u>to going</u> to Boston to visit my friends this weekend. **3.** Yes, I thanked him/her OR No, I didn't thank him/her <u>for picking up</u> my pen. **4.** Yes, I'm accustomed OR No, I'm not accustomed <u>to living</u> in a cold/warm climate. **5.** Yes, I'm excited OR No, I'm

not excited <u>about going</u> to Italy for a vacation.   **6.** Yes, I aplogized   OR   No, I didn't
apologize <u>for interrupting</u> Mehmet while he was speaking.   **7.** Yes, all of the students
participated   OR   No, all of the students didn't participate <u>in doing</u> pantomimes.
8. Yes, I know who is responsible   OR   No, I don't know who is responsible <u>for breaking</u>
the window.   **9.** Yes, I'm used to   OR   No, I'm not used <u>to having</u> my biggest meal in
the evening.   **10.** The hot weather prevents me <u>from running</u> every morning.
11. Yes, Peter complains   OR   No, Peter doesn't complain <u>about/of having</u> a lot of
homework to do.   **12.** Yes, I blame Susan   OR   No, I don't blame Susan <u>for staying</u>
home sick in bed last week.   **13.** S/he went to a baseball game <u>instead of studying</u>
grammar last night.   **14.** I wrote a few letters and read some news magazines <u>in addition</u>
<u>to studying</u> last night.

□ **EXERCISE 4, p. 301.   Using gerunds as the objects of prepositions. (Chart 14-2)**

You can read the beginning of a sentence and have one or two students finish it by calling
out their completions. Discuss any problems.

SAMPLE COMPLETIONS: **4.** by eating.   **5.** by drinking.   **6.** by looking it up in a
dictionary.   **7.** by watching TV.   **8.** by waving to me.   **9.** by calling an
exterminator.   **10.** by wagging her tail.   **11.** by sticking a knife in the toaster.
12. by coming home late at night.

CHART 14-4:   COMMON VERBS FOLLOWED BY GERUNDS

• This chart and the next exercises present just a few of the verbs that are followed by gerunds.
Some students, depending on their learning style, may want to memorize the list, but most
students will find it more effective to practice them orally and in writing until they begin to
"sound right."

□ **EXERCISE 5, p. 302.   Verbs followed by gerunds. (Chart 14-4)**

Encourage the students to use various tenses and to include interesting information in their
sentences. If they work in pairs, have them switch roles during the exercise.

SAMPLE RESPONSES: [Words already provided in the text are in *italics*.]
1. Sam *enjoyed watching TV* last night.   **2.** Would you *mind opening the window?*
3. James *quit eating desserts*.   **4.** James *gave up eating desserts* for six months.   **5.** Bill
finished eating dinner before he went out to play.   **6.** After Bill *got through eating dinner,* he
ran out to play.   **7.** When it *stops raining,* we can go to the beach.   **8.** Why did you
avoid answering my question?   **9.** I cannot *postpone doing my work* any longer.   **10.** I
have *put off doing my work* as long as I can.   **11.** We *delayed leaving on vacation* because of
the hurricane.   **12.** I must *keep working* or I won't get home until late tonight.
13. Ted *kept on working* through his lunch hour.   **14.** My sister must *consider getting a job*
if she wants to redecorate her kitchen this year.   **15.** She really doesn't want to *think*
about getting a job.   **16.** Let's *discuss going to a movie* this weekend.   **17.** We'll *talk*
about going to a movie when we meet for dinner this evening.   **18.** David *mentioned going*
to a concert instead of a movie.   **19.** Rita *suggested going on a picnic* if the weather is
nice.   **20.** I *enjoy listening to music* in the evening.

POSSIBLE COMPLETIONS: **2.** closing/opening   **3.** raining   **4.** running
5. taking/going on   **6.** studying   **7.** giving/having   **8.** laughing   **9.** hitting/
running into/colliding with   **10.** going   **11.** doing/starting   **12.** making
13. going   **14.** taking   **15.** being

CHART 14-5:   *GO* + GERUND

• Some grammarians disagree about the nature of these *-ing* words; are they gerunds or participles? For your students, terminology is much less important than idiomatic use. We will call these structures "gerunds."

• Definitions of some vocabulary items in the chart:
birdwatching = a hobby for people who enjoy identifying birds in natural habitats
bowling = an indoor sport in which a heavy ball is rolled toward 9 or 10 wooden pins to
    knock them down
camping = living in a tent or trailer/caravan for fun; "getting back to nature"
canoeing = floating/paddling on a river or lake in a small, simple boat called a "canoe"
    (pronounced /kənu/)
hiking = walking vigorously in the mountains or countryside (possibly while carrying
    equipment in a pack on one's back = *to go backpacking*)
jogging = running somewhat slowly for exercise
sailing = traveling on a lake or sea in a boat that has a sail or perhaps a motor for power
sightseeing = touring; traveling to see a famous or beautiful place
skinny dipping = swimming with no clothes on
sledding = in winter, going down a snowy hill using a sled, which is a wooden seat on metal
    bars that can slide quickly over the snow
snorkeling = swimming underwater with a face mask and breathing tube in order to watch fish
tobogganing = similar to sledding; a toboggan is a long, flat wooden structure to sit on while
    going down a snowy hill
window shopping = looking into shop windows, but perhaps not intending to buy anything

• A phrase similar in structure is *to go missing*, meaning "to disappear." For example: *In the mystery novel, a rich widow **went missing** and Sherlock Holmes had to use all his powers of deduction to find her. Go missing is principally British, but is also sometimes used in American English. Students may find it of interest.*

□ **EXERCISE 7, p. 304.   GO + gerund.   (Chart 14-5)**

Ask these questions in a natural, conversational way while students are looking at
Chart 14-5. Encourage them to respond with complete sentences.

ANSWERS: [These depend on students' experiences.]

□ **EXERCISE 8, p. 304.   GO + gerund. (Chart 14-5)**

The cuer, Speaker A, can be you the teacher, the leader of a small group, or one of a pair. For pair work, have the students switch roles halfway through.

ANSWERS: [These depend on students' creativity.]

CHART 14-6:   SPECIAL EXPRESSIONS FOLLOWED BY -*ING*

• In (a) and (b), the verb "have" means "to experience" something.

• The *-ing* verbs in these expressions are labeled "gerunds" in some grammar texts. The argument, however, for their being called present participles is strong. This text chooses simply to call them "*-ing* forms."

   Quite honestly, the grammar in this chart doesn't fit in neatly anywhere in the text. This chart is included in the unit on gerunds because this seems a logical place: certain verbs are typically followed by *-ing* forms, and the verbs and expressions in this chart share that characteristic.

□ **EXERCISE 9, p. 305.   Special expressions followed by -ING. (Chart 14-6)**

In items 1 through 12, there may be more than one possible completion, especially if one stretches one's imagination, but the items are constructed to produce one logical, typical completion. Items 13–16 are intended to produce free responses.

POSSIBLE COMPLETIONS: **2.** understanding   **3.** doing   **4.** waiting   **5.** taking
6. listening   **7.** going   **8.** getting   **9.** making   **10.** watching   **11.** eating
12. traveling/going/driving   [BrE: *travelling*]   **13.** doing . . . talking on the phone.
14. going to museums and Broadway shows   **15.** understanding the lecturers when they speak too fast   **16.** going to class and studying English

---

□ **EXERCISE 10, p. 306.   Special expressions followed by -ING. (Chart 14-6)**

The cuer can be the teacher, the leader of a small group, or one of a pair. In the second example, polish is pronounced /palɪš/ or /pɔlɪš/.

SAMPLE RESPONSES: [Words already provided in the text are in *italics*.]
1. I *have trouble remembering* phone numbers.   **2.** I *have been* standing at this counter for ten minutes *waiting* for a salesperson.   **3.** Anton *had a hard time learning* how to spell "Antarctica."   **4.** I enjoy *sitting* in the park and *thinking* about my girlfriend.   **5.** The children *have a good time playing* in the sandbox at the playground.   **6.** I was *lying* in the shade of a large tree *dreaming* about faraway places.   [Check the spelling of *lying*.]   **7.** I *have difficulty pronouncing* Mr. Krzyzewski's name correctly.   **8.** The teenagers *had fun singing and dancing* at the local club.   **9.** I *found someone studying* at my usual desk in the library.   **10.** Jack *spent* 30 minutes *chatting* with Ellen instead of studying for his chemistry test.   **11.** Don't *waste* money *trying* to win the lottery.   **12.** I *caught* my brother *taking* my car without my permission.

CHART 14-7: COMMON VERBS FOLLOWED BY INFINITIVES

• The passive examples (f) and (g) assume that students are familiar with the basic forms in Chapter 11. If they aren't, you may need to explain them, because the passive is used in Exercises 11 through 14.

• The alternative structures in the notes below this chart are important for the following exercise. You should call the students' attention to these sentences.

□ **EXERCISE 11, p. 307.   Verb + gerund or infinitive. (Charts 14-4 and 14-7)**

This exercise covers common verbs followed by a gerund and common verbs followed by an infinitive.

POSSIBLE COMPLETIONS: **3.** to get/look for   **4.** to complete/do/ finish   **5.** playing
6. to lend   **7.** to call/come   **8.** to finish/do   [*ASAP* = /eysæp/   OR   usually, the four letters: A-S-A-P]   **9.** holding/opening   **10.** to be . . . whispering/talking
11. getting . . . to wait   **12.** to use/consult   **13.** to write   **14.** not to touch
15. being/living   **16.** to be   **17.** to know   **18.** to write [also possible: *writing*]
19. to keep/have   **20.** to pass/take   **21.** to deliver/mail   **22.** to mail/accept
23. to find   **24.** to find   **25.** finding   **26.** finding   **27.** to take   [*Oregon* = /ɔrɪgən/]   **28.** taking

□ **EXERCISE 12, p. 309.   Verbs followed by infinitives. (Chart 14-7)**

The answers are in the form of reported (or indirect) speech. The cues are in quoted (or direct) speech. Chapter 12 contains Charts 12-6 and 12-7 on quoted and reported speech, but students probably don't need that lesson in order to complete this exercise. Students can understand that *verb + infinitive* is a way of reporting what someone has said. You may wish to point out the equivalency between modals/imperatives in quoted speech and *verb + infinitive* in reported speech. Or you may wish not to discuss the concept of quoted vs. reported speech at all.

   Show the students how item 1 was produced. Give them time to write their answers. Then review all their answers orally, with each student reading one answer aloud. Discussion can follow each item that causes difficulty.

POSSIBLE COMPLETIONS: [The verbs and the infinitives which follow them are underlined.]
2. The secretary <u>asked me to give</u> this note to Sue. I <u>was asked to give</u> this note to Sue.   **3.** My advisor <u>advised me to take</u> Biology 109. I <u>was advised to take</u> Biology 109.   **4.** When I went to traffic court, the judge <u>ordered me to pay</u> a fine. I <u>was ordered to pay</u> a fine.   **5.** The teacher <u>warned Greg to keep</u> his eyes on his own paper during the test. During the test, Greg <u>was warned to keep</u> his eyes on his own paper.
6. During the test, the teacher <u>warned Greg not to look</u> at his neighbor's paper. Greg <u>was warned not to look</u> at his neighbor's paper during the test.   **7.** At the meeting, the head of the department <u>reminded the faculty not to forget</u> to turn in their grade reports by the 15th. The faculty <u>was</u> (also possible: *were*) <u>reminded not to forget</u> to turn in their grade reports by the 15th.   **8.** Mr. Lee <u>told the children to be</u> quiet. The children <u>were told to be</u> quiet.   **9.** The hijacker <u>forced the pilot to land</u> the plane. The pilot <u>was forced to land</u> the plane.   **10.** When I was growing up, my parents <u>allowed me to stay</u> up late on Saturday night. When I was growing up, I <u>was allowed to stay</u> up late on Saturday

night.   **11.** The teacher <u>encouraged the students to speak</u> slowly and clearly. The students <u>were encouraged to speak</u> slowly and clearly.   **12.** The teacher <u>expects the students to come</u> to class on time. The students <u>are expected to come</u> to class on time.

□ **EXERCISE 13, p. 310.   Using infinitives to report speech. (Chart 14-7)**

You may want to allow students to work in small groups. Then, an individual can read the cue aloud rather dramatically, and two other students can read the reported forms. No *by*-phrase should be included in the answers.

EXPECTED RESPONSES: [Verbs and infinitives are <u>underlined</u>.]
2. The general <u>ordered</u> the soldiers <u>to surround</u> the enemy.   OR   The soldiers <u>were ordered</u> (by the general) <u>to surround</u> the enemy.   **3.** Nancy <u>asked</u> me <u>to open</u> the window.   OR   I <u>was asked</u> (by Nancy) <u>to open</u> the window.   **4.** Bob <u>reminded</u> me <u>not to forget</u> to take my book back to the library.   OR   I <u>was reminded</u> (by Bob) <u>not to forget</u> to take my book back to the library.   **5.** Paul <u>encouraged</u> me <u>to take</u> singing lessons.   OR   I <u>was encouraged</u> (by Paul) <u>to take</u> singing lessons.   **6.** Mrs. Anderson <u>warned</u> the children sternly <u>not to play</u> with matches.   OR   The children <u>were warned</u> sternly (by Mrs. Anderson) <u>not to play</u> with matches.   **7.** The Dean of Admissions <u>permitted</u> me <u>to register</u> for school late.   OR   I <u>was permitted</u> (by the Dean of Admissions) <u>to register</u> for school late.   **8.** The law <u>requires</u> every driver <u>to have</u> a valid driver's license.   OR   Every driver <u>is required</u> (by law) <u>to have</u> a valid driver's license.   **9.** My friend <u>advised</u> me <u>to get</u> some automobile insurance.   OR   I <u>was advised</u> (by my friend) <u>to get</u> some automobile insurance.   **10.** The robber <u>forced</u> me <u>to give</u> him all my money.   OR   I <u>was forced</u> (by the robber) <u>to give</u> him/the robber all my money.   **11.** Before the examination began, the teacher <u>advised</u> the students <u>to work</u> quickly.   OR   Before the examination began, the students <u>were advised</u> (by the teacher) <u>to work</u> quickly.   **12.** My boss <u>told</u> me <u>to come</u> to the meeting ten minutes early.   OR   I <u>was told</u> (by my boss) <u>to come</u> to the meeting ten minutes early.

□ **EXERCISE 14, p. 310.   Common verbs followed by infinitives. (Chart 14-7)**

This exercise follows the same pattern as Exercises 12 and 13. Students should now be able to use their own ideas to create appropriate sentences.

SAMPLE RESPONSES: [Words already provided in the text are in *italics*.]
1. The teacher *reminded me to finish* my composition and hand it in. I *was reminded to finish* my composition and hand it in.   **2.** The teacher *asked me to go* to the front of the classroom. I *was asked to go* to the front of the classroom.   **3.** The ticket *permitted me to have* two free glasses of wine at the art show. I *was permitted to have* two free glasses of wine at the art show.   **4.** My family *expected me to be* at the station when their train arrived. I *was expected to be* at the station when my family's train arrived.   **5.** The park ranger *warned me not to go* into the national forest alone. *I was warned not to go* into the national forest alone.   **6.** He also *advised me to take* a bottle of water and a compass. I *was* also *advised to take* a bottle of water and a compass.   **7.** My employer *told me to open* the mail by 11:00 every morning. I *was told to open* the mail by 11:00 every morning.   **8.** My doctor *encouraged me to visit* a warm, dry climate. I was *encouraged to visit* a warm, dry climate.   **9.** Our teacher *requires us to take* a test every week. We *are required to take* a test every week.

CHART 14-8: COMMON VERBS FOLLOWED BY EITHER INFINITIVES
OR GERUNDS

• The complex history of the English language—elements from German, French, Norse, etc.—has produced the parallel forms in Group A. Learners should be confident that using the infinitive or gerund with these verbs causes no substantial change in meaning that would in any way interfere with communication.

• Native speakers of English do not always agree on their uses of the forms in Group A. The differences are the result of regional variations in usage.

• The differences in meaning with Group B verbs are great, and students need practice in order to understand and use them appropriately. Using an infinitive instead of a gerund with one of these verbs causes a significant change in meaning.

□ **EXERCISE 15, p. 312. Gerund vs. infinitive. (Chart 14-8)**

The answers to this exercise will probably raise many questions that need to be discussed briefly. Therefore, it is best to discuss this exercise with the whole class.

ANSWERS: **2.** to leave/leaving **3.** to lecture/lecturing **4.** to swim/swimming **5.** to see/seeing **6.** to move/moving . . . to race/racing . . . to move . . . to race **7.** driving . . . taking [*to* is a preposition: *prefer X to Y*] **8.** driving/to drive . . . taking/ (to) take **9.** to turn **10.** being **11.** to give **12.** playing **13.** doing **14.** to do **15.** to do **16.** carrying **17.** watching **18.** to do **19.** to inform **20.** not listening **21.** to explain **22.** holding . . . feeding . . . burping . . . changing [AmE = *diapers;* BrE = *nappies*]

□ **EXERCISE 16, p. 314. Gerund vs. infinitive. (Chart 14-4 → 14-8)**

This is a cumulative review exercise of the grammar in the last five charts.

ANSWERS: **2.** cleaning **3.** to take **4.** to leave **5.** talking/to talk **6.** waiting . . . doing **7.** to stay . . . (to) paint **8.** quitting . . . opening **9.** to take **10.** looking . . . to answer **11.** postponing **12.** watching . . . listening **13.** to read/reading **14.** to go to camp/to go camping **15.** singing **16.** to take . . . to pay **17.** to stand **18.** not to wait

□ **EXERCISE 17, p. 315. Gerund vs. infinitive. (Charts 14-4 → 14-8)**

This is also a review exercise, but with free rather than controlled completions.

SAMPLE RESPONSES: [Words already provided in the text are in *italics.*]
1. Ms. Fisher *reminded* me *to finish* the marketing report before Friday. **2.** *We always had fun swimming* at the lake every summer. **3.** *Students are required to have* a laboratory notebook in Chemistry 101. **4.** *The counselor advised* Sharon *to take* an introductory math class. **5.** *I am trying to learn* French. **6.** Natasha *warned* me *not to open* my apartment door to strangers. **7.** *I like to go camping* in the Rocky Mountains. OR I *like going camping . . .* **8.** Roberto *was invited to go* to Surasuk's birthday party. **9.** Omar *promised not to tell* Mr. Stone that Toshi had cut class. **10.** *We aren't permitted to take* dogs into the student cafeteria. **11.** *My friend asked me not to tell* anyone about her illness. **12.** *When the wind began to blow/blowing,* we decided to return to our car.

13. *I must remember to call* my dad tonight.   **14.** Maria *told* me *not to worry about not being* dressed up for the dance.   **15.** Sergio *was told to be* at the meeting at six.   **16.** *I spent* five hours *writing* my last composition.

☐ EXERCISE 18, p. 315.   Gerund vs. infinitive. (Charts 14-4 → 14-8)

This is a quick review that requires uncomplicated sentences. After the pair work, you could turn the exercise into a quiz, with the students writing sentences from your spoken cues. You could make up additional items for a quiz.

Please note for the students that the exercise continues on p. 316.

ANSWERS: [These depend on students' creativity.]

☐ EXERCISE 19, p. 316.   Gerund vs. infinitive. (Charts 14-4 → 14-8)

This is a review exercise.

Items 21 and 22 should be fun for the students. Assure them that these sorts of sentences are not out of the ordinary.

ANSWERS: **1.** talking   **2.** to play . . . not to make   **3.** to look after   **4.** paying   **5.** chasing/to chase   **6.** going . . . to go   **7.** going skiing   **8.** not to smoke   **9.** not to know/not knowing   **10.** whistling . . . to concentrate   **11.** doing   **12.** to quit . . . (to) look for   **13.** to turn off [vaguely possible with different meaning: *turning off*]   **14.** to renew   **15.** not to wait   **16.** not to play   **17.** to call   **18.** convincing   **19.** to throw away . . . (to) buy   **20.** dropping out of . . . hitchhiking . . . trying to find   **21.** to tell . . . to call . . . going swimming   **22.** to ask . . . to tell . . . to remember to bring

---

CHARTS 14-9 AND 14-10:   REFERENCE LISTS OF VERBS FOLLOWED BY GERUNDS OR INFINITIVES

• These lists are for students to refer to, not to memorize. The following exercises and the *Workbook* provide a lot of practice, but learners don't have to learn the lists by heart. Some students, however, will sit down and try to memorize every word on every list no matter what you say. It doesn't seem to hurt them.

• Ask for and answer any questions about vocabulary.

• You could create an oral exercise using these charts. Select some of the sentences at random and ask students to put the verbs in their proper gerund or infinitive forms. For example:
TEACHER: (choosing #9 from Section A in Chart 14-10): *I don't care* (pause) *see that show.*
SPEAKER: *I don't care to see that show.*
TEACHER: (Perhaps repeat the correct answer. Then choose another item, e.g., #5 from Chart 14-9): *He avoided* (pause) *answer my question.*
SPEAKER: *He avoided answering my/your question.* Etc.

• These lists are not exhaustive, but do represent many of the most frequently used words that fall into these patterns.

□ EXERCISE 20, p. 320.   Gerund vs. infinitive.   (Charts 14-9 and 14-10)

This is a mechanical exercise so that students can focus on choosing the gerund or the infinitive after certain verbs. The whole class can answer together. As suggested in the book, you could then repeat the exercise, with individual students using their own words to complete each sentence.

ANSWERS:

1. doing it.	11. to do it.	21. to do it?	31. doing it.	41. doing it.
2. to do it.	12. to do it.	22. doing it?	32. to do it.	42. to do it.
3. to do it.	13. to do it.	23. doing it?	33. to do it.	43. doing it.
4. to do it.	14. doing it.	24. to do it.	34. to do it.	44. to do it.
5. to do it.	15. to do it.	25. doing it.	35. doing it.	45. to do it.
6. doing it.	16. to do it.	26. doing it.	36. to do it.	46. doing it?
7. doing it.	17. to do it.	27. to do it.	37. to do it.	47. to do it.
8. to do it.	18. to do it.	28. doing it.	38. doing it.	48. doing it?
9. doing it.	19. doing it.	29. to do it.	39. doing it?	49. to do it?
10. doing it.	20. to do it.	30. doing it?	40. doing it.	50. to do it.

□ EXERCISE 21, p. 321.   Gerund vs. infinitive.   (Charts 14-9 and 14-10)

ANSWERS: **1.** to bring   **2.** pronouncing   **3.** to eat   **4.** to hang up   **5.** to pull   **6.** to know   **7.** being   **8.** telling   **9.** to be   **10.** to do   **11.** to return . . . (to) finish   **12.** worrying   **13.** to play   **14.** telling   [*blabbermouth* = someone who talks too much, especially to tell secrets (a negative term)]   **15.** taking   **16.** to buy   **17.** to change   **18.** to have   **19.** being   **20.** hearing   **21.** promising to visit   **22.** to race   **23.** hoping . . . praying   **24.** to persuade . . . to stay . . . (to) finish

□ EXERCISE 22, p. 322.   Activity: gerund vs. infinitive.   (Charts 14-9 and 14-10)

This additional practice may not be necessary for all students or all classes. You might suggest that interested students pair up and work on it outside of class. Also, you could use it for quick review in the last five or ten minutes of class now and again.

ANSWERS: [These depend on students' creativity.]

□ EXERCISE 23, p. 322.   Activity: gerund vs. infinitive.   (Charts 14-9 and 14-10)

Refer to the *Introduction*, p. xix, on conducting games in the classroom.

CHART 14-11:   *IT* + INFINITIVE; GERUNDS AND INFINITIVES AS SUBJECTS

• You may need to point out that a gerund subject is singular and requires a singular form of the verb, e.g. *Playing games is fun*.

• The emphasis in Chart 14-11 and Exercises 24 to 27 is on the *it* + *infinitive* structure, a frequent pattern in both speech and writing.

• Of course, *it* + *gerund* is also possible, and some students may produce some examples. Also, an infinitive can be the subject of a sentence. Commend students if they use these correctly, but return their attention to the more common *it* + *infinitive* and *gerund as subject* patterns in this lesson.

EXERCISE 24, p. 323.   IT + Infinitive. (Chart 14-11)

SAMPLE SENTENCES: [The infinitives are <u>underlined</u>.]
2. It's important <u>to look</u> both ways before crossing a busy street.   **3.** It's not easy <u>to learn</u> a foreign language.   **4.** It's foolish <u>to dive</u> into water before checking its depth.
5. It must be interesting <u>to be</u> a foreign correspondent.   **6.** It's always a pleasure <u>to see</u> you.   **7.** It was clever of you <u>to buy</u> Microsoft stock when it was low.   **8.** It doesn't cost much money <u>to go</u> camping.   **9.** It's necessary <u>to have</u> a visa before you can travel to certain countries.   **10.** It takes time <u>to learn</u> how to play a musical instrument.

EXERCISE 25, p. 323.   IT + infinitive. (Chart 14-11)

NOTE: Substitute a pronoun or noun in place of *(someone)*.

This exercise has two purposes. One is to teach the correct location of the *for (someone)* phrase between the adjective and the infinitive. (For example, it is highly unusual or usually incorrect in English to say: "For me it is important to go." / "It for me is important to go." / "It is for me important to go.")

The other purpose is to demonstrate the meaning and use of the *for (someone)* phrase. It limits the meaning of a general statement. For example, item 2 ("It's easy to speak Spanish") is not true for most people, so it's necessary to limit that statement to some person or group ("It's easy for Roberto to speak Spanish because it's his native language. It isn't easy for Mr. Wu to speak Spanish because his native language is Chinese and he's studied very little Spanish.").

SAMPLE SENTENCES: **2.** It's easy for Maria to speak Spanish because it's her native language.   OR   It's easy for someone to speak Spanish if s/he learns it as a child.   **3.** It's important for Toshi to learn English because he wants to attend an American university.   OR   It's important for someone to learn English if s/he plans to work at a foreign embassy.   **4.** It's essential for international students to get a visa if they plan to study here.   OR   It's essential for someone to get a visa if s/he wants to visit Russia.   **5.** It's important for engineering students to take advanced math courses.   OR   It's important for someone studying engineering to take advanced math courses.   **6.** It's difficult for me to communicate with Mr. Wang.   OR   It's difficult for someone who does not know sign language to communicate with a deaf person.   **7.** It is impossible for Abdul to come to class because he is in the hospital.   OR   It is impossible for someone to come to class if s/he is out of town.   **8.** It's a good idea for us to study gerunds and infinitives because we get to practice ways of connecting ideas.   OR   It's a good idea for someone who wants to speak English fluently to study gerunds and infinitives.

EXERCISE 26, p. 324.   Gerunds as subjects. (Chart 14-11)

After giving the example, ask students to complete the same sentence with other gerund phrases. Ask for several different responses for each item so that students have a chance to think of meaningful sentences in this pattern. Encourage them to use a whole phrase (e.g., *climbing to the top of a mountain*), not just the gerund.

SAMPLE COMPLETIONS: **2.** Skiing down a steep mountain slope is hard.   **3.** Meeting new people can be interesting.   **4.** Visiting Prague was a good experience.   **5.** Does climbing a mountain with a heavy pack on your back sound like fun to you?   **6.** Raising children demands patience and a sense of humor.   **7.** Rebuilding an engine is a complicated process.   **8.** Chewing gum in public is considered impolite in my country.

☐ EXERCISE 27, p. 324. IT + infinitive; gerunds as subjects. (Chart 14-11)

Students must listen carefully to each other in this exercise. Student A's answer is used by Student B.

SAMPLE RESPONSES: **1.** It's dangerous to climb a mountain. Mountain climbing is dangerous. **2.** It's easy to ride a bike. Riding a bike is easy. **3.** It's impolite to interrupt someone. Interrupting someone is impolite. **4.** It is important to keep the peace. Keeping the peace is important. **5.** It is wrong to drive through a stop sign. Driving through a stop sign is wrong. **6.** It takes a lot of time to do a job well. Doing a job well takes a lot of time. **7.** It's a good idea to park your car close to the curb. Parking your car close to the curb is a good idea. **8.** Is it difficult to learn a foreign language? Is learning a foreign language difficult? [Note the word order in questions.]

☐ EXERCISE 28, p. 324. Activity: gerunds and infinitives. (Chapter 14)

This activity needs at least 15 minutes, probably longer.

If each group chooses a different story beginning, they can retell their stories later to the whole class.

As a followup activity, each group could hand in a written summary of its story. All infinitives and gerunds should be underlined. You could make copies of the stories for the whole class to read.

Chapter 15: GERUNDS AND INFINITIVES, PART 2

ORDER OF CHAPTER	CHARTS	EXERCISES	WORKBOOK
Infinitive of purpose: *in order to*	15-1	Ex. 1 → 3	Pr. 1
Adjectives followed by infinitives	15-2	Ex. 4 → 6	Pr. 2
Using infinitives with *too* and *enough*	15-3	Ex. 7 → 8	Pr. 3 → 4
Passive and past forms of infinitives and gerunds	15-4	Ex. 9	Pr. 5 → 9
Using gerunds or passive infinitives following *need*	15-5	Ex. 10 → 11	
Using a possessive to modify a gerund	15-6	Ex. 12 → 13	Pr. 10
Cumulative review		Ex. 14	Pr. 11
Using verbs of perception	15-7	Ex. 15 → 16	Pr. 12
Using the simple form after *let* and *help*	15-8	Ex. 17	
Using causative verbs: *make, have, get*	15-9	Ex. 18 → 20	Pr. 13
Cumulative review		Ex. 21 → 26	Pr. 14 → 18

General Notes on Chapter 15

• OBJECTIVE: Students will learn some special uses of gerunds, infinitives, and the simple form.

• APPROACH: The chapter begins with the infinitive of purpose and common structures that require infinitives. Then passive and past forms are presented. Next, some classes of verbs that are accompanied by other simple or *-ing* verb forms are presented. Finally, an extensive set of exercises provides a review of Chapters 14 and 15.

• TERMINOLOGY: The traditional term "infinitive" is used for *to* + *a verb* in its simple (i.e., non-finite or uninflected) form. A "gerund" is defined as "a word that ends in *-ing* and functions as a noun."

CHART 15-1:   INFINITIVE OF PURPOSE: *IN ORDER TO*

• Additional examples for the footnote:
General: *An encyclopedia is used for locating facts and information.*
Specific: *I used the encyclopedia to locate facts about India.*

General: *Knives are used for cutting or slicing.*
Specific: *My brother used a knife to cut his birthday cake.*

☐ **EXERCISE 1, p. 326.   Error analysis: IN ORDER TO.   (Chart 15-1)**

Allow students some time to find errors in the sentences, then lead the class in a discussion of their corrections. Perhaps introduce some items by asking a *why*-question, e.g., in item 1. "Why did you go out last night?"

ANSWERS:
2. Helen borrowed my dictionary ~~for~~ to look up the spelling of "occurred."
3. The teacher opened the window <u>to let</u> some fresh air in the room.
4. I came to this school <u>to</u> learn English.
5. I traveled to Osaka ~~for~~ to visit my sister.

☐ **EXERCISE 2, p. 327.   IN ORDER TO vs. FOR.   (Chart 15-1)**

This exercise contrasts the infinitive of purpose *(in order to)* with a prepositional phrase of purpose *(**for** + noun)*.
ERRATUM: In item 4, the word after *market* should be "to," not "for." This is corrected in subsequent printings.

SAMPLE COMPLETIONS: **3.** (some) bread and coffee.   **4.** buy (some) groceries.   **5.** have my annual checkup.   **6.** a checkup.   **7.** stay in (good physical) shape.   **8.** exercise and recreation.   **9.** get (some) gas/petrol.   **10.** (some) gas/petrol.

☐ **EXERCISE 3, p. 327.   IN ORDER TO.   (Chart 15-1)**

Students can try asking *why*-questions to determine whether *in order* is possible.

ANSWERS: **3.** Ø   **4.** in order   **5.** in order   **6.** in order   **7.** Ø   **8.** in order   **9.** Ø   **10.** in order   **11.** in order   **12.** in order   **13.** Ø   **14.** in order   **15.** Ø

CHART 15-2:   ADJECTIVES FOLLOWED BY INFINITIVES

• This list is not complete; other examples can be found in reference books on grammar. However, many of the most frequently used adjectives are included here.

• Many of these adjectives can be followed by other structures. For example:
I was *happy about going* to the circus. (preposition + gerund)
I was *happy watching* the clouds float by. (present participle)
It is not necessary to mention these structures to the learners at this point. Their focus should remain on *adjective + infinitive*.

• If students wonder why these particular adjectives, unlike others, are followed by infinitives, tell them that it's a traditional pattern developed during the long history of the English language.

□ EXERCISE 4, p. 328.   Adjectives followed by infinitives.   (Chart 15-2)

Students can call out completions. Encourage a variety of completions using the adjectives listed in Chart 15-2.

POSSIBLE COMPLETIONS: **2.** careful to lock my doors.   **3.** ready to go home.
4. eager to see my relatives again.   **5.** fortunate to have my family.   **6.** ashamed to ask anyone for a loan.   **7.** determined to succeed.   **8.** hesitant to accept it without the support of his wife and children.   **9.** delighted to accept the invitation.
10. shocked to learn that he had actually gotten a job! [*wayward* = going in undesirable directions; *be up to* = be doing something secretive or naughty]

□ EXERCISE 5, p. 329.   Adjectives followed by infinitives.   (Chart 15-2)

Tell Speaker A to listen carefully for an infinitive phrase in B's response and make sure it is correctly used. This is an "easy" exercise—except for that fact that often students have developed incorrect usages of this pattern, for example: *I'm eager for going on vacation.*

Another common problem with this pattern has nothing to do with infinitives. Some students even at this level still drop *be*. INCORRECT: *I happy to see my friend.* Tell Student A to be alert for that possible problem also.

It is also possible that this exercise is simply too easy for your class and can be skipped.

POSSIBLE ANSWERS: **1.** Yes. (Maria) is fortunate to have a lot of good friends.   **2.** Yes. I'm eager to go on vacation.   **3.** Yes. I was delighted to meet Yoko's husband.
4. Yes. I went to (Iceland) last summer. I was surprised to see Omar there too.   **5.** Yes. I am prepared to take the test tomorrow.   **6.** Yes. I am hesitant to ask (Yoko) a personal question.   **7.** Yes. I was relieved to find out that (Kim) was okay.   **8.** Yes. I was sorry to hear about (Jamal)'s accident.

□ EXERCISE 6, p. 329.   Adjectives followed by infinitives.   (Chart 15-2)

This is an expansion of Exercise 5, giving students more opportunity to communicate their own ideas. Some answers could be written.

You, the teacher, can choose to be Speaker A and lead a general discussion, pursuing interesting responses and encouraging students to expand on their answers. The exercise can also be used for group conversation. Although pairwork is also a possibility, a larger number of conversants might produce more interesting discussion. Item 1 is, as usual, a "starter item" that basically illustrates the exercise format. Item 2 is impersonal and allows students to concentrate on the pattern they're supposed to be using. Others that follow are more open-ended and personal, and are designed to stimulate discussion. For example, item 5 could serve as an opening for a fairly detailed discussion in which the students could share their personal difficulties and frustrations in using English—if they're not too reluctant to try to express that in English!

ANSWERS: [These depend on students' creativity.]

CHART 15-3:   USING INFINITIVES WITH *TOO* AND *ENOUGH*

• Learners of English often fail to understand that the word "too" before an adjective has a negative meaning, usually that something is excessive and that this causes a negative result. The speaker gives completely different information when using *very* or *too* followed by an infinitive.

☐ **EXERCISE 7, p. 330.   Using infinitives with TOO and ENOUGH. (Chart 15-3)**

Students must understand what a "negative result" is. In item 1, for example, the speaker obviously wants to buy a ring. But, because the ring is too expensive, the result is negative: he/she is <u>not able</u> to buy the ring.

POSSIBLE COMPLETIONS: **3.** I don't want to watch a video. It's too late to start watching a video.   **4.** I don't want to take a walk. It's too cold to take a walk.   **5.** I don't understand nuclear physics. Nuclear physics is too difficult to understand.   **6.** I can't meet my friend for lunch. I'm too busy to meet my friend for lunch.   **7.** My son can't stay home alone. My son is too young to stay home alone.   **8.** People can't climb the mountain. The mountain cliff is too steep to climb.   **10.** I can finish my homework. I'm very tired, but I'm not too tired to finish my homework.   **11.** I can carry my suitcase. My suitcase is very heavy, but it's not too heavy for me to carry.   **12.** I can talk to you for a few minutes. I'm very busy, but I'm not too busy to talk to you for a few minutes.

☐ **EXERCISE 8, p. 330.   Activity: using infinitives with TOO and ENOUGH. (Chart 15-3)**

Students' books should be closed. Therefore, you may need to repeat a cue or add some brief contextual information to help them understand the cue. This exercise intends to touch upon typical student misunderstandings in the use of *too* instead of *very* (e.g., INCORRECT: *My country is too beautiful*).

POSSIBLE ANSWERS:
1. She's very young. [Also possible: *She's old enough/not too young to begin walking and talking.*]
2. A child is too young to read a novel, but an adult is old enough to appreciate good literature. [Have the students come up with various ideas, then compare *too young* with *very young* in item 1.]
3. very [Note: In the negative, *too* and *very* can express the same idea: *It wasn't too good* and *It wasn't very good* = I didn't like it much. But here the cue says it <u>was</u> a good dinner.]
4. very [*It's too difficult* = It's impossible to learn, which is not true. Maybe give your students a pep talk and praise their progress.]
5. very [Ask your students if something can be "too clean."]
6. very   OR   too [depending on student's idea, with *too* implying negative result]
7. [demonstrate *enough* and *too*]
8. very
9. very [The highest mountain in the world is Mt. Everest: 5.5 miles, 8.9 kilometers above sea level; approximately 29,000 feet or 8,800 meters high.]
10. [Discuss placement of *enough*: when it follows a noun, it may seem somewhat formal or literary. In everyday English, it usually comes in front of a noun.]
11. a. We need more envelopes. [*enough* modifies the noun "envelopes."]
    b. We need larger envelopes. [*enough* modifies the adjective "big."]
    [Note for the learners how the difference in structure (i.e., the difference in word order here) conveys the difference in meaning.]
12. very
13. The sun is too bright to look at directly without special sunglasses.
14. You can't read if a room is too dark.
15. A cup is too full (to drink) if you can't lift it to your lips without spilling it.

• Chapter 11 presents the passive. You may wish to review the notions of "passive verb" and "*by*-phrase" with your students.

• Students may need to review the reference lists of verbs followed by infinitives or gerunds, pp. 318–319.

• ERRATUM: In the first printing, the labels are incorrect for (c) and (d): (c) is a PASSIVE INFINITIVE and (d) is a PASSIVE GERUND. This is corrected in later printings.

☐ **EXERCISE 9, p. 332.   Passive and past forms of infinitives and gerunds. (Chart 15-4)**

This exercise requires students to think about the meanings and forms of tenses, verbs that require infinitives or gerunds, and relationships in time. Allow plenty of time for them to prepare their answer to an item, then discuss any misunderstanding.

As the footnote on page 332 explains, sometimes a simple gerund can be used with a past tense main verb even though the gerund's action occurred earlier in time. This shows that the English language is changing—not everyone always uses these forms in the same way. But both forms are still in common use, so students need to learn their normal functions.

ANSWERS: **4.** to be invited   **5.** being understood   **6.** to be written   **7.** being hit   **8.** to be called   **9.** being elected   **10.** to have lost [also possible: *to be losing*]   **11.** being told   **12.** to be loved . . . needed   **13.** not having written / not writing [*swamped* = overwhelmed, flooded]   **14.** having met / meeting   **15.** having been injured / being injured   **16.** to have escaped   **17.** having gone / going   **18.** to have been invited

• British English can also use *want* in (c) and (d), but American English can use only *need* in those cases. For example: *The house wants painting* = BrE, but not AmE.

• There are dialectical differences in native-speaker preferences for using gerund vs. passive infinitive after *need*.

☐ **EXERCISE 10, p. 333.   Using gerunds or passive infinitives following NEED. (Chart 15-5)**

ANSWERS: **2.** to be changed/changing [AmE = *diaper;* BrE = *nappy*]   **3.** to be cleaned/cleaning . . . to clean   **4.** to be ironed/ironing   **5.** to be repaired/repairing   **6.** to take . . . to be straightened/straightening   **7.** to be picked/picking   **8.** to be washed/washing

☐ **EXERCISE 11, p. 334.   Gerunds vs. infinitives following NEED.   (Chart 15-5)**

Small groups could suggest answers, or you could assign this as a written exercise, requiring at least five sentences.

POSSIBLE ANSWERS:
The fence needs to be repaired/fixed/mended.
The grass needs to be mowed/mowing.
Trash needs to be picked up/picking up.
The wash(ing)/laundry needs to be hung up to dry.   OR   The clothes need to be hung up to dry. [The use of a gerund is not probable here; the sentence doesn't involve repairing or improving something, but rather, simply completing a task.] The chair and tricycle /traɪsɪkəl/ need to be repaired/need repairing.

CHART 15-6:   USING A POSSESSIVE TO MODIFY A GERUND

• This is another example of change in the English language. Formal usage keeps the traditional possessive form of the noun or pronoun before a gerund. Less formal usage permits the objective form.

• This chart does not present significantly important information to second language learners. It's not a point they typically have difficulty with, since both forms are correct. The chart is included because sometimes students (and sometimes teachers) have questions about this point; in addition, sometimes standardized tests have an item on this point and may deem the formal possessive form to be the only "correct" usage. This chart and subsequent exercise can be covered quickly.

☐ **EXERCISE 12, p. 334.   Using a possessive to modify a gerund.   (Chart 15-6)**

This exercise could be done in small groups, but it's probably more beneficial for the whole class to discuss the notion of differences between formal and informal usage.

Note the very informal use of *them* in item 5. It can be heard in native-speaker conversations, but some stylists and prescriptive grammarians would consider this usage to be unacceptable. If asked about it, advise your students according to your own standards of appropriate language use, or simply tell them, "When in doubt, use formal English and you can't go wrong."

ERRATUM: The last line on page 334 is missing. Item 8 should include a second sentence: "We should take advantage of *that fact.*" This is corrected in subsequent printings.

ANSWERS: **3.** We greatly appreciate your/you taking the time to help us.   **4.** The boy resented our/us talking about him behind his back.   **5.** Their   [very informal: *Them*] running away to get married shocked everyone.   **6.** I will no longer tolerate your/you being late to work every morning.   **7.** Sally complained about Ann's/Ann borrowing her clothes without asking her first.   **8.** We should take advantage of Helen's/Helen being here to answer our questions about the company's new insurance plan.

□ EXERCISE 13, p. 335.   Review: verb forms.   (Charts 14-1 → 15-6)

This exercise is quite long, so you might want to lead the class through it quickly. It takes about 10 minutes if the students have prepared it out of class.

ANSWERS: **1.** to be asked   **2.** drinking [*to* is a preposition]   **3.** washing   **4.** to relax   **5.** to answer   **6.** telling   **7.** beating   **8.** not being/not having been   **9.** to be awarded   **10.** to accept   **11.** getting . . . (in order) to help   **12.** to travel . . . (to) leave   **13.** Helping   **14.** to be liked . . . trusted   **15.** wondering   **16.** to be chosen / to have been chosen   **17.** Living   **18.** doing . . . to interrupt [*keep on* = continue (same as *keep*)]   **19.** to take/to have taken   **20.** (in order) to let   **21.** to cooperate   **22.** hanging [*hang out* = be together, socialize]   **23.** to turn   **24.** hearing/having heard   **25.** leaving . . . going . . . (in order) to study   **26.** asking/ having asked   **27.** driving . . . to drive   **28.** falling   **29.** (in order) to get   **30.** not being/not having been

□ EXERCISE 14, p. 336.   Review: gerunds and infinitives.   (Charts 14-1 → 15-6)

This is a cumulative review exercise of material from the first page of Chapter 14 to this point in the text's unit on gerunds and infinitives and related structures. The intention of this exercise is for you to elicit several oral completions of each item from the class and for you to reiterate the pertinent grammar point the item illustrates.

Alternatively, if you and your class are in a serious mood, responses could be written and exchanged with classmates for correction, or handed in. If handed in, errors could be compiled for an error-analysis review exercise of your own devising. It is sincerely to be hoped, however, that at this point in their study of this unit there will be minimal usage errors of the target structures.

Alternatively, if you and your class are in a more playful mood, you could present a special challenge by limiting the number of words in each response; for example, not fewer than eight words nor more than twelve—or exactly ten words if you want to make the task even more challenging.

Another possibility is for the students to draw a card from a stack you have prepared on which a number is written, or perhaps roll three dice, and then add that exact number of words to the sentence. You could divide the class into teams, somehow come up with a number for the length of a sentence, and see which group can respond first with a correct sentence with the correct number of words.

Making the exercise into a game can be fun and involving for the students. Another benefit is that students understand that they can shorten (by eliminating nonessential words), lengthen (by combining ideas into compound and complex structures), and otherwise manipulate sentences as needed when revising their own writing.

ANSWERS: [These depend on students' creativity.]

CHART 15-7: USING VERBS OF PERCEPTION

• The five physical senses are sight, hearing, touch, smell, and taste. This chart deals with the patterns of complementary verb use with the list of "verbs of perception" that express four of the five senses, all but taste.

• Since both the simple form and the *-ing* form are correct and often interchangeable, it is sometimes difficult to explain that there can be a difference in meaning. The chart attempts to make the difference easier to grasp, but for some students the distinction may seem unnecessarily subtle.

New users of English can't really make any sort of substantial communication error by using one form rather than the other, so the grammar points in this chart are not crucial. However, for those interested in the subtleties of how form affects meaning and how choice of form can make meaning more precise, the information in this chart will be of interest.

• In the terminology used in this text, the "simple form" of a verb is the form that is usually listed in a dictionary, the form with no tense or endings, i.e., the uninflected form.

SIMPLE VERB: *go, accept*

SIMPLE INFINITIVE: *to go, to accept*

□ **EXERCISE 15, p. 337. Using verbs of perception. (Chart 15-7)**

Identify the verb of perception in each item.

Make sure the students understand that the items in Part I illustrate the fact that in many situations either form of the complementary verb is correct and possible. There may be a little difference in meaning, but it is not of great significance. Explain the difference as best you can and let it go.

The items in Part II are intended to make clear the difference in meaning between the choice of the two forms in certain situations. Even so, the line between the two is sometimes very thin. Don't dwell on this.

Students can have fun demonstrating some of the situations in the entries, as if performing in a theater. Other students can describe the situation. For example (item 4), Carlos acts out being in an earthquake. Another student reports: "Carlos could feel the ground shake/shaking."

PART I POSSIBLE COMPLETIONS: **2.** sing/singing   **3.** walk/walking   **4.** shake/shaking
5. knock/knocking   **6.** take off/taking off . . . land/landing

PART II EXPECTED COMPLETIONS: **2.** slam [once, not continuously]   **3.** snoring
4. playing   **5.** call   **6.** walking   **7.** calling   **8.** play [AmE: *football;* BrE: *soccer*]   **9.** singing . . . laughing   **10.** land [*swat* = hit with something in one's hand]
11. burning   **12.** touch

□ **EXERCISE 16, p. 338. Activity: using verbs of perception. (Chart 15-7)**

This exercise demonstrates a common use of verbs of perception in everyday life.

As an extension of this exercise, you could take the students to another place (outside perhaps, or to another area of the class building) and ask them to describe their perceptions, encouraging them to observe closely and describe carefully what they hear and see.

ANSWERS: [These depend on students' creativity.]

CHART 15-8: USING THE SIMPLE FORM AFTER *LET* AND *HELP*

- The American English preference is (d), the simple form of a verb rather than an infinitive after *help*. The British English preference is (e), the infinitive after *help*.

- In the contraction "Let's"(c), the apostrophe indicates omission of the letter "u" in *Let us*. (See Chart 9-10, p. 169.) There is no other instance in English in which an apostrophe plus *-s* represents a contraction of *us*.

☐ **EXERCISE 17, p. 338. Using the simple form after LET and HELP. (Chart 15-8)**

The purpose of this exercise is to accustom the students to using simple forms after *let* and *help*. If additional practice is needed, you and the students can think of new sentences.

POSSIBLE COMPLETIONS: **2.** correct our own quizzes. [Note that there is no apostrophe in the verb "lets," and explain the difference between *lets* (simple present, third person singular form) and *let's* (imperative + contracted *us* = a unique expression).] **3.** borrow your sweater? **4.** tell you what to do. **5.** (to) find her mother in the supermarket. **6.** (to) locate the registrar's office. [Note: omitting *to* is preferable stylistically to avoid repetitiveness of the word "to."] **7.** interrupt you. **8.** (to) figure out how to operate this computer?

CHART 15-9: USING CAUSATIVE VERBS: *MAKE, HAVE, GET*

- A "causative" verb carries the meaning that something/someone produces (causes) a result. This may be a difficult concept in some cultures, and languages express the notion of causation in very different ways. Therefore, you may need to discuss the notion of causation with your students.

- The method of causation is expressed by choosing one of the three verbs: *make* = use force; *have* = request or order; *get* = use persuasion or perhaps trickery.

☐ **EXERCISE 18, p. 340. Causative verbs. (Chart 15-9)**

Each response should be discussed so that students understand (1) the verb form and (2) the meaning of the causative verb.

ANSWERS: **3.** write **4.** wash **5.** to clean [*clean out* = remove trash] **6.** cashed **7.** to go **8.** shortened **9.** redo [*redo* /ridu/ = do again] **10.** filled **11.** to lend **12.** removed [*a wart* = a raised spot of hard skin] **13.** cleaned **14.** cry **15.** to do **16.** take

☐ **EXERCISE 19, p. 341. Causative verbs. (Chart 15-9)**

POSSIBLE COMPLETIONS: **2.** go to bed when they don't want to. **3.** bring us a menu. **4.** changed. **5.** write on the chalkboard. **6.** (to) move into a new apartment. [*more than willing* = eager] **7.** print out two copies of my itinerary. **8.** laugh. **9.** go downtown alone. **10.** to replace our old refrigerator. [*landlady/landlord* = owner of a rented home]

☐ **EXERCISE 20, p. 341. Activity: causative verbs. (Chart 15-9)**

You may ask these questions in any sequence to promote conversational exchanges with students. Substitute more appropriate items for their circumstances, as necessary.

ANSWERS: [These depend on students' experiences.]

☐ **EXERCISE 21, p. 341. Error analysis: gerunds, infinitives, causatives. (Chapters 14 and 15)**

ANSWERS:
1. Stop <u>telling</u> me what to do! Let me ~~to~~ make up my own mind.
2. My English is pretty good, but sometimes I have trouble ~~to~~ <u>understanding</u> lectures at school.
3. When I entered the room, I found my wife ~~to~~ <u>crying</u> over the broken vase that had belonged to her great-grandmother.
4. Sara is going to spend (the) next year ~~for~~ studying Chinese at a unversity in Taiwan.
5. I went to the pharmacy <u>to have</u> my prescription ~~to be~~ filled.
6. You shouldn't let children <u>play</u> with matches.
7. When I got home, Irene was lying in bed <u>thinking</u> about what a wonderful time she'd had.
8. When Shelley needed a passport photo, she had her picture <u>taken</u> by a professional photographer.
9. I've finally assembled enough information <u>to begin</u> writing my thesis.
10. Omar is at the park right now. He is <u>sitting</u> on a park bench <u>watching</u> the ducks <u>swimming</u> in the pond. The sad expression on his face makes me ~~to~~ feel sorry for him.

☐ **EXERCISES 22 and 23, pp. 342–343. Review: verb forms. (Chapters 14 and 15)**

There are plenty of items in these exercises for additional practice of all the material in Chapters 14 and 15. You might do a few with the whole class, then let them do the rest in small groups. After enough time, discuss only those items which caused difficulty.

EX. 22 ANSWERS: **2.** trickling [*sweat* /swɛt/ = perspiration] **3.** to ignore **4.** drink [This is a well-known saying, meaning that you can show people what you think they should do, but you can't make them do it.] **5.** move **6.** play . . . joining **7.** being elected **8.** to be told **9.** have . . . join **10.** drive **11.** sipping . . . eating **12.** (in order) to let . . . run **13.** make **14.** talking **15.** being forced / to be forced to leave . . . (in order) to study . . . having **16.** being **17.** to have . . . to know . . . to handle **18.** Looking . . . realize . . . to be **19.** staying . . . getting **20.** having . . . adjusting

EX. 23 ANSWERS: **1.** being allowed **2.** Observing . . . climbing/climb . . . realize (that) **3.** (to) being surprised . . . planning **4.** to have been performed **5.** to be identified **6.** to pick **7.** having met/meeting . . . to be introduced [*do the honors* = perform the ritual] **8.** to have been considered/to be considered **9.** to sleep . . . thinking **10.** to force . . . to use . . . to feel . . . share **11.** being accepted . . . concentrating **12.** to persuade . . . to give . . . to cut [*cut down on* = reduce] . . . working . . . to retire . . . take . . . being dedicated **13.** to commute . . . moving . . . to give . . . to live . . . (in order) to be . . . doing . . . doing **14.** feel . . . to get . . . feeling . . . sneezing . . . coughing . . . to ask . . . to see . . . go **15.** chewing . . . grabbing [*grab* = snatch, catch hold of quickly] . . . holding . . . tearing . . . swallow **16.** to get . . . running . . . having . . . sprayed **17.** being treated . . . threatening to stop working . . . to listen **18.** being . . . being . . . to be understood . . . to bridge . . . teaching [*functionally illiterate* = unable to read basic information]

☐ EXERCISE 24, p. 345. Error analysis: gerunds, infinitives, causatives. (Chapters 14 and 15)

ANSWERS:

1. My parents made me ~~to~~ promise to write them once a week.
2. I don't mind ~~to~~ <u>having</u> a roommate. [Note the double letters in *roommate*.]
3. Most students want <u>to</u> return home as soon as possible.
4. When I went ~~to~~ shopping last Saturday, I saw a man ~~to~~ drive his car onto the sidewalk. OR . . . I saw a man <u>driving</u> his car <u>on</u> the sidewalk.
5. I asked my roommate to let me ~~to~~ use his shoe polish.
6. ~~To~~ <u>Learning</u> about another country ~~it~~ is very interesting. OR It is very interesting to learn about another country.
7. I don't enjoy ~~to~~ <u>playing</u> card games.
8. I heard a car door ~~to~~ open and <u>close</u>. OR I heard a car door ~~to~~ <u>opening</u> and closing.
9. I had my friend ~~to~~ lend me his car.
10. I tried very hard <u>not to</u> make any mistakes. OR I tried very hard to ~~don't~~ make <u>no</u> mistakes.
11. You should visit my country. It is <u>very</u> beautiful.
12. The music director tapped his baton <u>to begin</u> the rehearsal.
13. Some people prefer ~~to~~ <u>saving</u> their money to <u>spending</u> it. OR Some people prefer to save their money <u>than</u> (to) spend it.
14. The task of <u>finding</u> a person who could help us wasn't difficult.
15. All of us needed to <u>go</u> to the cashier's window.
16. I am looking forward to <u>going</u> ~~to~~ <u>swimming</u> in the ocean.
17. When <u>you're</u> planting a garden, it's important to ~~be~~ <u>know</u> about soils.
18. My mother always <u>makes</u> me ~~to be~~ slow down if she <u>thinks</u> I am driving <u>too</u> fast.
19. One of our fights ended up with <u>my</u>/me having to <u>be</u> sent to the hospital <u>for</u>/to get stitches.
20. Please promise not <u>to tell</u> anybody my secret.
21. I would appreciate ~~having~~ <u>hearing</u> from you soon.
22. Maria has never complained about <u>having</u> a handicap.
23. Lillian deserves to be <u>told</u> the truth about what happened last night.
24. Barbara always makes me <u>laugh</u>. She has a great sense of humor.
25. Ali <u>doesn't</u> speak Spanish, and Juan <u>doesn't</u> know Arabic. But they communicate well by <u>speaking</u> English when they <u>are</u> together.
26. I enjoyed ~~to~~ <u>talking</u> to her on the phone. I look forward to <u>seeing</u> her next week.
27. During a fire drill, everyone is required <u>to leave</u> the building.
28. <u>Skiing</u> in the Alps was a big thrill for me.
29. Don't keep ~~to be~~ <u>asking</u> me the same questions over and over.
30. When I entered the room, I found my young son <u>standing</u> on the kitchen table.

☐ EXERCISE 25, p. 347. Writing. (Chapters 14 and 15)

Students should be able to produce several informal paragraphs on a topic. After they finish, they or a partner might underline all the gerunds and infinitives.

All of the topics require use of more than one verb tense. Topic 1 is basically about the past, but might also include the present perfect. Topic 2 combines the present and the past. Topic 3 requires the present and either present perfect or past.

It is not necessary for students to answer each question directly. These questions are designed to stimulate recollections and other ideas for writing material.

□ EXERCISE 26, p. 347. Writing. (Chapters 14 and 15)

Examine the example introductory paragraph with your class. Have them find the gerunds, infinitives, and complementary simple forms: *buying, to have, to accompany, to help, had us look,* ("not to mention" is a set, idiomatic phrase), *to think, to go, to share . . . and (to) discuss.* This paragraph was adapted from one written by a student and represents typical use of these verb forms: moderately occasional but essential in a variety of situations in order to communicate one's meaning.

This exercise is intended for classes that include an introduction to English rhetoric in their goals and curriculum. This exercise deals with exposition of process, a fundamental form of English rhetoric. Instruction in English rhetoric is beyond the scope of this text, but the teaching of grammar and of writing are so closely linked and compatible that the text seeks to provide opportunites such as this for the teacher to exploit if so desired.

Encourage the students to use a personal experience in the introductory paragraph.

You might want to set a limit (350–500 words).

If you want a shorter composition, assign only a personal experience the writer has had that is related to one of the topics.

When marking the papers, focus on verb forms. Point out good usage as well as errors. Perhaps excerpt sentences or passages to be reproduced for class discussion.

Chapter 16: COORDINATING CONJUNCTIONS

ORDER OF CHAPTER	CHARTS	EXERCISES	WORKBOOK
Parallel structure	16-1	Ex. 1 → 6	Pr. 1 → 4
Paired conjunctions	16-2	Ex. 7 → 10	Pr. 5 → 6
Combining independent clauses with coordinating conjunctions	16-3	Ex. 11 → 12	
Cumulative review		Ex. 13	Pr. 7 → 9

General Notes on Chapter 16

• OBJECTIVE: This chapter gives students more choices for expressing related ideas. They will learn how English connects bits of information that are in a relationship of equality.

• APPROACH: Essentially, the chapter deals with the concept of parallelism. Two or more similar bits of information should be expressed in similar grammatical forms, according to the preferred style of written English. The chapter introduces the use of coordinating conjunctions and related rules for punctuation.

• TERMINOLOGY: A "conjunction" is a function word that serves as a connector or a linking word to join words, phrases, or clauses. This chapter deals with coordinating conjunctions, words that are used to create compound structures (e.g., compound subjects, compound verbs, compound sentences). In this text, correlative conjunctions (e.g., *both . . . and*) are called "paired conjunctions." Subordinating conjunctions (e.g., *when, because, if*) are used to create complex sentences and are dealt with in the following chapter.

CHART 16-1: PARALLEL STRUCTURE

• Using parallel structure is an economical way to include several bits of information in a single phrase or clause. The ability to use parallel structure is highly valued in spoken and written English, for conciseness is a cultural value in English-speaking countries. Other cultures may have other values.

• Problems with parallel structure are common in student writing.

• To understand parallel structure, learners need to understand the concept of the ellipsis: that certain words have been omitted from a sentence. The sentence can be understood without them because the omitted words are repetitive. English rhetoric does not value repetitiveness. Wordy and repetitive: *Steve is coming to dinner and his friend is coming to dinner.* In ellipsis, the repeated words *(be + coming to dinner)* are omitted and the verb is made to agree with the compound subject: *Steve and his friend are coming to dinner.*

    Write sentences without ellipsis on the board (e.g., *The man is wearing a hat and the man is wearing a coat. The woman is wearing her hat and the woman is holding her coat.*). Ask the students to omit any words they see that are repeated. Explain the grammatical source of the parallel structure.

• In a series, the last item is preceded by a conjunction (usually *and* or *or*). Many people place a comma before that conjunction (e.g., *an apple, a banana, and a pear*), but that is a matter of choice. Grammar books and style guides do not agree on whether that comma is required. This text uses the final comma so that the students can more clearly see each element of a serial parallel structure. In addition, spoken English patterns usually have a pause before the conjunction in this instance, and the comma reflects the pause.

☐ **EXERCISE 1, p. 348. Parallel structure. (Chart 16-1)**

> *ANSWERS:*
> **3.** She spoke <u>angrily</u> and <u>bitterly</u> about the war. [adverb + adverb]
> **4.** I <u>looked</u> for my book but <u>couldn't find</u> it. [verb + verb]
> **5.** I hope <u>to go</u> to that university and <u>study</u> under Dr. Liu. [infinitive + infinitive]
> **6.** In my spare time, I enjoy <u>reading</u> novels or <u>watching</u> television. [gerund + gerund]
> **7.** He <u>will leave</u> at eight and <u>arrive</u> at nine. [verb + verb]
> **8.** He <u>should have broken</u> his engagement to Beth and <u>married</u> Sue instead. [verb + verb]

☐ **EXERCISE 2, p. 349. Parallel structure. (Chart 16-1)**

Ask the students to explain the grammatical functions of the parallel words. This may lead to a review of basic terminology (noun, verb, adjective, preposition, etc.) and how to recognize the various forms. Anyone having difficulty with this should review Appendix Unit A.

ANSWERS: **2.** Mary is opening the door and (is) greeting her guests.   **3.** Mary will open the door and (will) greet her guests.   **4.** Alice is kind, generous, and trustworthy.   **5.** Please try to speak more loudly and clearly.   **6.** He gave her flowers on Sunday, candy on Monday, and a ring on Tuesday.   **7.** While we were in New York, we attended an opera, ate at marvelous restaurants, and visited some old friends.   **8.** He decided to quit school, (to) go to California, and (to) find a job. [Note: *To* is usually not repeated in parallel infinitives unless the sentence is long and complicated. In a series, if the second *to* (*to go* in item 8) is included, the third *to* (*to find*) should be included also.]   **9.** I am looking forward to

going to Italy and eating wonderful pasta every day.   [Note: Point out that *to* is a preposition here, followed by a gerund.]   **10.** I should have finished my homework and (should have) cleaned up my room.   **11.** The boy was old enough to work and (to) earn some money.
12. He preferred to play baseball or (to) spend his time in the streets with other boys.
13. I like coffee but not tea.   **14.** I have met his mother (**,**) but not his father.
15. Jake would like to live in Puerto Rico (**,**) but not (in) Iceland.

□ **EXERCISE 3, p. 350.   Parallel structure.   (Chart 16-1)**

Students might enjoy working in pairs to complete these sentences. Then you can ask for several versions of each item from the class. Exercises 3 and 4 could also be assigned as out-of-class homework now that the students understand parallel structure.

POSSIBLE COMPLETIONS: **2.** the food—I like to become acquainted with the people, (the) customs, and (the) food of other countries.   **3.** the noise—I dislike living in a city because of the air pollution, (the) crime, and (the) noise.   **4.** economic—We discussed some of the social, political, and economic problems of the United States.   **5.** a warm climate—Hawaii has a warm climate, many interesting tropical trees and flowers, and beautiful beaches.   **6.** is a good leader—Mary Hart would make a good president because she is a good leader, works effectively with others, and has a reputation for integrity and independent thinking.

□ **EXERCISE 4, p. 351.   Parallel structure.   (Chart 16-1)**

Students may find item 8 difficult to complete.

POSSIBLE COMPLETIONS: **2.** competent [adjective]   **3.** said, "Good morning." [verb phrase]   **4.** reading the newspaper [-*ing* verb]   **5.** leave for work [verb]
6. Swimming at the lake [gerund]   **7.** hiking on mountain trails [gerund]
8. supportive of those who are in trouble / generous to those in need / kind to people down on their luck [adjective]

□ **EXERCISE 5, p. 351.   Error analysis: parallel structure.   (Chart 16-1)**

ANSWERS:
1. By obeying the speed limit, we can save energy, lives, and <u>money</u>.
2. My home offers me a feeling of security, <u>warmth</u>, and love.
3. The pioneers labored to clear away the forest and <u>plant</u> crops.
4. When I refused to help her, she became very angry and <u>shouted</u> at me.
5. In my spare time, I enjoy taking care of my aquarium and <u>working</u> on my stamp collection.   OR   In my spare time, I enjoy taking care of my aquarium and ~~to~~ I work on my stamp collection.
6. With their keen sight, fine hearing, and ~~they have a~~ refined sense of smell, wolves hunt elk, deer, moose, and caribou.
7. All plants need light, ~~to have~~ a suitable climate, and an ample supply of water and minerals from the soil.
8. Slowly and <u>cautiously</u>, the firefighter ascended the burned staircase.
9. The Indian cobra snake and the king cobra use poison from their fangs in two ways: by injecting it directly into their prey or ~~they~~ (by) spitting it into the eyes of the victim.
10. On my vacation, I lost a suitcase, broke my glasses, and ~~I~~ missed my flight home.
11. When Anna moved, she had to rent an apartment, make new friends, and ~~to~~ find a job.

☐ EXERCISE 6, p. 352.   Error analysis: Parallel structure.   (Chart 16-1)

ERRATUM: The mischievous misprint gremlins misspelled "analysis" in the title of this exercise. This is corrected in later printings.

ANSWERS:

What do people in your country think of bats? Are they mean and scary creatures, or are they symbols of happiness and <u>luck</u>?

In Western countries, many people have an unreasoned fear of bats. According to scientist Dr. Sharon Horowitz, bats are <u>beneficial and harmless mammals</u>. "When I was a child, I believed that a bat would attack me and <u>tangle</u> itself in my hair. Now I know better," said Dr. Horowitz.

Contrary to popular Western myths, bats do not attack humans and <u>are</u> not blind. Although a few bats may be infected, they are not major carriers of rabies or ~~carry~~ other dread diseases. Bats help natural plant life by pollinating plants, spreading seeds, and ~~they~~ <u>eating</u> insects. If you get rid of bats that eat overripe fruit, then fruit flies can flourish and <u>destroy</u> the fruit industry.

According to Dr. Horowitz, bats make loving, ~~pets, and they are~~ trainable, and ~~are~~ gentle pets. Not many people, however, are known to have bats as pets, and bats themselves prefer to avoid people.

CHART 16-2:   PAIRED CONJUNCTIONS: *BOTH . . . AND;*
NOT ONLY . . . BUT ALSO; EITHER . . . OR;
NEITHER . . . NOR

• There are two important grammar points here: (1) subject–verb agreement and (2) parallel structure. Both are practiced in the following exercises.

• Some native speakers of English have trouble using these structures correctly (according to formal English preferences); learners can expect to be confused sometimes, too. In actual usage of *neither . . . nor,* native speakers often use a plural verb with two singular subjects (e.g., *Neither my mother nor my sister* **are** *here. Neither my brother nor I* **were** *interested*). This usage is not presented in the text because it seems unnecessarily confusing for the learners. You may wish to mention it, though, perhaps with the caveat "When in doubt, use formal English."

• Another point not mentioned in the text is that when there are two independent clauses connected by *not only . . . but also,* the first independent clause usually (but not always) has inverted subject–verb word order. (When a sentence begins with a negative, the subject and verb are often inverted. See Appendix Chart D-3, p. A20.) Example: *Not only* **does John go** *to school full time, but he also has a full-time job.* You may or may not wish to introduce this point to your students.

☐ EXERCISE 7, p. 353.   Paired conjunctions.   (Chart 16-2)

Ask the students to explain how they chose *is* or *are.*

ANSWERS: **2.** is   **3.** is   **4.** are   **5.** is   **6.** are   **7.** are   **8.** are

□ EXERCISE 8, p. 353.   Error analysis: paired conjunctions. (Chart 16-2)

ANSWERS: [The paired conjunctions are underlined.]
1. John will call either Mary or Bob.   OR   Either John or Bob will call Mary.   **2.** Sue saw not only the mouse but also the cat.   OR   Not only Sue but (also) the cat saw the mouse.
3. Both my mother and (my) father talked to the teacher.   OR   My mother talked to both my teacher and my father.   **4.** Either Mr. Anderson or Ms. Wiggins **is** going to teach our class today.   **5.** I enjoy reading not only novels but also magazines.   **6.** Oxygen is plentiful. Both air and water contain oxygen. [*Air* and *water* are equals; they are both substances that contain oxygen. They are the two items to join in a parallel structure. *Oxygen* and *water* are not parallel substances.]

□ EXERCISE 9, p. 354.   Paired conjunctions. (Chart 16-2)

For an advanced class, conduct this as a teacher-led exercise with students' books closed. Group or pair work is also possible, followed by a quick written quiz using one item from each section.
      Both . . . and is used more frequently than *not only . . . but also. Not only . . . but also* tends to mean that something is surprising or especially interesting. Note that "Yes" is the required answer in the first three groups of items, but "No" is the answer with *neither . . . nor.*

PART I ANSWERS: **2.** Yes, both the driver and the passenger were injured in the accident.
3. Yes, both wheat and corn are grown in Kansas.   **4.** Yes, he both buys and sells used cars.   **5.** Yes, I had both lunch and dinner with my friends.   **6.** Yes, the city suffers from both air (pollution) and water pollution.

PART II ANSWERS: **8.** Yes, not only his cousin but also his mother-in-law **is** living with him.   **9.** Yes, not only my country but also the United States **has** good universities. [*The United States* is one country; therefore, the verb is singular. See Chart 6-5, p. 92.]   **10.** Yes, I lost not only my wallet but also my keys.   **11.** Yes, she not only goes to school but also has a full-time job.   **12.** Yes, he bought not only a coat but also a new pair of shoes.

PART III ANSWERS: **14.** Yes, I'm going to give my friend either a book or a pen for her birthday.   **15.** Yes, either my sister or my brother will meet me at the airport.
16. Yes, they can either go swimming or play tennis.   **17.** Yes, I'm going to vote for either Mr. Smith or Mr. Jones.   **18.** Yes, I'll go to either New Orleans or Miami for my vacation.

PART IV ANSWERS: **20.** No, neither her husband nor her children **speak** English.
21. No, neither the students nor the teacher **is** wide awake today.   **22.** No, they have neither a refrigerator nor a stove for their new apartment.   **23.** No, she enjoys neither hunting nor fishing.   **24.** No, the result was neither good nor bad.

□ EXERCISE 10, p. 355.   Paired conjunctions. (Chart 16-2)

ANSWERS: [The paired conjunctions are underlined.]
2. Both Ron and Bob **enjoy** horseback riding.   OR   Not only Ron but also Bob **enjoys** horseback riding.   **3.** You can have either tea or coffee.   **4.** Neither Arthur nor Ricardo **is** in class today.   **5.** Both Arthur and Ricardo **are** absent.   OR   Not only Arthur but also Ricardo **is** absent.   **6.** We can either fix dinner for them here or take them to a restaurant. [*Fix dinner* = prepare dinner.]   **7.** She wants to buy either a Chevrolet or a Toyota.   **8.** Both the leopard and the tiger **face** extinction.   **9.** Neither the library nor the bookstore **has** the book I need.   **10.** We could either fly or take the train.

11. The president's assistant will <u>neither confirm nor deny</u> the story.   12. <u>Both coal and oil</u> **are** irreplaceable natural resources.   OR   <u>Not only coal but also oil</u> **is** an irreplaceable natural resource.   13. <u>Both smallpox and malaria</u> **are** dangerous diseases. 14. <u>Neither her roommates nor her brother</u> **knows** where she is.   15. According to the news report, it will <u>either snow or rain</u> tonight.

> **CHART 16-3:   COMBINING INDEPENDENT CLAUSES WITH COORDINATING CONJUNCTIONS**
>
> • Formal English usually requires a comma preceding the conjunction when it connects two independent clauses. Example (e) is generally not favored in formal English, but is common in informal writing such as letters to friends and family.
>
> • Another term for a "run-on sentence" is a "comma splice" when a comma is used in place of a period. Run-on sentences are a common problem in student writing (native and non-native alike).
>
> • Advanced students may be interested to know that it is possible to use commas between independent clauses <u>in a series</u>: *Janet washed the windows, Bob swept the floor, and I dusted the furniture.* INCORRECT: *Janet washed the windows, Bob swept the floor.*
>
> • Another conjunction could be added to this section if you wish. The connector "then" is frequently used in the pattern of coordinating conjunctions between two independent clauses:
> *Remove the book from the shelf yourself,* ***then*** *take it to the librarian to check it out.*
> *Stir the flour and milk,* ***then*** *add two eggs and a cup of sugar.*
> *Buy your ticket at the counter,* ***then*** *proceed to the gate.*
> *We ate,* ***then*** *we started home.* (This example is taken from the *Random House Webster's College Dictionary.)*
>
> NOTE: Some English stylists may not approve using a comma and *then* to connect two independent clauses, preferring to use a period and a capitalized *Then*.

☐ EXERCISES 11 and 12, pp. 356–357.   Combining independent clauses with coordinating conjunctions. (Chart 16-3)

Exercise 11 should be done as seatwork in about five to eight minutes. After reviewing the answers with you, the students could continue with Exercise 12 as seatwork or homework. Exercise 11 is intended to help you explain the chart. Exercise 12 is intended as practice for the students.

EX. 11 ANSWERS: **2.** The teacher lectured. **The** students took notes.   **3.** The teacher lectured**, and** the students took notes. [The comma is not required between two short clauses. Also possible, informally: period and capitalized *And* . . . .]   **4.** Elena came to the meeting**,** but Pedro stayed home. [The comma is not required. Also possible: period and capitalized *But* . . . .]   **5.** Elena came to the meeting. **Her** brother stayed home.   **6.** Her academic record was outstanding**,** yet she was not accepted by the university.   **7.** I have not finished writing my term paper yet. **I** will not be finished until sometime next week. **8.** *(no change)* [*for* is a preposition, not a conjunction, here.]   **9.** We had to go to the grocery store**,** for there was nothing in the house to fix for dinner.   **10.** Kostas didn't have enough money to buy an airplane ticket**,** so he couldn't fly home for the holiday.

EX. 12 ANSWERS:

1. A thermometer is used to measure temperature. **A** barometer measures air pressure.
2. Daniel made many promises, but he had no intention of keeping them.
3. I always enjoyed mathematics in high school, so I decided to major in it in college.
4. Anna is in serious legal trouble, for she had no car insurance at the time of the accident.
5. Last night Martha had to study for a test, so she went to the library. [A comma after *night* is possible but not required.]
6. The ancient Egyptians had good dentists. **A**rchaeologists have found mummies that had gold fillings in their teeth.
7. Both John and I had many errands to do yesterday. **J**ohn had to go to the post office and the bookstore. **I** had to go to the post office, the travel agency, and the bank.
8. I did not like the leading actor, yet the movie was quite good on the whole.
9. The team of researchers has not finished compiling the statistics yet. **T**heir work will not be made public until later.
10. We have nothing to fear, for our country is strong and united.
11. He slapped his desk in disgust. **H**e had failed another examination and had ruined his chances for a passing grade in the course.
12. I struggled to keep my head above water. **I** tried to yell for help, but no sound came from my mouth.
13. The earthquake was devastating. **T**all buildings crumbled and fell to the earth.
14. It was a wonderful picnic. **T**he children waded in the stream, collected rocks and insects, and flew kites. **T**he teenagers played an enthusiastic game of baseball. **T**he adults busied themselves preparing the food, supervising the children, and playing a game or two of volleyball.
15. Some people collect butterflies for a hobby. **T**hese collectors capture them with a net and put them in a jar that has poison in it. **T**he dead butterflies are then mounted on a board.
16. Caterpillars eat plants and cause damage to some crops, but adult butterflies feed principally on nectar from flowers and do not cause any harm.
17. The butterfly is a marvel. **I**t begins as an ugly caterpillar and turns into a work of art.
18. The sight of a butterfly floating from flower to flower on a warm sunny day brightens anyone's heart. **A** butterfly is a charming and gentle creature. [It's possible to put a comma between *warm* and *sunny* to separate two descriptive adjectives; it would replace the word *and* between two adjectives of equal status.]

NOTE: Items 19 and 20 are intended to review the patterns and punctuation of adverb clauses as presented in Chapter 5 as a way of previewing the material soon to come in Chapter 17. The suggestion is that you take a moment here to prepare the students for the coming chapter.

19. When cold weather comes, some butterflies travel great distances to reach tropical climates.
20. Butterflies are admired throughout the world because they are beautiful. **T**hey can be found on every continent except Antarctica. [Point out that the period after *beautiful* shows which independent clause the adverb clause *(because they are beautiful)* should be linked to. With improper punctuation, the reader doesn't know exactly what relationships the writer intended. Following are examples of <u>improper</u> punctuation of adverb clauses: (a) *I should have stayed home. Because I wanted to see my friends. I went to the meeting.* (b) *I should have stayed home because I wanted to see my friends I went to the meeting.* Proper punctuation clarifies the writer's intent, which may be either of the following: (a) *I should have stayed home because I wanted to see my friends.*   OR (b) *Because I wanted to see my friends, I went to the meeting.* Of course, the addition of other connectors and combining complex and compound structures could also greatly help to clarify the writer's meaning, e.g., *I should have stayed home because I wanted to see my friends, but I went to the meeting anyway.*   OR   *I should have stayed home, but because I wanted to see my friends, I went to the meeting.]*

☐ EXERCISE 13, p. 358. Writing. (Chapter 16)

If possible, have the students write the first draft quickly in class. Then ask them to take that home and tighten it up. Request that both the first and second drafts be submitted to you.

Reproduce some of the more successful attempts at tightening writing style through good use of parallelism; discuss them with the class.

Some students may not want to produce two versions of the same paragraph, but you can assure them that most people—even very experienced and skilled authors—use this method of improving their writing. Revision with an eye toward conciseness is an essential process in producing good writing in English.

Chapter 17: ADVERB CLAUSES

ORDER OF CHAPTER	CHARTS	EXERCISES	WORKBOOK
Introduction	17-1	Ex. 1 → 2	Pr. 1 → 3
Using adverb clauses to show cause and effect	17-2	Ex. 3 → 4	Pr. 4
Using *even though*	17-3	Ex. 5 → 7	Pr. 5
Using *while* and *whereas*	17-4	Ex. 8 → 9	Pr. 6
If-clauses	17-5	Ex. 10	Pr. 7
Using *whether or not* and *even if*	17-6	Ex. 11 → 12	Pr. 8
Using *in case* and *in the event that*	17-7	Ex. 13	Pr. 9
Using *unless*	17-8	Ex. 14 → 15	
Using *only if*	17-9	Ex. 16 → 18	Pr. 10 → 12
Review		Ex. 19	Pr. 13

General Notes on Chapter 17

• OBJECTIVE: Learning to use adverb clauses extends one's ability to communicate complex information and show relationships between ideas.

• APPROACH: Adverb clauses of time are presented in Chapter 5; they are reviewed briefly here in the first two exercises of this chapter.

   This brief chapter focuses on the other three common functions of adverb clauses to express relationships of (1) cause and effect, (2) contrast, and (3) "if–then" conditions (except for contrary-to-fact conditional sentences, which are covered in Chapter 20).

• TERMINOLOGY: As noted in the footnote to Chart 17-1, in this text "subordinating conjunctions" (e.g., *when*, *because*) are called "words that introduce adverb clauses." Coordinating and correlative conjunctions (Chapter 16) link equal, parallel elements; subordinating conjunctions link a dependent structure to an independent one.

CHART 17-1: INTRODUCTION

• Students have learned about two other kinds of dependent clauses: adjective clauses (Chapter 13) and noun clauses (Chapter 12). You might review the characteristics of dependent clauses: they must contain *a subject + a verb;* they cannot stand alone as a sentence.

• Incomplete sentences consisting of a solo adverb clause are a common problem in student writing. INCORRECT: *He went to bed.* ***Because he was sleepy.*** However, such incomplete sentences are common in conversation in response to a *why*-question:
 A: *Why did he go to bed?*
 B: ***Because he was sleepy.***

☐ **EXERCISE 1, p. 360. Adverb clauses. (Chart 17-1)**

Give students time to add punctuation in their books. Then lead a quick run-through of the items, or have pairs of students compare their work.

Many of the items in this exercise require an understanding of the uses of periods and commas as presented in Chapter 16 (Coordinating Conjunctions). Items 12 and 13 contain incidental material covered in Chapters 12 (Noun Clauses) and 13 (Adjective Clauses).

Items 5–9 are related to the picture.

ANSWERS: [The adverb clauses are <u>underlined</u>.]
2. <u>When it began to rain,</u> he closed the windows. **3.** He closed the windows <u>when it began to rain.</u> **4.** <u>As soon as the rain began,</u> the children wanted to go outdoors. **T**hey love to play outside in the warm summer rain. **I** used to do the same thing <u>when I was a child.</u> **5.** Jack got to the airport early. <u>After he checked in at the airline counter,</u> he went to the waiting area near his gate. **H**e sat and read <u>until his flight was announced.</u>
6. Jack walked onto the plane, found his seat, and stowed his bag in an overhead compartment. **7.** <u>Before the plane took off,</u> he fastened his seat belt and put his seat in an upright position. **8.** Jack's wife doesn't like to fly <u>because she gets nervous on airplanes.</u> **9.** <u>When Jack and his wife go on vacation,</u> they have to drive or take the train <u>because his wife is afraid of flying.</u> **10.** I had a cup of tea <u>before I left for work this morning,</u> but I didn't have anything to eat. **I** rarely eat breakfast. **11.** <u>After Ellen gets home from work,</u> she likes to read the newspaper. **S**he follows the same routine every day after work. **A**s soon as she gets home, she changes her clothes, gets a snack and a drink, and sits down in her favorite chair to read the newspaper in peace and quiet. **S**he usually has about half an hour to read the paper <u>before her husband arrives home from his job.</u>
12. <u>When you speak to someone</u> [*who is hard of hearing* = adjective clause], you do not have to shout. **I**t is important to face the person directly and speak clearly. **M**y elderly father is hard of hearing, but he can understand me <u>if I face him, speak slowly, and say each word clearly.</u> **13.** Greg Adams has been blind <u>since he was two years old.</u> **T**oday he is a key scientist in a computer company. **H**e is able to design complex electronic equipment <u>because he has a special computer</u> [*that reads, writes, and speaks out loud* = adjective clause]. **H**is blindness neither helps nor hinders him. **I**t is irrelevant to [*how well he does his job* = noun clause].

☐ **EXERCISE 2, p. 361. Review of adverb clauses of time. (Chapter 5 and Chart 17-1)**

This can be done as seatwork while you walk around the classroom and offer help, or it could be assigned as homework. It could also be done orally. One of the challenges of this exercise is appropriate verb tense usage.

SAMPLE COMPLETIONS: **1.** Since I came to this city, I've met a lot of nice people.
2. Just as I was falling asleep last night, a mosquito buzzed in my ear and woke me up.
3. I'll help you with your homework as soon as I finish washing the dishes.   **4.** I was late.
By the time I got to the airport, my plane had already taken off.   **5.** One of my friends
gets nervous every time she has to perform in public.   **6.** I will be here until I have
completed my education.   **7.** I will remember my wedding day as long as I live.
8. I heard the phone ring while I was in the shower.   **9.** Once summer comes, the traffic
on the highway becomes heavier.   **10.** Shortly before I put supper on the table, the cat
demanded to be fed.   **11.** I have been in this city for three years. By the time I leave,
I will be able to speak English fluently.   **12.** The last time I was with my family, I was 24
years old.   **13.** The next time you see them, you'll be 28.   **14.** I will be with you just
as soon as I finish checking this inventory.   **15.** Not long after I bought the car, I ran
over a nail and got a flat tire.   **16.** I had already finished supper when you telephoned.
17. Whenever I'm late for an important meeting, I get nervous.   **18.** Ever since I was a
child, I've been afraid of snakes.

CHART 17-2:   USING ADVERB CLAUSES TO SHOW CAUSE AND EFFECT

• There are differences among the ways to say "because." *Because* makes the most direct or
explicit cause-and-effect statement. *Since* means "because it is a fact that" or "seeing that it is
true that." For example: *Since you've done this before* (a known fact), *could you please show me
how? Because,* but not *since,* can ask about an unknown cause. For example: *Did he stay home
because he was tired? Now that* is special to present-time, known reasons. It indicates that a
situation has changed.

• Punctuation follows the same guidelines with these adverb clauses as with others. (And they
are only guidelines, not rules. There are wide stylistic variations in comma usage with adverb
clauses. This text simply presents the most usual patterns.)

• Other cause-and-effect subordinating conjunctions you may wish to introduce in an
advanced class are *as, as/so long as,* and *inasmuch as.* They are similar to *since:* they express a
cause that is a known fact.
  As has many uses. Students might be interested in knowing that one use is to express
cause and effect. In their own writing, however, they might prefer to use *because, since,* or *now
that* in order to ensure clarity.
  Inasmuch as is generally found only in formal writing and is relatively infrequent.

☐ **EXERCISE 3, p. 362.   Using adverb clauses to show cause and effect.   (Chart 17-2)**

You might ask for two different versions of the response to a few items to show the use of a
comma whenever the adverb clause precedes the independent clause.

ANSWERS: [The adverb clauses are underlined.]
3. Cold air hovers near the earth <u>because it is heavier than hot air</u>.   **4.** <u>Since you paid
for the theater tickets</u>, please let me pay for our dinner.   **5.** <u>Now that Larry is finally
caught up on his work</u>, he can start his vacation tomorrow. [*be caught up on* = have no tasks left
to do]   **6.** <u>Because our TV set was broken</u>, we listened to the news on the radio.
7. My brother got married last month. <u>Now that he's a married man</u>, he has more
responsibilities.   **8.** <u>Since oil is an irreplaceable natural resource</u>, we must do whatever
we can in order to conserve it.   **9.** Do you want to go for a walk <u>now that the rain has
stopped</u>?   **10.** Many young people move to the cities in search of employment <u>since</u>

there are few jobs available in the rural areas.   11. Now that the civil war has ended, a new government is being formed.   12. Since ninety-two thousand people already have reservations with an airline company for a trip to the moon, I doubt that I'll get the chance to go on one of the first tourist flights.

☐ **EXERCISE 4, p. 363.   Using adverb clauses to show cause and effect. (Chart 17-2)**

SAMPLE COMPLETIONS: [The adverb clauses are underlined.]
1. Now that I've finally finished cleaning my room, I can watch TV.   2. The teacher didn't collect the papers because the exercise is not going to be graded.   3. Since it's too expensive to fly across the country, we are going by bus.   4. Jack can't stay out all night with his friends now that he is working the night shift.   5. Since we don't have class tomorrow, we can stay up later tonight.

**CHART 17-3:   EXPRESSING CONTRAST (UNEXPECTED RESULT):
USING *EVEN THOUGH***

• The general category of "contrast" is defined as "unexpected result" here to help the students compare *because* and *even though,* and also to help them understand the meaning of contrast (i.e., that something is in some way different from something else) as the term is used in the text.

• Other forms of *even though* are *although* and *though*. (See Chart 19-6.) The differences are negligible.

☐ **EXERCISE 5, p. 364.   Using EVEN THOUGH. (Chart 17-3)**

Compare the related pairs of sentences: 1 and 2, 3 and 4, 5 and 6, and 7 and 8. Give students a chance to comprehend the information in both sentences before discussing them.

ANSWERS: **3.** even though   **4.** because   **5.** Even though   **6.** Because
7. even though   **8.** because   **9.** even though   **10.** even though   **11.** because
12. Even though . . . because

☐ **EXERCISE 6, p. 364.   Using EVEN THOUGH. (Chart 17-3)**

Before responding, the students need a moment to decide whether the "truthful" answer is *Yes* or *No.* Then they must construct a complete sentence. The result is a fairly realistic dialogue. You can easily assume the role of Speaker A, but in a large class, group work may be preferable.

ANSWERS: [The adverb clause can come before or after the main clause.]
1. Yes, even though I wasn't tired, I went to bed. [*Anyway* is similar in meaning to *even though,* showing an unexpected result.]   **2.** No, (. . .) didn't wake up even though the telephone rang many times.   **3.** Yes, even though the food was terrible, I ate it.
4. Yes, even though I didn't study, I passed the test.   **5.** No, I didn't say home even though the weather is terrible (today).   **6.** No, even though I fell down the stairs, I didn't get hurt.   **7.** Yes, I still feel tired even though I took a nap. [*took a nap* = slept for a short time during the day]   **8.** No, even though I told the truth, no one believed me.   **9.** Yes, even though I turned on the air conditioner, it's still hot in here.   **10.** No, even though I mailed the letter three days ago, it still hasn't arrived/it hasn't arrived yet.   **11.** No, I

can't afford to buy an airplane even though I have a lot of money.   **12.** Yes, even though my grandmother is ninety years old, she's still young at heart.   **13.** Yes, I laughed at (. . .)'s joke even though I didn't understand it.   **14.** Yes, I'm still cheerful even though (all those terrible things happened).

□ **EXERCISE 7, p. 365.   Using EVEN THOUGH and BECAUSE.   (Charts 17-2 and 17-3)**

These answers use the past tense, but other tenses are possible.

Items 11 and 12 may be quite challenging, so you could give special praise for good responses.

SAMPLE COMPLETIONS: **3.** Because it was a beautiful day, I went fishing.   **4.** Even though it was a work day, I went fishing.   **5.** Even though there were very few customers in the store, we decided to stay open until 9:00 P.M.   **6.** Because there were very few customers in the store, we closed early.   **7.** I wore heavy gloves because the temperature was below freezing.   **8.** Even though my feet were killing me and my head was pounding, I finished running the marathon.   **9.** Even though I was speeding, I didn't get a traffic ticket. **10.** Even though I was tired, I finished my homework because my essay was due the next day. **11.** Even though I didn't like baked beans when I was small, I always finished them because I wanted dessert.   **12.** Because we didn't have a television set while I was growing up, I watched TV at my neighbor's house even though my parents didn't approve.

CHART 17-4:   SHOWING DIRECT CONTRAST: *WHILE* AND *WHEREAS*

• *Whereas* and *while* can appear at the beginning of either clause with no change of meaning. *Whereas* is somewhat formal and of relatively low frequency. *Whereas* is included in the text mostly as a way of defining this use of *while,* distinguishing it from its use in time clauses and phrases.

While has two different meanings: (1) at the same time and (2) whereas.
   (1) *While (he was) swimming, he got very tired.*
   (2) *While fire is hot, ice is cold.*

• In British English, *whilst* is another form of *while. Whilst* is fairly formal.

□ **EXERCISE 8, p. 366.   Using WHILE and WHEREAS.   (Chart 17-4)**

ERRATUM: Item 6 should read "Jack is an interesting storyteller and conversationalist, whereas his brother _____." This is corrected in subsequent printings. *On the other hand* was reorganized into Chapter 19 in this third edition; the inclusion of *on the other hand* in this exercise slipped by the author.

ANSWERS: **2.** D.   **3.** C.   **4.** C.   **5.** B.   **6.** B.

□ **EXERCISE 9, p. 366.   Using WHILE and WHEREAS.   (Chart 17-4)**

Two or more students should give different versions of each item. Every sentence should contain a comma before the second adverb clause.

POSSIBLE ANSWERS: **2.** Some people are tall, whereas others are short. [also possible: move *whereas* to the first clause]   **3.** . . . while others prefer to live in town/in the city/in urban areas.   **4.** . . . others know one or more foreign languages.   **5.** . . . a rat is large. **6.** . . . is always cold.   **7.** and **8.** *(free response)*

CHART 17-5: EXPRESSING CONDITIONS IN ADVERB CLAUSES: *IF*-CLAUSES

• As with adverb clauses of time (see Chapter 5), it is incorrect to use the future tense (i.e., *will / be going to*) in an *if*-clause. An exception, however, occurs when the speaker is trying to arrange an exchange of promises: *If you'll do it, I'll do it.*

• All of the examples and exercise items in this unit on "condition" (17-5 through 17-9) are in present or future time. Chapter 20 picks up the use of other verb forms in conditional sentences.

□ **EXERCISE 10, p. 367. IF-clauses. (Chart 17-5)**

Several students could give answers for each item. Encourage them to be creative or humorous. The main point is to use present verbs in the *if*-clause.

ANSWERS: [These depend on students' creativity.]

CHART 17-6: ADVERB CLAUSES OF CONDITION: USING *WHETHER OR NOT* AND *EVEN IF*

• Students sometimes wonder about the difference between *even though* and *even if*. *Even though* deals with actual, present-time events or states; *even if* deals with possible future conditions. *Even though the weather is cold (today)* = the weather is cold. *Even if the weather is cold (tomorrow)* = the weather may be cold. In some contexts, the distinction blurs: *Even if you don't like pickles, you should try one of these.*

□ **EXERCISE 11, p. 368. Using WHETHER OR NOT and EVEN IF. (Chart 17-6)**

You should read the cue to the class so they understand the situation. It isn't necessary to use the exact words from the book; just describe the situation. Then ask students to complete the sentences logically.

ANSWERS:
2. Sam laughs at the jokes:
   a. whether they're funny or not.   b. even if they're not funny.
3. You have to hand in your examination paper:
   a. whether you're finished or not.   b. even if you're not finished.
4. We're going to go camping in the mountains:
   a. whether it snows or not.   b. even if it snows.
5. Max can go to school:
   a. whether or not he gets a scholarship.   b. even if he doesn't get a scholarship.
6. My grandfather wears his gray sweater:
   a. whether or not the weather is cold.   b. even if the weather is hot.
7. I'm going to marry Harry:
   a. whether you approve or not.   b. even if you don't approve.

☐ EXERCISE 12, p. 369.　Using WHETHER OR NOT and EVEN IF.　(Chart 17-6)

SAMPLE COMPLETIONS:　**1.** We're not going to the park today even if the weather improves. **2.** Even if she apologizes to her supervisor, Maria may lose her job. **3.** Getting that job depends on whether or not you can speak English. **4.** I'm going to help you whether you want me to or not. **5.** I won't tell you even if you beg me. **6.** I'm really angry! Maybe he'll apologize, and maybe he won't. It doesn't matter. Even if he tells me he's really sorry, I won't forgive him! **7.** I'm exhausted. Please don't wake me up even if the house catches on fire. **8.** I'm not going to go with him to the boxing match even if he begs me. **9.** Even if it rains, I'm going to take my morning walk. **10.** I'm going to quit school whether my parents like it or not.

CHART 17-7:　**ADVERB CLAUSES OF CONDITION: USING *IN CASE* AND *IN THE EVENT THAT***

- Often *in case* and *in the event that* are synonomous, as in the examples in the chart and the exercises.

　　However, there are also differences you may or may not wish to bring up in class. *In case* is used to say that something may possibly happen and that is the reason why something else is done: *I'll take my purse with me in case we decide to stop at the store.* In other words, the reason I'm doing one thing (taking my purse) is that something else might happen (we might decide to stop at the store). *In the event that* could also possibly be used in this example, but *in case* would be more likely.

　　In the event that is used to talk about a possible future event when the speaker is planning what to do if it occurs. *In the event that more than 40 students sign up for the class, we'll divide it into two sections.*

- British English has another use of *in the event* in formal English. It is not followed by a *that*-clause; it is a transition followed by a comma. It expresses an unexpected result or the idea that "this is what really happened instead." For example:
　　They had planned to go swimming. In the event, they went to a movie because it rained.

An American English speaker would use *instead* or *as it turned out* rather than *in the event* in this context.

- Some scientific and philosophical texts use *in case* to mean "in the specific circumstance or example." This is often followed by a *that*-clause.

☐ EXERCISE 13, p. 369.　Using IN CASE and IN THE EVENT THAT.　(Chart 17-7)

In these sentences, students should take the role of "I." In other words, they are just changing the form of your sentence, not having a dialogue with you. Responders can alternate between *in case* and *in the event that* or simply use whichever one seems more comfortable.

ANSWERS:　**2.** In case / In the event that you need to see me, I'll be in my office tomorrow morning around ten. **3.** In case / In the event that you need more information, you can call me. **4.** In case / In the event that you have any more questions, ask Dr. Smith. **5.** In case / In the event that Jack calls, please tell him that I'm at the library. **6.** In case / In the event that you're not satisfied with your purchase, you can return it to the store.

SAMPLE COMPLETIONS: **7.** . . . you'll have to go to the library. **8.** . . . you lose your credit cards. **9.** . . . my parents decide to come for a visit. **10.** . . . it rains. [*just adds a bit of emphasis*] **11.** . . . the refugees can at last return to their homes. **12.** . . . please start without me. **13.** . . . it malfunctions.

CHART 17-8: ADVERB CLAUSES OF CONDITION: USING *UNLESS*

• Trying to distinguish between *until* and *unless* for the students can be difficult. *Unless* expresses a condition that is required for a particular result. *Until* expresses a time relationship—but also expresses a condition required for a result. It is no wonder that students may be confused when they compare the following: *You can't drive unless/until you're sixteen. Class can't start unless/until the teacher arrives. I don't eat unless/until I'm hungry.*

• The verb in the *unless*-clause is usually positive, but it could be negative. For example:
  A: *Will I see you at the theater tonight?*
  B: *Yes, unless I can't go.*

☐ **EXERCISE 14, p. 370. Using UNLESS. (Chart 17-8)**

Expect some students to have difficulty with *unless*. You may want to write the answers on the chalkboard so that everyone can focus and the exercise can proceed more slowly.

ANSWERS: **2.** You can't travel abroad unless you have a passport. **3.** You can't get a driver's license unless you're at least sixteen years old. **4.** Unless I get some film, I won't be able to take pictures when Ann and Rob get here. **5.** You'll get hungry during class unless you eat breakfast.

☐ **EXERCISE 15, p. 371. Using UNLESS. (Chart 17-8)**

SAMPLE COMPLETIONS: **2.** I'm sorry, but you can't see the doctor unless you have an appointment. **3.** I can't graduate from school unless I pass all my courses. **4.** That food will spoil unless you put it in the refrigerator. **5.** Unless it rains, we plan to have the birthday party in the backyard. **6.** Certain species of animals will soon become extinct unless we stop destroying their habitats. **7.** I will have to look for another job unless I get a raise [BrE: *rise*] in salary. **8.** Tomorrow I'm going to call my sister unless I hear from her on e-mail today. **9.** The political situation in (. . .) will continue to deteriorate unless the opposing sides commit to ending the hostilities and creating a lasting peace. **10.** He doesn't say anything unless the teacher calls on him. **11.** Unless you start learning how to use the Internet, the modern world will pass you by.

CHART 17-9: ADVERB CLAUSES OF CONDITION: USING *ONLY IF*

• No commas are used when *only if / only when / only after* clauses begin a sentence.

☐ **EXERCISE 16, p. 371. Using ONLY IF. (Chart 17-9)**

You should set up the situation in each item so that the students understand it. It is not necessary to use exactly the same words that are in the book; just explain it briefly and naturally. Make up similar items using your students' names and situations.

ANSWERS: **2.** You can go to the party only if you have an invitation. **3.** You can attend this school only if you have a student visa. [A visa is required by some countries for students coming from other countries.] **4.** Jimmy chews gum only if he's sure his mother won't find out. **5.** We will go to the movie only if you want to (go). **6.** Water will freeze only if the temperature reaches 32°F / 0°C [F = Fahrenheit /fɛrənhait/; C = Celsius /sɛlsiəs/]
7. Only if you study hard **will you** pass the exam. **8.** Only if you have a ticket **can you** get into the soccer stadium. **9.** Only if Jake's homework is finished **can he** watch TV in the evening. **10.** Only if I get a job **will I** have enough money to go to school.
11.–13. (*free response*)

☐ EXERCISE 17, p. 372.   Using UNLESS and ONLY IF. (Charts 17-8 and 17-9)

Two students could give different responses to each item, as in the example.

ANSWERS: **2.** I can't pay my bills unless I get a job. I can pay my bills only if I get a job. **3.** Your clothes will get clean only if you use soap. Your clothes won't get clean unless you use soap. **4.** I can't take any pictures unless I buy some film. I can take pictures only if I buy some film. **5.** I don't wake up unless the alarm clock rings. I wake up only if the alarm clock rings. **6.** Eggs won't hatch unless they're kept at the proper temperature. Eggs will hatch only if they're kept at the proper temperature. [*hatch* = produce baby chicks] **7.** Don't borrow money from friends unless you absolutely have to. Borrow money from friends only if you absolutely have to. **8.** Anna doesn't talk in class unless the teacher asks her specific questions. Anna talks in class only if the teacher asks her specific questions.

☐ EXERCISE 18, p. 372.   Adverb clauses of condition. (Charts 17-6 → 17-9)

Do this exercise orally as a quick review. One student could answer, and another could then indicate the necessary punctuation in the sentence. Every answer should contain the two given ideas about rain and the party (unless you wish to encourage more creativity).

ANSWERS: [These depend on students' creativity.]

☐ EXERCISE 19, p. 373.   Activity: adverb clauses. (Chapter 17)

EXPANSION: After B completes A's sentence, A could paraphrase the whole sentence using a different connecting word/expression (e.g., "You wanted to fly a kite, but you went to class so you could improve your English").

ANSWERS: [These depend on students' creativity.]

Chapter 18: REDUCTION OF ADVERB CLAUSES TO MODIFYING ADVERBIAL PHRASES

ORDER OF CHAPTER	CHARTS	EXERCISES	WORKBOOK
Modifying adverbial phrases	18-1 → 18-4	Ex. 1 → 7	Pr. 1 → 5
Using *upon* + *-ing*	18-5	Ex. 8	Pr. 6
Cumulative review		Ex. 9 → 11	Pr. 7
General review, Chapters 16 → 18		Ex. 12	Pr. 8 → 9

General Notes on Chapter 18

• OBJECTIVE: Students learn the meaning and use of adverbial phrases that modify the subject of a sentence. These phrases are primarily a feature of written English.

• APPROACH: This chapter draws a parallel with Chapter 13, where adjective phrases are introduced. Adverb clauses and reduced adverbial phrases are illustrated and practiced with special attention to avoiding dangling modifiers. The chapter ends with a review of Chapters 16–18.

• TERMINOLOGY: A "dangling participle" is one type of dangling modifier.
   Unsure of himself, *the right words stuck in Bob's throat.*
   = a dangling modifier (but not a dangling participle).

   Being unsure of himself, *the right words stuck in Bob's throat.*
   = a dangling participle that can also be called by the more inclusive term "dangling modifier."

CHARTS 18-1 AND 18-2: CHANGING TIME CLAUSES TO MODIFYING ADVERBIAL PHRASES

• These modifying phrases are often called "participial phrases" because the main word is a present participle (*-ing* form) or sometimes a past participle (*-ed* form, conveying a passive meaning). If the phrase doesn't modify the subject of the main clause, the unacceptable result is called a "dangling participle"—the participle has nothing to modify, so it dangles (hangs) unattached to any other word. For example:
   While walking by the lake, a fish jumped out of the water.

Obviously, the fish wasn't walking! But in this sentence *walking* must refer to *fish*, so the whole thing is ungrammatical (as well as unscientific).

• In Chart 18-2, the word "since" has its time-related meaning (see Chart 5-2), not its cause-and-effect meaning. Learners are sometimes confused about this. Just tell them that sometimes two different vocabulary items have the same spelling, like *fall* (autumn) vs. *fall* (drop down).

• Call attention to (f) in Chart 18-2 so that students see that a phrase may either precede or follow the main clause. Note the punctuation in each case.

□ **EXERCISE 1, p. 375.** **Changing time clauses to modifying adverbial phrases.**
                                   (Charts 18-1 and 18-2)

You could use the first few items of this exercise for chart reinforcement and then turn it over to group work in which the students can teach each other.

ANSWERS: **3.** Before <u>I</u> came to class, <u>I</u> had a cup of coffee. *Before coming to class*, I had a cup of coffee. **4.** Before <u>the student</u> came to class, <u>the teacher</u> had already given a quiz. *(no change)* **5.** Since <u>I</u> came here, <u>I</u> have learned a lot of English. *Since coming here*, I have learned a lot of English. **6.** Since <u>Bob</u> opened his new business, <u>he</u> has been working 16 hours a day. *Since opening his new business*, Bob has been working 16 hours a day. **7.** After <u>Omar</u> (had) finished breakfast, <u>he</u> left the house and went to his office. *After finishing / having finished breakfast*, Omar left the house and went to his office. **8.** <u>Alex</u> hurt his back while <u>he</u> was chopping wood. Alex hurt his back *while chopping wood*. **9.** <u>You</u> should always read a contract before <u>you</u> sign your name. You should always read a contract *before signing your name*. **10.** Before <u>the waiter</u> came to the table, <u>I</u> had already made up my mind to order shrimp. *(no change)* **11.** Before <u>you</u> ask the librarian for help, <u>you</u> should make every effort to find the materials yourself. *Before asking the librarian for help*, you should make every effort to find the materials yourself. **12.** While <u>Jack</u> was trying to sleep last night, a <u>mosquito</u> kept buzzing in his ear. *(no change)* **13.** While <u>Susan</u> was climbing the mountain, <u>she</u> lost her footing and fell onto a ledge several feet below. *While climbing the mountain*, Susan lost her footing and fell onto a ledge several feet below. **14.** <u>The Wilsons</u> have experienced many changes in their lifestyle since <u>they</u> adopted twins. The Wilsons have experienced many changes in their lifestyle *since adopting twins*. **15.** After <u>I</u> heard Mary describe how cold it gets in Minnesota in the winter, <u>I</u> decided not to go there for my vacation in January. *After hearing Mary describe how cold it gets in Minnesota in the winter*, I decided not to go there for my vacation in January.

**CHART 18-3:   EXPRESSING THE IDEA OF "DURING THE SAME
                 TIME" IN MODIFYING ADVERBIAL PHRASES**

• Compare modifying participial phrases at the beginning of a sentence with gerund subjects (sometimes a point of confusion for leaners).

   Gerund subjects: ***Walking*** *down that street alone at night **is** dangerous.*
                    Hiking *through the woods **is** an enjoyable way to get exercise.*

• Point out that the position of certain modifying phrases can determine meaning. Compare those in (c) and (d) in this chart with the following:

   I ran into an old friend (who was) walking down the street.
   We saw a bear (that was) hiking through the woods. (The concept of a bear "hiking" may be
      an imaginative, creative use of that verb.)

The modifier should be as close as possible to the noun that it modifies.

CHART 18-4: EXPRESSING CAUSE AND EFFECT IN MODIFYING ADVERBIAL PHRASES

• The important point for learners to understand is that the grammatical structure itself (without function words) expresses a cause-and-effect meaning.

• In many cases, an initial modifying participial phrase combines the ideas of "during the same time" and "because"—as the students will discover in Exercise 2.

• To point out that *being* expresses cause and effect in this structure, have the students compare the meanings of the following two sentences.

   (1) *Chicago, a large city, has a crime problem.* (*a large city* = an appositive, reduced adjective clause that gives identifying information about the noun: *Chicago, which is a large city, has . . . .* Cause and effect may be implied, but is not stated.)

   (2) *Chicago, being a large city, has a crime problem.* (a clear cause-and-effect relationship)

☐ EXERCISE 2, p. 376. Modifying adverbial phrases. (Charts 18-3 and 18-4)

See the *Introduction*, p. xix, for suggestions for using discussion-of-meaning exercises.

ANSWERS: **1.** *while* **2.** *because* **3.** *while* **4.** *because* **5.** a blending of the meanings of *while* and *because* **6.** *because* **7.** *because* **8.** *while* **9.** *while* **10.** *because* **11.** *because* **12.** a blending of the meanings of *while* and *because*

☐ EXERCISE 3, p. 377. Modifying adverbial phrases. (Chart 18-4)

This exercise emphasizes that these modifying phrases convey a cause-and-effect meaning without the word "because." In the example, call attention to the structure of the negative phrase and to the necessity of identifying the subject in the main clause. Point out that these phrases modify the subject of the main clause.

ANSWERS: **2.** *Believing that no one loved him,* **the little boy** ran away from home.
3. *Not paying attention to where she was going,* **Rosa** stepped into a hole and sprained her ankle. **4.** *Having forgotten to bring a pencil to the examination,* I had to borrow one.
5. *Being a vegetarian,* **Chelsea** does not eat meat. **6.** *Having (already) flunked out of school once,* **Mike** is determined to succeed this time.

☐ EXERCISE 4, p. 377. Modifying adverbial phrases. (Charts 18-2 → 18-4)

This exercise is a summary review of Charts 18-2, 18-3, and 18-4. It is helpful to point out repeatedly that these phrases modify the subject of the main clause.

ANSWERS: **1.** *Before talking to you,* **I** had never understood that formula. **2.** *Not wanting to spend any more money this month,* **Larry** decided against going to a restaurant for dinner. **3.** *After reading the chapter four times,* **I** finally understood the author's theory.
4. *Remembering that everyone makes mistakes,* **I** softened my view of his seemingly inexcusable error. **5.** *Since completing his Bachelor's degree,* **he** has had three jobs, each one better than the last. **6.** *While traveling across the United States,* **I** could not help being impressed by the great differences in terrain. **7.** *Before gaining national fame,* **the union leader** had been an electrician in a small town. **8.** *Enjoying the cool evening breeze and listening to the sounds of nature,* **we** lost track of time. **9.** *Having never flown in an airplane before,* **the little girl** was surprised and a little frightened when her ears popped. [You can hear a small "pop" in your head when air pressure is released, often by yawning slightly.] **10.** *Before becoming vice-president of marketing and sales,* **Peter McKay** worked as a sales representative.

□ **EXERCISE 5, p. 378. Modifying adverbial phrases. (Charts 18-3 and 18-4)**

In this exercise, the students have to make modifying phrases while being careful to avoid dangling participles. Strongly emphasize that these phrases modify the subject of the main clause.

Discuss the implied meanings of the adverbial phrases: *because, while,* and a blending of the two.

ANSWERS: **2.** *Hearing that Nadia was in the hospital,* **I** called her family to find out what was wrong. **3.** *(no change)* **4.** *Living a long distance from my work,* **I** have to commute daily by train. **5.** *Living a long distance from her work,* **Heidi** has to commute daily by train. **6.** *(no change)* **7.** *Not wanting to inconvenience my friend by asking her to drive me to the airport,* **I** decided to take a taxi. **8.** *Sitting on a large rock at the edge of a mountain stream,* **I** felt at peace with the world. **9.** *Being a married man,* **I** have many responsibilities. **10.** *Trying his best not to cry,* **the little boy** swallowed hard and began to speak. **11.** *Keeping one hand on the steering wheel,* **Anna** opened a can of soda pop with her free hand. **12.** *(no change)* **13.** *Recognizing his face but having forgotten his name,* **I** just smiled and said, "Hi." **14.** *(no change)* **15.** *(Being) Convinced that she could never learn to play the piano,* **Anna** stopped taking lessons.

□ **EXERCISE 6, p. 378. Modifying adverbial phrases. (Charts 18-3 and 18-4)**

Students should say or write the whole sentence, not just the number and letter from the columns.

ERRATUM: Item 9 in Column A should read: "She has done very well in her studies." This is corrected in later printings.

ANSWERS: **1.** [+ G] Having sticky pads on their feet, flies can easily walk on the ceiling. **2.** [+ J] Having worked with computers for many years, Ed has an excellent understanding of their limitations as well as their potential. **3.** [+ I] (Having been) Born two months prematurely, Mary needed special care for the first few days of her life. **4.** [+ D] Having done everything he could for the patient, the doctor left to attend other people. **5.** [+ A] Having never eaten / Never having eaten Thai food before, Sally didn't know what to expect when she went to the Thai restaurant for dinner. **6.** [+ H] Having no one to turn to for help, Sam was forced to work out the problem by himself. [*Turn to someone (for help/advice)* = ask, depend on] **7.** [+ C] Being an endangered species, rhinos are protected by law from poachers who kill them solely for their horns. [*rhino* /ra̲ino/ = rhinocerus /ra̲inəsərəs/] **8.** [+ B] (Being) Able to crawl into very small spaces, mice can hide in almost any part of a house. **9.** [+ E] Having done very well in her studies, Nancy expects to be hired by a top company after graduation. **10.** [+ F] (Being) Extremely hard and nearly indestructible, diamonds are used extensively in industry to cut other hard minerals.

□ **EXERCISE 7, p. 379. Modifying adverbial phrases. (Charts 18-1 → 18-4)**

ANSWERS: **3.** *(no change)* **4.** *Because* **I** *was too young to understand death,* **my mother** gave me a simple explanation of where my grandfather had gone. **5.** *(no change)* **6.** *While* **I** *was working in my office late last night,* **someone** suddenly knocked loudly at my door and nearly scared me to death! **7.** *After* **we** *(had) hurried to get everything ready for the picnic,* **it** began to rain just as we were leaving. **8.** *While* **I** *was walking across the street at a busy intersection,* **a truck** nearly ran over my foot.

CHART 18-5: USING *UPON* + *-ING* IN MODIFYING ADVERBIAL PHRASES

• These phrases are more common in formal writing than in conversation.

☐ **EXERCISE 8, p. 380. Using UPON + -ING. (Chart 18-5)**

The answers may use either ***upon*** or ***on***.

ANSWERS: **2.** *Upon crossing* the marathon finish line, Tina fell in exhaustion. **3.** *Upon looking* in my wallet, I discovered I didn't have enough money to pay my restaurant bill. **4.** I bowed my head *upon meeting* the king. **5.** *Upon re-reading* the figures, Sam found that he had made a mistake. **6.** . . . *Upon discovering* it was hot, the small child jerked his hand back, ... **7.** Mrs. Alexander nearly fainted *upon learning* that she had won the lottery. **8.** *Upon finishing* the examination, bring your paper to the front of the room. **9.** . . . *Upon hearing* my name, I raised my hand to identify myself. **10.** . . . *Upon hearing this*, Cook grabbed his telescope and searched the horizon.

☐ **EXERCISE 9, p. 381. Review: modifying adverbial phrases. (Chapter 18)**

ANSWERS: **5.** *Before leaving* on my trip, I checked to see what shots I would need. **6.** *(no change)* **7.** *Not having understood* the directions, I got lost. **8.** My father reluctantly agreed to let me attend the game *after talking/having talked* it over with my mother. **9.** *Upon discovering / Discovering* I had lost my key to the apartment, I called the building superintendent. **10.** *(no change)* **11.** Garcia Lopez de Cardenas accidentally discovered the Grand Canyon *while looking* for the legendary Lost City of Gold. **12.** *(no change)* **13.** *After having to wait* for more than half an hour, we were finally seated at the restaurant. **14.** *Before getting accepted* on her country's Olympic running team, Maria had spent most of the two previous years in training. **15.** *Not paying* attention to his driving, George didn't see the large truck until it was almost too late.

☐ **EXERCISE 10, p. 382. Review: modifying adverbial phrases. (Chapter 18)**

When the students use an adverbial phrase, be sure that the subject is clearly identified in the main clause.

ANSWERS:

1. . . . When Watson heard words coming from the machine, he immediately realized that their experiments had at last been successful.
   → Hearing words coming from the machine, = *adverb phrase*

   . . . After Bell had successfully tested the new apparatus again and again, he confidently announced his invention to the world.
   → After having / Having successfully tested the new apparatus again and again, = *adverb phrase*

   . . . Because they believed the telephone was a toy with little practical application, most people paid little attention to Bell's announcement.
   → Believing the telephone was a toy with little practical application, = *adverb phrase*

2. . . . Because many people believe that wolves eagerly kill human beings, they fear them.
   → Believing that wolves eagerly kill human beings, = *adverb phrase*

   . . . Because they are strictly carniverous, wolves hunt large animals. . . .
   → Being strictly carnivorous, = *adverb phrase*
   [*mainstay* = most important food or source of support]

. . . Because it was relentlessly poisoned, trapped, and shot by ranchers and hunters, the timber wolf, ...

→ Having been / Being relentlessly poisoned, trapped, and shot by ranchers and hunters, = *adverb phrase*

. . . In the 1970s, after they realized a mistake had been made, U.S. lawmakers passed laws to protect wolves.

→ In the 1970s, after realizing / after having realized / having realized that a mistake had been made, = *adverb phrase*

. . . Today, after they have been unremittingly destroyed for centuries, they are found in few places, ...

[*unremittingly* = persistently, ceaselessly]

→ Today, after having been / after being / having been unremittingly destroyed for centuries, = *adverb phrase*

☐ **EXERCISE 11, p. 383.   Review: modifying adverbial phrases. (Chapter 18)**

POSSIBLE COMPLETIONS: **1.** After having finished my work, I decided to take a long walk.   **2.** Before going to Canada, I had never seen snow.   **3.** Since coming to this school, I have met a lot of interesting people.   **4.** Sitting in the park the other day, Mustafa saw a squirrel with a red tail.   **5.** Having heard a strange noise in the other room, the babysitter called a neighbor to help him investigate.   **6.** Being new on the job, I felt very unsure of myself.   **7.** Being the largest city in the United States, New York is a favorite tourist destination.   **8.** Upon reaching our destination, we leapt out of the car and ran toward the lake.   [The past tense of *leap* is either *leaped* /lipt/ or *leapt* /lɛpt/.]   **9.** Receiving no answer when he knocked on the door, the mail carrier took the registered package back to the post office.   **10.** Exhausted by the long hours of work, the medical student was too tired to eat his dinner and went straight to bed.

☐ **EXERCISE 12, p. 384.   Error analysis: general review. (Chapters 16, 17, and 18)**

ANSWERS:

2. Because our leader could not attend the meeting, ~~so~~ it was canceled.   OR
   ~~Because~~ Our leader could not attend the meeting, so it was canceled.
3. My wife and I like to travel. [Stylistically it is generally preferred that the pronoun "I" be second in a compound subject, though grammatically "I and my wife" is possible.]
4. I always fasten my seat belt before ~~to~~ starting the engine.   OR   I always fasten my seat belt before ~~to~~ I start the engine.
5. I don't like our classroom **b**ecause it is hot and crowded. I hope we can change to a different room.   OR   I don't like our classroom. It is hot and crowded. I hope we can change to a different room.
6. Since / Because the day was very warm and humid, ~~for that~~ I turned on the air conditioner.
7. Upon ~~I~~ learning that my car couldn't be repaired for three days, I was very distressed.
8. Because I missed the final examination ~~because~~, the teacher gave me a failing grade.   OR   Having missed the final examination, I received a failing grade.
9. Both my sister and (my) brother are going to be at the family reunion.
10. I hope my son will remain/remains in school until he finishes his degree.
11. My brother has succeeded in business because ~~of~~ he works hard. [*Because vs. because of* is introduced in Chapter 19, Chart 19-1. This item should appear in the following chapter, not here—but since it's here, through an oversight on the part of the author during the reorganization of this edition, the item can be profitably used to introduce the chart on the next page.]
12. Luis stood up, turned toward me, and spoke so softly that I couldn't hear what he said.
13. I was lost. I could ~~not~~ find neither my parents nor my brother.
14. Since she had studied Greek for several years, Sarah's pronunciation was easy to understand. [A phrase (*Having studied* . . .) is not possible because the subjects *(she* and *pronunciation)* are not the same.]

Chapter 19: CONNECTIVES THAT EXPRESS CAUSE AND EFFECT, CONTRAST, AND CONDITION

ORDER OF CHAPTER	CHARTS	EXERCISES	WORKBOOK
Preview		Ex. 1	
Using *because of* and *due to*	19-1	Ex. 2 → 3	Pr. 1 → 2
Using transitions to show cause and effect: *therefore* and *consequently*	19-2	Ex. 4 → 6	Pr. 3
Summary of patterns and punctuation	19-3	Ex. 7 → 8	Pr. 4
Other ways of expressing cause and effect: *such . . . that* and *so . . . that*	19-4	Ex. 9 → 11	Pr. 5 → 6
Expressing purpose: using *so that*	19-5	Ex. 13* → 16	Pr. 7
Review: cause and effect			Pr. 8
Showing contrast (unexpected result)	19-6	Ex. 17 → 22	Pr. 9 → 11
Showing direct contrast	19-7	Ex. 23 → 26	Pr. 12
Review: cause/effect and contrast			Pr. 13
Expressing conditions: using *otherwise* and *or (else)*	19-8	Ex. 27 → 28	Pr. 14
Summary of connectives: cause and effect, contrast, condition	19-9	Ex. 29 → 32	Pr. 15
Review		Ex. 33* → 40	Pr. 16 → 17

* ERRATA: The exercises in this chapter were misnumbered. Exercise numbers 12 and 39 were inadvertently omitted. To avoid confusion in classes where some students are using one printing of the text and others a later printing, the numbering will not be changed. Congratulate alert students for noticing that exercise numbers 12 and 39 are absent and assure them that the author and editors truly regret the error.

• OBJECTIVE: Students practice combining ideas into compound and complex sentences using various connectives. This gives them flexibility in communicating complex information, especially in written English.

• APPROACH: This chapter presents many ways to show relationships between ideas. This is a semantic as well as grammatical approach focusing on the meaning of certain conjunctions. The first section deals with cause-and-effect relationships. Next is a section on contrasts. Finally, ways of expressing a condition and outcome are presented, a unit which anticipates the focus of Chapter 20. Matters of punctuation are also included. At the end of the chapter, Chart 19-9 summarizes the structures and connectives presented in Chapters 16 through 19.

• TERMINOLOGY: The term "connective" includes expressions that serve to connect independent clauses to other coordinate or subordinate structures. This broad term includes words and phrases that are variously called "adverbial transitions," "subordinating conjunctions," "subordinators," "coordinating conjunctions," "conjunctive adverbs," "logical connectors," and "conjuncts" of various types.

☐ **EXERCISE 1, p. 385.   Preview. (Charts 19-1 → 19-3)**

Allow a few minutes for students to identify and correct all the errors in these sentences prior to discussion.

ANSWERS:
1. Because ~~of~~ Rosa's computer skills were poor, she was not considered for the job.
2. Rosa's computer skills were poor. **T**herefore, she was not considered for the job. [OR . . . poor; therefore, she . . . (See footnote to Chart 19-3 in the student book.)]
3. Because Rosa's computer skills were poor, ~~therefore~~ she was not considered for the job. OR ~~Because~~ Rosa's computer skills were poor. **T**herefore, she was not considered for the job. [OR . . . poor; therefore, she . . .]
4. Because Rosa's computer skills were poor, ~~so~~ she was not considered for the job. OR ~~Because~~ Rosa's computer skills were poor, so she was not considered for the job.
5. Due to her poor computer skills, Rosa was not considered for the job ~~therefore~~.
6. ~~Consequently~~ Rosa's computer skills were poor. <u>Consequently</u>, she was not considered for the job. OR <u>Because</u> Rosa's computer skills were poor, she was not considered for the job.

CHART 19-1:   USING *BECAUSE OF* AND *DUE TO*

• A common error is for a learner to begin an adverb clause with *because of*.
     INCORRECT: *He stayed home because of he was ill.*

• A "phrasal preposition" is a phrase that functions as a single preposition.

• Traditionally, a distinction has been made between *because of* and *due to: because of* is used adverbially *(He stayed home because of illness)*, and *due to* is used adjectivally *(His absence is due to illness)*. In current usage, *due to* is also used with verbs: *He stayed home due to illness.* (But *because of* is not used adjectivally following *be*. INCORRECT: *His absence is because of illness.*)

• *Owing to* is used in the same ways as *because of* and *due to,* more in spoken than written English.

• Note that punctuation rules are the same for these phrases as for adverb clauses.

☐ EXERCISE 2, p. 386.   Using BECAUSE and BECAUSE OF.   (Charts 17-2 and 19-1)

The key to choosing the correct answer here is recognizing whether a clause or a noun phrase follows it.

ANSWERS: **3.** because   **4.** because of [*sprained* = twisted but not broken]   **5.** Because of   **6.** Because [*a flight of stairs* = the steps between two floors]   **7.** because of [*a famine* = a time of great hunger due to lack of food]   **8.** because of [*dilapidated* /dɪlǽpɪdetəd/ = broken-down, deteriorated]

☐ EXERCISE 3, p. 386.   Using BECAUSE OF and DUE TO.   (Chart 19-1)

Students need to create noun phrases, not clauses, for these answers.

ANSWERS: **2.** the heavy traffic   **3.** his wife's illness   **4.** Dr. Robinson's excellent research on wolves   **5.** the noise in the next apartment   **6.** circumstances beyond my control

---

CHART 19-2:   USING TRANSITIONS TO SHOW CAUSE AND EFFECT: *THEREFORE* AND *CONSEQUENTLY*

• Students sometimes ask, "Why are these two words used so differently from *so* if they mean the same?" There is no satisfactory answer except: "It's traditional in English to use them in this way." Languages develop patterns; certain words fit certain patterns, and certain words do not.

• Have the students identify which of the related ideas is the "cause" and which is the "effect"—*not studying* is the cause; *failing* is the effect.

• If your students are advanced and are interested in conventions of formal writing, you could include teaching the use of the semicolon at this point. Otherwise, the semicolon can simply remain in the footnote to Chart 19-3 as a minor point of information for those who may be interested.

• The name "Al" in these examples is a short form of Albert or Alfred.

☐ EXERCISE 4, p. 387.   Using THEREFORE and CONSEQUENTLY.   (Chart 19-2)

Give the class time to write this exercise as seatwork. It is a straightforward exercise on written forms. They are asked to practice all three forms of each sentence. You might ask students to write the sentences on the board. You might show the punctuation on the chalkboard or on pieces of cardboard (pasteboard):

∼∼∼ . Therefore, ∼∼∼ . ∼∼∼ . ∼∼∼ , therefore, ∼∼∼ . ∼∼∼ . ∼∼∼∼∼ , therefore.

∼∼∼ . Consequently, ∼∼∼ . ∼∼∼ . ∼∼∼ , consequently, ∼∼∼ . ∼∼∼ . ∼∼∼∼∼ , consequently.

ANSWERS:
1. A storm was approaching. Therefore, the children stayed home.
   A storm was approaching. The children, therefore, stayed home.
   A storm was approaching. The children stayed home, therefore.
2. I didn't have my umbrella. Consequently, I got wet.
   I didn't have my umbrella. I, consequently, got wet.
   I didn't have my umbrella. I got wet, consequently.

Students can write these items on the chalkboard for everyone to discuss, or they can read them aloud and indicate where they used punctuation and capital letters.

EX. 5 ANSWERS: **1.** Because it was cold, she wore a coat.   **2.** *(no change)*   **3.** Because of the cold weather, she wore a coat.   **4.** *(no change)*   **5.** The weather was cold. Therefore, she wore a coat.   **6.** The weather was cold. She, therefore, wore a coat.   **7.** The weather was cold. She wore a coat, therefore.   **8.** The weather was cold, so she wore a coat.

EX. 6 ANSWERS: **1.** Pat always enjoyed studying sciences in high school. Therefore, she decided to major in biology in college.   **2.** Due to recent improvements in the economy, fewer people are unemployed. [i.e., fewer than before]   **3.** Last night's storm damaged the power lines. Consequently, the town was without electicity for several hours.
4. Because of the snowstorm, only five students came to class. The teacher, therefore, canceled the class.   **5.** *(no change)* [It's important for students to understand that long sentences do not necessarily require internal punctuation.]

CHART 19-3:   SUMMARY OF PATTERNS AND PUNCTUATION

• Students are learning structural distinctions in the use of coordinating conjunctions, subordinating conjunctions, adverbial prepositional phrases, and conjunctive adverbs by using cause-and-effect sentences as models. The patterns and terminology ("conjunction," "adverb clause," "preposition," "transition") they are learning here will transfer to the following units on opposition and condition. The term "conjunction" in this chart is used to refer to "coordinating conjunctions"; include the term "coordinating" if you think it helps your students make distinctions among the differing patterns.

• A wall chart, cards, or a transparency of the patterns and punctuation may prove useful not only here but also for the charts and exercises in the rest of this chapter. For example:

Adverb clause, ⌒⌒ . ⌒⌒ adverb clause.	Prepositional phrase, ⌒⌒ . ⌒⌒ prepositional phrase.
⌒⌒ . Transition, ⌒⌒ . ⌒⌒ . ⌒⌒ , transition, ⌒⌒ . ⌒⌒ . ⌒⌒ , transition.	⌒⌒ , conjunction ⌒⌒ .

• When some students discover the semicolon (see the chart footnote), they tend to use it everywhere. You might point out that it is not often used, even by professional writers. (If students overuse it, tell them to look at any English text and see how many semicolons they can find. Chances are they will find very few.) Many native speakers are unsure about its correct use. A period (full stop) is usually acceptable or even preferable.

• You might call attention to the relationship between a comma in written English and a slight pause in spoken English. [*Riddle:* What's the difference between a cat and a comma? *Answer:* A cat has claws at the end of its paws, and a comma is a pause at the end of a clause.]

☐ **EXERCISE 7, p. 389.   Showing cause and effect. (Chart 19-3)**

Assign each item for one student to write all of its possible patterns on the board. Insist on perfect punctuation and capitalization. (Include the semicolon only if it seems appropriate for your class.) Have the rest of the class offer suggestions and corrections. Let students who think they see an error go to the board and correct it.

Another option is to have the students work in small groups to produce one communal paper that everyone in the group agrees is perfect.

PART I ANSWERS:

2. The weather was bad. <u>Therefore</u>, we postponed our trip.   OR   We, <u>therefore</u>, postponed our trip.   OR   We postponed our trip, <u>therefore</u>.

3. <u>Since</u> the weather was bad, we postponed our trip.   OR   We postponed our trip <u>since</u> the weather was bad.

4. The weather was bad, <u>so</u> we postponed our trip.

5. <u>Because of</u> the bad weather, we postponed our trip.   OR   We postponed our trip <u>because of</u> the bad weather.

6. The weather was bad. <u>Consequently</u>, we postponed our trip.   OR   We, <u>consequently</u>, postponed our trip.   OR   We postponed our trip, <u>consequently</u>.

7. <u>Due to the fact that</u> the weather was bad, we postponed our trip.   OR   We postponed our trip <u>due to the fact that</u> the weather was bad.

PART II ANSWERS:

1. <u>Because of</u> her illness, she missed class.   OR   She missed class <u>because of</u> her illness.

2. <u>Because</u> she was ill, she missed class.   OR   She missed class <u>because</u> she was ill.

3. She was ill. <u>Consequently</u>, she missed class.   OR   She, <u>consequently</u>, missed class. OR   She missed class, <u>consequently</u>.

4. She was ill, <u>so</u> she missed class.

5. <u>Due to the fact that</u> she was ill, she missed class.   OR   She missed class <u>due to the fact that</u> she was ill.

6. She was ill. <u>Therefore</u>, she missed class.   OR   She, <u>therefore</u>, missed class. OR She missed class, <u>therefore</u>.

☐ **EXERCISE 8, p. 390.   Showing cause and effect. (Charts 19-2 and 19-3)**

ANSWERS:

2. Emily has never wanted to return to the Yukon to live <u>because of</u> the severe winters.   OR   <u>Because of</u> the severe winters, Emily has never wanted to return to the Yukon to live.

3. It is important to wear a hat on cold days <u>since</u> we lose sixty percent of our body heat through our head.   OR   <u>Since</u> we lose sixty percent of our body heat through our head, it is important to wear a hat on cold days.

4. When I was in my teens and twenties, it was easy for me to get into an argument with my father, <u>for</u> both of us can be stubborn and opinionated.

5. <u>Due to the fact that</u> a camel can go completely without water for eight to ten days, it is an ideal animal for desert areas.   OR   A camel is an ideal animal for desert areas <u>due to the fact that</u> it can go completely without water for eight to ten days.

6. Bill's car wouldn't start. Therefore, he couldn't pick us up after the concert.   OR   **He**, <u>therefore</u>, couldn't pick us up after the concert.   OR   **He** couldn't pick us up after the concert, <u>therefore</u>.

7. Robert did not pay close attention to what the travel agent said when he went to see her at her office last week, <u>so</u> he had to ask many of the same questions again the next time he talked to her.

8. A tomato is classified as a fruit, but most people consider it a vegetable <u>since</u> it is often eaten in salads along with lettuce, onions, cucumbers, and other vegetables.   OR   <u>Since</u> it is often eaten in salads along with lettuce, onions, cucumbers, and other vegetables, a tomato is classified as a fruit.

9. <u>Due to</u> consumer demand for ivory, many African elephants are being slaughtered ruthlessly. <u>Consequently,</u> many people who care about saving these animals from extinction refuse to buy any item made from ivory. OR Many people who care about saving these animals from extinction, <u>consequently,</u> refuse to buy any item made from ivory. OR Many people who care about saving these animals from extinction refuse to buy any item made from ivory, <u>consequently.</u>

10. <u>Because</u> most 15th-century Europeans believed the world was flat and that a ship could conceivably sail off the end of the earth, many sailors of the time refused to venture forth with explorers into unknown waters. OR Many sailors of the 15th century refused to venture forth with explorers into unknown waters <u>because</u> most Europeans of the time believed the world was flat and that a ship could conceivably sail off the end of the earth. [*conceivably* = possibly; *venture forth* = go out into a new, possibly dangerous area]

CHART 19-4: OTHER WAYS OF EXPRESSING CAUSE AND EFFECT: *SUCH . . . THAT* AND *SO . . . THAT*

• Often in conversation we don't add a clause with *that* after using *so*. The word "so" then seems to mean "very" with additional emphasis. For example:
  A: *Did you enjoy that book?*
  B: *Yes, it was **so** interesting!*

This implies a clause with *that,* such as ". . . *so* interesting *that* I couldn't stop reading until I finished the whole book."
  Other examples: *I'm **so** tired. I've never been this tired before.*
               *I'm **so** glad to meet you.*
               *Everyone was **so** relieved when the hurricane changed course and went back out to sea.*
  This colloquial use of *so* is not appropriate in most expository writing.

• *Such* can also be used to mean "very": *It's such a beautiful day today!* = *It's a very beautiful day today.*

☐ **EXERCISE 9, p. 391. Using SUCH . . . THAT and SO . . . THAT. (Chart 19-4)**

The object of this exercise is to clarify the points in the chart. Lead a discussion, calling attention to the difference in patterns between a modified noun (e.g., *expensive car*) and a modifier alone (e.g., *expensive*).

ANSWERS: **3.** It was <u>such</u> an expensive car <u>that</u> we couldn't afford to buy it.   **4.** The car was <u>so</u> expensive <u>that</u> we couldn't afford to buy it.   **5.** The weather was <u>so</u> hot <u>that</u> you could fry an egg on the sidewalk.   **6.** During the summer, we had <u>such</u> hot and humid weather <u>that</u> it was uncomfortable just sitting in a chair doing nothing.   **7.** We're having <u>such</u> beautiful weather <u>that</u> I don't feel like going to work.   **8.** Ivan takes everything in life <u>so</u> seriously <u>that</u> he is unable to experience the small joys and pleasures of daily living.   **9.** I've met <u>so</u> many people in the last few days <u>that</u> I can't possibly remember all of their names.   **10.** Tommy ate <u>so</u> much candy <u>that</u> he got a stomachache. /stəməkek/
11. There was <u>so</u> little traffic <u>that</u> it took us only ten minutes to get there.   **12.** In some countries, <u>so</u> few students are accepted by the universities <u>that</u> admission is virtually a guarantee of a good job upon graduation. [*virtually* = really, actually]

☐ EXERCISE 10, p. 392. Using SUCH . . . THAT and SO . . . THAT. (Chart 19-4)

Be sure that students say the whole sentence, not just the letter from Column B.

ANSWERS: **2.** [H] Karen is <u>such</u> a good pianist <u>that</u> I'm surprised she didn't go into music professionally. **3.** [G] The radio was <u>so</u> loud <u>that</u> I couldn't hear what Michael was saying. **4.** [J] Small animals in the forest move about <u>so</u> quickly <u>that</u> one can barely catch a glimpse of them. [*barely* = hardly; *a glimpse* = a quick look] **5.** [B] Olga did <u>such</u> poor work <u>that</u> she was fired from her job. **6.** [A] The food was <u>so</u> hot <u>that</u> it burned my tongue. **7.** [E] There are <u>so</u> many leaves on a single tree <u>that</u> it is impossible to count them. **8.** [F] The tornado struck with <u>such</u> great force <u>that</u> it lifted automobiles off the ground. [*a tornado* = a whirlwind, a cyclone] **9.** [K] Grandpa held me <u>so</u> tightly when he hugged me <u>that</u> I couldn't breathe for a moment. **10.** [D] <u>So</u> few students showed up for class <u>that</u> the teacher postponed the test. **11.** [I] Sally used <u>so</u> much paper when she was writing her report <u>that</u> the wastepaper basket overflowed. [*overflow* = spill over the top]

☐ EXERCISE 11, p. 392. Using SO . . . THAT. (Chart 19-4)

Students should use their creativity in this exercise, even exaggerating some of their information. This is a common use of *so/such . . . that,* sometimes for a humorous effect.

CHART 19-5: EXPRESSING PURPOSE: USING *SO THAT*

• In **conversation**, it is common for a dependent *so that*-clause to be used in answer to a *why*-question:
    A: *Why did you cut class yesterday morning?* [*cut class* = not go to class]
    B: *So (that) I could cram for a test in my afternoon class.* [*cram* = study hard at the last possible moment]

In **writing**, a dependent clause must never stand alone; it must be joined grammatically to an independent clause: *I cut class so that I could cram for a test.*

• The word "that" does not have full pronunciation as a conjunction. (This is perhaps why it is so often omitted.) It is said very quickly and with a lower voice. The vowel is reduced to a very short sound /ðət/.

• The difference between the coordinating conjunction "so" and the subordinating conjunction "so (that)" is a little tricky to explain. Students generally don't confuse the two in their own production. To avoid unnecessary confusion, the text does not compare the two; some students get so involved in trying to distinguish "purpose" from "cause and effect" that general confusion results, at least in the experiences of the writers of this *Teacher's Guide*. Other teachers may have more productive results in presenting a comparison of these two uses of *so*.

• Advanced students might want to know that *so as to* is a more formal, less frequent alternative to *in order to*. Example: *The law was changed so as to protect people more equitably.*

☐ EXERCISE 13, p. 393. Using SO THAT. (Chart 19-5)

Begin with the four examples so that everyone gets accustomed to the pattern. Then give the students some individual time to work out the rest. During discussion, the responder should choose only one form of the answer, not try to say all the possible forms.

ERRATUM: There is no Exercise 12 in this chapter. To avoid confusion in classes that may be using texts from different printings, the numbering is not corrected in subsequent printings.

ANSWERS: **5.** Please be quiet <u>so (that)</u> I can hear what Sharon is saying.   **6.** I asked the children to be quiet <u>so (that)</u> I could hear what Sharon was saying.   **7.** I'm going to cash a check <u>so (that)</u> I have / will have enough money to go to the market.   [AmE = *check;* BrE = *cheque*]   **8.** I cashed a check yesterday <u>so (that)</u> I would have enough money to go to the market.   **9.** Tonight Ann and Larry are going to hire a babysitter for their six-year-old child <u>so (that)</u> they can go out with some friends.   **10.** Last week, Ann and Larry hired a babysitter <u>so (that)</u> they could go to a dinner party at the home of Larry's boss.   **11.** Be sure to put the meat in the oven at 5:00 <u>so (that)</u> it will be/is ready to eat by 6:30.
12. Yesterday, I put the meat in the oven at 5:00 <u>so (that)</u> it would be ready to eat by 6:30.
13. I'm going to leave the party early <u>so (that)</u> I will be able to get a good night's sleep tonight.   **14.** When it started to rain, Harry opened his umbrella <u>so (that)</u> he wouldn't get wet.   **15.** The little boy pretended to be sick <u>so (that)</u> he could stay home from school.   **16.** A lot of people were standing in front of me. I stood on tiptoes <u>so (that)</u> I could see the parade better.

☐ EXERCISE 14, p. 394.   Using SO THAT. (Chart 19-5)

One emphasis in this exercise is on the verb forms used in the *so that*-clause. Students could work in pairs or groups.

ANSWERS: **2.** [+ F] I turned on the radio <u>so that</u> I could listen to the news.   **3.** [+ A] I need to buy some detergent <u>so that</u> I can wash my clothes.   **4.** [+ C] Roberto fixed the leak in the boat <u>so that</u> it wouldn't sink. [*fix* = repair, mend]   **5.** [+ I] Mr. Kwan is studying the history and government of Canada <u>so that</u> he can become a Canadian citizen.   **6.** [+ B] Mrs. Gow put on her reading glasses <u>so that</u> she could read the fine print at the bottom of the contract. [*fine* = very small]   **7.** [+ H] Jane is taking a course in auto mechanics <u>so that</u> she can fix her own car.   **8.** [+ J] Omar is working hard to impress his supervisor <u>so that</u> he will be considered for a promotion at his company.
9. [+ E] Po is saving his money <u>so that</u> he can travel in Europe next summer.   **10.** [+ G] During the parade, Toshi lifted his daughter to his shoulder <u>so that</u> she could see the dancers in the street.

☐ EXERCISE 15, p. 394.   Using SO THAT. (Chart 19-5)

Students could work alone or in pairs, then write sentences on the chalkboard for discussion.

POSSIBLE COMPLETIONS: **1.** . . . I can make out this check.   **2.** He needs to study diligently . . . .   **3.** . . . I wouldn't miss the news.   **4.** . . . he wouldn't be hit by the speeding bus.   **5.** Samir set his alarm clock . . . .   **6.** . . . I can see more of the countryside.   **7.** I went over to his house . . . .   **8.** Spiro works at two jobs . . . .
9. . . . she can get a better job.   **10.** They prepared lots of delicious food . . . .
11. . . . he could make a downpayment on a car.   **12.** Finish your chores early . . . .

☐ EXERCISE 16, p. 395.   Summary: cause and effect. (Charts 19-2 → 19-5)

Encourage the students to think up interesting, even humorous sentences. Some students have fun making up sentences about their class, using their classmates' names.

You could have students in small groups work out answers together. You could have students write sentences on the board. You could open each item to brainstorming, eliciting as many sentences as you can. You could assign the whole exercise to be written as homework and handed in to you, or have the students correct each other's papers before they are handed in to you.

Another option is to have Speaker A give Speaker B a word to include in a sentence that Speaker B makes up.

SPEAKER A: *Use "now that." Include the word "green."*
SPEAKER B: *Now that chalkboards are green, they are no longer called blackboards.*

The students could be divided into two teams. A student from Team A could give a student on Team B a conjunction from Exercise 16 plus a word or phrase to include. Team B could write the sentence on the board. Team A could judge its correctness. If it's correct (in all aspects, including punctuation and spelling), Team B gets a point. If it's not correct and Team A recognizes that, Team A gets a point and Team B gets no points. If it's not correct and Team A does not recognize that, nobody gets any points. (You can make up any rules you wish, perhaps giving one point for correct spelling, one point for correct punctuation, and two points for correct sentence structure. Whatever the rules of the game, the purpose is for the students to be engaged and have fun while they're practicing English.)

ANSWERS: [These depend on students' creativity.]

CHART 19-6: SHOWING CONTRAST (UNEXPECTED RESULT)

• This chart presents a number of synonyms. Point out their semantic similarities and grammatical differences. It is assumed that the students understand these structural differences and the grammatical labels from their study of Chapters 16 and 17 as well as Chart 19-3.

• A common error is the use of both *although* and *but* to connect two ideas within a sentence.
    INCORRECT: ***Although*** *it was raining,* ***but*** *we went to the zoo.*

• The text does not mention that *though* can be used as a final position adverb: *I was hungry. I didn't eat anything though.* Advanced students may be curious about this usage. It is used mainly in spoken English.

• *Nonetheless* is not frequently used.

☐ **EXERCISE 17, p. 395.   Showing opposition (unexpected result).   (Chart 19-6)**

PART I ANSWERS: **4.** but   **5.** Nevertheless   **6.** Even though   **7.** even though
8. but   **9.** Nevertheless

PART II ANSWERS: **10.** However   **11.** yet   **12.** Although   **13.** yet
14. Although   **15.** However

☐ **EXERCISE 18, p. 396.   Showing contrast (unexpected result).   (Chart 19-6)**

ANSWERS:
   2. Anna's father gave her some good advice, but she didn't follow it.
   3. Even though Anna's father gave her some good advice, she didn't follow it.
   4. Anna's father gave her some good advice. She did not follow it, however.
   5. Thomas was thirsty. I offered him some water. He refused it.
   6. *(no change)*
   7. Thomas was thirsty. **Nevertheless,** he refused the glass of water I brought him.
   8. Thomas was thirsty, yet he refused to drink the water that I offered him.

☐ **EXERCISE 19, p. 397. Showing contrast (unexpected result). (Chart 19-6)**

Use a wall chart (or something similar) of patterns and punctuation as suggested for use with Chart 19-3 (p. 199 of this *Guide*).

SAMPLE ANSWERS: [Not every possible variation is included.]
   1. We went for a walk even though it was raining.
      It was raining, but we went for a walk anyway.
      It was raining. Nevertheless, we went for a walk.
      We went for a walk in spite of the rain.
      We didn't go for a walk because it was raining.
   2. Although his grades were low, he was admitted to the university.
      His grades were low, yet he was still admitted to the university.
      His grades were low. Nonetheless, he was admitted to the university.
      Despite his low grades, he was admitted to the university.
      Because of his low grades, he wasn't admitted to the university.

☐ **EXERCISE 20, p. 397. Showing contrast (unexpected result). (Chart 19-6)**

Since students will have to think of logical completions, you might assign this to be written as seatwork or homework prior to discussion. Then the whole class can compare alternative answers, perhaps "voting" to choose the most creative ones.

POSSIBLE COMPLETIONS: **1.** I had a cold, but I went to class anyway. **2.** Even though I had a cold, I felt I had to finish my work. **3.** Although I didn't study, I did well on the test. **4.** I didn't study, but I did well on the test anyway. **5.** I got an "A" on the test even though I hadn't done any extra studying. **6.** Even though Howard is a careful driver, he had an accident. **7.** Even though the food they served for dinner tasted terrible, I finished my plate because I didn't want to hurt my hosts' feelings. **8.** My shirt still has coffee stains on it even though I have washed it twice. **9.** I still trust him even though he lied to me. **10.** Even though he was drowning, no one tried to save him. **11.** Although I tried to be very careful, I spilled the coffee because my cup was too full. **12.** Even though Ruth is one of my best friends, I didn't tell her about my plans to elope with my boyfriend. **13.** It's still hot in here even though I opened a window. **14.** Even though I had a big breakfast, I was hungry by eleven o'clock.

☐ **EXERCISE 21, p. 398. Showing contrast (unexpected result). (Chart 19-6)**

You may need to review with your class the last section of Chart 19-6. Point out that the prepositions are followed by noun objects, but *the fact that* is followed by a clause.

SAMPLE SENTENCES:
   2. I like living in a dorm in spite of / despite the noise. OR I like living in a dorm despite the fact that / in spite of the fact that it is noisy.
   3. In spite of / Despite the hard work, they enjoyed themselves. OR In spite of the fact that / Despite the fact that the work was hard, they enjoyed themselves.
   4. They wanted to climb the mountain in spite of / despite the danger. OR They wanted to climb the mountain in spite of the fact that / despite the fact that it was dangerous.
   5. In spite of / Despite the extremely hot weather, they went jogging in the park. OR In spite of the fact that / Despite the fact that the weather was extremely hot, they went jogging in the park.
   6. He is unhappy in spite of / despite his vast fortune. OR He is unhappy in spite of the fact that / despite the fact that he has a vast fortune.

□ **EXERCISE 22, p. 398.   Showing contrast (unexpected result).   (Chart 19-6)**

POSSIBLE COMPLETIONS: **1.** I didn't particularly want to see that play, but I went anyway. **2.** He is very old, yet he still plays tennis at 6 o'clock every morning.   **3.** The plane took off 20 minutes late. Nevertheless, we arrived on schedule.   **4.** Even though she wanted a new bike for her birthday, the little girl was happy to get a new doll.   **5.** I wanted to go somewhere exotic for my vacation. However, I had to go back home because it was my mother's 60th birthday.   **6.** The teacher dismissed the class when they had completed the test even though the hour wasn't over.   **7.** Although my daughter is only three years old, she knows all the words to the "Alphabet Song."   **8.** She never went to school. However, she has done very well in her job despite her lack of education.   **9.** Despite the fact that my sister was visiting, I went to bed early.   **10.** I have decided to go to Thailand even though I can't speak a word of Thai.

CHART 19-7:   SHOWING DIRECT CONTRAST

• Students may notice that *however* is included in both Chart 19-6 and 19-7. *However* can express "unexpected result," as in Chart 19-6. It is also used to express direct contrast and has the same meaning as *on the other hand*. (A look in a dictionary would show students that there are still more uses of *however*.)

□ **EXERCISE 23, p. 399.   Showing direct contrast.   (Chart 19-7)**

Either transition is possible. Various placements are possible. Discuss punctuation. (Patterns with semicolons are not given below but are, of course, possible.)

POSSIBLE COMPLETIONS:
1. Florida has a warm climate. *However,* Alaska has a cold climate.   OR   Florida has a warm climate. Alaska, *on the other hand,* has a cold climate.
2. Fred is a good student. His brother, *however,* is lazy.   OR   Fred is a good student. His brother, *on the other hand,* is lazy.
3. In the United States, gambling casinos are not legal in most places. *However,* in my country it is possible to gamble in any city or town.   OR   In the United States, gambling casinos are not legal in most places. In my country, *on the other hand,* it is possible to gamble in any city or town.
4. Sue and Ron are expecting a child. Sue is hoping for a boy. *However,* Ron is hoping for a girl.   OR   Sue is hoping for a boy. Ron, *on the other hand,* is hoping for a girl.
5. Old people in my country usually live with their children. *However,* the old in the United States often live by themselves.   OR   The old in the United States, *on the other hand,* often live by themselves.

□ **EXERCISE 24, p. 399.   Showing direct contrast.   (Chart 19-7)**

POSSIBLE COMPLETIONS: **2.** the United Kingdom drive on the left-hand side.   **3.** sister's apartment is always neat.   **4.** makes friends easily and is very popular. [*keeps to herself* = is often alone and doesn't readily share her thoughts and feelings with others.]   **5.** know about only house pets.   **6.** is easy to cut and shape.   **7.** is very outgoing.   **8.** some people are ambidextrous, which means that they can use either hand equally well.

□ EXERCISE 25, p. 399. Activity: expressing direct contrast. (Chart 19-7)

In this exercise, you could focus primarily on the grammar and go through the items rather quickly, or you could develop the exercise into an activity designed to encourage the sharing of information about the students' countries in comparison with the United States. Some options:

(1) Ask for volunteers for each item, concentrating on how to express direct opposition.

(2) Assign each student one item to present orally to the class to initiate open discussion on that topic.

(3) Assign national groups to make oral presentations.

(4) Have the students discuss all of the items in small groups.

(5) Open all of the items for a "brainstorming" class discussion; follow with a composition that compares and contrasts the U.S. and the student's country. (You might point out that almost any one of these items alone could be the topic of an entire composition.)

(6) In a multinational class, open discussion could also be followed by a short composition in which the students write about what they have learned and heard, both about the U. S. and about other countries represented in the class.

If students are not familiar with contrasts between their country and the U.S., they could choose two other countries or perhaps regions within their own country.

ANSWERS: [These depend on students' life experiences.]

□ EXERCISE 26, p. 400. Showing cause and effect and contrast. (Charts 19-1, 19-2, 19-7, and 19-8)

ANSWERS: 2. because   3. despite the fact that / even though / although   4. because of   5. now that   6. ,however,   7. .However, OR , but   8. .Therefore, 9. ,however,   10. , but [also possible: *although/whereas*]   11. although / even though / despite the fact that [*critical* = crucial, very important]

CHART 19-8: EXPRESSING CONDITIONS: USING *OTHERWISE* AND *OR (ELSE)*

• As a transition, *otherwise* is common in contrary-to-fact conditional sentences. Its use is discussed again in Chapter 20 ("Conditional Sentences and Wishes").

• *Otherwise* can also function as an adverb meaning "differently" (e.g., *Johns thinks that Mars is inhabited. I believe otherwise.*). *Otherwise* can also mean "except for that/other than that" (e.g., *I have a broken leg, but otherwise I'm fine*). The text asks the students to focus on the use of *otherwise* only as a conjunctive adverb, but advanced students might be curious about these other uses.

□ EXERCISE 27, p. 401. Using OTHERWISE and OR (ELSE). (Chart 19-8)

Note that only the present tense is used in the *if*-clauses. When the *if*-clause is transformed to a simple sentence in this exercise, a modal with a future meaning (e.g., *will, must*) or future phrasal modal (e.g., *be going to, have to*) is needed.*

Some responses could use *or else* for variety. Discuss punctuation.

POSSIBLE SENTENCES: **2.** You should / had better / have to / must leave now. Otherwise, you'll be late for class. **3.** You should / had better / have to / must go to bed. Otherwise, your cold will get worse. **4.** You should / had better / have to / must have a ticket. Otherwise, you can't get into the theater. **5.** You should / had better/ have to / must have a passport. Otherwise, you can't enter that country. **6.** Tom should / had better / has to / must get a job soon. Otherwise, his family won't have enough money for food. **7.** You should / had better / have to / must speak both Japanese and Chinese fluently. Otherwise, you will not be considered for that job. [Subject and verb are in normal order with *otherwise*.] **8.** Mary should / had better / has to / must get a scholarship. Otherwise, she cannot go to school. **9.** I am going to / should / had better / have to / must wash my clothes tonight. Otherwise, I won't have any clean clothes to wear tomorrow.

□ EXERCISE 28, p. 402. Expressing conditions. (Charts 17-5 → 17-9 and 19-8)

ERRATUM: The title for Ex. 28 should read: "Expressing conditions." This is corrected in later printings.

POSSIBLE COMPLETIONS: **1.** I am going to finish this report even if it takes me all night. **2.** We have no choice. **W**e have to go by train whether we want to or not. **3.** I will go to the concert with you only if you will come to the basketball game with me next week. **4.** Eric is very inconsiderate. **H**e plays his CD player even if his roommate is trying to sleep. **5.** I can't hang this picture unless you tell me if it's level. **6.** Tomorrow I'd better get to the store. **O**therwise, we will run out of food. **7.** You should take your umbrella in case it rains. **8.** I will help you move your piano only if no one else is available. **9.** I will be happy to attend your party unless you have also invited my ex-wife. **10.** You must take all your final exams. **O**therwise, you can't graduate.

CHART 19-9: SUMMARY OF CONNECTIVES: CAUSE AND EFFECT, CONTRAST, CONDITION

• Congratulate your students on knowing how to use all these expressions. Make them aware of how much they have accomplished.

□ EXERCISES 29 and 30, pp. 402–403. Summary of connectives. (Chart 19-9)

These exercises should proceed rather easily because the students don't have to create any content, just manipulate word order and punctuation. Students generally treat this type of exercise as a word game.

You could go through the exercises quickly with the whole class, or the students could have fun working together. You might want to do the first few items with the whole class to show them how to proceed, then you could have them work in pairs or small groups. You should walk around to give assistance as needed, perhaps suggesting where

---

*See Chart 10-10 of the student book, p. 199 (Summary Chart of Modals and Similar Expressions).

students might look in the text to find the answer to a problem. As a final step, you could open the exercises for general class discussion, answering any questions and settling any disputes.

EX. 29 POSSIBLE COMPLETIONS:

2. I failed the exam because I did not study.
3. Although I studied, I did not pass the exam.
4. I did not study. **Therefore,** I failed the exam.
5. I did not study. **However,** I passed the exam.
6. I studied. **Nevertheless,** I failed the exam.
7. Even though I did not study, I (still) passed the exam.
8. I did not study, so I did not pass the exam.
9. Since I did not study, I did not pass the exam.
10. If I study for the test, I should pass it.
11. Unless I study for the test, I am sure to fail it.
12. I must study. **Otherwise,** I will surely fail the exam.
13. Even if I study, I may still fail.
14. I did not study. **Consequently,** I failed the exam.
15. I did not study. **Nonetheless,** I passed the exam.
16. I will probably fail the test whether I study or not.
17. I failed the exam, for I did not study.
18. I have to study so that I won't fail the exam.
19. Only if I study will I pass the exam. [Note the inverted subject–verb order.]
20. I studied hard, yet I still failed the exam.
21. You'd better study, or else you will fail the exam.

EX. 30 EXPECTED COMPLETIONS:

1. Because I was not hungry this morning, I did not eat breakfast.
2. Because I ate breakfast this morning, I'm not hungry now.
3. Because I was hungry this morning, I ate a large breakfast.
4. I did not eat breakfast this morning even though I was hungry.
5. Although I was hungry this morning, I didn't have time to eat breakfast.
6. I was hungry this morning. **Therefore,** I ate breakfast.
7. I was hungry this morning. **Nevertheless,** I didn't eat breakfast.
8. I was so hungry this morning that I ate a large breakfast.
9. I was not hungry this morning, but I ate breakfast anyway.
10. I ate breakfast this morning even though I wasn't hungry.
11. Since I did not eat breakfast this morning, I am hungry now.
12. I ate breakfast this morning. **Nonetheless,** I am hungry.
13. I was not hungry, so I didn't eat breakfast.
14. Even though I did not eat breakfast this morning, I'm not hungry now.
15. I never eat breakfast unless I'm hungry.
16. I always eat breakfast whether or not I'm hungry.
17. I eat breakfast even if I'm not hungry.
18. Now that I have eaten breakfast, I'm not hungry.
19. I eat breakfast only if I'm hungry.
20. I ate breakfast this morning, yet I'm hungry now.
21. Even if I am hungry, I don't eat breakfast.
22. I was not hungry. **However,** I ate breakfast this morning.

☐ EXERCISE 31, p. 404. Summary of connectives. (Chart 19-9)

This exercise could be turned into a game. A student could make a sentence (orally or on the chalkboard), and the rest of the class could "vote" on its correctness. (Weaker students should be assigned easy items or paired with stronger students.) The class should have fun with this exercise and be impressed with their own recently acquired skills in using these words and structures.

ANSWERS: [These depend on students' creativity.]

□ EXERCISE 32, p. 404.   Summary of connectives.   (Chart 19-9)

After practicing the previous exercises, students could do this exercise as written seatwork or homework prior to discussion. Encourage them to use recently learned vocabulary and idioms in their answers. Later, you could copy some of their sentences for everyone to discuss.

POSSIBLE COMPLETIONS:
1. While some people are optimists, others are pessimists.
2. Even though he drank a glass of water, he was still thirsty.
3. Even if she invites me to her party, I will not go.
4. I have never been to Hawaii. **My** parents, however, have visited there twice.
5. I couldn't open the car door, for my arms were full of packages.
6. I need to borrow some money so that I can pay my rent on time.
7. The airport was closed due to fog. **Therefore,** our plane's departure was postponed.
8. The landing field was fogged in. **Therefore,** the airport was closed.
9. As soon as the violinist played the last note at the concert, the audience burst into applause.
10. Since neither my roommate nor I know how to cook, we took our visiting parents out to dinner.
11. I am not a superstitious person. **Nevertheless,** I don't walk under ladders. A paint can might fall on my head.
12. The crops will fail unless we get some rain soon.
13. Just as I was getting ready to eat dinner last night, the phone rang.
14. We must work quickly. **Otherwise,** we won't finish before dark.
15. Some children are noisy and wild. **My** brother's children, on the other hand, are very quiet and obedient.
16. According to the newspaper, now that hurricane season has arrived, we can expect bad weather at any time.
17. Ever since I can remember, my niece Melissa has been called "Missie" by her family.
18. Although my grades were high, I didn't get the scholarship.
19. The United States has no national health care, whereas Great Britain has socialized medicine.
20. I was tired. **However,** I felt I had to stay awake because I was babysitting.   OR   I was tired; however, I felt I had to stay awake because I was babysitting.
21. You must pay an income tax whether or not you agree with how the government spends it.
22. I was listening hard. **Nevertheless,** I could not understand what the person who was speaking was saying because she was standing too far from the microphone. [Note for the students that this last sentence contains a noun clause, adjective clause, and adverb clause—and congratulate them for their ability to handle such complex sentence structures!]

□ EXERCISE 33, p. 405.   Error analysis: general review.   (Chapters 16 → 19)

ANSWERS:
1. Unless I study very hard, I will <u>not</u> pass all of my exams.
2. My shoes and pants got <u>muddy even</u> though I walked carefully through the wet streets.
3. My neighborhood is quiet and safe. **However,** I always lock my doors.
4. Although I usually don't like Mexican food, ~~but~~ I liked the food I had at the Mexican restaurant last night.   OR   ~~Although~~ I usually don't like Mexican food, but I liked the food I had at the Mexican restaurant last night.

5. Although my room in the dormitory is very small, ~~but~~ I like it **b**ecause it is a place where I can be by myself and <u>study</u> in peace and quiet.   OR   ~~Although~~ My room in the dormitory is very small, but I like it **b**ecause it is a place where I can be by myself and <u>study</u> in peace and quiet.

6. <u>Even though</u> I prefer to be a history teacher, I am studying in the Business School in order ~~for I can~~ <u>to</u> get a job in industry.   OR   Despite <u>the fact that I prefer</u> to be a history teacher, I am studying in the Business School in order ~~for I can~~ <u>to</u> get a job in industry.

7. A little girl approached the cage. **H**owever, when the tiger <u>showed</u> its teeth and <u>growled</u>, she <u>ran</u> to her mother **b**ecause she was frightened.

8. Many of the people (who are) working to save our environment think that they are fighting a losing battle **b**ecause big <u>business and</u> the government have not joined together to eliminate pollution.

9. The weather was so cold that I <u>didn't</u> like to leave my apartment.   OR   The weather <u>is</u> so cold that I don't like to leave my apartment.

10. I have to study four hour**s** every day because ~~of~~ my courses are difficult / because of my <u>difficult</u> courses ~~are~~ / because <u>of the difficulty</u> of my courses.

11. On the third day of our voyage, we sailed across a rough sea before ~~to~~ <u>reaching</u> the shore.

12. I can't understand the lectures in my psychology class. **T**herefore, my roommate lets me borrow her notes.

13. According to this legend, a man went in search of a hidden village. **H**e finally found it after <u>walking</u> two hundred miles.

14. <u>Because</u> my country ~~it~~ is located in a subtropical area, ~~so~~ the weather is hot.   OR   My country ~~it~~ is located in a subtropical area, so the weather is hot.

15. I will stay <u>in</u> the **U**nited **S**tates for two more year**s** **b**ecause I want to finish my degree before <u>going / I go</u> home.

☐ EXERCISE 34, p. 406.   Activity: connectives. (Chart 19-9)

EXPANSION ACTIVITY: Choose one item. Tell each group to make the longest grammatically correct sentence they can. Ask that the sentences be written on the board with the number of words counted. Give the group with the longest correct sentence a "prize" (e.g., applause, one-minute early dismissal from class). This is just a word game whose main purpose is fun. If your class doesn't benefit from competition, don't award a prize. Instead, praise each group's efforts equally. (When setting up a "make-the-longest-correct-sentence word game," limit the number of adjectives and adverbs to ten or less.)

☐ EXERCISE 35, p. 407.   Review: punctuation and capitalization. (Chapters 13 and 16 →19)

Discuss how important correct punctuation and capitalization are to readers of written prose. These run-on sentences without correct internal punctuation make it difficult for readers to grasp the meaning quickly and accurately.

ANSWERS:
2. Although a computer has tremendous power and speed, it cannot think for itself. **A** human operator is needed to give a computer instructions, for it cannot initially tell itself what to do.

3. Being a lawyer in private practice, I work hard, but I do not go into my office on either Saturday or Sunday. **I**f clients insist upon seeing me on those days, they have to come to my home.

4. Whenever the weather is nice, I walk to school, but when it is cold or wet, I either take the bus or get a ride with one of my friends. **E**ven though my brother has a car, I never ask him to take me to school because he is very busy. **H**e has a new job and has recently

gotten married, so he doesn't have time to drive me to and from school anymore. **I** know he would give me a ride if I asked him to, but I don't want to bother him.

5. The common cold, which is the most widespread of all diseases, continues to plague humanity despite the efforts of scientists to find its prevention and cure. **E**ven though colds are minor illnesses, they are one of the principal causes of absence from school and work. **P**eople of all ages get colds, but children and adults who live with children get them the most. **C**olds can be dangerous for elderly people because they can lead to other infections. **I** have had three colds so far this year. **I** eat the right kinds of food, get enough rest, and exercise regularly. **N**evertheless, I still get at least one cold a year.

6. Whenever my father goes fishing, we know we will have fish to eat for dinner, for even if he doesn't catch any, he stops at the fish market on his way home and buys some.

☐ **EXERCISE 36, p. 408.   Review: showing relationships.   (Chapters 5 and 16 → 19)**

This is a review of several chapters; congratulate the students on how much they have learned about combining several ideas through the use of a variety of connectives and complex–compound structures.

EXPECTED ANSWERS:

2. <u>If</u> you really mean what you say, I'll give you one more chance, <u>but</u> you have to give me your best effort. <u>**O**therwise</u>, you'll lose your job.

3. <u>Due to</u> the bad weather, I'm going to stay home. <u>**E**ven if</u> the weather changes, I don't want to go to the picnic.

4. <u>Even though</u> the children had eaten lunch, they got hungry in the middle of the afternoon. <u>**T**herefore</u>, I took them to the market <u>so that</u> they could get some fruit for a snack <u>before</u> we went home for dinner.

5. <u>**W**hereas</u> Robert is totally exhausted after playing tennis, Marge isn't even tired <u>in spite of the fact</u> that she ran around a lot more during the game. [*even* = surprisingly not]

6. <u>**W**hile</u> many animals are most vulnerable to predators when they are grazing, giraffes are most vulnerable when they are drinking. **T**hey must spread their legs awkwardly in order to lower their long necks to the water in front of them. <u>**C**onsequently</u>, it is difficult and time-consuming for them to stand up straight again to escape a predator. <u>**H**owever</u>, once they are up and running, they are faster than most of their predators. /prɛdətər/

7. <u>Even though</u> my boss promised me that I could have two full weeks, it seems that I can't take my vacation after all <u>because</u> I have to train the new personnel this summer. <u>**I**f</u> I do not get a vacation in the fall either, I will be angry.

8. <u>**S**ince</u> education, business, and government are all dependent on computers, it is advisable for all students to have basic computer skills <u>before</u> they graduate from high school and enter the work force or college. <u>**T**herefore</u>, a course called "Computer Literacy" has recently become a requirement for graduation from Westside High School. <u>**I**f</u> you want more information about this course, you can call the academic counselor at the high school.

☐ **EXERCISE 37, p. 409.   Review: showing relationships.   (Chapters 5 and 13 → 19)**

POSSIBLE COMPLETIONS:

1. I woke up this morning with a sore throat. Nevertheless, I went to work because I had to finish an important report.

2. I love cats. My sister, on the other hand, prefers dogs.

3. When a small, black insect landed on my arm, I screamed because it had startled me. [*startle* = surprise suddenly]

4. I don't eat desserts because I'm watching my weight. However, I had a piece of chocolate cake last night because it was my sister's birthday.

5. Even though I told my supervisor I would finish the report by tomorrow, I really need another day to do a good job.

6. According to the newspaper, now that the speed limit has been raised, there will be more traffic accidents. Therefore, people will have to drive more carefully than ever before.

7. Since neither the man who gave me the information nor the manager was in, I said I would call back another time.

8. When people who are critical find fault with others, they should try to be more patient because no one is perfect.

9. Since I didn't know whose sweater I had found, I took it to the "Lost and Found" department.

10. Even though the book which I was reading was overdue, I kept it until I had finished reading it. [*overdue* = past the deadline for returning it to a library]

11. What did the woman who came to the door say when you told her you weren't interested in her political views?

12. If what he said is true, we can expect more rain soon.

13. Because the man who donated his art collection to the museum wishes to remain anonymous, his name will not be mentioned in the museum guide.

14. Even though she didn't understand what the man who stopped her on the street wanted, she tried to be helpful.

15. Now that all of the students who plan to take the trip have signed up, we can reserve the hotel rooms.

16. Since the restaurant where we first met has burned down, we will have to celebrate our anniversary somewhere else.

☐ **EXERCISE 38, p. 410. Error analysis: general review. (Chapters 1 → 19)**

This is a summary review exercise containing grammar covered in Chapters 1 through 19. It intends to challenge the grammar knowledge and proofreading skills that students have acquired during the course. Students need time, in or out of class, to edit these sentences prior to discussion.
  Some errors are in spelling.
  All of these items are adapted from student writing.

POSSIBLE ANSWERS: [Spelling and punctuation revisions are in **bold**; sentence structure revisions are underlined; a forward slash (/) indicates a second correct revision.]

1. We went shopping after <u>we</u> ate / after eating dinner**,** **b**ut the stores were closed**.** OR
   . . . **B**ut the stores were closed**.** We had to go back home even <u>though</u> we hadn't found what <u>we were</u> looking for.

2. I want <u>to</u> explain that I know <u>a lot</u> of gramm**ar,** but <u>my problem is that I don't know</u> enough <u>vocabulary</u>.

3. When I got lost in the bus station**,** a kind man helped me**.** **H**e explained how to read the huge bus schedule on the wall**,** **t**ook me to the window to buy a ticket**,** and showed me <u>where my bus was</u>**.** **I** will always appreciate his kindness.

4. I had never <u>understood</u> the <u>importance</u> of <u>knowing</u> English ~~language~~ **u**ntil I worked at a large, international company.

5. <u>When</u> I was young**,** my father found an American woman to teach <u>my brothers and me</u> English, but when we <u>moved</u> to <u>another</u> town**,** my father wasn't able to find <u>another</u> teacher for <u>another</u> five years.

6. I was surprised to see the room that I was given at/in the dormitory **b**ecause there <u>wasn't</u> any furniture and <u>it was</u> dirty.

7. When I <u>met</u> Mr. Lee for the first time, we played ping pong at the student center**.** **Even** though we <u>couldn't</u> communicate very well, ~~but~~ we had a good time.

8. Because the United States is a large ~~and also big~~ country, ~~it means that they're various kinds of people live there and~~ it has a diverse population.

9. My grammar class ~~was~~ <u>started</u> at 10:35. When the teacher <u>came</u> to class, she returned the last quiz to my classmates and <u>me</u>. After <u>that,</u> we ~~have~~ had another quiz.

10. If a wife has ~~a~~ <u>to</u> work, her husband should share the <u>housework</u> with her. If both of them help, the <u>housework</u> can be <u>finished</u> much faster.

11. The first time I went skiing**,** I was afraid to go down the hill**,** **b**ut somewhere ~~from~~ a little ~~corner of~~ voice in my head kept shouting, "Why not? Give it a try. You'll make it!" After <u>standing</u> around for ten minutes without moving**,** <u>I finally decided to</u> go down that hill.

12. *Possible revision:* This is a story about a man <u>who</u> had a big garden. One day he was sleeping in his garden. <u>When</u> he woke up**,** **h**e ate some fruit**,** ~~Then he~~ picked some apples**,** and ~~he~~ walked to a small river ~~and~~ <u>where</u> he saw a beautiful woman ~~was~~ on the other side. ~~And~~ **H**e gave her some apples, and ~~then~~ she gave him a loaf of bread. The two of them walked back to the garden. ~~Then~~ **S**ome children came and ~~were~~ <u>played</u> games with him. Everyone was laughing and smiling. <u>But when</u> one child destroyed a flower, ~~and~~ the man became angry and ~~he~~ said to them, "Get out of here**!**" <u>S</u>o the children ~~left~~ and the beautiful woman left. Then the man built a wall around his garden and would not let anyone in. He stayed in his garden all alone for the rest of his life.

☐ EXERCISE 40, p. 411. Activity: general review. (Chapters 1 → 19)

Students could discuss this topic before writing about it. Since it is a topic most students have probably not thought about before, a pre-writing sharing of ideas will result in better compositions.

ERRATUM: There is no Exercise 39 in this chapter. To avoid confusion in classes that use texts from different printings, the numbering is not corrected in subsequent printings.

Chapter 20: CONDITIONAL SENTENCES AND WISHES

ORDER OF CHAPTER	CHARTS	EXERCISES	WORKBOOK
Basic verb form usage in conditional sentences	20-1 → 20-4	Ex. 1 → 10	Pr. 1 → 2
Review		Ex. 11 → 14	Pr. 3 → 4
Other verb forms in conditional sentences	20-5 → 20-6	Ex. 15 → 16	Pr. 5 → 6
Conditionals without *if*-clauses	20-7 → 20-8	Ex. 17 → 19	Pr. 7 → 9
Review		Ex. 20 → 24	Pr. 10 → 11
Using *as if/as though*	20-9	Ex. 25	Pr. 12
Verb forms following *wish*	20-10 → 20-11	Ex. 26 → 32	Pr. 13 → 14
Review		Ex. 33	Pr. 15 → 17

General Notes on Chapter 20

• OBJECTIVE: Conditional sentences are among the most useful forms for communicating suppositions about events or situations that are contrary to reality. Students who learn to form these clauses correctly will add a very important dimension to their ability to understand and use English in order to communicate complex information in both speech and writing.

• APPROACH: Since verb forms are used for distinctions of meaning in conditional sentences, the chapter begins with a summary of their use in presenting factual and contrary-to-fact information. Then variations in conditional sentences are introduced, including the use of *as if* and *as though*. The chapter ends with a unit on expressing wishes. Many of the exercises in this chapter provide opportunities for students to communicate their own ideas.

• TERMINOLOGY: An *if*-clause is also called a "clause of condition."

□ **EXERCISE 1, p. 412.   Preview: conditional sentences.   (Charts 20-1 → 20-4)**

As a preview, this exercise asks learners to understand the meaning of conditional sentences. Give them a few moments to complete the exercise, then lead a discussion.
   As you discuss items in subsequent exercises in this chapter, ask the same kinds of questions posed in this exercise to make sure your students understand the meanings of the conditional sentences.

ANSWERS: **2.** a. no   b. yes   c. no   **3.** a. yes   b. no   c. yes   **4.** a. no   b. yes
5. a. yes   b. no   c. no   **6.** a. no   b. yes   **7.** a. yes   b. no   **8.** a. no   b. no
c. yes

CHART 20-1: OVERVIEW OF BASIC VERB FORMS USED IN CONDITIONAL SENTENCES

• This chart summarizes the information in the next three charts. It is helpful to have a wall chart or transparency of these verb forms for you to point at and the students to refer to during discussion of the exercises. When information about using progressives and other modals is introduced in later charts, this basic chart can be expanded to include them.

• It is assumed that the students are somewhat familiar with conditional sentences. You might introduce this chapter with an oral exercise in which you ask leading questions: *What would you do if there were a fire in this room? What would you have done if you hadn't come to class today? What would you do if I asked you to stand on your head in the middle of the classroom? If you were a bird/cat/mouse/etc., how would you spend your days? etc.*

• Some students may think that conditional sentences are odd and unimportant. Assure them that conditionals are common, in daily conversation as well as writing. They are the only way to express some ideas. You might mention that one situation in which they are especially common is sports broadcasting (e.g., *If Smith hadn't fallen down, he would have scored easily*).

□ **EXERCISE 2, p. 413. Basic verb forms in conditional sentences. (Chart 20-1)**

Using the chart, focus attention on the true/untrue distinction. Then point out the verb tenses in each type of clause. Relate these to the time phrases in this exercise.

You or a student could read aloud the situation. Then a volunteer could complete the statement.

ANSWERS: **2.** have . . . will write   **3.** had . . . would write   **4.** had . . . would write   **5.** had had . . . would have written

CHARTS 20-2 AND 20-3: TRUE AND UNTRUE (CONTRARY TO FACT) IN THE PRESENT OR FUTURE

• Conditional sentences have a sort of "truth value" in the mind of the speaker. The *if*-clause contains a condition under which, **in the speaker's opinion,** an expected result might or might not occur. The result-clause can state the speaker's prediction of an outcome.

• Like adverb clauses of time, an *if*-clause usually does <u>not</u> contain a future tense verb, *will* or *be going to*. This is a fact about English usage that must be learned, even though it might seem illogical to some students. A language is not a logical set of scientific formulas or rules; it is a complex, flexible instrument of communication based on traditions and preferences. Students should understand this point by the time they complete this book.

• In everyday conversation, the subjunctive use of *were* instead of *was* with singular subjects is more typical of American than British English. Favoring formal usage, the text encourages the use of *were*, but either is correct. [See examples (b) and (c) in Chart 20-3.]

• Some learners find this sentence fun: *I would if I could, but I can't, so I won't.* It captures the distinction between the conditional and the factual.

□ EXERCISE 3, p. 415. True in the present or future. (Chart 20-2)

Encourage students to refer to the chart if necessary. There are a lot of rules to keep in mind, but the form of each question in this exercise shows the form of the answer.

□ EXERCISE 4, p. 415. Present or future conditional sentences. (Charts 20-2 and 20-3)

Pairs of items in this exercise are related, showing true and untrue conditional statements. ("Untrue" does not mean that the speaker is lying, of course. It means that he or she is speaking of some situation that does not or cannot truly exist. The situation is hypothetical, not real. Untrue is defined as "contrary to fact" or "the opposite of what is true and real.")

Students could work on two items at a time. After a minute or so, lead them in a discussion of the correct forms and the differences in meaning. Try to help them understand that the speaker communicates an opinion about the truth value by his/her choice of verb forms. Ask leading questions about the truth value throughout: e.g., *Am I (the speaker) going to bake an apple pie? Do I have enough apples? Do I know if I have enough apples? Do I want to bake an apple pie?*

ANSWERS: **2.** would bake **3.** have **4.** had **5.** is **6.** were **7.** would not be . . . were **8.** floats / will float **9.** were . . . would not exist **10.** does not arrive **11.** were . . . would not want **12.** would human beings live . . . were [*eradicated* / ɪrǽdɪketəd/ = eliminated, destroyed] **13.** disappears / will disappear **14.** had . . . would have to . . . would not be

□ EXERCISE 5, p. 416. Activity: present or future untrue conditions. (Chart 20-3)

These sentences are meant simply to give the students some ideas to play around with using conditional sentences.

□ EXERCISE 6, p. 417. Activity: present conditionals. (Chart 20-3)

This is an exercise in discussing a hypothethical situation, the typical use of conditional sentences. You might note for the students that the *if*-clause doesn't need to be repeated in each answer but that the result clause, nonetheless, uses conditional verb forms.

The illustration is included to help students visualize the numbers of people they're talking about.

ANSWERS: [The conditional verbs are in **boldface**.]

If there **were** only one village on earth and (if) it **had** exactly 100 people, 51 of them **would be** women and 49 of them **would be** men.

More than half of the people in the village (57 of them) **would be** from Asia, the Middle East, and the South Pacific. Twenty-one of them **would be** from Europe, 14 from the Western Hemisphere, and 8 from Africa.

Half the people in the village **would suffer** from malnutrition.

Thirty of the villagers **would be** illiterate. Of those 30, 18 **would be** women and 12 **would be** men.

Only one person in the village of 100 people **would have** a college education.

Six of the villagers **would own** half of the village's wealth. The other half of the wealth **would be shared** among the remaining 94 villagers.

Thirty-three of the people **would be** below 15 years of age, while 10 **would be** over 65.

- Looking back at past times, we know whether events really occurred or not. Using conditional sentences, we can talk about hypothetical past events and results that would have or could have occurred had certain conditions been present.

- It is possible to use *would* in *if*-clauses.
  Examples: *If you'd try harder, you'd learn more.*
  If you would've told me about it, I could've helped you.
  The text does not teach this usage because it is not possible in all situations and is generally considered nonstandard, especially in formal written English.

□ EXERCISE 7, p. 418.   Conditional sentences. (Charts 20-1 → 20-4)

In this exercise, three similar sentences are grouped together up to item 10. Lead students in a discussion of the differences in form and meaning among the grouped sentences.

ERRATUM: Two consecutive items both appear as number 10. The second of these (at the top of page 419) should be number 11. This is corrected in subsequent printings.

ANSWERS: **1.** have **2.** had **3.** had had **4.** will go **5.** would go **6.** would have gone **7.** is **8.** were . . . would visit **9.** had been . . . would have visited **10.** had realized . . . would not have made **11.** had read . . . would not have washed **12.** B: would/could have come . . . [*would/could have* is not repeated] washed . . . had told A: would have come . . . had called

□ EXERCISE 8, p. 419.   Untrue in the past. (Chart 20-4)

This is a pattern practice, with controlled responses, so students can easily check on one another's verb form usage and work out the answers together if need be. You could, of course, choose to lead the exercise yourself if you think it's too difficult for your students.

Often speakers add emphasis to the word *had* in the *if*-clause in responses that begin with *But if.*

ANSWERS: **1.** But if I had known (that my friend was in the hospital), I would have visited her. **2.** But if I had known (that you'd never met my friend), I would have introduced you. **3.** But if I had known (that there was a meeting last night), I would have gone. **4.** But if I had known (that my friend's parents were in town), I would have invited them to dinner. **5.** But if I had known (that you wanted to go to the soccer game), I would have bought a ticket for you. **6.** But if I had known (that you were at home last night), I would have visited you. **7.** But if I had known (that my sister wanted a gold necklace for her birthday), I would have bought her one. **8.** But if I had known (that you had a problem), I would have offered to help.

□ EXERCISE 9, p. 420.   Untrue conditionals. (Charts 20-3 and 20-4)

Students should be able to respond orally. If that is too difficult, they could do the exercise as written seatwork, then glance at their written answers when they respond orally.

Most speakers add emphasis to the first auxiliary in the *But if*-clause.

ANSWERS: **2.** But if there were a screen on the window, there wouldn't be so many bugs in the room. **3.** But if I had had enough money, I would have bought a bicycle. **4.** But if I did have enough money, I would buy a bicycle. **5.** But if you had listened to me, you wouldn't have gotten into so much trouble. **6.** But if she had not received immediate medical attention, she would have died. **7.** But if she had passed the entrance examination, she would have been admitted to the university. **8.** But if we had stopped at the service station, we wouldn't have run out of gas.

☐ **EXERCISE 10, p. 420.   Untrue conditional sentences.   (Charts 20-3 and 20-4)**

Students could begin with *But if,* using the pattern in Exercises 8 and 9. Then they should add emphasis to the first auxiliary.

POSSIBLE COMPLETIONS: **1.** If I had been absent from class yesterday, I would have missed a quiz. **2.** If I had enough energy today, I would go jogging in the park. **3.** If ocean water weren't salty, we could drink it. **4.** If our teacher didn't like his/her job, he/she would change professions. **5.** If people had wings, we wouldn't have to rely on cars or airplanes for transportation. **6.** If you had asked for my opinion, I would have given it to you. **7.** If water weren't heavier than air, the earth as we know it couldn't exist. **8.** If most nations didn't support world trade agreements, international trade would be impossible.

☐ **EXERCISE 11, p. 421.   Review: conditional sentences.   (Charts 20-1 → 20-4)**

These items are past, present, and future. Students must identify the time and also the truth value, then use appropriate verb forms. They should be given time to do this as seatwork or homework before discussing their answers.

ANSWERS: **1.** were . . . would tell   **2.** had had . . . would have taken   **3.** have . . . will give   **4.** had . . . wouldn't have to   **5.** had been . . . wouldn't have bitten **6.** would we use . . . didn't have   **7.** doesn't rain . . . will die . . . die . . . will go [*draught* /draut/]   **8.** had not collided /kəlaidəd/ . . . would not have become . . . would be . . . still existed . . . would be

☐ **EXERCISE 12, p. 422.   Untrue conditionals.   (Charts 20-3 and 20-4)**

You could use this as a books-closed oral exercise to stimulate discussion. Lead students through the examples first.

    As an alternative format, Student A could make a true statement and then Student B could make a conditional sentence about that statement.

ANSWERS: [These depend on students' creativity.]

☐ **EXERCISE 13, p. 422.   Conditional sentences.   (Charts 20-1 → 20-4)**

Substituting an auxiliary for a verb phrase to avoid unnecessary repetition isn't explained in the text, as the students are assumed to be familiar with these patterns. However, some students may have difficulty with this exercise. Its purpose is to prepare for the next oral exercise, so you should take time now for discussion of the patterns.

    In speaking, the word in each blank space should be given emphasis followed by a slight pause.

    NOTE: In items 9 and 12, BrE tends to use *got*—*wouldn't have **got** infected* and *would have **got** worried*—where AmE prefers *gotten.*

ANSWERS: **4.** did   **5.** weren't   **6.** had   **7.** were   **8.** didn't   **9.** had **10.** didn't   **11.** weren't   **12.** hadn't

☐ **EXERCISE 14, p. 423. Conditional sentences. (Charts 20-1 → 20-4)**

Use this as a teacher-led, books-closed oral exercise if you prefer.

ANSWERS: [These depend on students' creativity.]

CHART 20-5:	**USING PROGRESSIVE VERB FORMS IN CONDITIONAL SENTENCES**

• If students are unclear about the function and meaning of progressive verb forms, you might conduct a review of the relevant parts of Chapters 1 through 3. A "progressive situation" is one in which an activity is (was / will be / would be) in progress during or at a particular time.

☐ **EXERCISE 15, p. 423. Using progressive verb forms in conditional sentences. (Chart 20-5)**

These answers should be spoken with emphasis on *be* or the first auxiliary.

ANSWERS: **2.** But if she were here, the child wouldn't be crying. **3.** But if you had been listening, you would have understood the directions. **4.** But if he hadn't been driving too fast, he wouldn't have gotten a ticket. **5.** But if I hadn't been listening to the radio, I wouldn't have heard the news bulletin. **6.** But if it weren't broken, Grandpa would be wearing it. **7.** But if you hadn't been sleeping, I would have told you the news as soon as I heard it. **8.** But if I weren't enjoying myself, I would leave.

CHART 20-6: USING "MIXED TIME" IN CONDITIONAL SENTENCES

• Most books don't point out this usage, but it is very common in both speech and writing. It is assumed the students have control of the basic conditional verb forms outlined in Chart 20-1 and are ready to practice variations that are common in actual usage: progressive verb forms, mixed time, use of other modals, omission of *if,* implied conditions.

☐ **EXERCISE 16, p. 424. Using "mixed time" in conditional sentences. (Chart 20-6)**

EXPANSION ACTIVITY: Have Speaker A make a statement about his/her past activities. Have Speaker B say what s/he would have done if s/he were Speaker A. Example:
SPEAKER A: *I ate dinner at the student cafeteria last night.*
SPEAKER B: *If I were you, I would have eaten at Luigi's Restaurant on 5th Street.*

ANSWERS: **2.** But if you hadn't left the door open, the room wouldn't be full of flies. **3.** But if you had gone to bed at a reasonable hour last night, you wouldn't be tired this morning. **4.** But if I had finished my report yesterday, I could begin a new project today. **5.** But if she had followed the doctor's orders, she wouldn't be sick today. **6.** But if I were you, I would have told him the truth. **7.** But if I knew something about plumbing, I could/would fix the leak in the sink myself. **8.** But if I hadn't received a good job offer from the oil company, I would seriously consider taking the job with the electronics firm.

CHART 20-7: OMITTING *IF*

- Of the three examples in this chart, the one with *had* is the most commonly used in both conversation and writing.

- The example with *should* is somewhat formal usage.

- The example with *were* is less frequent than the others, especially in conversation. *Was* is not substituted for *were* in this pattern.

☐ EXERCISE 17, p. 425. Omitting IF. (Chart 20-7)

This is a simple transformation exercise designed to help students become familiar with the pattern. You or a student could read the item aloud, then another could change it to the new pattern. Or students could do this in pairs.

ANSWERS: **2.** Were I you, I wouldn't do that. **3.** Had they realized the danger, they would have done it differently. **4.** Were I your teacher, I would insist (that) you do better work. **5.** Should you change your mind, please let me know immediately. **6.** She would have gotten the job had she been better prepared. **7.** Were I you, I would look for another job. **8.** Should you need to reach me, I'll be at the Hilton Hotel in Seoul. **9.** Had they not dared to be different, the history of civilization would have to be rewritten. **10.** Should there be a global nuclear war, life on earth as we know it would end forever.

CHART 20-8: IMPLIED CONDITIONS

- These examples show one of the most common uses of conditional verb forms. A result-clause does not always come neatly attached to an *if*-clause in actual usage. Many of the uses of *would* and *could* in daily conversation express results of implied conditions. In writing, one condition expressed near the beginning of a composition can affect verb forms throughout. In Exercise 6 in this chapter (concerning the village of 100 people), one *if*-clause in the first sentence sufficed to require the use of conditional verb forms in all the result-clauses in all the remaining sentences.

☐ EXERCISE 18, p. 425. Implied conditions. (Chart 20-8)

An understanding of implied conditions expands students' communicative repertoire.

ANSWERS: **3.** I would have answered the phone *if I had heard it ring.* **4.** I couldn't have finished the work *if you hadn't helped.* **5.** I would have gone to Nepal last summer *if I had had enough money.* **6.** *If I had not stepped on the brakes,* I would have hit the child on the bicycle. **7.** *If Olga had not turned down the volume on the tape player,* the neighbors probably would have called to complain about the noise. **8.** Tarek would have finished his education *if he had not had to quit school and find a job.*

☐ EXERCISE 19, p. 426. Implied conditions. (Chart 20-8)

Students might enjoy working in pairs or small groups to complete these sentences. They could write a few good ones on the chalkboard for discussion.

SAMPLE ANSWERS:
1. I would have finished my report before I left work yesterday, but I didn't have time.
2. I couldn't have paid for my trip to New Zealand without my parents' help.
3. I would buy a Ferrari, but I don't have enough money.
4. I ran out of time. Otherwise, I would have finished my report before the meeting.
5. I could go to an Italian restaurant with my friends tonight, but I don't want to.
6. I would have gone to the meeting, but I didn't know about it.
7. Without water, all life on earth would die.
8. I set my alarm for six every morning. Otherwise, I would be late to work.
9. I set my alarm for six this morning. Otherwise, I would have been late to work.
10. I would have invited your brother to join us for dinner, but I didn't know he was in town.

☐ **EXERCISE 20, p. 426.   Review: conditional sentences.   (Charts 20-1 → 20-8)**

Encourage the use of contractions (e.g. *wouldn't, hadn't*), especially in the dialogues.

ANSWERS: 1. would/could spend   2. would/could have sent   3. is completed
4. weren't snowing   5. would have gone   6. would be   7. were . . . would
be   8. had not been sleeping   9. would forget . . . were not   10. did not
outnumber . . . could not eat   11. A: were not   B: would be sleeping   12. were . . .
would not be   ["Boy!" is an exclamation of surprise. It does not refer to anyone, male or female.
"You said it!" = I agree with you completely.]   13. would not be . . . had   14. would have
been   ["Hi" is an informal "Hello."]   15. would not ride   ["No way!" = Definitely not.   OR
That's impossible.]   16. would not have come . . . had known   17. will tell

☐ **EXERCISE 21, p. 427.   Review: conditional sentences.   (Charts 20-1 → 20-8)**

This could be written, then read aloud and discussed by the class. Alternative versions
could be presented and evaluated.

SAMPLE COMPLETIONS: 1. If it hadn't rained yesterday, we would have had our barbecue
outdoors.   2. If it weren't raining, we would be going to the park today.   3. You would
have passed the test had you studied for it.   4. Otherwise, we would have missed the
turn.   5. Without electricity, modern life would be very different.   6. If you hadn't
reminded me about the meeting tonight, I would have forgotten about it.   7. Should
you need any help, please ask me for assistance.   8. If I could choose any profession I
wanted, I would be a marine biologist.   9. If I were at home right now, I would be
taking a nap.   10. Without your help yesterday, I could not have finished painting the
kitchen.   11. Were I you, I would finish my degree before returning home.
12. What would you do if you had a chance to go to the moon?   13. If I had the chance
to live my childhood over again, I would keep a diary.   14. Had I known the test would
be so easy, I would not have stayed up late studying for it.   15. Can you imagine what
life would be like if humans had never invented the wheel?

☐ **EXERCISE 22, p. 428.   Activity: conditional sentences.   (Charts 20-1 → 20-8)**

The purpose of this exercise is to prompt spontaneous, interactive use of conditional
sentences. Your task is to set up a situation for a student to respond to. It isn't necessary to
use the exact words in the book, and you may wish to substitute other situations that are
more familiar to your students. The responses should usually begin: "I would (have) . . . ."
     You could ask for more than one response to an item. Sometimes people have quite
different reactions to the same situation.
     This exercise could be done in small groups, with only the leaders having open books.
Pair work is also an option.

ANSWERS: [These depend on students' creativity.]

□ **EXERCISE 23, p. 429.   Activity: conditional sentences. (Charts 20-1 → 20-8)**

POSSIBLE ANSWERS:
1. If Ron didn't have a dinner meeting with a client, he could/would go to the ball game with Jim after work tonight. If Jim asks Ron to go to another ball game some other time, Ron might go.
2. Tommy wouldn't have got(ten) into a lot of trouble if he hadn't taken his pet mouse to school / if he hadn't let his friend Jimmy put the mouse in the teacher's desk drawer.
3. If Ivan hadn't already borrowed Dan's saw and never returned it, Ivan wouldn't be embarrassed (now) to borrow Dan's axe. If Ivan had been more careful, he wouldn't have lost the saw. If Ivan asked Dan for his axe, Dan probably wouldn't lend it to him.

□ **EXERCISE 24, p. 430.   Activity: conditional sentences. (Charts 20-1 → 20-8)**

When assigning this exercise, you may want to set some limits such as how many topics each student should write about, how long the writing should be, and how many conditional sentences should be included.

It's excellent practice for you also to write this assignment. If you do it before you assign it to the students, you can get some idea of how challenging it is for them. This helps you design reasonable limits for the length of their writing. You could also share your writing with the class as a model of native-speaker rhetoric.

> **CHART 20-9:   USING *AS IF/AS THOUGH***
>
> • The word "like" is often difficult for learners because it has many functions and meanings. The notes in this chart are useful in pointing out two common uses of *like*. However, the emphasis in the chart and the exercises is on *as if/as though,* not *like.*

□ **EXERCISE 25, p. 430.   Using AS IF/AS THOUGH. (Chart 20-9)**

Be sure that students understand that even though they change a negative sentence to a positive form, they do not change its meaning or "truth value." The example should make this clear, but you might want to be sure the students understand it correctly.

Vocabulary Note: Most items in this exercise contain common sayings or idioms. The meanings should be clear from the contexts.

ERRATUM: Item 4 (at the top of page 431) is misnumbered "2." This is corrected in subsequent printings.

ANSWERS: **2.** as if/as though it were her native tongue.   **3.** as if/as though you'd seen a ghost.   **4.** as if/as though they were people.   **5.** as if/as though he were a general in the army.   **6.** as if/as though I had climbed Mt. Everest.   **7.** as if/as though he doesn't have a brain in his head.   **8.** as if/as though we had known each other all of our lives.
9. as if/as though a giant bulldozer had driven down Main Street. [*a bulldozer* = a large piece of earth-moving equipment]   **10.** as if/as though I had wings and could fly.   **11.** as if/as though he would burst.   **12.** would . . . would . . . would . . . would

CHART 20-10:   VERB FORMS FOLLOWING *WISH*

• Noun clause verbs following *wish* are in a past form. The past form signifies "contrary to fact"—just as it does in conditional sentences in *if*-clauses. Discuss verb relationships:

"true" situation	→	"wish" situation
simple present	→	simple past
present progressive	→	past progressive
simple past	→	past perfect
present perfect	→	past perfect
will	→	*would*
am/is/are going to	→	*was/were going to*
can	→	*could*
could + simple form	→	*could have* + past participle

• *Wish* can also be followed by an infinitive, e.g.: *I wish to know the results of the test as soon as possible.* In this instance, *wish* is usually a more formal way of saying *want,* or a more direct (possibly impolite or imperious) way of saying *would like.*

• The subjunctive use of *were* instead of *was* with *I/he/she/it* is considered formal by some, standard by others.

• Some teachers like to compare *hope* and *wish.* See notes in this *Teacher's Guide* for Chart 20-11.

☐ EXERCISE 26, p. 432.   Verb forms following WISH. (Chart 20-10)

This exercise is a quick check on the students' understanding of Chart 20-10. If the students seem to be having difficulty, make up additional items to illustrate verb form usage in noun clauses following *wish*.

ANSWERS: **2.** were shining   **3.** had gone   **4.** knew   **5.** had told   **6.** were wearing   **7.** had   **8.** had gone   **9.** could   **10.** would lend   **11.** were coming   **12.** weren't going to give   **13.** could meet   **14.** had come   **15.** were lying

☐ EXERCISE 27, p. 433.   Activity: verb forms following WISH. (Chart 20-10)

If possible, students' books should be closed. Repeat your question if necessary, and give them time to construct an answer.

ANSWERS: [These depend on students' creativity.]

☐ EXERCISE 28, p. 433.   Verb forms following WISH. (Chart 20-10)

Only an auxiliary (helping) verb is required in each item. British and American English differ somewhat in usage. For example:
  3. *I can't sing well, but I wish I **could*** (AmE).   OR   *. . . I wish I **could do*** (BrE).
  4. *I didn't go, but I wish I **had*** (AmE).   OR   *. . . I wish I **had done*** (BrE).
  5. *He won't . . ., but I wish he **would*** (AmE).   OR   *. . . I wish he **would do*** (BrE).

ANSWERS: [The answers given here are American usage, also understandable in Britain. These shortened forms are used mainly in spoken English.]
  6. had   **7.** could   **8.** did   **9.** had   **10.** could   **11.** would   **12.** were   **13.** had   **14.** did   **15.** were

CHART 20-11: USING *WOULD* TO MAKE WISHES ABOUT
THE FUTURE

- When speakers want something to happen in the future and think it is possible, they usually use **hope** to introduce their idea: *I hope they (will) come.* When they want something to happen but think it is probably not possible, they'd probably use **wish**: *I wish they would come.*

- A common mistake is the use of **will** in the noun clause following **wish**:
  INCORRECT: *I wish they will come.*

☐ **EXERCISE 29, p. 434.   Using WOULD to make wishes. (Charts 20-10 and 20-11)**

Two students can read the cues. Then you can ask the questions, and volunteers can answer them.

ANSWERS: **1.** Rita wishes (that) it would stop raining. Yoko also wishes it would stop raining.   **2.** Anna wishes Yoko would come to the concert. Anna wishes Yoko would change her mind.   **3.** Bob's mother wishes he would shave off his beard. Bob probably wishes his mother wouldn't try to tell him what to do.   **4.** Helen wishes Judy would pick up after herself, wash her dirty dishes, pick up her clothes and other stuff, and make her bed. Judy probably wishes Helen wouldn't nag her to pick up after herself. [*nag* = bother with constant questions]

☐ **EXERCISE 30, p. 435.   Using WISH. (Charts 20-10 and 20-11)**

Give the class a few minutes to prepare their answers. Then you might have individuals answer the first four items, and have pairs read the dialogues.
    ERRATUM: In item 9B, the word "not" should be omitted. This is corrected in subsequent printings.

ANSWERS: **1.** were . . . were   **2.** had come . . . had come . . . would have had
3. weren't . . . were not . . . could/would go   **4.** had paid   **5.** had   **6.** would turn
7. A: were lying   B: were   **8.** A: didn't have   B: were   **9.** had   **10.** had not
gone   **11.** would tell   **12.** A: were wearing   B: had known

☐ **EXERCISE 31, p. 436.   Using WISH. (Charts 20-10 and 20-11)**

You should set up the questions so that students are eager to share their wishes and dreams with the class. If some of the items are not appropriate to your students, you might substitute others. It isn't necessary to use the exact words in the book; just ask the question in an interesting way.

ANSWERS: [These depend on students' creativity.]

☐ EXERCISE 32, p. 436. Using WISH. (Charts 20-10 and 20-11)

You can lead this discussion, or break the class into groups or pairs.

ANSWERS: [These depend on students' creativity.]
6. [Note: The word "teleportation" may not be in the students' dictionaries. It is a sci-fi (science fiction) term that means sending something to a receiving unit by breaking it down into molecules and then reassembling it in its original form.]

☐ EXERCISE 33, p. 437. Activity: conditionals and wishes. (Chapter 20)

These questions can prompt the spontaneous use of conditional sentences in a lively discussion. Encourage diversity of opinion.

ANSWERS: [These depend on students' creativity.]

Appendix: SUPPLEMENTARY GRAMMAR UNITS

ORDER OF CHAPTER	CHARTS	EXERCISES	WORKBOOK
Subjects, verbs, and objects	A-1	Ex. 1 → 2	Pr. 1 → 2
Prepositions and prepositional phrases	A-2	Ex. 3 → 4	Pr. 3 → 4
Adjectives and adverbs	A-3 → A-4	Ex. 5 → 7	Pr. 5 → 7
The verb *be* and linking verbs	A-5 → A-6	Ex. 8	Pr. 8 → 9
Review		Ex. 9	
Forms of yes/no and information questions	B-1	Ex. 10	Pr. 10
Question words	B-2	Ex. 11 → 12	Pr. 11 → 14
Shortened yes/no questions	B-3	Ex. 13	
Negative questions	B-4	Ex. 14	Pr. 15
Tag questions	B-5	Ex. 15 → 16	Pr. 16
Contractions	C	Ex. 17	Pr. 17
Using *not* and other negative words	D-1	Ex. 18	Pr. 18
Avoiding double negatives	D-2	Ex. 19	Pr. 19
Beginning a sentence with a negative word	D-3	Ex. 20	Pr. 20
Preposition combinations with adjectives and verbs	E	Ex. 21 → 24	Pr. 21 → 26
Connectives to give examples	F-1	Ex. 25 → 26	
Connectives to continue the same idea	F-2	Ex. 27	
Review of verb forms		Ex. 28 → 30	

• PURPOSES: Teachers and students need a common vocabulary of grammar terms so that they can identify and discuss the patterns they are using in English. Also, every language learner needs to use a dictionary, and every dictionary uses grammar terms.

Have the students look in their dictionaries to find abbreviated labels such as "n," "v," "vi," "vt," "adj," "adv," "prep."

Also, have the students look up words that have various uses, such as *fast* and *crown,* and have them note the grammatical labels. Being able to recognize the grammatical function of a word in a sentence can help one find the appropriate definition. For example, if one sees that *fast* is used as a verb in the sentence "He fasted for three days," it makes looking up the meaning easier. Similarly, if one is unsure of the use of, for example, *crown* as a verb *(Napoleon crowned himself emperor. The dentist crowned two of my teeth. The festival was crowned by a dazzling display of fireworks.),* a dictionary can provide valuable usage information.

• USES: The textbook assumes that your students are already familiar with basic grammar terminology, but often it is helpful for them to review these concepts, either on their own or at your direction.

At the beginning of the English course, you could show your students the Appendix and suggest how to use it on their own. Also refer them to the selfstudy practices in the *Workbook.* You may want to cover some of the Appendix units as part of your regular teaching syllabus or in connection with related units in the chapter material.

• NOTE ON PHRASAL VERBS: A supplementary unit on phrasal verbs (two-word and three-word verbs such as *give up* or *catch up with*) can be found in the accompanying *Workbook* for *Understanding and Using English Grammar.* Phrasal verbs were deleted from the Appendix in the third edition because there was not space in the text to give phrasal verbs their just due. (One of the regrets of any author is that not everything can be included in a textbook.) Phrasal verbs require minimal grammatical explanation, after which learning them is largely a matter of vocabulary acquisition. Students interested in learning phrasal verbs should be referred to the *Workbook* or to one of several available texts that give phrasal verbs a thorough and informative presentation.

UNIT A: Basic Grammar Terminology

CHART A-1:   SUBJECTS, VERBS, AND OBJECTS

• The text assumes that its users are familiar with the terms "noun," "verb," "adjective," "adverb," and "preposition" as well as the terms "subject" and "object." Some students need to review this basic terminology so that you and they share a common vocabulary for discussing sentence structures.

• A noun or pronoun can have several functions in a sentence: subject, direct or indirect object, or object of a preposition. Sometimes these categories confuse learners.

• It is also sometimes confusing for students that the term "verb" is used to refer to the part of speech a word is (noun, *verb,* adjective, adverb) and, as well, to refer to the function of a word in a sentence (subject, *verb,* object).

   Look at the first item in Exercise 1 as an example. To elicit what part of speech a word is, ask "What kind of word is 'politician'?" Answer: A noun. To elicit the grammatical function of a word, ask "How is 'politician' used in the sentence?" Answer: It's the subject.

• You might point out to the students that transitive and intransitive verbs are noted "v.t." and "v.i.," respectively, in most dictionaries. The *Collins COBUILD English Language Dictionary* notes transitive verbs as "V + O" and intransitive verbs as "V."

   This terminology, "transitive" and "intransitive," is used in the text for two principal reasons: (1) It draws attention to an important feature of English verbs (i.e., that they may or may not be followed by an object), and hence to the two most common variations in the fundamental structure of the simple sentence in English (S + V and S + V + O); and (2) it is useful in the teaching of the passive voice, where only transitive verbs can be used (since the subject of a passive verb also functions as the object of the verb's action).

• Some common verbs that are usually or always intransitive: *agree, appear, arrive, come, cost, cry, die, exist, fall, flow, go, happen, laugh, live, occur, rain, rise, seem, sit, sleep, sneeze, snow, stand, stay, talk, wait, walk.*

☐ EXERCISE 1, p. A2.   Subjects, verbs, and objects.   (Chart A-1)

Use this exercise to discuss the labels "noun," "verb," "subject," and "object."

   Most students should be able to identify each structure quickly. If not, perhaps they need to review a more basic English textbook. This is not intended to be at all challenging.

ANSWERS:

　　　　　　S　　　　V　　　　　　　O
2. The <u>mechanic</u> <u>repaired</u> the <u>engine</u>.

　　　　　　　　S　　　　V　　　　　　　O
3. Those <u>boxes</u> <u>contain</u> old <u>photographs</u>.

　　　　　　S　　　　V　　　　　　O
4. The <u>teacher</u> <u>canceled</u> the <u>test</u>.

　　　　　　　S　　　　V　　　　　　　O
5. An <u>earthquake</u> <u>destroyed</u> the <u>village</u>.

　　　　　S　　　V　　　O
6. All <u>birds</u> <u>have</u> <u>feathers</u>.

   List of nouns: *politician, taxes, mechanic, engine, boxes, photographs, teacher, test, earthquake, village, birds, feathers.*

☐ EXERCISE 2, p. A2. Transitive vs. intransitive verbs. (Chart A-1)

Students need to determine whether or not the verb is followed by an object. The main focus of this exercise is to promote recognition of simple sentence structure, and secondarily to clarify the terminology of "transitive" and "intransitive." You might want to mention that *trans* comes from Latin and is a prefix meaning "across": a transitive verb is like a bridge across a river, connecting the subject and the object. The prefix "in-" means "not": *intransitive* means "not transitive." Other common words with *trans*: *transportation, transform, transfer, transatlantic, translate, transmit.*

ANSWERS: **3.** divided = VT   **4.** sneezed = VI   **5.** happened = VI   **6.** bought = VT   **7.** won = VT   **8.** won = VI   **9.** disappeared = VI; shone = VI   **10.** boiled = VT; made = VT; drank = VT

CHART A-2:   PREPOSITIONS AND PREPOSITIONAL PHRASES

• A preposition is a kind of "cement" that connects a noun or pronoun to other parts of an English sentence. Many languages have no prepositions, so these small English words can be very difficult to understand and explain. To get across the importance of these words, take a simple sentence such as "I walked ____ my father" and complete it with as many different prepositions as possible: *I walked with, toward, into, beside, behind, like, on(!), under(?), around, (etc.) my father.*

• In (d) notice that a comma is customary before the subject of the sentence. This comma signals that an element has been moved to the front of the sentence, and the speaker's voice will usually rise a bit before the comma.

• A few prepositions consist of short phrases; examples of "phrasal prepositions":

because of	*in the middle of*	*out of*
instead of	*in back of*	*according to*
in (the) front of	*ahead of*	*due to*

• Students need to be able to identify prepositions in the chapters on gerunds and infinitives, the passive, modal auxiliaries, and adjective clauses in particular, but also in many other units.

☐ EXERCISE 3, p. A3. Identifying prepositions. (Chart A-2)

Again, this is not supposed to be a challenging exercise. If it is extremely confusing and seems arcane for some students, they may need a more basic textbook than *Understanding and Using English Grammar* or may need tutoring in the structure of the simple sentence and its terminology prior to beginning the text. Also, depending on the students' proficiency needs in speech and writing, it is possible that such students would benefit from a different approach to language teaching, one in which grammar is not explicitly taught.

ANSWERS:

                                      P   **O of P**
  2. The waiter cleared the dirty dishes <u>from our table</u>.

                   P   **O of P**
  3. I parked the car <u>in the garage</u>.

               P   **O of P**
  4. Trees fell <u>during the violent storm</u>.

$$\overset{\text{P}}{}\overset{\text{O of P}}{}\overset{\text{P}}{}\overset{\text{O of P}}{}$$

5. Cowboys depended <u>on horses</u>   <u>for transportation</u>.

$$\overset{\text{P}}{}\overset{\text{O of P}}{}\overset{\text{P}}{}\overset{\text{O of P}}{}$$

6. We walked <u>to the park</u>   <u>after class</u>.

□ EXERCISE 4, p. A3. Sentence elements. (Charts A-1 and A-2)

ANSWERS:

    S   VT   O   PP

3. <u>Sally</u> <u>wore</u> her blue <u>suit</u> <u>to the meeting</u>.

      S   VT   O

4. <u>Beethoven</u> <u>wrote</u> nine <u>symphonies</u>.

    S   VI   PP

5. <u>Bells</u> <u>originated</u> <u>in Asia</u>.

    S   VT   O   PP

6. <u>Plants</u> <u>need</u> a reliable <u>supply</u> <u>of water</u>.

    S   VT   O   PP   PP   PP

7. <u>We</u> <u>enjoyed</u> the <u>view</u> <u>of snowy mountains</u> <u>from the window</u> <u>of our hotel room</u>.

     S   VT   PP   PP   PP   S

8. The <u>child</u> <u>sat</u> <u>between her parents</u> <u>on the sandy beach</u>. <u>Above her</u>, an <u>eagle</u>

   VI   PP

<u>flew</u> <u>across the cloudless sky</u>.

CHARTS A-3 AND A-4: ADJECTIVES AND ADVERBS

- Have the class call out words they think are adjectives and make sentences with these words.

- In general, adjectives are placed before nouns in English.

- Another common pattern places an adjective after the verb *be* (see Charts A-5 and A-6):
  - (a) *The student is intelligent.*
  - (b) *The children were hungry.*

- Chart A-4 summarizes only the basic form and placement of adverbs. There are many other phenomena related to adverbs, but they are not included here.

□ EXERCISE 5, p. A5. Nouns, verbs, adjectives, adverbs. (Charts A-1 → A-4)

ANSWERS:

    ADJ   ADV   ADJ

2. A <u>small</u> child cried <u>noisily</u> in the <u>third</u> row of the theater.

    ADJ   ADV

3. The <u>eager</u> player waited <u>impatiently</u> for the start of the game.

    ADV   ADJ

4. An <u>unusually</u> <u>large</u> crowd came to the concert.

    ADV   ADJ   ADJ

5. Arthur <u>carefully</u> repaired the <u>antique</u> vase with <u>special</u> glue.

    ADV   ADJ   ADJ   ADV

6. On <u>especially</u> <u>busy</u> days, the telephone in the <u>main</u> office rings <u>constantly</u>.

Nouns: *fire, house, child, row, theater, player, start, game, crowd, concert, Arthur, vase, glue, days, telephone, office.*
Total nouns = 16
Verbs: *spread, cried, waited, came, repaired, rings.*
Total verbs = 6

☐ **EXERCISE 6, p. A5.   Adjectives and adverbs. (Charts A-3 and A-4)**

Call attention to the footnote on usage of *well* and *good*. These may be confusing, even to native speakers of English.

ANSWERS: **1.** careless . . . carelessly   **2.** easy . . . easily   **3.** softly . . . soft
4. quietly   **5.** well . . . good

☐ **EXERCISE 7, p. A5.   Midsentence adverbs. (Chart A-4)**

Ask the students to use these adverbs in their usual positions. Point out that using them in other positions is possible and serves to focus attention on them; e.g., ***Never*** *has Erica seen snow.* (See Chart D-3.) ***Often*** *Ted studies at the library in the evening. Ann **often** is at the library in the evening, too. Fred has finished studying for tomorrow's test **already**.*

ANSWERS: [Verbs and adverbs are <u>underlined</u>.]
2. Ted <u>often studies</u> at the library in the evening.   **3.** Ann <u>is often</u> at the library in the evening, too.   **4.** Fred <u>has already finished</u> studying for tomorrow's test.   **5.** Jack <u>is seldom</u> at home. [also possible for emphasis: *seldom is*]   **6.** <u>Does he always stay</u> there?
7. He <u>often goes</u> into town to hang around with his buddies. [*buddy* = a close friend, a pal]
8. You <u>should always tell</u> the truth.

CHARTS A-5 AND A-6:   THE VERB *BE* AND LINKING VERBS

• Some grammar books call *be* a linking verb. In British English, a linking verb is called a "link verb."

• The key point here for learners to understand is that *be* can function in two ways:
   (1) as the main verb in a sentence (a, b, c) and
   (2) as the auxiliary element in a verb phrase (d, e, f).

☐ **EXERCISE 8, p. A6.   Linking verbs. (Charts A-3 → A-6)**

ANSWERS: **1.** easy . . . easily   **2.** comfortable   **3.** carefully   **4.** sad
5. cheerfully . . . cheerful   **6.** carefully . . . good [*Taste* can be either transitive or intransitive.]   **7.** quiet . . . quietly   **8.** dark

☐ **EXERCISE 9, p. A7.   Nouns, verbs, adjectives, adverbs, prepositions.**
        (Charts A-1 → A-6)

This exercise can be used in class discussion to make sure that the students understand the basic terminology used in the textbook. The exercise can be expanded by asking them to identify words in addition to those that are underlined. The material can also be used to discuss sentence structure; you could focus on the elements of a simple sentence or preview the compound–complex structures. (Some teachers like to diagram sentences for their students.) In addition, you could ask the class to discuss punctuation and capitalization.

2. Whales = *noun*
   mammals = *noun*
   breathe = *verb**
   air = *noun*
3. dive = *verb*
   deeply = *adverb*
   beneath = *preposition*
   surface = *noun*
   under = *preposition*
   water = *noun*
   for = *preposition*
4. migrations = *noun*
   among = *preposition*
   swim = *verb*
   from = *preposition*
   to = *preposition*
   icy = *adjective*

5. highly = *adverb*
   trainable = *adjective*
   intelligent = *adjective*
   sensitive = *adjective*
   refused = *verb*
   Finally = *adverb*
   immediately = *adverb*
   took = *verb*
   shared = *verb*
6. smell = *noun*
   poor = *adjective*
   eyesight = *noun*
   extremely = *adverb*
   wide = *adjective*
   range = *noun*
   of = *preposition*
   sounds = *noun*
   use = *verb*
   sound = *noun*

7. with = *preposition*
   clicks = *noun*
   whistles = *noun*
   songs = *noun*
   gather = *verb*
   around = *preposition*
   communicate = *verb*
   through = *preposition*

UNIT B: Questions

CHART B-1:   FORMS OF YES/NO AND INFORMATION QUESTIONS

• Note the special form of questions with *who* as subject.

☐ **EXERCISE 10, p. A9.   Forms of yes/no and information questions. (Chart B-1)**

The purpose of this mechanical exercise is for students to review the word order of questions using a variety of verb forms.

SUGGESTION: Draw a chart on the chalkboard with the following headings:

Q Word + Auxiliary + Subject + Main Verb + Rest of the Sentence

Then ask students to fit each element of a question sentence into the chart. This makes clear the position of each element in a question. For example:

Q Word + Auxiliary + Subject + Main Verb + Rest of the Sentence

	Does	she	stay	there?
Where	does	she	stay?	

---

* Point out the spelling and pronunciation of *breathe* (verb) and *breath* (noun), or have the students look this information up in their dictionaries. Also note that in this sentence *live* is an adjective and *young* is a noun. You might ask students to find these particular uses of these two words in their dictionaries. Mention that it can be helpful to determine the grammatical function of a word in order to know which definition and pronunciation to look for in a dictionary.

To clarify the use of a question word as the subject of a question, also have the class form questions with *who*.

Q Word + Auxiliary + Subject + Main Verb + Rest of the Sentence
Who   stays   there?

As a variation, you could divide the class into thirds. Group 1 reads the cue, Group 2 asks the yes/no question, then Group 3 asks the information question. You could have four groups, with Group 4 asking the question with *who*. Rotate the groups after two responses so that everyone has a chance to use each question type. The exercise is mechanical, but it can be turned into a game.

ANSWERS: [All three types are included here.]
1. Does she stay there? Where does she stay? Who stays there?
2. Is she staying there? Where is she staying? Who is staying there?
3. Will she stay there? Where will she stay? Who will stay there?
4. Is she going to stay there? Where is she going to stay? Who is going to stay there?
5. Did they stay there? Where did they stay? Who stayed there?
6. Will they be staying there? Where will they be staying? Who will be staying there?
7. Should they stay there? Where should they stay? Who should stay there?
8. Has he stayed there? Where has he stayed? Who has stayed there?
9. Has he been staying there? Where has he been staying? Who has been staying there?
10. Is John there? Where is John? Who is there?
11. Will John be there? Where will John be? Who will be there?
12. Has John been there? Where has John been? Who has been there?
13. Will Judy have been there? Where will Judy have been? Who will have been there?
14. Were Ann and Tom married there? Where were Ann and Tom married? Who was married there?
15. Should this package have been taken there? Where should this package have been taken? What should have been taken there?

CHART B-2:   QUESTION WORDS

• This chart is for consolidation and review. It is intended for reference, not memorization. In order to acquaint the students with its contents, spend a little time discussing it in class, including modeling spoken contractions (e.g., *When'd they arrive?*). After you discuss it, have the students close their books; give answers from the ANSWER column (adapting them to your class) and have the students supply possible questions. Examples:

TEACHER: David's   [OR   Yoko's, Olga's, Ali's, Roberto's, etc.]
SPEAKER: Whose . . . ?
TEACHER: Yesterday.
SPEAKER: When . . . ?
TEACHER: Dark brown.
SPEAKER: What color . . . ?

• Point out that an informal alternative for *Why* is *How come*. With *How come*, the subject and verb are not inverted. Compare: *Why did you go there?*
How come you went there?

☐ **EXERCISE 11, p. A11.   Information questions. (Charts B-1 and B-2)**

ERRATUM: Item 18 should read "Because the traffic was heavy. I was late because the traffic was heavy." This is corrected in subsequent printings.

ANSWERS: **1.** Who is that letter from?   **2.** Who wrote that letter?   **3.** Whose coat is that? [Check the spelling of *whose* (not *who's*).]   **4.** When are Alice and John going to get married?   **5.** What color are her eyes?   **6.** What color is her hair?   **7.** What kind of tea would you like? OR What would you like?   **8.** What do you usually drink with your breakfast?   **9.** What made her sneeze?   **10.** How long does it usually take you to eat breakfast?   **11.** How did you get to the airport?   **12.** What does the boy have in his pocket? [also possible: *What has the boy in his pocket?*]   **13.** How many brothers and sisters do you have? [also possible: *How many . . . have you?*]   **14.** Where did you grow up?   **15.** How long does it take to get there by plane?   **16.** What kind of novels do you like to read? OR What do you like to read?   **17.** Which chapters will the test cover? OR What will the test cover?   **18.** Why were you late? OR How come you were late? [Note the subject–verb order after *How come*.]   **19.** How long has she been sick?   **20.** How many people are you going to invite to your party?   **21.** Which camera should I buy?   **22.** Who discovered radium?   **23.** What are we doing?   **24.** How's everything going?

☐ **EXERCISE 12, p. A12.   Activity: asking questions. (Charts B-1 and B-2)**

This can be a fun exercise. Students can role-play their dialogues for the rest of the class, who can listen specifically for correct question forms.

ANSWERS: [These depend on students' creativity.]

CHART B-3:   SHORTENED YES/NO QUESTIONS

• These forms are used only in casual conversation, not formal situations.

☐ **EXERCISE 13, p. A12.   Shortened yes/no questions. (Chart B-3)**

ANSWERS: [Subjects and auxiliary verbs which need to be added are <u>underlined</u>.]   **2.** <u>Are you</u> expecting someone?   **3.** <u>Did you</u> stay up late last night?   **4.** <u>Have you</u> ever been there before?   **5.** <u>Are you</u> nervous? [*Who me?* can be interpreted as a shortened form of *Who(m) do you mean? Do you mean me?*]   **6.** <u>Do you</u> want a cup of coffee?   **7.** <u>Have you</u> heard any news about your scholarship?   **8.** A: <u>Are you</u> hungry? B: Yeah. <u>Are</u> you?

CHART B-4: NEGATIVE QUESTIONS

• Negative questions are seldom found in nonfiction writing (other than as rhetorical questions). They are principally conversational, expressing emotions and opinions.

• The speaker of a negative question has an opinion about a situation. Asking the negative question is a signal to the listener. The speaker expects a certain answer, but the listener has to answer truthfully. Sometimes, therefore, the answer is unexpected. Even with native speakers, this can cause confusion, so the questioner may have to ask another question for clarification. See example (e):

    A: What happened? Didn't you study?
    B: Yes. (Meaning: That is what happened.)
    A: I'm confused. Did you study or didn't you?
    B: No, I didn't.

□ **EXERCISE 14, p. A14. Negative questions. (Chart B-4)**

> *ANSWERS:* **1.** No. [= No, I wasn't hungry.] **2.** A: Aren't you hungry? B: Yes.
> **3.** A: Didn't you sleep well? B: No. **4.** A: Doesn't it rise in the east? B: Yes,
> Annie. **5.** A: Don't you recognize him? B: No. **6.** A: Didn't he say he would be
> here by 4:00? B: Yes. **7.** A: Aren't you having a good time? B: No. **8.** B: Isn't
> the Mississippi the longest? A: No.

CHART B-5: TAG QUESTIONS

• Tag questions are an important element in English language conversation. They help establish communication because they invite a response from another person. Using the questions incorrectly can, therefore, cause confusion and disrupt communication. Students should be aware of the importance of using tag questions correctly.

• Ask the students to make sentences beginning with "I'm not sure, but I think. . . ." Then have them turn that statement of opinion into an inquiry with a tag question that indicates their belief. For example: *I'm not sure, but I think we're going to have a test on question forms tomorrow.*

→ *We're going to have a test on question forms tomorrow, aren't we?* OR *I'm not sure, but I think Venus is the second closest planet to the sun.*
→ *Venus is the second closest planet to the sun, isn't it?*

    To elicit negatives in the main rather than tag verb, have the students begin a sentence with "It is my understanding that . . . not . . . ." For example: *It is my understanding that we're not going to have a test tomorrow.* → *We're not going to have a test tomorrow, are we?*

• There is another aspect of questions you may wish to mention to your class. Asking questions without using question word order or tags is common in everyday speech: the speaker simply uses interrogative intonation (voice rising at end). Demonstrate for the students: *Mary is here? Mary isn't here? She'll be here at ten? They won't be here? You can't come? You've never been to Paris? You live with your parents? Etc.*

☐ EXERCISE 15, p. A15. Tag questions. (Chart B-5)

Most of the items here would typically have a rising intonation. Of course, some could be said with a falling intonation.
> ERRATUM: Item 15 should read "There is something wrong with Jane today, _____?" This is corrected in subsequent printings.

ANSWERS: **2.** isn't she **3.** will they **4.** won't you **5.** are there **6.** isn't it **7.** isn't he **8.** hasn't he **9.** doesn't he [also possible: *hasn't he*] **10.** can they **11.** won't she **12.** wouldn't she **13.** are they **14.** have you **15.** isn't there **16.** can't they **17.** did they **18.** did it **19.** aren't I **20.** isn't it

☐ EXERCISE 16, p. A16. Tag questions. (Chart B-5)

Perhaps you could tell the students which intonation to use for certain items. Or you could allow them to choose rising or falling intonation and then explain their choices. Or you could simply concentrate on the grammar and pay scant attention to intonation.

ANSWERS: **1.** , isn't it? **2.** , isn't he/she? **3.** , doesn't he/she? **4.** , is there? **5.** , doesn't/hasn't he/she? **6.** , didn't you? **7.** , hasn't she/he? **8.** , did you? **9.** , have they? **10.** , don't they? **11.** , can she/he? **12.** , is she/he? **13.** , won't it? **14.** , do they? **15.** , didn't you? **16.** isn't there? **17.** , isn't he/she? **18.** , shouldn't you? **19.** , does he/she? **20.** , didn't she/he? **21.** , don't/haven't we? **22.** , haven't you? **23.** , won't he/she/they/you? **24.** , have they? **25.** , aren't I? **26.** , doesn't it?

UNIT C: Contractions

CHART C: CONTRACTIONS

• Understanding contractions is very important for anyone who hears native speakers of English talking.

• Make sure the students understand that the quotation marks around the contractions are NOT written.

• Mention the possibility that learners may have difficulty with auxiliary verbs in their own speech and writing because they don't always hear them in normal, rapidly spoken English. Unstressed contracted forms may be barely discernable to the inexperienced, unaware ear.

☐ EXERCISE 17, p. A17. Contractions. (Chart C)

Have the students listen carefully to your oral production. Students enjoy trying to copy the teacher's model, but the emphasis should be on their <u>hearing</u> the contractions you say.

PART I ANSWERS: **1.** "friend's" **2.** "friends're" **3.** "Tom's" /tamz/ **4.** "students've" /studəntsəv/ **5.** "Bob'd" /babəd/ **6.** "Bob'd" **7.** "Ron'll" / ranəl/ **8.** "window's" /windouz/ **9.** "windows're" /windouzər/ **10.** "Jane's" **11.** "boys've" /boizəv/ **12.** "Sally'd" /sælid/ **13.** "Sally'd"

14. "Who's" /huz/   **15.** "Who're" /huər/   **16.** "Who's"
17. "What've" /hwətəv/   **18.** "What'd" / hwətəd/   **19.** "What'd" /wətəd/
20. "What'd"   **21.** "Why'd" /hwaid/   **22.** "When'll" /hwɛnəl/   **23.** "How long'll"
/lɔŋəl/   **24.** "Where'm" /hwɛrəm/   **25.** "Where'd" /hwɛrd/

UNIT D: Negatives

CHART D-1:   USING *NOT* AND OTHER NEGATIVE WORDS

- A note on pronunciation of some contractions:
    1. Do not pronounce the letter "l" in *could(n't)*, *should(n't)*, *would(n't)*, etc. They should sound like "good."
    2. Do not pronounce the letter "t" in *mustn't.*
    3. Pronounce the letter "s" in *hasn't*, *isn't*, and *doesn't* like the letter "z."

- Examples in (c) show word order in negative verbs.

- The important difference between *not* and *no* is shown in (f) and (g).

- The footnote explains *ain't* for students who may be curious about its use.

☐ EXERCISE 18, p. A18.   Using NOT and NO. (Chart D-1)

The purpose of this exercise is to show students two equally correct ways to make a negative statement. The form with *no* is generally more formal. Caution students against double negatives.

ANSWERS: **2.** no . . . not . . . not   **3.** No   **4.** no   **5.** not . . . not   **6.** no
7. not   **8.** no   **9.** no . . . no [This is a common saying that means "I can keep a secret" or "I prefer to keep my opinion to myself."]   **10.** not   **11.** no   **12.** not

---

CHART D-2:   AVOIDING DOUBLE NEGATIVES

- Some native speakers of English use double negatives regularly in their speech, so students might hear double negatives and wonder if they are grammatical. Double negatives are considered to be nonstandard usage and may reflect disadvantageously on one's educational background. However, they are sometimes used for a humorous or theatrical effect.

□ EXERCISE 19, p. A20.   Error analysis: double negatives.   (Chart D-2)

ANSWERS: [The first answer is more frequently used.]

2. I didn't see <u>anybody</u>.   OR   I <u>saw</u> nobody.
3. I <u>can</u> never understand him.   OR   I can't <u>ever</u> understand him.
4. He doesn't like <u>either</u> coffee <u>or</u> tea.   OR   He ~~doesn't~~ <u>likes</u> neither coffee nor tea.
5. I didn't do <u>anything</u>.   OR   I <u>did</u> nothing.
6. I <u>can</u> hardly hear the radio.   OR   I can't ~~hardly~~ hear the radio.
7. We couldn't see <u>anything</u> but sand.   OR   We <u>could</u> see nothing but sand.
8. Methods of horse training <u>have</u> barely changed at all in the last eight centuries.   OR   Methods of horse training haven't ~~barely~~ changed at all in the last eight centuries.

CHART D-3:   BEGINNING A SENTENCE WITH A NEGATIVE WORD

• This inversion is principally a literary device. Advanced students may find it interesting. Intermediate students may well ignore it.

□ EXERCISE 20, p. A20.   Negative words.   (Chart D-3)

ANSWERS: 2. Seldom do I sleep past seven o'clock.   3. Hardly ever do I agree with her.   4. Never will I forget the wonderful people I have met here.   5. Never have I known Rosa to be dishonest.   6. Scarcely ever does the mail arrive before noon.

UNIT E: Preposition Combinations

CHART E: PREPOSITION COMBINATIONS WITH ADJECTIVES AND VERBS

• This list is for reference, not memorization. Other combinations exist.

• ERRATUM: The chart should read (under the "E" column): "excel in, **at**." The omission of *at* is corrected in subsequent printings.

□ EXERCISES 21–24, pp. A22–A23.   Prepositions.   (Chart E)

Students might want to try to complete these exercises without looking at the list.

EX. 21 ANSWERS: 2. to   3. for   4. from   5. for   6. (up)on   7. from   8. in/at   9. to   10. in [also possible: *at*]   11. of   12. from   13. for [*care for* = like]   14. about it [*care about* = be concerned about]   15. of

EX. 22 ANSWERS: **1.** for **2.** to **3.** (up)on **4.** from **5.** of **6.** of [*take care of* = pay attention to] **7.** about **8.** with **9.** (up)on **10.** for [*Whom* is very formal; *who* is acceptable.] **11.** from **12.** to **13.** for **14.** of **15.** for

EX. 23 ANSWERS: **1.** with **2.** of **3.** to **4.** of **5.** at **6.** from **7.** with **8.** in [*in* an area] **9.** at [*at* a specific location] **10.** from **11.** for [= hope for] **12.** of **13.** at/with **14.** with **15.** to

EX. 24 ANSWERS: **1.** to . . . for **2.** from **3.** with **4.** to **5.** (up)on **6.** of [also possible: *from*] **7.** (up)on **8.** for . . . to **9.** about [also possible: *of*] **10.** of [also possible: *about*] **11.** of **12.** to [also possible: *with* or *toward(s)*] **13.** of **14.** with **15.** to [also possible: *with*]

UNIT F: Connectives to Give Examples and to Continue an Idea

CHART F-1: CONNECTIVES TO GIVE EXAMPLES

- Giving examples is important in English rhetoric; general statements need specific support for clarity and persuasiveness.
- The abbreviation "e.g." is a written form only, never spoken.

☐ **EXERCISE 25, p. A24. Giving examples. (Chart F-1)**

ANSWERS: [These depend on students' creativity.]

☐ **EXERCISE 26, p. A25. Using SUCH AS. (Chart F-1)**

Students can use their knowledge of many things to complete these sentences. You might ask more than one student to give relevant examples for an item. They enjoy giving examples from their own experience or knowledge.

The commas are already given so that students can concentrate on meaning.

POSSIBLE COMPLETIONS: **2.** such as bread and butter. **3.** such as a Honda or Volkswagen. **4.** such as cancer and heart disease. **5.** such as Iran and Venezuela **6.** as tennis and soccer. **7.** as the printing press and the computer chip . . . such as the atomic bomb and bacterial weapons **8.** such as when I'm sick or when I'm trying to solve a difficult problem. **9.** such as history and mathematics . . . such as languages and science are difficult. **10.** such as when I'm at a theater or when I'm talking on the phone **11.** such as three and eleven . . . such as six and ten **12.** such as German and French . . . such as Chinese and Arabic

---

CHART F-2: CONNECTIVES TO CONTINUE THE SAME IDEA

- One other transition in this pattern is *besides that.* Example:

  She's an excellent teacher. Besides that, students really like her.

This transition is usually used when listing points in an argument in order to persuade someone. (In this example, you might be trying to persuade an administrator to give the teacher a promotion or a salary increase.) Informally, *that* is sometimes dropped: *She's an excellent teacher. Besides, students really like her.*

- Ask the students to give additional examples using *beside* vs. *besides* in order to clarify the point.

☐ EXERCISE 27, p. A26. Connectives to continue the same idea. (Chart F-2)

Since these items are rather long and several answers are possible, students should prepare their answers (seatwork or homework). Then you can lead a discussion of good alternatives and the required punctuation.

POSSIBLE COMBINATIONS: **1.** <u>Furthermore</u>, it has interesting special features. **2.** <u>In addition</u>, you should read as many magazines in English as you have time for. Watching television can <u>also</u> be helpful. **3.** <u>Moreover</u>, a housing shortage has developed. <u>In addition</u>, there are so many automobiles . . . . **4.** Physical exercise is <u>also</u> essential. <u>In addition</u>, sleep and rest should not be neglected.

UNIT G: Verb Form Review Exercises

☐ EXERCISES 28–30, pp. A26–A28. General review of verb forms. (Chapters 1 → 20)

At the end of the book, these three exercises give students an opportunity to evaluate their understanding and control of verb forms in English. The exercises cover verb forms presented in Chapters 1 through 20. They should be prepared before discussion, as either seatwork or homework.

EX. 28 ANSWERS:
  1. had never spoken [also possible: *never spoke*]
  2. hadn't come
  3. be
  4. wouldn't have come
  5. was stamped
  6. will probably continue / is probably going to continue . . . lives
  7. will have been
  8. going
  9. Having heard
  10. sitting / who is sitting
  11. have been produced
  12. would give / was going to give / is going to give
  13. have known . . . met . . . was working [also possible: *worked*]
  14. had been . . . would have met
  15. were made
  16. have been standing . . . are
  17. would change . . . (would) decide
  18. understood / could understand
  19. Being . . . was respected / is respected
  20. would not exist [also possible: *could not exist*]

EX. 29 ANSWERS: **1.** coming . . . has learned **2.** had already given **3.** apply / should apply **4.** would have been / would be **5.** would be / was going to be **6.** Sitting . . . watching **7.** had been informed **8.** was completely destroyed . . . had gone **9.** embarrassing **10.** were **11.** invited **12.** puzzled . . . puzzling . . . give . . . figure **13.** has been **14.** working . . . can/will be solved **15.** call

ERRATUM: In lines 22 and 23, the pronoun "I" is erroneously repeated. This is corrected in subsequent printings.

(1) finish / have finished taking
(2) will also finish / will also have finished
  . . . have ever had
(3) have learned
(4) had anticipated / anticipated . . .
  coming
(5) Living . . . going
(6) have given [also possible: *has given*]
(7) to encounter . . . (to) interact
(8) would like
(9) arrived . . . knew
(10) needed . . . (in order) to
  communicate
(11) couldn't find . . . would use / used
(12) (in order) to communicate
(13) Knowing
(14) was
(15) to make
(16) became
(17) Hoping to improve
(18) (to) understand . . . appearing
(19) were saying / said
(20) bored
(21) think
(22) were experiencing / experienced
(23) was doing
(24) had wanted / had been wanting . . .
  living
(25) studying

(26) began . . . had
(27) Not knowing
(28) to expect
(29) excited . . . finding
(30) chose . . . introduced
(31) sitting . . . talking
(32) were
(33) spoke / had to speak
(34) wouldn't / couldn't / didn't understand
  . . . was saying
(35) was pleasantly surprised . . .
  responded
(36) took . . . building
(37) progressed . . . found
(38) asked . . . spoke
(39) were
(40) hesitated to ask
(41) even interrupted . . . had never been
(42) not to be surprised
(43) sharing
(44) learning
(45) was
(46) am
(47) hadn't come . . . wouldn't have been
(48) could have / would have
(49) knew
(50) had . . . to make
(51) would be

ERRATA for the First Printing of the *UUEG* Student Book

The following errors appeared in the first printing of the *UUEG* student book (third edition). They have been corrected in subsequent printings. This list may be helpful for those of you who are teaching from the first printing. The page numbers refer to student book pages.

CHAPTER 1, Ex. 3, p. 3:   Items 3 and 4 were accidentally combined. Item 4 should read "What are you going to do tomorrow?"

CHAPTER 2, Ex. 12, p. 21:   The last blue chart heading should read /əd/, not /əz/.

CHAPTER 5, Ex. 7, p. 71:   Item 12 has as its intended completion the habitual past *used to go*. Presentation of the habitual past was deleted from the Third Edition of this book because it is covered thoroughly in *Fundamentals of English Grammar (FEG* = the black book). But this exercise item mistakenly did not get changed in the revision. Instead of being deleted in a reprint, the item will remain here with the suggestion that the teacher use this as an opportunity to review the habitual past. If students need more information, refer them to *FEG* by Azar.

CHAPTER 6, Ex. 2, p. 85:   The second column in Group C contains two items numbered 30. Instead of 30 through 34, the second column should be numbered 30 through 35.

CHAPTER 7, Chart 7-4, p. 107:   The first line on the right in this chart should read ". . . chairs are items that can **be** counted."

CHAPTER 10, Ex. 10 , p. 183:   The first five speakers in the CONVERSATION should be A, B, A, B, then **C** (not A).

CHAPTER 11, Ex. 6, p. 213:   Item 4 should read "Someone has given Maria a promotion at her job as a computer programmer at Microsoft."

CHAPTER 11, Ex. 15, p. 224:   The example should read (*name of a person*) \ offer.

CHAPTER 13, Ex. 2, p. 269:   Item 5 should read "The man is standing over there. Ann brought him to the party."

CHAPTER 13, Ex. 9, p. 274:   In the footnote to item 3, the last word should be "those," not "x."

CHAPTER 13, Ex. 21, p. 282:   There should be no commas in item 8.

CHAPTER 15, Ex. 2, p. 327:   In item 4, the word after *market* should be "to," not "for."

CHAPTER 15, Chart 15-4, p. 331:   The labels are incorrect for (c) and (d): (c) is a PASSIVE INFINITIVE and (d) is a PASSIVE GERUND.

CHAPTER 15, Ex. 12, p. 334:   The last line on page 334 is missing. Item 8 should include a second sentence: "We should take advantage of *that fact.*"

CHAPTER 16, Ex. 6, p. 352:   The mischievous misprint gremlins misspelled "analysis" in the title of this exercise.

CHAPTER 17, Ex. 8, p. 366:   Item 6 should read "Jack is an interesting storyteller and conversationalist, whereas his brother _____." *On the other hand* was reorganized into Chapter 19 in this Third Edition; the inclusion of *on the other hand* in this exercise slipped by the author.

CHAPTER 18, Ex. 6, p. 379:   Item 9 in Column A should read "She has done very well in her studies."

CHAPTER 19, Ex. 12 and 39:   These exercise numbers do not appear in this chapter. To avoid confusion in classes that may be using texts from different printings, the numbering will NOT be corrected in subsequent printings.

CHAPTER 19, Ex. 28, p. 402:   The title for Exercise 28 should be "Expressing conditions." The chart reference should be: (Charts 17-5 → 17-9 and 19-8).

CHAPTER 20, Ex. 7, p. 418:   Two consecutive items appear as number 10. The second of these (at the top of page 419) should be number 11.

CHAPTER 20, Ex. 25, p. 430:   Item 4 (at the top of page 431) is misnumbered 2.

CHAPTER 20, Ex. 30, p. 435:   In item 9B, the word "not" should be omitted.

APPENDIX, Ex. 11, p. A11:   Item 18 should read "Because the traffic was heavy. I was late because the traffic was heavy."

APPENDIX, Ex. 15, p. A15:   Item 15 should read "There is something wrong with Jane today, _____?"

APPENDIX, Chart E, p. A21:   The chart should read (under the "E" column): "excel in, **at**."

APPENDIX, Ex. 30, p. A28:   In lines 22 and 23, the pronoun "I" is erroneously repeated.

Index

1